AUCKLAND INTERNATIONAL COLLEGE
85 Airedale Street
P O Box 3966, Shortland Street
Auckland
New Zealand

theory of
knowledge

AUCKLAND
INTERNATIONAL
COLLEGE

If you find this book please return it to Auckland International College
(AIC). Ph. (09) 309 4480.

Copy Number:

Student Name	Teacher initial
Kay lu ☺	WB
Samuel Qin	As
Ji Ho Choi · ʿᵒʸ ᵕ 𝄞	

IB
DIPLOMA
PROGRAMME

theory of knowledge

Nicholas Alchin

HODDER MURRAY

© Nicholas Alchin, 2003

First published 2003
by Hodder Murray, a member of the Hodder Headline Group
338 Euston Road
London NW1 3BH

Reprinted 2003, 2004 (twice), 2005 (twice)

Layouts by Jenny Fleet
Artwork by Countryside Illustrations
Typeset in Meridien by Wearset Ltd, Boldon, Tyne and Wear
Printed and bound in Malta

A catalogue entry for this title is available from the British Library

ISBN 0 7195 7865 5
Teacher's Book ISBN 0 7195 7866 3

Contents

Preface viii

CHAPTER 1 What are we trying to do? 2
Resource file 12

CHAPTER 2 The natural sciences 14
Resource file 28

CHAPTER 3 The arts 30
Resource file 46

CHAPTER 4 Mathematics 52
Resource file 66

CHAPTER 5 Rationalism: the use of reason 72
Resource file 92

CHAPTER 6 The social sciences 94
Resource file 119

CHAPTER 7 History 124
Resource file 138

CHAPTER 8 Empiricism: the use of the senses 146
Resource file 163

CHAPTER 9 Paradigms and culture 168
Resource file 192

CHAPTER 10 Language 198
Resource file 202
Resource file 225

CHAPTER 11 Ethics 230
Resource file 249

CHAPTER 12 Politics 252
Resource file 272

CHAPTER 13 Religion 274
Resource file 291

CHAPTER 14 Feelings, emotions and intuition 292
Resource file 314

CHAPTER 15 Where do we go from here? 316

Acknowledgements 321
Index 323

"*You are a human being. And so you have a philosophical view of existence — whether you realise it or not. About this you have no choice. But there is a choice to be made about your philosophy, and it can be put in these terms: is your philosophy based on conscious, thoughtful and well-informed reflection? Is it sensitive to, but not chained by, the need for logical consistency? Or have you let your subconscious amass an ugly pile of unexamined prejudices, unjustified intolerances, hidden fears, doubts and implicit contradictions, thrown together by chance but integrated by your subconscious into a kind of mongrel philosophy and fused into a single, solid weight, like a ball and chain in the place where your mind's wings should have grown?*

It is not the answer that enlightens but the question."

Eugène Ionesco

Preface

Most people read non-fiction books to find out about non-fiction – to find out some facts about a certain subject, or perhaps, at the very least, the opinions of the author, who is presumably an expert in the field. You may well take this approach with academic books, which are very often packed with facts and opinions. If so, reading this book may prove to be a frustrating experience. It is certainly non-fiction (although there are fictional articles in it) but it does not, in general, try to convey information. You will learn some facts, and some opinions about them, but you will probably not **learn** many answers – these you have to **find** yourself. This book is about important questions, and what might make a good answer, but most of all it is about you deciding what **your** answers are. These questions are concerned with **knowledge** – what you know, how you know it, and whether what you know is likely to be true or not.

Some questions that have interested people over the centuries include:

- What is right and what is wrong?
- What is love?
- What is good art?
- Will science tell us everything?
- Can I trust my senses?
- How do people invent maths?
- How can we tell how people lived a long time ago?
- Could the world be an illusion?
- Why can people and animals think when rocks can't?
- Why do some things seem logical when others do not?
- What is life?
- How did the Universe start?
- How will it all end?
- Is there life after death?
- Is there a God?

You can see that there are some big issues involved, and some of the questions are very much open to debate (which ones these are is certainly open to debate itself!). I can't pretend to answer any of them definitively, but I will provide an introductory framework for a thoughtful reader looking for ways to approach these and other questions. I indicate certain ways in which we might look for an answer and certain problems that naturally arise when we try to do so. As a result, we shall see that some questions may have definite answers while others seem too difficult to answer by reason or by experiment. The important thing to remember is that all interesting questions started off in this latter state (when we call them **philosophical** questions), but over time some manage to get moved into the former state (when we call them geography, physics, history, or whatever). I believe that we should keep thinking about the questions, and deepening our understanding of them – only then can we hope to find the right answers. Doing this is an exciting and never-ending journey, and I hope to help you along the way.

My aim has been to provide a broad coverage of themes and ideas rather than to follow any particular thread to its bitter end. This may prove frustrating at times, but the further reading lists at the end of each chapter provide a guide to further material. This text is, therefore, simplified, but hopefully not simplistic. It is in no sense 'complete', and at the end you may feel rather dissatisfied, as if you have eaten only the starter to a wonderful meal. That is good, because the final answers, and in some cases, the final questions, must be yours.

1 What are we trying to do?

Shall I teach you what knowledge is? When you know a thing, to recognise that you know it; and when you do not know a thing, to recognise that you do not know it. That is knowledge.
Confucius

Where there is shouting there is no true knowledge.
Leonardo da Vinci

NOTHING IN ALL THE WORLD IS MORE DANGEROUS THAN SINCERE IGNORANCE AND CONSCIENTIOUS STUPIDITY.
Martin Luther King

Mediocre minds usually dismiss anything which reaches beyond their own understanding.
Francois de La Rochefoucald

Education is learning what you didn't even know you didn't know.
Daniel J. Boorstin

It is very good for a man to talk about what he does not understand; as long as he understands that he does not understand it.
G. K. Chesterton

Those who are convinced they have a monopoly on The Truth always feel that they are only saving the world when they slaughter the heretics.
Arthur M. Schlesinger, Jr

A very popular error – having the courage of one's convictions; rather it is a matter of having the courage for an attack upon one's convictions.
Anon

THERE ARE MANY WHO KNOW MANY THINGS, YET ARE LACKING IN WISDOM.
Democritus

The most important truths are likely to be those which . . . society at that time least wants to hear.
W. H. Auden

Never assume the obvious is true.
William Safire

The criterion of truth is that it works even if nobody is prepared to acknowledge it.
Ludwig von Mises

Aims

By the end of this chapter you should:

- understand that, perhaps contrary to what you have so far found in your formal education, certainty and truth are not easily found
- recognise that there are many dubious pieces of 'knowledge' available and that even the word of a world authority is no guarantee of truth
- understand that 'certainty' is a matter of degree and that some opinions are better than others
- be able to give at least an initial definition of 'knowledge' and distinguish between 'knowledge' and 'belief'
- be able to list and give a simple critique of different reasons for saying that you 'know' something
- be able to discuss how these different reasons relate to the standard academic subjects.

Introduction

You have probably been in full-time education for a number of years, and in that time you have acquired a vast amount of knowledge. With the help of your teachers and your textbooks, the number of facts you know and the depth of your knowledge are probably amazing. What is more, you are learning more and more, and will probably go on to do so for several more years. In the sciences, for example, many of you will know about Einstein's theories. Einstein is widely regarded as one of the greatest geniuses of all time, and yet the physicists among you will be writing about his ideas in your exams. In English literature, many of you will be able to analyse and discuss Shakespeare, possibly the greatest English playwright the world has ever seen and will ever see. The same goes for any other subject; you will be studying ideas that only thinkers of great genius could develop.

When you scale that up to all the people alive today, you realise that the amount of knowledge out there is truly staggering. What is more, you have access to so much of it. You want to know what animals were walking the Earth two hundred million years ago? Look it up in a book. You want to know what it's like in Antarctica in the middle of winter? Watch a documentary. And it's getting better all the time – with newspapers, magazines, TV and the internet, you can find out all about the world without leaving the comfort of your own home. And what could be more reliable than journalism and the internet?

Well, recent headlines that have been seen in one, admittedly less than illustrious, newspaper include 'Woman Eaten by Fur Coat!' and 'Alien Base Found on Dark Side of Moon!'. The latter is especially interesting, as when it was pointed out that NASA pictures showed no such base, the newspaper ran an 'Alien Base Mysteriously Disappears!' story. The internet, too, is hardly a totally trustworthy source of information – just look for the 'Elvis is alive and well and working as a plumber in Bolivia' websites! So can we trust the information that we have?

I can imagine what you are thinking at this stage: that these are stupid examples. Only really gullible people would believe stories as ridiculous as these, and nobody with any sense would make errors as obvious. So now consider the following predictions. They are slightly different from the newspaper headlines in that they are all claims about the future, but they still tell us something about the possibility of error.

- *There is no likelihood that humans will ever tap the power of the atom.*
  Robert Millikan, Nobel Prize Winner in Physics (1923)
- *The atom bomb will never go off and I speak as an expert.*
  Admiral W. Leahy, advisor to the US President (1945)
- *I think there will be a world market for five computers.*
  Thomas Watson, founder of IBM (1958)
- *By 2000 women will wear pants, men will wear skirts, both sexes will go bare-chested (weather permitting) and clothes will be see-through.*
  Rudi Gernreitch, American fashion expert (1970)
- *The internet will never take off.*
  Bill Gates, founder of Microsoft (1988)

So it isn't just stupid people who get things wrong. Perhaps there are errors in what you are told every day, even in what you are reading now. It could be that what you learn in school isn't totally correct. So when I said that you have a lot of knowledge, maybe I should have been more careful. How much of what you know is true?

> **A** Identify something that you have been told, which you believed at the time but which you now recognise is false. How did you find out the truth?
>
> **B** Think of some things about which you are absolutely certain. Is anyone else certain about them, too?
>
> **C** What is the difference between 'I am certain that . . .' and 'It is certain that . . .?'

So when and how do you know if something is true? In relation to your studies, which of your subjects is the most reliable, and why? Does this reliability come at a cost? Answering these questions is the central theme of this book, and sometimes the answers can be quite surprising; they can force us to look at the world in a different way. As a brief example, let's consider how much we know in light of how long we have been around. Those of you who study history may sometimes feel overwhelmed at the massive length of human history. Geographers often comment how the impact of humans can be felt all over the world, even in the remotest places. These are both very valid perspectives. We humans dominate the Earth. In many ways, we are the supremely powerful species on Earth at the moment – there's no doubt about that.

But let's look at it slightly differently. Suppose you took the whole history of the Universe and compressed it into one year. (The year has been constructed on current estimates that the Universe is 15 billion years old; that the Earth is 4.55 billion years old; that humans developed around two million years ago. These figures are controversial and almost certainly wrong, but we don't know by how much! So take this example in the spirit in which it is meant!) So now it is 12.00p.m., 1 January, and the Universe began exactly one year ago. How long would we have been around for? Let's examine the cosmic calendar.

Current theory suggests that our galaxy formed on 1 May. It took another four months, to 9 September, until our solar system appeared. A few days later, the Earth was formed, around 14 September. After life begins on 25 September, it may seem like things are speeding up, but it then takes until 12 November for the oldest photosynthetic plants to develop, and it isn't until 1 December that there is a significant quantity of oxygen in the atmosphere. So for the first eight-and-a-half months, there was no Earth, and even then for another two-and-a-half months there was no conceivable way for humans, had they been around, to survive. But at least now we are beginning to approach human history...

Although there was oxygen in the atmosphere, fish did not develop until 19 December; trees followed soon after on 23 December, and the first dinosaurs turned up on 24 December. Mammals arrived on 26 December, and had to live with the dinosaurs until 28 December when it seems that a massive comet struck the Earth, causing major climatic change. The dinosaurs, unable to cope with this, died out, and the age of the mammals started. Humans appeared on 31 December. All of human history, therefore, happened on the last day of the year. Well, at least we have a day (remember that the dinosaurs had four!). Or do we?

In fact, probably not. Humans developed rather late in the day, around 10.50p.m. Current belief is that Peking Man first used fire in a controlled way at 11.46p.m., and at 11.59p.m. cave paintings started being created in Europe. Things happen in a rush now, with agriculture transforming the human way of life at 11.59.20, and the alphabet allowing detailed communication through generations at 11.59.51. The modern calendar began at 11.59.56 with the birth of Christ. The great Mayan civilisation and Chinese Sung Dynasty came and went at 11.59.58, and one second later, at 11.59.59, the modern technological world was born with the Renaissance and Industrial Revolution.

On the cosmic scale, therefore, it is only in the last fraction of a second, on the last day in the entire year that anyone alive today has existed, that you were born. Most people feel this to be profoundly humbling. And where does it leave humans' feelings of grandeur, sense of power and sense of certainty?

A What is the humans' place in the Universe? How likely is it that humans have found out any profound truths about the Universe?
B What are humankind's greatest successes?
C Does it really matter how long we have been around?

Some people think that the cosmic calendar analogy calls into question our certainties and our claims to knowledge. Certainly, it alerts us to the fact that our point of view is just one, perhaps very recent and very modest, perspective and it gives us good reason to approach grand claims to knowledge with some humility. However, we have skirted around the subject for long enough. We need to find out what knowledge actually is before we begin properly to question it.

What is knowledge?

This may seem like a ridiculous question. We all know what knowledge is, don't we? Well, maybe, but explaining it may prove to be a little tricky. Let's think about a couple of examples where we use the word 'know'. What do you make of the person who claims that they know that the Sun is pulled across the sky by six chameleon-like horses who blend into the sky so well that they are invisible? Or about my knowledge that I am, in fact, the secret hybrid product of an alien/human experiment? Can we really say we 'know' such things?

Most people would say that these beliefs are not knowledge because they are not true. We wouldn't say that people knew the Earth was flat; we would say that they believed it, but that they were proven wrong. Similarly, children cannot know, but can only believe, that Santa Claus is coming to town. There is a difference between belief and knowledge.

> **A** We have suggested that you can believe something without knowing it. Is it possible to know something without believing it?
>
> **B** Is knowledge the same as true belief? Can you imagine a case where someone believes something which is true, but where we would not say that she knows it?
>
> **C** One night my watch broke at 11.51, but I didn't realise. I was asleep at the time, and when I woke up I just put the watch on without looking at it. The next time I looked at it, it was, by chance, 11.51. I believed it was 11.51, and it was, in fact, 11.51. So did I know it? If not, why not?

In answer to question C, most people would say that I did not know it was 11.51, and that it was just a fluke. But this means something is wrong with saying knowledge is true belief. I believed it was 11.51, and it was true that it was 11.51. So why didn't I know it was 11.51?

Let's consider another example. Imagine that you find a long-lost manuscript detailing a conversation between two scholars, Joseph and Daniel, from the Middle Ages. The text starts:

'Joseph! I have made a great discovery! The Earth is round, not flat as everyone believes!'

Immediately your eyes light up! You have a fantastic new historical document. Excitedly, you read on:

'What rubbish Daniel. Anyone can see that the Earth is flat. The Greeks may have written something about a round Earth, but we have moved on since then. We know it is flat. Why are you saying this?'
'I have compelling evidence; no-one can deny it.'
'Go on then, tell me what brilliant discovery you have made.'

You are breathless with excitement – what evidence has Daniel found? Will he talk about the shadow cast by the Earth on the moon, or about ships vanishing on the horizon?

'Its wonder lies in its very simplicity! Take off your shoes and look at your feet – they are curved on the bottom! Your feet have arches! What is the reason for that? It can only be that in your childhood, when you walked around without shoes, your feet were moulded to the shape of the round Earth!'

Deflated and disappointed, you realise that Daniel did not know the Earth was round at all! He believed it, and it is true, but he didn't know it because his reasons were not adequate – his belief was unjustified. In the case of my faulty watch (above), I did not know that it was 11.51 because my justification would have rested on a false assumption – that my watch was working. So perhaps we may define knowledge as justified, true belief.

A Does the 'justified, true belief' definition fit our understanding of the term 'knowledge', or does it wrongly include or exclude anything? That is, can you think of a situation where either:

- someone might have justified, true belief but we wouldn't say that they knew something
- someone did not have justified, true belief but we would say they knew something?

So is the 'justified, true belief' definition absolutely correct? It has been suggested that to define knowledge like this is not very helpful – and for a very simple reason. If we claim to know something then we believe it, and we believe it to be justified and to be true. But how do we know if it is really justified and/or really true? You should see the problem here – we are trying to define knowledge in terms of justification and truth, but we are having to use the concept of knowledge in doing so! Our definition has become circular, and ultimately unhelpful.

A Molière once wrote that a sleeping potion worked by virtue of its 'dormitive faculty'. How is this related to what was said in the previous paragraph?

B Can you find a solution to the problem that defining knowledge as 'justified, true belief' may be a circular definition?

If we approach the issue in a slightly different way, then the problem of justification is not as serious as we thought. Rather than saying 'this is justified' or 'this is not justified', maybe we should talk about the **validity** of the justification – for example, 'poor justification', 'strong justification' or 'excellent justification' – leading to 'stronger' and 'weaker' forms of knowledge.

A What sort of justifications would lead to 'strong' knowledge or 'weak' knowledge?

B Revisit the examples in this section and describe the validity of the justifications. Is the 'knowledge' 'strong' or 'weak'?

C Which of your school subjects give you 'strong knowledge'? Which give you 'weak knowledge'?

How do we proceed from here? We have been arguing about the meaning of words for a little too long (this is something that, rightly or wrongly, philosophers are often accused of doing!). Perhaps we need to start looking at examples of what we consider to be knowledge, and see how we justify these claims. So let us take our tentative definition of 'justified, true belief' at face value and, while we remain aware that it is a limited definition, let's use it to set out the parameters of our inquiry. If knowledge is justified, true belief then we must examine what we believe, how we justify our beliefs and whether or not they are likely to be true. Let's start with a simple question.

What types of knowledge are there?

It is very easy to read, often in reputable newspapers, that news is about facts, and opinions on those facts. **Facts** are disputable (for example, we can argue about the number of computers sold in India in 1999) but there is a right and a wrong answer. **Opinions** are rather different – you may hear it said that an opinion can never be wrong because everybody is entitled to their own opinion. The notion of freedom is sometimes interpreted as meaning that anyone's opinion is as good as anyone else's.

This is actually pure nonsense. Suppose you are a keen runner, but you break your leg in an accident. Your leg is put in plaster for a month, and when the plaster is removed you are keen to start training straightaway. In my opinion, you should start training immediately, and push yourself really hard, ignoring any pain, until you are as fit as you were before the accident. In your doctor's opinion, you should take things very slowly, and stop as soon as you feel any pain.

Which opinion is better? Clearly, the one that is based on reason and experience. This is the kind of opinion most important to educated people, and the kind we will concentrate on in this course. Most people would agree that some opinions are better than others – the difficult thing is to decide how to tell a good opinion from a bad one. In the case of the injured runner, it seems reasonable to trust a doctor, as she will have better reasons for her judgement than a lay person.

We might plausibly argue that there are three types of questions.

- Questions that have one correct answer. Example: how many atoms of hydrogen are there in a water molecule?
- Questions that have many possible answers but which require justification and reasoned judgements. Example: what is the best way to tackle the developing world's debt problem?
- Questions that have no correct answer but depend totally on the person answering the question. Example: which type of chocolate tastes best?

Sometimes it is possible to argue about which category a question falls into – for example, 'Is this painting good art?' Some people might put it in the third category while some might choose the second. If in doubt, it is worth assuming that it is a question worthy of debate and exploring how a discussion develops. If it turns out to be pure personal choice, with nothing to be said for one side more than the other, then it will probably turn out to be a short and boring discussion! If you find yourself coming up with reasons that appeal to 'universal' intellectual standards, such as clarity, consistency, honesty, factual accuracy and so on, then the question is certainly a 'type two' question.

It is the appeal to 'universal' intellectual standards which is important, and it is these standards which we shall be looking at in some detail. (Of course, we might argue about 'universal' but to argue at all requires some agreement.) The standards mean that we can at least try to make coherent intellectual progress towards a well-reasoned and justified answer with even the hardest questions.

A Do you think three categories of question are enough? Are there any others you could add?

B For each of the following questions, decide which of the three categories of knowledge the answer fits into.

■ How many planets are there in the solar system?
■ Who is the Singaporean minister with responsibility for education?
■ When was the French Revolution?
■ Is it wrong to kill?
■ What is the colour of the nearest wall?
■ Does God exist?
■ Are you happy?
■ Is your teacher happy?
■ Is one plus one always two?
■ Does violence on television contribute to violence in the community?
■ Was Hitler a good leader?
■ Can a male doctor know more about childbirth than a mother of ten children?
■ Is it possible to know something but be unable to say what it is that you know?
■ Will science eventually tell us how and why the Universe started?

C Three categories may not really seem to do the variety of questions justice. If we want to analyse different types of knowledge, it might be helpful to be more specific. What categories might you divide knowledge up into?

Good reasons

In answering the questions above, you have begun to justify your thinking. In one sense, this whole book is about justifying our thoughts on various topics; about arguing for what we believe in. We naturally do this all the time – when we explain why we want to see a particular film, how we solved a maths problem, or the nature of our religious beliefs. For such an important topic, it is surprising that we usually spend so little time examining whether or not our reasons are actually good reasons, or if some types of reasons are better than others. In fact, most of us probably don't even know the different types of reasons that we have, so this must be our starting point.

A Below is a rather dubious list of things that I might claim to know, and another list of reasons that I might give to support these pieces of knowledge. Match the reasons to the claims.

Claims   **Reasons**
- I know that the sky is blue because
  I can see it.
- I know that $1 + 1 = 2$.
- I know that it is wicked to murder a   **Value judgement**
  person.   **Faith**
- I know that I have a fear of spiders.   **Memory**
- I know that I went out for a run   **Authority**
  yesterday.   **Intuition**
- I know that what the doctor said is true.   **Revelation**
- I know that women are more emotional   **Sense perception**
  than men.   **Logic**
- I know exactly what God wants of me.   **Self-awareness**
- I know that I am going to Heaven.   **Common knowledge**
- I know that a lake is more beautiful   **Instinct**
  than a sewage works.
- I know that I love my brother.

B Are there any other ways to justify things that we know?
C Are any of these ways of knowing really the same thing?
D Which of these do you think are the most reliable ways of finding the truth? Justify your answer.

We can argue about the distinctions, differences and overlaps between the categories given here as there are several possible ways to categorise knowledge. For our purposes, we will suggest that sense perception and logic form two vital categories, and later on we shall see how they arise naturally from an examination of everyday and academic knowledge.

Where do we go from here?

We have seen that there may be good reasons to think carefully about what we claim to know; that knowledge is a multi-faceted and complex concept and humans are only recent additions to the Universe. What hope do we have for certainty and truth when we are so limited? And yet, we seem to have made so much progress, even in the short time we have been around. Our societies are radically different to those of any animals; we know how the stars shine and we have the power to destroy the Earth. So far we have even had the wisdom not to! Have we overplayed the weaknesses of humankind?

Perhaps in our quest for truth we should be a little more positive and look at what we *do* know rather than what we do not. Maybe we should turn our attention to what seems to be the triumphant model for certainty in today's world – the natural sciences.

Further reading

At this stage, any text that takes a thoughtful, reflective and wide-ranging approach to knowledge will be very helpful. Excellent, short and accessible essays on topics as diverse as propaganda, art, Santa Claus, God and truth can be found in Martin Gardner's *Order and Surprise* (Oxford University Press, 1983) and *The Whys of a Scrivening Philosopher* (Oxford University Press, 1985). For a more philosophical but delightfully readable and very short introduction, you might try Thomas Nagel's *What Does It All Mean?* (Oxford University Press, 1989). By the same author, *Mortal Questions* (Cambridge University Press, 1979) is much more advanced but equally fascinating. For a look at the whole concept of knowledge, it is hard to find a better introduction than Stephen Cade Hetherington's *Knowledge Puzzles* (Westview Press, 1996). In terms of relevant fiction, Robert Pirsig's *Zen and the Art of Motorcycle Maintenance* (Bodley Head, 1974) takes an unusual but compelling approach to some of the issues, and the dazzling stories, essays and parables in Jorge Luis Borges' *Labyrinths* (Penguin, 1964) defy description, providing a unique and paradoxical window on the everyday world.

Ghosts

An extract from *Zen and the Art of Motorcycle Maintenance* by Robert M. Pirsig.

'Let's tell stories,' Chris says. He thinks for a while. 'Do you know any good ghost stories? The kids in our cabin used to tell ghost stories at night.'

'You tell us some,' John says.

And he does. They are kind of fun to hear. Some of them I haven't heard since I was his age. I tell him so, and he wants to hear some of mine, but I can't remember any.

After a while he says, 'Do you believe in ghosts?'

'No,' I say.

'Why not?'

'Because they are *un*-sci-en-*ti*-fic.'

The way I say this makes John smile. 'They contain no matter,' I continue, 'and have no energy and therefore, according to the laws of science, do not exist except in people's minds.'

The whiskey, the fatigue and the wind in the trees start mixing in my mind.

'Of course,' I add, 'the laws of science contain no matter and have no energy either and therefore do not exist except in people's minds. It's best to be completely scientific about the whole thing and refuse to believe in either ghosts or the laws of science. That way you're safe. It doesn't leave you very much to believe in, but that's scientific too.'

'I don't know what you're talking about,' Chris says.

'I'm being kind of facetious.'

Chris gets frustrated when I talk like this, but I don't think it hurts him.'

'One of the kids at YMCA camp says he believes in ghosts.'

'He was just kidding you.'

'No he wasn't. He says that when people haven't been buried right, their ghosts come back to haunt people. He really believes in that.'

'He was just spoofing you,' I repeat.

'What's his name?' Sylvia says.

'Tom White Bear.'

'Ah, American Indian!' I laugh. 'I guess I'm going to have to take that back a little,' I say. 'I was thinking of European ghosts.'

'What's the difference?'

John roars with laughter. 'He's got you,' he says.

I think a little and say, 'Well, Indians sometimes have a different way of looking at things, which I'm not saying is completely wrong. Science isn't part of the Indian tradition.'

Chris thinks a little and says, 'Tom White Bear said that his mother and father told him not to believe all that stuff. But his grandmother whispered to him that it was true anyway, so he believes it.'

He looks at me pleadingly. He really *does* want to know things sometimes. Being facetious is not being a very good father. 'Sure,' I say, reversing myself, 'I believe in ghosts.'

Now John and Sylvia are looking at me peculiarly. I see that I'm not going to get out of this one easily and brace myself for an explanation.

'It's completely natural,' I say, 'to think of people who believed in ghosts as ignorant. The scientific point of view has wiped out every other point of view to such an extent that they seem primitive, so that today if a person talks about ghosts or spirits he is considered ignorant or maybe nutty. It's all but completely impossible to believe in a world where ghosts can actually exist.'

John nods his head and I continue.

'My own opinion is that the intellect of modern man isn't that superior. IQs aren't that different. Those Indians and other believers in ghosts were just as intelligent as we are, but the context in which they thought was completely different. Within their context of thought, ghosts and spirits are as real as atoms, particles, photons and fields are to a modern man. In *that* sense I believe in ghosts and spirits too.'

'What?'

'Oh, the laws of physics and of logic ... the number system ... the principles of algebra. These are ghosts. We just believe in them so that they seem thoroughly real.'

'They seem real enough to me,' John says.

'I don't get it,' says Chris.

So I go on. 'For example, it seems completely natural that gravitation and the law of gravitation existed before Isaac Newton. It would sound nutty to think that until the seventeenth century there was no law of gravity.'

'Of course.'

'So when did this law start? Has it always existed?'

John is frowning, wondering what I am getting at.

'What I'm driving at,' I say, 'is the notion that before the beginning of the Earth, before the sun and the stars were formed, before the primal generation of anything, the law of gravity existed.'

'Sure it did.'

'What, sitting there, having no mass, no energy of its own, not in anyone's mind because there wasn't anyone – this law still existed?'

Now John doesn't seem so sure.

'If that law existed,' I say, 'I honestly don't know what a thing has to do to be non-existent. It seems to me that the law of gravity has passed every test for non-existence that I can think of. No mass, no energy, unknown to anyone ... I can't think of a single scientific attribute of existence that it has. And yet it is still "common sense" to believe that it existed.'

John says, 'I guess I'd have to think about it.'

'Well I predict that if you think about it long enough you will find yourself going round and round and round and round until you finally reach the only possible, rational conclusion. The law of gravity *did not exist* before Isaac Newton. No other conclusion makes sense.'

John and Chris sit silently, foreheads creased in confusion. I continue anyway.

'And what that means is that the law of gravity exists nowhere except in people's heads! It's a ghost! We are all of us very arrogant and conceited about running down other people's ghosts but just as ignorant and barbaric and superstitious about our own!'

'So why does everybody believe in the law of gravity then?' asks John.

'Mass hypnosis. In a very orthodox form known as "education".'

'That's absurd.' John shakes his head. He pours me another drink, puts his hand over his mouth and in a mock aside says to Sylvia, 'You know, most of the time he seems like such a normal guy.'

I counter, 'That's the first normal thing I've said in weeks. Most of the time I'm feigning twentieth-century lunacy just like you are. So as not to draw attention to myself.'

'But I'll repeat it for you,' I go on. 'We believe that the disembodied words of Isaac Newton were sitting in the middle of nowhere billions of years before he was born, and that he somehow magically *discovered* these words. They were always there, even before the Universe, when they applied to nothing. And when the Universe began, then they applied to it? That, John, is ridiculous.'

'The problem, the contradiction that scientists are stuck with, is that of *mind*. Mind has no matter or energy, but they can't escape its predominance over everything we do. Logic exists in the mind. Numbers exist only in the mind. I don't get upset when scientists say that ghosts exist in the mind. It's that *only* that gets me. Science is *only* in your mind too, it's just that that doesn't make it bad. Or ghosts either.'

They are looking at me so I continue: 'Laws of nature are human inventions, like ghosts. Laws of logic, laws of mathematics are also human inventions, like ghosts. The whole blessed thing is a human invention, including the idea that it *isn't* a human invention! The world has no existence whatsoever outside the human imagination. It's all a ghost, and in antiquity it was recognised as a ghost – the whole blessed world we live in. It's run by ghosts. We see what we see because ghosts *show* it to us, ghosts of Moses and Christ, and Buddha, Plato, Einstein and so on. Isaac Newton is a very good ghost. One of the best. Your "common sense" is nothing more than the voices of thousands of these ghosts from the past. Ghosts and more ghosts. Ghosts trying to find their place among the living.'

John looks too much in thought to speak. But Sylvia is excited. 'Where do you get these ideas?' she asks.

I am about to answer, but do not. I have a feeling of having pushed it to the limit, maybe beyond, and it is time to drop it.

After a while John says, 'It'll be good to see the mountains and the high country again.'

'Yes it will,' I agree. 'One last drink to that!'

A Why does the narrator think that the laws of nature are in the mind? Do you agree?

B Did the force of gravity exist before Newton? Did the law of gravity exist before Newton? Can the one exist without the other?

C The narrator states that the word 'only' irritates him. Explain why. Do you agree?

The progress of science is strewn, like an ancient desert trail, with the bleached skeletons of discarded theories which once seemed to possess eternal life.
Arthur Koestler

The notion of absolute truth is shown to be in poor correspondence with the actual development of science. Scientific truths are better regarded as relationships holding in some limited domain.
David Bohm

IN QUESTIONS OF SCIENCE THE AUTHORITY OF A THOUSAND IS NOT WORTH THE HUMBLE REASONING OF A SINGLE INDIVIDUAL.
Galileo Galilei

Science is built with facts just as a house is built with bricks, but a collection of facts cannot be called a science any more than a pile of bricks can be called a house.
Henri Poincaré

ALL OUR SCIENCE, MEASURED AGAINST REALITY, IS PRIMITIVE AND CHILD-LIKE – AND YET IT IS THE MOST PRECIOUS THING WE HAVE.
Albert Einstein

In science the primary duty of ideas is to be useful and interesting; even more than 'true'.
Wilfred Trotter

When a distinguished but elderly scientist states that something is possible, he is almost always right. When he states that something is impossible, he is very probably wrong.
Arthur C. Clarke

The most incomprehensible thing about the world is that it is comprehensible.
Albert Einstein

Far more marvellous is the truth than any artists of the past imagined! What men are poets who can speak of Jupiter as a man, but if he is an immense spinning sphere of methane and ammonia must be silent?
Richard Feynman

Everything you've learned in school as 'obvious' becomes less and less obvious as you begin to study the Universe. For example, there are no solids in the Universe. There's not even a suggestion of a solid. There are no absolute continuums. There are no surfaces. There are no straight lines.
R. Buckminster Fuller

All science is either physics or stamp collecting.
Ernest Rutherford

By the end of this chapter you should:

- **understand what elements are often said to make up the classical scientific method (with examples, preferably some of your own)**
- **recognise the limits and problems of the classical scientific method and appreciate that the growth of scientific knowledge is a complex phenomenon that cannot be rigidly defined**
- **know what makes a claim a scientific claim and the meaning of the term 'pseudo-science'**
- **appreciate the meaning of 'truth' in a scientific context**
- **be able to discuss the interplay between science and other areas, such as the arts and religion**
- **appreciate that the scientific way of thinking may have important consequences for our beliefs in other areas.**

Introduction

The natural sciences are one of humankind's great achievements. In popular culture to hear that something is 'scientifically proven' is almost the same thing as hearing that it is 'definitely true' and science has certainly achieved many wonderful, and terrible, advances in recent history. In a search for reliable knowledge, science must rank high on any list. After all, we trust scientific beliefs with our lives every time we get in a car or aeroplane, use a lift or eat processed foods. So what is it about the natural sciences that make them so special?

There are few people who answer this question as well as Richard Feynman, a visionary physicist who fundamentally changed our understanding of nature. He wrote:

The things with which we concern ourselves in science appear in a myriad of forms, and with a multitude of attributes. For example, if we stand on the shore and look at the sea, we see the water, the waves breaking, the foam, the sloshing motion of the water, the sound, the air, the winds and the clouds, the sun and the blue sky, and light; there is sand and there are rocks of various hardness and permanence, colour and texture. There are animals and seaweed, hunger and disease, and the observer on the beach; there may be even happiness and thought. Any other spot in nature has a similar variety of things and influences. It is always as complicated as that, no matter where it is. Curiosity demands that we ask questions, that we try to put things together and try to understand this multitude of aspects as perhaps resulting from the action of a relatively small number of elemental things and forces acting in an infinite variety of combinations.

For example: Is the sand other than the rocks? That is, is the sand perhaps nothing but a great number of very tiny stones? Is the moon a great rock? If we understood rocks, would we also understand the sand and the moon? Is the wind a sloshing of the air analogous to the sloshing motion of the water in the sea? What common features do different movements have? What is common to different kinds of sound? How many different colours are there? And so on. In this way we try gradually to analyse all things, to put together things which at first sight look different, with the hope that we may be able to reduce the number of different things and thereby understand them better.

A few hundred years ago, a method was devised to find partial answers to such questions. Observation, reason, and experiment make up what we call the scientific method.

What do we mean by 'understanding' something? We can imagine that this complicated array of moving things which constitutes 'the world' is something like a great chess game being played by the gods, and we are observers of the game. We do not know what the rules of the game are; all we are allowed to do is to watch the playing. Of course, if we watch long enough, we may eventually catch on to a few of the rules. Knowing the rules of the game is what we mean by 'understanding'. Even if we knew every rule, however, we might not be able to understand why a particular move is made in the game, merely because it is too complicated and our minds are limited. If you play chess you must know that it is easy to learn all the rules, and yet it is often very hard to select the best move or to understand why a player moves as he does. So it is in nature, only much more so; but we may be able at least to find all the rules. Actually, we do not have all the rules now. (Every once in a while something like castling is going on that we still do not understand.) Aside from not knowing all of the rules, what we really can explain in terms of those rules is very limited, because almost all situations are so enormously complicated that we cannot follow the play of the game using the rules, much less tell what is going to happen next. We must, therefore, limit ourselves to the more basic question of the rules of the game. If we know the rules, we consider that we 'understand' the world.

You find here, in a nutshell, what many scientists believe science to be. You may be surprised to hear them wax lyrical about curiosity, awe, beauty, rigour, honesty and humility – but contrary to some stereotypes science can inspire lofty emotion! This isn't that surprising – it is, after all, a human endeavour.

Occasionally, you hear science spoken of in an arrogant fashion, with disdain for 'non-scientific' thoughts or processes, but this usually says more about the speaker than about science. Feynman again:

We must, incidentally, make it clear from the beginning that if a thing is not a science, it is not necessarily bad. For example, love is not a science. So, if something is said not to be a science, it does not mean that there is something wrong with it; it just means that it is not a science.

A Explain the game analogy that Feynmann uses to explain the aims of science.
B Do you think the analogy is a good one? Explain your answer.
C How does this fit in with your science lessons at school?

The 'scientific method'

We found that the theory did not fit the facts; and we were delighted, because this is how science advances.

O. R. Frisch

Let us look now, in some more detail, at what makes science so special. As Feynman says, **observation**, **reason**, and **experiment** make up what we call the **scientific method**. It is also very important that the observations, reasoning, and experiments can be **repeated and checked independently** by other observers. If you and your friends are the only ones to have seen or understood something, then it doesn't count as science.

Your sighting of a UFO last year is not likely to be accepted by scientists. If the UFO had really been there, radar equipment would have picked it up, and it would have been reported. Your report has not received independent experimental confirmation where there should have been, so your claim is not scientific. That is not to say that it is definitely false, just that it is highly likely to be false. (Of course, it may be that UFOs have the ability to hide from radar; we cannot rule this out – when we have so-called Stealth technology it hardly seems impossible to believe that visiting extra-terrestrials also have it. However, the point stands   we must look to the evidence and evaluate it. Most scientists believe that the evidence is unconvincing, and that the best explanations do not involve aliens.)

We will say a little bit more about experimental confirmation later on, but here we return to Feynman to talk about one other key element of science, namely **imagination**.

But what is the source of knowledge? Where do the laws that are to be tested come from? Experiment itself helps to produce these laws, in the sense that it gives us hints. But also needed is imagination to create from these hints the great generalisations – to guess at the wonderful, simple, but very strange patterns beneath them all, and then to experiment to check again whether we have made the right guess.

We can examine these ideas with reference to the following two simple claims:

(a) The Earth is flat.
(b) The Earth is round.

Were these scientific claims at the time they were made? Let us first turn to claim (a).

At the time, it was certainly observed that the Earth was flat. We are not talking about there being a few mountains here and there, but the fact that, on the whole, the Earth seemed flat. People certainly did their reasoning: things on a slope have a tendency to slide down the slope, so if the Earth weren't flat, people would start sliding at some stage. But this is not what happens. So at this stage, thinking that the Earth was flat was a reasonable scientific belief. Here we have the first indication that science and truth are not necessarily intimately related.

But what about testing claim (a)? People did that, too. They travelled over land and over sea. Some went to look for the edge of the planet, since there should be one assuming the Earth has finite size. The fact that they did not find an edge helped a great deal in the eventual rejection of claim (a).

Now let's look at claim (b). Here one clearly needed some imagination. At the time, there was no direct observation available. But there were hints: perhaps the moon is not a disc painted on the sky but a solid sphere a long way off; perhaps our Earth is similar to it. Also, no edge to the Earth was ever found, and on the contrary, there were strange reports of sightings of similar land found by sailing east and sailing west. So someone used some imagination and made a bold move: suppose that the Earth is round.

Now what? We need to test this claim experimentally. How do we do that without aeroplanes and satellites? We reason and think of possible consequences, and then test those consequences. One immediate consequence of a round Earth is that there should be a horizon. If boats disappear over the horizon, their mast should disappear last. Also, we should be able to see further the higher up we go.

These consequences were known to be correct experimentally. After all, boats always had somebody high up in the mast, so that they could look further. These consequences could not be explained in a straightforward manner with claim (a). The first seed of doubt was sown. The distance to the horizon is easy to measure experimentally: all it takes is you, a friend and a small boat. It turns out to be about 5 km if your eyes are 2 m above sea level. Now we can use some mathematics and lo and behold, we find the size of the Earth! The radius should be about 6000 km.

So by simply applying reason, we see that claim (b) implies precise limitations on the size of our planet! If it is round, then its radius better be 6000 km, or, equivalently, its circumference should be about 40,000 km. Could this claim be tested experimentally? Well, it could certainly have proved false. That is, it could have been **falsified**. If people had been able to sail 50,000 km west without returning to the start, claim (b) would have been in trouble. But the fact of the matter was that the 40,000 km circumference tallied quite well with the earlier suspicions of having reached the same land from two different directions. Of course, it could be that the Earth isn't a sphere but an egg shape, and that the voyages which seemed to confirm a circumference of 40,000 km were only good for one particular direction. On the basis of theory and evidence so far discussed, we can't be sure.

This is the essence of scientific truth: it can never be proved experimentally that a claim is correct, but it can be proved that it's wrong (in which case it is said that the theory has been falsified). This might seem a little strange because it is easy to assume that scientific laws have been proven but, in fact, they have not. No matter how good our theories are, there is always the possibility that they will be shown to be incomplete, or even downright wrong. Even if a theory has been tested a million times, there may be an exception lurking around the corner. This is why we say that science has an **inductive** component (see Chapter 5 for more on induction). We must assume that our laws will continue into the future, even though we cannot justify this assumption, except by noting that we have little alternative!

It does not follow that we reckon all our theories are wrong – far from it. Scientists have tried very hard to disprove them, in some cases for hundreds of years, and they have failed. The longer a theory has resisted falsification, the more confident we feel about it. That is what Einstein meant when he said: *'Truth is what stands the test of time.'*

Now we know, for example, that:

(c) The Earth is not exactly round, but it is actually a bit wider at the equator.

Does that mean that claim (b) was wrong, just like claim (a)? This is an interesting point. It leads to the question, 'How much of today's science is wrong? If it is wrong, why does it work so well?' Perhaps right and wrong are not good ways of describing science; perhaps truth is not what science gives us at all.

What is clear is that a scientific claim is a claim that should lend itself to experiment. We should be able to devise an experiment that could falsify the claim. It is precisely here that we can differentiate between a scientific claim and a non-scientific one.

A Decide whether or not these are scientific claims:

1 The Earth is flat.
2 The Earth is not exactly round, but it is actually a bit wider at the equator.
3 UFOs regularly visit Earth to abduct humans for experimentation.
4 God created the world in seven days approximately 5000 years ago.
5 God created the Universe.
6 God did not create the Universe.
7 In some remote areas of China, there are people who can jump higher than 10 m.
8 In some remote areas of China, there are people who can jump higher than 10 m, but their society is so secretive that they will never permit outside observers to witness it.
9 Love is more important to human beings than anything else.
10 If you ask people what they find most important in a multiple-choice question, and you include love as a possible answer, then more than 75 per cent will put love at the top of their list.
11 Saying 'I love you' to your partner.
12 Picasso's painting 'Cannes, 4 a.m.' is a beautiful piece of art.

Discuss these with others to see if you can agree.

Remember that to say that a claim is not scientific does not mean that it is not important. Some of the claims above provide evidence of that – clearly arts, religion, and emotion are some of the most important ways of giving meaning to people's lives. The point is that a claim can only be called scientific if it lends itself to scrutiny and rigorous testing. This is a very difficult requirement, but it is precisely the strict adherence to this principle that accounts for the enormous and rapid progress made by science.

A If science never proves anything right, why do we trust it so much?
B Think about the science you learn at school. How likely do you think it is that it is wrong or incomplete? What about the science you read about in magazines such as *Nature*, *New Scientist* or *Scientific American*?

Another important aspect of scientific statements is best illustrated by example. Suppose the time is now one second past 9.00a.m. Consider these statements:

- It is 9.00a.m.
- It is between 3.00a.m. and 3.00p.m.

Both are testable by checking a reliable watch, and so both are scientific claims. The latter statement is, in fact, true, but very unlikely to be useful, whereas the former is false but probably accurate enough for almost any purpose. This clearly shows that there is more to a scientific statement than the requirement that it can be tested. There is also the issue of how much information a statement contains. A highly informative but incorrect theory (the former) is better than a vague but less informative theory (the latter). It may seem odd that a false statement is of more use than a true one – and this may lead us to question precisely what we mean by 'true' and 'false' in this context – but the answer to that question will have to wait until after we have looked at not just the scientific statements, but the scientists themselves.

Science as a human endeavour

A new scientific truth does not win by convincing its opponents and making them see the light, but rather because its opponents eventually die and a new generation grows up that is familiar with it.

Max Planck

The astronomer Carl Sagan argued that the success of science is similar to the success of democracy – both thrive on transparency and in both science and democracy the most effective road to progress is to give everyone the opportunity to have a look at the data. Everyone has the right to contribute, but only the ideas that deliver the goods carry the day. If your ideas don't stand the test of experiment, they'll be ruthlessly demolished, even if your name is Einstein (the work done by Einstein in the latter half of his life is considered ill-conceived by the majority of physicists). Perhaps this is what distinguishes science from other disciplines – because scientists rely on experiment, they can reject most of the rubbish! It does not accumulate and get in the way of new, better ideas.

The idea of testing theories and the value placed on scepticism are central to science. Attempts to prove Einstein, Newton, Darwin and all the other great (and not so great) scientists wrong are a central part of the scientific endeavour. After all, is there a better way to convince someone that a theory is valid than to try, but fail, to prove it wrong?

There is an important difference here between science and some other systems that claim to explain something about the Universe. The institutions of science have built-in sceptics – the scientists themselves! It is the sceptics who refuse to accept the current theory, who come up with their own ideas and persuade others that they are right, who win fame, fortune and success. We might usefully contrast this with other areas where scepticism is sometimes regarded as suspicious, and to be avoided.

Sagan goes on to ask:

'How is it possible that so many people distrust science, but are willing to put their trust in horoscopes and fortune tellers?'

Science tells you: here's what we've got. If you don't agree, show us where we're wrong, and we'll not only accept it, but cherish you as the bringer of new insights. Compare this to the leaders of the local cult or your local astrologist, who tell you:

'I cannot explain it to you in ways that you can test and unambiguously confirm, but I have the truth. Trust me and believe me; the truth has been revealed to me.'

Why is it that so many people prefer to trust one person who makes non-accountability his trademark rather than trust a community that has made self-criticism and scepticism its main virtue? Perhaps the answer to this is that we have so far been talking about science as it should be practised ideally. Of course, science is carried out by humans, and that means that it should also be studied as a human endeavour, with all that entails.

Perhaps the most interesting aspect of science as a human endeavour has been explored by Thomas Kuhn, a scientist himself, and also an historian and philosopher of science. Kuhn argued that, contrary to what we have said so far, scientists do not work by falsification. Arguing not just on philosophical grounds, but as a matter of historical fact, he suggested that scientists hold some fundamental beliefs (paradigms) so strongly that they are sometimes not prepared to allow them to be falsified; they may ignore or disbelieve findings which seem to disprove them.

Kuhn's classic example is the paradigm of the Earth at the centre of the Universe with the planets and the Sun orbiting in circles. This paradigm was technically falsified by Galileo and Kepler. According to a strictly rational scientific process, we might expect their findings to have been greeted enthusiastically, but it took a long time for their findings to be accepted. Another example is the theory of continental drift (which states that the continents 'slide around' on the surface of the Earth), which was laughed at by the geological community for years before finally being accepted.

The key point here is that, when doing experiments, it is very difficult to know how to interpret the results. When you find a result that seems to indicate that a widely held theory is false, what do you do? Of course, you assume that it is your mistake – and you check the evidence carefully. Even if you can't find the error, which of the possible explanations is more likely:
(a) that you have failed to spot the error
(b) that the famous theory is wrong?

Well, that depends on many things. Once there is enough evidence, the scientific community will accept that a theory has been falsified. But what is enough evidence? That is a question which cannot be answered by science – it is a value judgement that individuals make according to their own personalities and idiosyncrasies. There are emotional reasons, too (perhaps some scientific advances are felt to be threatening), and the feelings of the scientific community are of paramount importance. Kuhn stresses, for the first time, the social nature of science.

Consider another example: in 1926, after 25 years of skilful and patient work by physicist D. C. Miller, in which many thousand repetitions of the Michelson–Morley experiment (to measure the speed of light) produced results clearly inconsistent with Einstein's theory of relativity, he addressed the American Physical Society, explaining his results. At face value, Miller falsified relativity, but was the theory abandoned or even brought into serious question by the community? It was not. In fact, his results evoked nothing but expressions of regret that such a fine experimental physicist should waste his professional career generating data in which no-one was interested. What seems to have been at stake was the professional skill of the scientist rather than the hypothesis he thought he was testing! So the claim that 'experiment is always the final arbiter of a theory' needs some qualification. The philosopher Michael Polanyi writes:

It is the normal practice of scientists to ignore evidence which appears incompatible with the accepted system of scientific knowledge, in the hope that it will eventually prove false or irrelevant.

Many scientists have echoed this. Erasmus Darwin, brother of Charles, said, *'If the facts won't fit in, why so much the worse for the facts.'* Paul Dirac, Nobel Prize-winning physicist, said, *'It is more important to have beauty in one's equations than to have them fit the experiment.'*

Crucially, this view deposes science from its objective, value-free status. After Kuhn's analysis we tend to see science as very much a human activity, flawed and multi-faceted. Expecting a perfect truth-seeking mechanism from flesh-and-blood people is, perhaps, asking a little too much.

Let us not, however, get too carried away. The natural sciences have made many magnificent and unprecedented achievements, and we should not pretend that they are completely irrational. Although science is a human activity performed by a human community, it seems to work most of the time. This is truer now than at any time in the past. Today, the greatest dream of many scientists is to prove a theory wrong, since that is how progress is made and fame is won! While conservatism was part and parcel of science a few centuries ago, many scientists would say that things have moved on and that today 'difficult' experimental data would not be ignored. Early last century, it took Einstein less than fifteen years to win the world over to his radically new ideas. Likewise, when Feynman proved previous theories wrong and proposed new ones, they were accepted within a few years. Conversely, when 'cold fusion' was proposed a few years back, experimenters all over the world immediately took up the challenge (of course, the trillions of dollars that were available to the finders of cold fusion may have had something to do with it, too). After a tumultuous few months of conflicting results, the scientific community came to the consensus that the phenomenon of 'cold fusion' was simply an error or a hoax: the crucial results could not be duplicated. 'Cold fusion' did not pass the stringent test of experiment.

To overturn a theory now requires less time than it ever did before. But let us not forget that scientists are humans.

A If you did an experiment that seemed to have falsified the theory of conservation of energy, what would you do?

B What does this imply for the roles of experiment and falsification in the progress of science?

C If what Kuhn says is true, is this a positive or negative description of science? What might it mean for the commonly-held notion of the methods of science as yielding facts and truths?

D Do you think that Kuhn's model is an accurate description of science?

Science – a universal tool?

Science is nothing but trained and organised common sense.

T. H. Huxley

As we've seen, the method of science is widely applicable, but we haven't made clear what distinguishes the **natural** sciences from other sciences. Natural scientists have a far easier job than **social** scientists (such as economists or social psychologists) because their claims can be defined very precisely. For example, compare a physicist with an economist who has great difficulty in even obtaining precise definitions (what does 'the economy will react adversely to the imposition of currency controls' really mean, in absolutely accurate terms?). This is not economists' fault. Their subject is plagued by many variables that cannot be independently controlled by experiment, and the environment they are trying to describe is continually changing (for example, a society with widespread internet access may react differently to one without). This is in stark contrast to chemists, who keep working and combining the same 100-odd atoms. If nature had decided to work the way economics works, it would introduce a few new atoms every year! The amazing thing about nature is that, as far as we can tell, its underlying laws are **unchanging**. It goes without saying that it is far easier to work in a fixed environment than in an everchanging one. This is the luck of natural scientists, and is another reason for the rapid progress in their fields.

The fact that the natural sciences study an environment that is believed to have fixed laws marks another distinction: it allows researchers in these fields to keep on digging for the underlying foundations and thereby reduce their theories to fewer and more basic terms. To make progress in the natural sciences means to make things simpler – for example, phenomena like wind, sound and heat, what keeps a solid together, and the principles of cooling and pressure are all manifestations of the same underlying truth, that the world is made up of molecules. Going one step deeper, one asks what molecules are made of, and so on. But progress in economics, for example, has led to greater complexity and an increasing list of exceptions to general rules.

The fact that the laws of the natural sciences are undergoing continuous reduction is also the reason why we have so far restricted our discussion of the natural sciences to physics. The basic laws of chemistry, for example, can be understood with physics (with quantum mechanics, to be precise). The laws of biology are essentially chemical in nature, so arguably they also reduce to physics ultimately. Geology is another discipline in which the underlying principles are physical in nature. In short, the deepest underlying rules of all natural sciences ultimately reduce to physics. However, please remember Feynmann's words at the beginning of this chapter. We're not saying that by knowing everything about physics we will also know everything about biology. After all, knowing the rules of chess does not mean you know how to play! There is a distinction between reductionism and elimination – when a subject is reduced to physics is does not necessarily mean that we have found out everything about that subject.

A 'People fall in love because of their psychological make-up. Psychology reduces to biology; biology to anatomy; anatomy to chemistry; chemistry to physics. So to be the best psychologist you can be, you should study physics.' On what grounds would you accept or reject this statement?

B Read the final paragraph above carefully and imagine that at some future date we eventually find all the laws of nature – 'the rules of the game'. What would that mean for our ability to make things and control the world?

C We have considered at least four aspects of sciences – inductivism, falsification, paradigms and creativity. Think of some examples of each aspect. What are the respective roles of each component? Are any components more important than others? What are the problems with each aspect?

D Some sciences are increasingly taking a **holistic** approach whereby they try to avoid **reduction**. Does this mean that they are still sciences, or have they become something else?

E Think back over your science education. What did you learn about the way science works?

F Are the theories in this chapter realistic about the way sciences work?

G Are they the way sciences *should* work?

H Ask any scientists you know what they think makes the natural sciences so special.

'Right', 'wrong' and scientific 'truth'

Even if by chance he were to utter The final truth, he would himself not know it: For all is but a woven web of guesses.

Xenophanes

One of the greatest triumphs of the natural sciences is Einstein's theory of general relativity. Combining spectacular creativity, brilliant reasoning, bold conjectures and dramatic experimental confirmation, it seems to be all that science should be.

But what if Einstein was wrong? The history of science is full of theories that once seemed 'right', but which we now know are 'wrong'. Famously, the Earth is not flat, atoms are not the smallest particles, and Mars has no canals on it. Some of today's science seems so outrageous (chaos theory tells us that a butterfly flapping its wings can cause a hurricane on the other side of the world!) that surely it is just a matter of time before today's beliefs are superseded and discarded. So why shouldn't Einstein be wrong?

Well, most scientists believe that eventually Einstein will be proven 'not right'. But 'not right' does not mean 'wrong'. This can lead to confusion because we tend to think of science as black and white. We can argue about shades of grey in the arts, or perhaps the social sciences, but we tend to think of 'truth' and 'certainty' in physics. However this may be incorrect. Dividing the scientists into the 'bad guys' (who tried hard, but got it wrong) and the 'good guys' (who got it right) is a little too simple.

Of course, Einstein is the archetypal 'good guy'. He managed to solve problems that even the great Newton got wrong. Strange then, that Newton's 'wrong' ideas are still used by NASA for satellites and space shuttles. Why do all our daily experiences (apples falling and the like) obey his rules? Why does the moon still orbit according to Newton's formulas? Newton's laws *work*. How can they be wrong?

> **A** If Newton's ideas were wrong, why are they still used? Can wrong theories make correct predictions?
> **B** What are the meanings of 'wrong' and 'correct' in the previous question?

The answer to the apparent contradiction between Newton and Einstein is surprisingly simple. Einstein generally *agrees* with Newton; in fact, the only point of disagreement is over issues that Newton never considered (such as speeds extremely close to the speed of light, or near objects with intense gravitational fields). That is, Einstein built on Newton's theories, added to them and took them to new levels of complexity and sophistication. If Newton had been completely wrong, Einstein could not have been right. To say that Einstein 'disproved' Newton is to miss the point of the process – without Newton, there could not have been Einstein.

'Right' and 'wrong' therefore may not be useful ways to describe scientific theories. Physicist David Bohm puts it well:

The notion of absolute truth is shown to be in poor correspondence with the actual development of science. Scientific truths are better regarded as relationships holding in some limited domain.

New ideas rarely mean abandoning old ideas completely. Rather they stretch, expand and build upon old ideas. Scientists used to argue about whether light was a wave or a particle. It turns out (so we now think) that it is both. The new theory of light does not disprove either old one, rather it unites and enlarges them.

This simple point is often lost in the very human desire to categorise ideas as 'right' or 'wrong'. We like clarity and easy answers and we tend to shy away from more complex notions if we can. This means that we sometimes see a 'scientific revolution' when there was really a slow evolution of scientific theory. Physicist Hendrik Casimir writes:

The gradual evolution of new theories will be regarded as revolutions by those who, believing in the unrestricted validity of a physical theory, make it the backbone of a whole philosophy.

'Right' ideas are ideas that lead to other ideas and, that seem to make deep and unexpected connections to other areas of knowledge. Sometimes they lead to a new explanation of a familiar phenomenon. 'Wrong' ideas, by contrast, do not lead anywhere.

By this definition, several 'wrong' ideas are 'right'. We could say that those scientists who once thought that the Earth was flat were 'wrong', but it may be more accurate to say that their theories were limited. If you walk around town, it seems pretty flat. It is all just a matter of perspective (you should be reminded of Newton and Einstein again here). 'The Earth is flat' is 'right' when you are in town. But if you need to travel by aeroplane, then you need to take a larger, wider perspective. You need to expand your theory to take more cases into account. That doesn't mean you were wrong before. It just means that you were only right in some cases.

In other words, 'wrong' means limited. It means that you haven't got the whole story. It doesn't mean that the theory has no value and is useless. We can say that most scientific ideas are 'wrong' as long as we understand what 'wrong' really means. As ever, a thorough understanding of language is essential.

So in all likelihood, Einstein was wrong. He was not able to see all the possible problems or consequences of his theories. He was not omniscient! In fact, anyone who claims to have the absolute truth is probably not in the business of science. 'Right' and 'wrong', in that sense, do not really enter into the scientific process. They are only matters of dogma.

A In your own words explain the difference between 'right' and 'wrong' suggested here. Do you agree?

B According to this way of thinking, what is scientific 'truth'? Is this different to the way we use the word 'truth' in everyday speech?

C Are 'right' and 'wrong' used in the same way in maths, the arts or other disciplines?

Where do we go from here?

As we noted in the introduction to this chapter, it would be foolish to deny that the natural sciences have made, and are still making, astonishing progress in understanding the way the Universe works. They even seem to be telling us something about where we came from and our place in the Universe. But can the sciences ever tell it all? Can they ever tell us something about our daily lives and the human experiences which fill them? Many would say not, arguing that even if we knew every single physical detail about the Universe that it was possible to know, we would not know, for example, what it would be like to be someone else. Nor could any science, no matter how advanced, explain what it feels like to be in pain, or in love, or to taste coffee or wine. The argument seems to have a lot of force – maybe the sciences can never do that for us. Can any other discipline?

To some, the answer is obvious. Where do we regularly seem to 'touch' another human and transcend what has been called our 'egocentric predicament'? The only place, surely, is the arts, and it is to these we now turn.

Further reading

The recent explosion in popular science writing means that you are spoiled for choice in this area, and any good bookshop will have a whole section devoted to the philosophical implications of the natural sciences.

In terms of the scientific method itself, Alan Chalmers' *What is This Thing Called Science?* (Open University Press, 1979) is an accessible but detailed and lively overview. John Hosper's *An Introduction to Philosophical Analysis* (Prentice Hall, 1957) chapter 4, also provides a very brief but interesting overview. Karl Popper's *The Logic of Scientific Discovery* (Hutchinson, 1968) and *Conjectures and Refutations* (Routledge and Kegan Paul, 1969) are classics, though a more accessible introduction to his work can be found in the marvellous and very short *Popper* by Bryan Magee (Fontana Modern Masters, 1969). Thomas Kuhn's *The Copernican Revolution* (Random House, 1959) and *The Structure of Scientific Revolutions* (University of Chicago Press, 1970) are also very readable and entertaining. On the issue of science and truth, John Ziman's *Reliable Knowledge* (Cambridge University Press, 1978) is helpful. On the links between science and religion (and interludes into the nature of time, free will, miracles, mind and self) a great starting point is Paul Davies' *God and the New Physics* (Pelican, 1984) or *The Mind of God* (Penguin, 1992). The whole concept of laws of science and their nature is explored in John Barrow's *The World Within the World* (Oxford University Press, 1988). The possible limits of science are discussed lucidly and entertainingly in both John Horgan's *The End of Science* (Abacus, 1996) and John Barrow's *Impossibility* (Vintage, 1999). Carl Sagan's *The Demon Haunted World* (Ballentine Books, 1996) is a classic call for us not to take these limits too far.

On science and uncertainty

An essay from *Discover*, by Lewis Thomas.

SCIENCE and technology, hailed just a few years back as the sure solutions for all our increasingly complex societal problems, are both in trouble these days. Part of the difficulty is that the two enterprises, really quite separate, generally seem so tightly linked as to be one thing: the nuclear bomb and energy plants are scientific accomplishments; chemical waste products are the droppings of science; the increased levels of CO_2 in the Earth's atmosphere are pumped there by science; and now we have genetic engineering, computers playing high-class chess, satellites capable of photographing the tears on up-turned faces, overpopulation of the planet by older and older people blocking options for the young. Soon enough we will have to begin worrying about traffic accidents on Mars.

If you concentrate on technology, it can seem as though science has developed into the mightiest force in the affairs of mankind, and is getting out of hand and beyond control because of the overwhelming power of piled-up mountains of new information. There are uncomfortable doubts in the public mind about the risks entailed by learning so much so fast. Soon there will be earnest proposals that science

should be slowed down by law to regulate the enterprise more tightly, with agencies deciding in advance that there are some things that human beings are better off not knowing. There is concern that research, left to itself, driven by its implacable reductionism, will quickly penetrate all the great mysteries and we will be left with nothing to contemplate but the nasty little details of a monstrous machine. There is a genuine apprehension that science may be taking the meaning out of life.

But if you concentrate on science, it is in real life not like this at all. We are nowhere near comprehension. The greatest achievements in the science of this and the last century are themselves the sources of more puzzlement than human beings have ever experienced. Indeed, it is likely that these times will be looked back on as the time when science provided the first close glimpse of the profundity of human ignorance. We have not reached solutions; we have only begun to discover how to ask questions.

Science is founded on uncertainty. Each time we learn something new and surprising the astonishment comes with the realisation that we were wrong before. The body of science is not, as is sometimes thought, a huge coherent mass of facts, neatly

arranged in sequence, each one attached to the next by a logical string. In truth, whenever we discover a new fact it involves the elimination of old ones. We are always, as it turns out, fundamentally in error.

I cannot think of a single field in biology or medicine in which we can claim genuine understanding, and it seems to me the more we learn about living creatures, especially ourselves, the stranger life becomes. I do not understand modern physics at all, but my colleagues who know a lot about the physics of very small things, like the Universe, seem to be running into one queerness after another, from puzzle to puzzle.

The sense of strangeness and ambiguity is the best evidence that science is working. The world is not a simple place, nor are we simple instruments. We should have known this long ago, but we found it easier in earlier centuries to tell tales to each other, powerfully explanatory but based on pure guesswork, and generally mistaken. Now that we have made a beginning of sorts, it is becoming clear that nothing is clear. I believe that the exploration of nature, given the spectacular human gift of insatiable curiosity, will never be concluded. I cannot for the life of me imagine a time when all our questions will do more than raise new questions, with new astonishments for answers.

It is a risky business, science. Not only do you have to start your work by assuming the existence of wrongness, you must count on a very high probability of being wrong in your own experiments, running into dead ends, finishing the work with that greatest of scientific disasters, a 'trivial' observation. It takes the greatest skill, and a measure of courage, to turn your imagination completely loose and this is the mandatory first step. You make up a story to explain whatever it is that you are curious about and then you design an experiment to test the story, building in all the controls that you can think of in order to make sure that your wish to be right, just this once, will not influence the outcome. This, by the way, is where the greatest danger lies; you can wish too hard for it to be garden path and overlook the plainest evidence of a blind alley. I do not know of a chancier profession.

It is true that scientists have not done a very good job of explaining what they are up to, but this is not because of any reluctance to display their accomplishments; they tend to brag all over town, to anyone willing to listen. The real trouble is that the public knows too little, and is told by the scientists too little, about the ignorance of science itself.

This has nothing at all to do with the applications of science. The ignorance I have in mind is of another order, unrelated to usefulness, not connected with our capacity as a species to solve practical problems. There are questions of the agenda of modern science that need answering simply for better comprehension, and for the wisdom of a future society.

We know a lot about the structure and function of the cells and fibres of the human brain, but we haven't the ghost of an idea about how this extraordinary organ works to produce awareness; the nature of consciousness is a scientific problem, but still an unapproachable one. We can make good educated guesses about the origin of life on this planet; it must have started, we think, as single-celled creatures resembling today's bacteria, but we have no way of tracking back to the events preceding this first cell, nor can we lay out an orderly scheme for explaining the nearly four billion years of evolutionary process from such a cell to ourselves.

We do not know how the first cells of an embryo, starting from the fusion of an egg and a sperm, sort themselves out with infallible precision into the systems of differentiated cells of a baby, each cell in possession of all the information needed for a complete baby but with most of that information switched off so that it can only become, say, a skin cell or a brain cell. We do not know how normal cells are transformed into cancer cells; we know the names of some of the chemicals, and types of radiation that can launch this process, but the nature of the process itself eludes us.

· We know that songbirds have centres on the left sides of the brain for the generation of bird song, and we suspect that this may somehow be related to the lateralisation of speech centres in our own brains, but we do not understand language itself. Indeed, language is so incomprehensible a problem that the language we use for discussing the matter is itself becoming incomprehensible. We do not know what holds us together as a social species; it is a mystery that we are so dependent on each other, in search all our lives for affection, and yet so willing to destroy each other when assembled in larger groups; the failure of nations to conduct their affairs with anything resembling the humanity we expect from each other as individuals is, somehow, a biological problem still beyond our reach. We do not understand the process of dying, nor can we say anything clear, for sure, about what happens to human thought after death.

In short, we are an ignorant species, new to the Earth, still juvenile, still in the earliest stages of inquiry, bound by our very nature to discover more about ourselves and the life around us in which we are, like it or not, embedded. It is in our genes to understand the Universe if we can, to keep trying even if we cannot, and to be enchanted by the act of learning all the way.

But we have a long way to go.

Every artist dips his brush in his own soul, and paints his own nature into his pictures.
Henry Ward Beecher

ART IS EITHER PLAGIARISM OR REVOLUTION.
Paul Gauguin

The fashionable oppish and popish forms of non-art today bear as much resemblance to exuberant creativity . . . as the noise of a premeditated fart bears to the trumpet voluntary of Purcell.
Lewis Mumford

These are bagpipes. I understand the inventor of the bagpipes was inspired when he saw a man carrying an indignant, asthmatic pig under his arm. Unfortunately, the man-made sound never equalled the purity of the sound achieved by the pig.
Alfred Hitchcock

Without music life would be a mistake.
Friedrich Nietzsche

Acting is not being emotional, but being able to express emotion.
Kate Reid

Imaginative literature in the service of rebellion, or satanism, quickly sinks into exhibitionism or obscurity. Imaginative literature as the expression of a deeply apprehended truth, poetry which interprets to a man the myth of his own age, can in the hands of Dante, of Shakespeare, of Cervantes, of Camões and of Goethe, help to raise the level of a whole civilisation.
J. M. Cohen

ART IS NOT A HANDICRAFT, IT IS THE TRANSMISSION OF FEELING THE ARTIST HAS EXPERIENCED.
Leo Tolstoy

I passionately hate the idea of being with it, I think an artist has always to be out of step with his time.
Orson Welles

Beauty is excrescence, superabundance, random ebullience, and sheer delightful waste to be enjoyed in its own right.
Donald Culross Peattie

Remember that the most beautiful things in the world are the most useless; peacocks and lilies, for example.
John Ruskin

By the end of this chapter you should:

- appreciate possible definitions and descriptions of the central characteristics of the arts
- be able to defend what you think are the standards of artistic judgement
- understand how the arts fit into the human experience
- be able to discuss the possible status of artistic knowledge, as opposed to other forms of knowledge
- appreciate various theories of the role of truth in the context of the arts.

Introduction

For much of our lives, we are concerned with the nitty gritty business of staying alive – if not by growing our own crops, raising our own animals or constructing our own homes, then by participating in an economy which allows us to have these things done for us by others. Sustenance, shelter and other such fundamental human needs are, by definition, vital for us, but once these basic needs have been achieved, we find that there is a universal human tendency to look for that which is beyond mere survival. In his famous **hierarchy of needs**, the psychologist Maslow ordered our requirements in the following pyramid, where each need can be addressed only once those below it have been fulfilled.

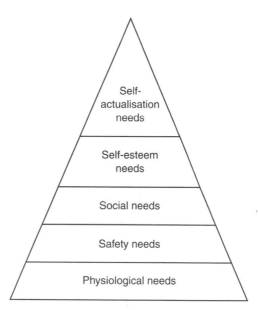

The top level, self-actualisation, may seem a little obscure, but it means something like 'fulfilment' at a deep level. The same idea has been echoed many times throughout history. The psychologist Carl Jung wrote:

The supreme goal of man is to fulfil himself as a creative, unique individual according to his own unique potentialities and within the limits of reality.

Similarly, in the eighteenth century, one of the founding figures of America, John Adams, wrote:

I must study politics and war so that my sons may have liberty to study mathematics and philosophy. My sons ought to study mathematics, philosophy, geography, naval architecture, navigation, commerce and agriculture in order to give their children a right to study painting, poetry, music, architecture, statuary, tapestry and porcelain.

These claims that creativity, and its embodiment in the arts, is the highest and noblest human impulse is a sentiment that many would echo. If we accept it, then Adams' view that other forms of knowledge are mere means to that end might seem to be a logical conclusion. Certainly, it would suggest that a close look at what the arts actually do would be in order. What do the arts bring us that mathematics does not? What can we learn from the arts that is beyond the reach of the sciences?

A little reflection on our own lives quickly shows the pervasive nature of the arts. Evidence of the artistic impulse can be found almost everywhere – in what we wear, what music we listen to, what television programmes we watch, what books we read, what food we eat and what jobs we choose. In every recorded culture around the world, people have produced works of art to adorn their homes, to beautify their clothes, to decorate their bodies, and generally to enhance their experience of life. In this we seem to differ from other animals, whose activities are centred only around the **function** of objects, and not their **form**.

So we have two burning reasons to study the arts. The desire to create some sort of art seems to be a universal (some have argued **defining**) human trait, and the artistic impulse may be among the loftiest of human drives.

A Do you think that the notion of a hierarchy of needs is meaningful? If so, is Maslow's model the correct one? If not, why not – surely we all have biological needs that we must satisfy before other needs can be met?

B What is the role of the arts in the hierarchy that Maslow has identified? Is this role universal across different cultures?

C If you accept Maslow's hierarchy, which is more important – the lowest level of the pyramid or the top level? Construct arguments to support both views.

What is art?

Life beats down and crushes the soul and art reminds you that you have one.

Stella Adler

Before we consider how to define or evaluate the importance of art, we need to decide what may or may not be legitimately called 'works of art'. We should not restrict our attention purely to painting, poetry, or any other particular form, and when we refer to 'the arts' or 'art' it will not be with reference to any particular medium. However, in expanding our vision of the arts we are immediately faced with the problem of where to stop. It would be difficult to say that *everything* is art, but once we go beyond the obvious art forms it is very hard to know where to draw the line.

A Which of the following twenty items are works of art? Justify your choice.

- *Sunflowers* by Vincent van Gogh.
- A mass-produced urinal entitled *Fountain*, chosen and displayed, but not designed or created, by Marcel Duchamp.
- An untitled white piece of canvas.
- A superb rock concert.
- The song *Happy Birthday*.
- A superb sportsman running 100 m.
- A perfect copy of *Sunflowers* sold for $3 in a market.
- A beautiful mountain.
- A poem generated by a computer.
- Einstein's general theory of relativity.
- A white piece of canvas entitled *A Foggy Day*.
- An extremely funny cartoon.
- Mozart's *Clarinet Concerto*.
- A perfect copy of *Sunflowers* hung in a gallery and called *The Perfect Copy*.
- *King Lear* by William Shakespeare.
- The Taj Mahal in Agra, India.
- A sheep cut in two and preserved in a glass container.
- Some old bricks and timber randomly arranged and entitled *Building Site*.
- The ballet *Swan Lake* by Tchaikovsky.
- A white piece of canvas entitled *Hiroshima*.

You may find some of the following concepts helpful in your discussions:

value   creativity   truth   intention   enlightenment splendour   reality   perspective   accuracy   elegance   form realism   novelty   empathy   beauty   emotion   passion wisdom   interpretation   education   wonder   awe

When we ask what art is, we need to be clear about what sort of answer we are hoping to find. If we mean 'What sort of things are called art?' then we have an empirical issue – the question is about how and in what contexts people use the word 'art'. In this sense, the answer will be descriptive of how the world is. On the other hand, and perhaps far more interestingly, if we mean 'What sort of things *should* we call art?' then we have entered a different area for this question cannot be answered purely by reference to a description of the world. In order to answer the question in this sense, we are required to make a judgement, and the answer will indicate how we think the world should be.

This split between descriptive and prescriptive modes of analysis is often found when we consider human activity (in the human sciences, the terms '**positive**' and '**normative**' are used) and it raises the problem of criteria, or standards, by which to judge. If we have a theory in, say, the natural sciences, then we can, in principle, perform experiments to test the theory. The standard of judgement is clear and unambiguously stated; theory must conform to experiment. Now the natural sciences are not without their difficulties, as we have seen, but there are universally accepted standards because we know what the natural sciences are about. Broadly speaking, they are about finding out how the physical world works, and so they appeal to the physical world (that is, experiment) as the arbiter of success. The contrast with the arts could not be more clear. There are no universally accepted standards because there is no universal agreement as to the subject matter of the arts. What are they about? What are they trying to do?

So before we can even begin to address the question of good or bad art, we need to think about precisely what it is that art attempts to do. Only then might we be in a position to see whether or not any particular piece has achieved its intended goals.

Several suggestions have been made about the purpose of the arts. It is often suggested that **the arts are a way of expressing emotion**. We certainly engage in those art forms which give us the emotion of pleasure in one way or another. This is consistent with the commonly held belief that 'beauty is in the eye of the beholder'. Since we are the only ones who can be sure of the emotions we are feeling perhaps, by extension, we are the only ones capable of saying which are good and bad pieces of art **for us**. This idea also seems to fit well with the stereotypical art/science divide – the (often implicit) argument being that if science is objective and emotion free, then art must be subjective and emotion laden. Certainly, much art is either directly about emotions or evokes strong emotions within us.

A Find several pieces of art in different media (for example, architecture, music, painting, poetry, plays, sculpture), good and bad, which evoke emotion.

B If the purpose of art is to evoke emotion, then what are the best forms of art?

C Would this definition of the purpose of art include things which we would not wish to include, or exclude things we would not wish to exclude?

D In light of this, to what extent is communication of emotion a useful characterisation of art?

This emotional theory is, however, far from a complete explanation of the purpose of the arts. Another theory suggests that **the arts imitate nature or the world** (this theory is also called the **mimetic theory of art**). Indeed, we all know that it takes great skill to draw or paint a realistic scene. If we take this as a requirement of art, then photography would seem to be one of the highest forms as it can arguably capture more detail than any picture. But is the old cliché 'the camera never lies' really true? We all know that a photographer has to select his picture from an almost infinite range of possibilities; to take a particular set of photos is to miss the other possibilities. But which set tells the truth? One also wonders if there is room for music and dance in this conception of the arts.

These days to speak of an artist as an imitator would be an insult, and although we can appreciate the skills required to do an incredibly realistic still life, it seems rather limiting that art should aim for accurate representation of that which exists in the world. This seems to be missing the point of art. When a visitor to Matisse's studio asked, 'Surely the arm of that woman is too long?', he replied, 'Madam, you are mistaken. That is not a woman; that is a picture.'

Certainly few painters today would say that their main goal is to imitate nature or the 'real world', and they would be quick to correct this attitude in others. Nevertheless, terms such as 'non-representational', 'vivid', and 'abstract' have their roots in this mimetic conception of art and much abstract art is loosely based in the material world. In the cubist movement of art, for example, a single picture might show several superimposed images of a person's face, each one viewed from a different angle. Obviously this is not realistic, but the artist might have been acknowledging the fact that any single image of the face cannot possibly capture its 'reality' and trying to give a 'truer' representation of the face than the one we see from a single, limited perspective. Arguably, even when we stray from nature, we implicitly affirm its central role in our thinking; we use nature as the baseline against which to compare the alternatives. If art was totally unrelated to the world in which we live, then it would be very difficult to see why we should find it so important.

Imitating the world is also rather an ambiguous idea – for example, does showing how something looks exactly make a good imitation? Some paintings have been called masterpieces precisely because they go beyond appearances and seem to capture what the thing really is not just what it looks like. It has been said that Picasso painted chickens that were in some sense more chicken-like than any 'real' chicken – he somehow captured the essence of 'chicken-ness'. Is this imitating the world or not? Perhaps there is more to artistic 'truth' than mere accuracy.

A Find several pieces of art which imitate nature.
B If the purpose of art is to imitate nature, what are the best forms?
C Would this definition of the purpose of art include things which we would not wish to include, or exclude things we would not wish to exclude?
D In light of this, to what extent is mimesis a useful characterisation of art?
E What do you think might be the aims of a typical photographer? Are they different from the aims of the artist?

Another ancient tradition is that of **art teaching us what is right**. If art does not tell us how the world is then perhaps it tells us how it should be. A famous example is Picasso's *Guernica*, which depicts the slaughter and mayhem caused by fascists in Spain. The picture alerts us to a moral issue; it is an immediate and powerful way of saying that something is wrong, and that the world should be different. Certainly as a medium, art is often able to say some things in a more powerful way than the truthful but limited statement, 'Many people were killed by fascists in

Spain.' (So can art be considered a language?) This is not to say that art should consist of direct moral instruction; rather it can heighten moral awareness in a subtle and perhaps more profound way. Recently an artist hung aborted fetuses as earrings from a mannequin. There was an outcry that this was a deeply immoral thing to do; that it showed no respect for human dignity or the sanctity of life. However, it could also be argued that the piece was attempting to make a profoundly moral point – that in our materialistic society children are treated as fashion accessories, available if we want them and disposable if we do not. The art conveys the message in a powerful and striking way that words cannot.

Oscar Wilde famously disagreed in *The Picture of Dorian Gray* where he wrote:

There is no such thing as a moral or an immoral book. Books are well written or badly written. That is all.

However, many have since suggested that art which broadens our experience must, of necessity, inform our understanding of how we should live. Certainly many, if not most, books, plays and films involve some moral perspective. The writer and philosopher Iris Murdoch has argued that appreciation of the arts, and beauty in particular, allow us to transcend some of the empirical and rational problems of the human condition; they allow us to rise above our petty and individual selves, and that this must be the first step towards a meaningful morality.

By opening our eyes we do not necessarily see what confronts us. We are anxiety-ridden animals. Our minds are continually active, fabricating an anxious, usually self-preoccupied, often falsifying veil, which partially conceals the world. Our states of consciousness differ in quality, our fantasies and reveries are not trivial and unimportant, they are profoundly connected with our energies and our abilities to choose and act. And if quality of consciousness matters, then anything which alters consciousness in the direction of unselfishness, objectivity and realism is to be connected with virtue.

This is a difficult idea. Murdoch suggests that by altering our states of consciousness, as the arts surely do, they are of necessity linked with our moral perspectives. On a similar practical level, philosopher Martha Nussbaum has argued that literature enhances our moral understanding not only by encouraging us to look outside ourselves, but also by engendering a sympathetic and emotional identification with characters (perhaps suggesting that the emotional and moral approaches are not as distinct as they might, at first, seem). It is this identification which can then contribute to the growth of the reader.

We have never lived enough. Our experience is, without fiction, too confined and too parochial. Literature extends it, making us reflect and feel about what might otherwise be too distant for feeling. The importance of this for both morals and politics cannot be underestimated.

A Describe some art which has affected your moral outlook. Why did it do so?

B Does this view of the purpose of art capture what we think should and should not be categorised as art?

C According to this model, what are the highest and lowest forms of art?

D What are the links between emotional and moral feelings that are engendered by the arts?

While acknowledging that the arts can offer moral insights, many have felt that the identification of art with morality is not helpful. Arguing that the arts can do so much more than offer only moral insights, they suggest that **art offers insights into the human condition**. Perhaps this explanation allows us to see why the arts are regarded as a mark of civilisation, why they offer something glorious and profound. If they offer us a way to make sense of what is a confusing natural world, a way to interpret our emotions and those of others, or a guide to the nature of morality, then they are indeed to be valued! This characterisation of the arts seems to encompass the others so far suggested, and suffuses them with a meaning and purpose which resonates more warmly with our experience of great works of art. It may not be the ultimate description of the arts, but it may bring into sharp relief exactly what forms of knowledge and truth are offered by the arts, and explain why they are held in such high regard. Perhaps other disciplines give us 'knowledge' but we turn to the arts to broaden our emotional and intellectual boundaries.

A Look at the list of items on page 33 and suggest what the pieces might tell us about the human condition.

B Describe some art which has moved you profoundly in some way.

C According to this model, what are the highest and lowest forms of art?

This view of the arts immediately raises several important questions concerning the nature of artistic truth and experience, but before we can consider these questions in a meaningful way, we need to address another fundamental issue.

Does it all come down to opinion?

I'd like to hear your opinion on this piece of Beethoven. And remember, it is not Beethoven who is being examined here.

Paul Strathern

When someone tells us that their favourite piece of music is better than ours, we might well shrug, point out that 'beauty is in the eye of the beholder' and be content to leave it there. The idea that each person can judge equally well and that no opinion is more valid that any other seems quite common – it seems to be based in both everyday experience and common sense. In the eighteenth century, the philosopher David Hume wrote:

Beauty is no quality in things themselves: it exists merely in the mind that contemplates them; and each mind perceives a different beauty ... to seek the real beauty is as fruitless an inquiry, as to pretend to ascertain the real sweet or the real bitter. According to the disposition of the organs, the same object may be both sweet and bitter . . . It is very natural, and even quite necessary to extend this axiom to mental, as well as bodily taste.

This view that art is not a tangible product but a state of mind has also been expressed by the art critic and philosopher John Dewey:

In common conception, the work of art is often identified with the building, book, painting or statue in its existence apart from the human experience. Since the actual work of art is what the product does with and in experience, the result is not favourable to understanding.

Of course, beauty and art are not the same thing (so Hume and Dewey may need a little interpretation) but we can immediately see the force of what they are saying. Whenever we talk about art, we tend to suggest tentatively 'I like it' or 'It speaks to me' rather than state dogmatically 'It is good art'. Conscious of our own cultural, class and gender perspectives and aware of the socially constructed nature of value and of art, we would not want to be seen to be suggesting that we have access to the 'truth' about art, or that we are privy to deep insights about art. We might even argue that there is no such thing as truth in this context.

However, a little critical reflection on our own aesthetic and everyday experience might give us reason to question this rather stereotyped account. To suggest that a railway is on a par with *Hamlet*, or that an opera is no better than the sound of elevator music, is surely ridiculous. Outside the philosophical arena, no one would seriously defend such a view. Similarly, if we really believe that there are no standards in art, then it is very difficult to see why the arts are taught, studied, examined and graded, or how there can be great, mediocre and poor pieces of art.

It seems that when the objects concerned are relatively close on some scale of merit then we pretend there is no such scale, but when they are far apart we are all happy to consent to its existence. Now this rather strange phenomenon needs to be explained, and there seem to be two alternatives. Either all artistic judgement comes down to personal opinion, or there are some standards by which all art is measured.

A If the arts are about personal opinions then why do we, as a society, rate some art as much better than others? Why are some pieces that were created centuries ago still well known today? Could the sound of my pet dog vomiting really be great art?

B If there are objective standards by which to measure the arts, then what are they? Do you think your standards are universally applicable? And what is the basis for your choice of those particular standards?

C It has been suggested that A and B are only two options on the question of artistic standards. Is this true? Are there any other alternatives or distinctions which might be helpful?

The fact that there are art critics seems to suggest that some standards are worth listening to. The fact that more often than not the critics are in broad agreement might suggest that there are standards of judgement. Anyone who has ever sat an art, music or drama examination knows that some standards do exist. A discussion of balance and tone in paintings, or of harmony and structure in music, would be out of place here, but the existence of the terms means, surely, that we can make judgements. These discussions are relevant not only for 'high' arts – every time we see a film we use standards which are not just arbitrary, but which are centrally linked to the quality of the film. We may talk about the special effects, or the characterisation, or another aspect of the film, but these are qualities about which there is general agreement.

A Think about your own experiences in art or music lessons. Are there standards which you attempt to meet?
B Are your judgements about art as good as those of an expert?
C Is there universal agreement about the standards of judgement? If not, why not?

It may be that even after thinking long and hard about this, we still find that our position is inconsistent; we believe that some art is better than others, objectively, but we believe that there are no objective standards by which to judge! The difference between good and bad art has been described as indefensible but also indispensable, and perhaps it is so. If this is the case, then maybe we should accept the inconsistent nature of our beliefs and stop worrying about it. After all, this mirrors the often ambiguous nature of art itself.

When Oscar Wilde quipped, *'There are two ways of disliking art; one is to dislike it; the other, to like it rationally,'* he may have hit the nail on the head. It has often been suggested that certain human truths cannot be expressed in the language of rationality – perhaps the arts attempt to address these truths, if such things exist. Maybe scientists and philosophers cannot maintain inconsistent positions, but artists can embrace them as part of the artistic process itself! That is not to say that art has to be irrational – the laws of logic are not lightly tossed aside – but perhaps we should acknowledge what has been called 'an organic connection between form and content' and rest content with the idea that the language of communication must reflect the substance of the message. If we hold contradictory beliefs, then we can smile and remember the words of the great scientist Neils Bohr: *'The opposite of a correct statement is a false statement. The opposite of a profound truth may well be another profound truth.'* Perhaps this is no bad thing. Maybe there is no shame in the rule of the subjective in the arts; if the artist cannot escape to the safe, objective and impersonal haven that other scholars may crave, so be it. That is not to say that there are no standards of judgement, that nothing distinguishes the genuine from the misbegotten (which is, roughly, the 'true' from the 'false'). Whatever your thoughts on the issue of artistic standards, it is worth asking yourself why people feel strongly about the arts. Art critic Ted Cohen's answer leads us back to the whole nature of art, and on to the meaning of truth and knowledge within the arts:

I am ... trying to understand why I (or anyone for that matter) would ever seriously care to deny or assert that something is art. I have gotten this far: when I feel like insisting or denying that something is art it is because I wish to insist on or resist the idea that the thing is to be taken seriously, that there is a kind of obligation to recognise the thing as a significant item in my life.

And I have gotten this much further: to explain the significance of the thing in my life I must suppose that it also has a place, or deserves to have a place, in the lives of others. That's as far as I've gotten.

> **A** Are the arts important? If so, is this despite or because of the problem of finding the standards by which to judge them?
> **B** What place does rationality have in the arts?
> **C** What are the standards of artistic judgement?
> **D** Which people are best qualified to judge the arts? What qualities should they possess?

The arts, experience, and the nature of artistic truth

Poetry begins in delight and ends in wisdom.

Robert Frost

Several philosophers have suggested that the arts are not related to truth and knowledge. It has been argued that the language of the poet is close in nature to a grunt or a stamp of the foot; it is non-cognitive, conveys no knowledge and is unrelated to truth. Others in the same tradition have taken similar, though less extreme positions. The once influential philosopher A. J. Ayer, while agreeing that art has nothing to do with knowledge, notes that:

a work of art is not necessarily the worse for the fact that ... [it is] ... literally false ... If the author writes nonsense, it is because he considers it most suitable for bringing about the effects for which his writing is designed.

This is an interesting position – Ayer suggests that in the arts 'nonsense' and statements which are 'literally false' may be the best way to achieve certain effects. So if we take these effects to be truth and knowledge of some sort, as many have done, this means that we are using falsehoods as the best way to find truth! Perhaps this is what Picasso meant when he said, *'Art is a lie that gives us the truth, at least the truth we are given to understand.'* This seemingly ridiculous assertion is well worth pursuing. Consider this famous piece from Shakespeare's *Macbeth*. Having just been told that his wife is dead Macbeth says:

Life's but a walking shadow, a poor player
That struts and frets his hour upon the stage,
And then is heard no more; it is a tale
Told by an idiot, full of sound and fury
Signifying nothing.

Let us examine this extract for meaning, truth and knowledge. *Life's but a walking shadow...* No, it is not. This is false.

...a poor player that struts and frets his hour upon the stage and then is heard no more... No, the vast majority of us do not act, and we do not go on stage. Those of us who do so probably spend significantly more than an hour there.

...it is a tale told by an idiot... No, life is not a story, and it is unlikely that an intellectually-impaired person is involved.

...full of sound and fury... There is sound in life, and some fury, but clearly life cannot be literally full of anything, any more than life can have a colour.

...signifying nothing... Well, my life is certainly significant to me, even if to nobody else. Again, this is false!

On this reading, the passage contains no truth. Is it therefore meaningless and without merit? Most would agree that to say so would be to misunderstand profoundly the point of the arts, and that it is this literal analysis, not the passage, which is without real meaning. The flaw lies in the conception of knowledge and truth that is at the root of the analysis. We have tacitly assumed that by 'truth' we mean literal truth (this is also sometimes referred to as scientific truth, although this may be based on a misunderstanding of scientific truths) or truth that is verifiable in some sense. But if we try to reduce art to a series of truth statements, are we not diminishing it? To anyone who has ever felt undercurrents of insignificance or absurdity in their life, Macbeth's words speak a deep and vitally human truth. The artistic truth is different from the literal truth, but it is not without value for that.

That is not to suggest that literal truth has no place in the arts – Dickens describes certain aspects of Victorian London in great detail and Homer is an important historical source for the Trojan War, but this is only incidental to their value as arts. Our artistic appreciation of Dickens and Homer is not based on the accuracy of their factual accounts (more detailed and accurate accounts may not be art at all). Broadening our experience of situations where we were not personally present is no bad thing, but it does not require art to do that. If we prefer an account of Homer's to that of the historian, it is precisely because it goes beyond what actually happened in the Trojan War and in some way informs us about something in the present – our own experience. The condition of humans is a very different thing to the human condition, and it is knowledge of the latter with which the arts should be concerned.

Let us look again at the passage from *Macbeth*.

Life's but a walking shadow... So at times it seems shallow and fragile, and perhaps feels like it's just a copy of something real. Haven't we all felt that at times?

...a poor player that struts and frets his hour upon the stage and then is heard no more... Well, this refers to the sensation of playing a role in a play, and of having a rather small and worthless part, but nevertheless never being quite sure of your lines. Again, many of us have been there!

...it is a tale told by an idiot... If life is a play then it certainly does make you wonder sometimes about the sanity of the playwright!

...full of sound and fury signifying nothing... No matter what we do, how we struggle, or how much we try to fight it, we will all die and be forgotten. Even if we are remembered, what will that signify? Nothing.

Now it would be possible to write out what the passage means in a sense which contained literal truths. It might start, 'There are times when, to some people, life seems shallow and unreal...'. The passage would then conform to a strict notion of truth, but it would also be a rather dull statement not worth re-reading. Yet when Shakespeare has Macbeth say the literally false passage in the context of the play, when his wife is dead and his life is falling to pieces, it is a profound and moving sentiment that has provided insight and, yes, truth of sorts, to people for hundreds of years. Art critic John Tomlinson summed it up when he wrote:

An insight which might take a moment to express literally, and which would seem trite in speech, may strike us as a profound truth about the human condition when conveyed through, say, the medium of opera.

This approach stresses the role of the arts in expressing that which cannot be expressed **directly**, but which we can perhaps hint at. The writer Franz Kafka said, *'all things resist being written down'*, and perhaps he meant that *meaning* is constructed in our minds partly on the basis of the language we use. So if we want to communicate a profound human truth then we need a profound human medium to do so. Literal analysis is not enough. Martha Nussbaum writes:

There may be some views of the world ... that emphasise the world's surprising variety, its complexity and mysteriousness, its flawed and imperfect beauty, that cannot be adequately stated in the language of conventional philosophical prose – a style remarkably flat and lacking in wonder – but only in a language and in forms more complex, more allusive...

We should not think that truth in the sense that we have mentioned it is in any way mystical, or divorced from everyday experience. It is not something confined to Shakespeare and the most refined forms of opera, though it is surely to be found there in great measure. The greatest art should inform and enrich our interactions with the world. The writer Robert Dessaix has gone so far as to suggest that, *'Once you've read Tolstoy and Turgenev, for example, you will simply love differently.'* Nussbaum again:

Novels do not function ... as pieces of 'raw' life: they are a close and careful interpretative description. All living is interpreting; all action requires seeing the world as something. So in this sense no life is 'raw' and ... throughout our living we are, in a sense, makers of fictions. The point is that in the activity of literary imagining we are led to imagine and describe with greater precision, focusing our attention on each word, feeling each event more keenly – whereas much of actual life goes by without that heightened awareness, and is thus, in a certain sense, not fully or thoroughly lived ... So literature is an extension of life not only horizontally, bringing the reader into contact with events or locations or persons or problems he or she has not otherwise met, but also, so to speak, vertically, giving the reader experience that is deeper, sharper and more precise than much of what takes place in life.

Perhaps this conception allows us to suggest that profound art is art which provides us with meaningful experience, either in its own right, or as a way to reinterpret or re-experience our own experiences. In this sense we can see why the arts are subjective – they speak to us about our own experiences – but also see why there is so much agreement as so many of our experiences and inner worlds are common. Arthur Danto has related this to the original Greek concept of mimesis:

Hamlet and Socrates, though in praise and deprecation respectively, spoke of art as a mirror held up to nature. As with many disagreements in attitude, this one has a factual basis. Socrates saw mirrors as but reflecting what we can already see . . . and [therefore] of no cognitive benefit whatever. Hamlet, more accurately, recognised a remarkable feature of reflecting surfaces, namely that they show us what we could not otherwise perceive – our own face and form . . . and so art, in so far as it is mirrorlike, reveals us to ourselves.

Of course, there are other views. We might argue that experience is indeed 'raw' and cannot be interpreted, only misinterpreted. To exist 'in the moment' is the true experience – all else is secondary. To think that we can have experience *through* art, or indeed *through* anything may be mistaken – perhaps the whole point of experience is that it is unmediated and immediate. Film critic Michael Norman mentions Samuel Fuller, a Second World War veteran and war film director, who said that the only way to recapture the experience of war on film is to put a machine gun behind the screen and gun down the audience! His point is clear and powerful – the experience of war through a film can never be the same as the real thing. Norman writes of the seductive nature of the war film, and arguably this point is applicable in the widest sense:

Everything on the screen is bigger, brighter, louder, more beautiful, more desolate, more dangerous and more sensual than anything in life . . . the truth is that war movies are not about war; they are about our fantasies of war . . . they are the images we can't summon on our own or are too afraid to imagine. They are the stories we need to hear, the explanation we require to deal with the mysteries of living. Without war movies we would be left only with the truth and truth is simply too terrible to tell.

A What are the different possible senses of the word 'truth' that have been described here? Are these mutually exclusive? Are there any other forms of truth?

B Identify a piece of art which has communicated some truth to you, in the non-literal sense that we have discussed. What precisely is that truth? Define/explain it as precisely as you can. Is it possible to do so?

C How is it that the medium of art manages to convey these truths if they cannot be expressed in a literal way?

We have so far made the claim that the arts convey an important type of truth. Needless to say, not everyone agrees. A common objection is that there is no truth in the arts because the arts are all just a matter of opinion. Whether or not this is correct is for you to decide. A more interesting objection is that the arts are far more important than any concept of truth. Perhaps the insistence that we find some sort of knowledge in the arts is a reflection of today's obsession with information and facts. Maybe we should drop our rational approach and take the arts for what they are (whatever that may be). Douglas Morgan puts it beautifully:

Remember, if you can, that breathless final moment when you have moved intensively with heart and mind through a quartet of Brahms or Bartók. You have hoped, expected, feared, been lifted, lowered, fulfilled and disappointed, and now, inevitably, the voices together sing one rich climactic chord. You as a person vibrate, suspended, with the vibrating sound.

Now imagine your neighbour leaning towards you anxiously and expectantly, to ask, 'Quickly now, tell me what you learned from that music. What information did it communicate to you?' Such a neighbour deserves only an icy glare of disdain. He is projecting learning, knowledge, and truth into an area of human experience where it has no natural or necessary place. Learning, knowledge and truth are no less valuable because their value is not exclusive. There really are other goods in the world than these, and there really is no need to invent such bogus kinds of truth as poetic or pictorial or even musical truth for art to wear as certificates of legitimacy.

A What does Morgan mean by his last sentence? Is there really no such thing as artistic truth?

B If this view is correct, what is the value of the arts?

Where do we go from here?

The arts have proven to be at least as slippery as the sciences! As we were hoping to use them to fill the gaps left by the sciences, this is probably no bad thing. As to whether or not we have succeeded in doing so, that's up to you.

However, we cannot deny that the arts offer us something different to science. They seem to connect with us, and to allow us to connect to each other in a very human way. This benefit has, however, come with a cost – we have lost much of any objective claim to certainty that we may once have had. What can we do about this? Probably little, as far as the arts go, but perhaps we should look elsewhere. If it is certainty we seek in our quest for truth, what things are most certain?

To many, mathematics, with its abstract and even inhuman theorems, contrasts totally with the subjective world of the arts, and it is to this area that we now direct our attention.

Further reading

An extremely powerful introduction to the social and political relevance of the arts is John Berger's very readable and short *Ways of Seeing* (Penguin, 1972), based on the BBC television series. The best general philosophical introduction I know of is chapter 10 of Donald Palmer's wonderful *Does the Centre Hold?* (Mayfield, 1991). Chapter 4 of Martin Gardner's *The Whys of a Philosophical Scrivener* (Oxford University Press, 1983) directly addresses the issue of aesthetic relativism. The links between the arts and the natural sciences are controversially explored in Edward Wilson's *Consilience* (Vintage, 1999). A tremendous consideration of the relationship between the arts and truth is in Douglas Morgan's *Must Art Tell the Truth?* (Journal of Aesthetics and Art Criticism, vol 26, 1967). In fiction, I have been charmed and enlightened by Alain de Botton's *How Proust Can Change Your Life* (Vintage, 1998). For the thoughts of the critics, a great overview is Carolyn Korsmeyer (ed.) *Aesthetics: The Big Questions* (Blackwell, 1998). Many of the original expressions of aesthetic theory from down the ages and across the cultures can be found in David Cooper, Peter Lamarque and Crispin Sartwell (eds) *Aesthetics: The Classic Readings* (Blackwell, 1997).

Is 'beauty' just 'biology'?

Most people who have seen a peacock's tail in full plumage think it is a very beautiful thing. And it seems that peahens agree – females mate with only one male, and when they have a choice they seem to choose the male with the most elaborately decorated tail. This may seem like an aesthetic choice in the animal kingdom, but perhaps the peahens are wilier than they appear to be because studies have shown that only healthy peacocks can maintain stunning tails. This means that the peahens are actually choosing mates with strong resistance to disease and who are therefore better able to pass on this trait. For penguins there is a similar story – the females prefer chubby males, which may seem charming, but is actually based in cold reason. As the males warm the eggs for weeks, it makes a lot of sense to choose one with large fat reserves. In the case of flies and birds it seems that symmetry is important. This is readily explained by noting that evading predators and catching prey is a good deal easier when both wings are the same size.

Of course, we humans are far more sophisticated. Or are we? We all know from everyday experience that looks count, and the huge cosmetics and fashion industries rely on our need to look good. This is not a recent development; it seems that every culture examined has put high store by physical beauty. We may dismiss preening as unimportant, and declare the higher value of inner beauty, but we still check the mirror as we go out. And with good reason. 'Judging beauty involves looking at another person,' says psychologist Devendra Singh, 'and figuring out whether you want your children to carry that person's genes.'

A traditional idea is that beauty varies from race to race and from time to time, but recent studies have challenged this notion. It seems that there are certain traits that are considered attractive by all – regardless of race, culture, age or class. That is not to say that we can yet define exactly what these things are, but it seems that they are not as obvious as a woman's legs or man's muscles, and may be more closely related to extremely subtle cues such as bone structure or weight distribution around the body.

This new research may turn up some ugly facts about humans – but that doesn't mean that they aren't true. And of course here we need to distinguish between fact and value – whatever the facts are, that says nothing about our values. They physical qualities of health and fertility are independent of the human quality of moral worth. The best we can say is that if we are to understand ourselves then we need to examine ourselves. If in doing so we find ugly facts then we may be better placed to overcome what may be ugly urges within us.

Of course, no-one would argue that we all have identical tastes. In cold countries a tan may be considered attractive while light skin is all the rage in equatorial zones. But while fashions come and go, there seem to be some underlying universal constants. Psychologists who asked English, Chinese and Indian women to rate pictures of Greek men found that there was almost unanimous agreement. Similarly, whites, Latinos and Asians all seemed to have similar preferences. Perhaps most surprisingly, it has been shown that even babies share a sense of beauty! Experiments which involved showing three- and six-month-old babies pairs of photos – one considered attractive by adults and one considered unattractive – suggested that infants gaze significantly longer at the attractive faces. When the children are relatively untouched by popular culture, adverts and upbrining, this seems to suggest that our perception of 'beauty' is built in in an unexpected way.

So if we have built-in rules, what are they? Perhaps the most obvious one is that we find health attractive, and physical infirmity unattractive. No-one finds rotting teeth and weeping wounds a turn-on; and why is being on the college basketball or rugby team a sign of status that being on the chess team is not? Perhaps a less obvious trait is symmetry. We are rather more like the Japanese scorpion flies, for whom symmetry is a good predictor of mating success, than we might like to think.

Psychologists Randy Thornhill and Steven Gangstead took seven measurements of body symmetry (for example, breadth of feet, length of ears) from hundreds of college-age men and women, and used these to generate a 'symmetry score'. Each subject also filled in intimate, detailed and personal questionnaires. The results were astonishing – the most symmetrical males had started

The ideas in this article by Nick Alchin are based on those expressed by Geoffrey Cowley in *The Biology of Beauty* (*Newsweek*, 3 June 1996).

having sexual relationships three to four years before the others, and for both men and women, the degree of symmetry was well correlated with a number of previous sexual partners. Further experiments with 86 couples have shown that women with highly symmetrical partners were twice as likely to have an orgasm during intercourse (it is possible that this may help conception by assisting sperm on their eggward-journey), and separate surveys show that extremely symmetrical men are less attentive to their partner and more likely to cheat on them (interestingly, this finding did not apply to women).

Of course, we do not often get a chance to measure the symmetry of the feet of the people we meet – so how can these findings be explained? Thornhill argues that symmetry is just one of a range of attractive features. It seems that facial symmetry is associated with larger, more muscular and healthier bodies, and more dominant personalities. It seems that, just like the scorpion flies, females bet on symmetry because it is a sure way of predicting the ability of the male in a wide range of tasks.

But what about widely-held beliefs about the differences between men and women? Most people would probably agree that, while both sexes place value on appearance, it matters more to men. There may be good reasons for this. Most men can produce sperm, but actually conceiving and bearing a child is, or at least has been over the history of humankind, a far riskier business. Women will have relatively few opportunities to be parents, so they need to attract the right man. Men can afford to be less picky. And there appears to be evidence that a woman's body is an accurate indicator of potential mate value.

Boys and girls have roughly the same waistline. At puberty, however,

while the boys add muscle and bone, girls also add roughly 35 pounds of fat – enough to nourish a baby and support the mother during a pregnancy. The curves produced by this fat say a lot about the ability to reproduce easily, and a waist-hip ratio (WHR) of 0.6 to 0.8 tends to result for healthy, fertile women. Almost anything that interferes with fertility – obesity, malnutrition, pregnancy and menopause – will change this crucial ratio. That is not to say that women outside the range cannot have children – they can, and they do, but with greater difficulty. Data from *in vitro* fertilisation programmes suggest that for a ten per cent increase in WHR, chances of conception decrease by 30 per cent. So for men looking for children (consciously or not), choosing the optimally curved woman seems to be an important business.

What is really interesting is that throughout the ages, whether fat has been fashionable, or slimness sexy, the WHR of women who are considered attractive has remained the same. Devendra Singh measured the WHR for *Playboy* centrefolds from 1923 to 1990, and though the models changed shape considerably, the WHR stayed within the extremely narrow range of 0.68–0.72. Even the extremely thin 1960s model Twiggy had a WHR of 0.73. It would be interesting to compare today's beauties to this standard. Singh has shown line drawings of differently shaped women to males from age 8 to 85 from different nationalities, ages and backgrounds, and the favourite figure by far is of average weight with a WHR of 0.7.

To some, this is powerful evidence of the similarities between us and the rest of the animal kingdom. Others believe it is pure fantasy, arguing that if sexual attraction were just about genetics then there would be no

place for homosexuality or celibacy. 'People make decisions; they are free agents' goes the argument; there are no overall explanations for behaviour. But this makes rather a straw man of the case we have seen, which does not seek to explain everything in terms of reproductive success. It cannot explain homosexuality or celibacy – but nor can it explain scuba-diving or carpentry. Of course, we have a multitude of designs, schemes and desires – but that doesn't mean that we do not have deeply-rooted needs for sexual relationships, and no-one could deny that physical attractiveness forms an important part of desire. If we are to understand a complex world then we need to know our own (subconscious) biases and preferences.

Still, the findings are disturbing. We all know that we are not perfect; in some cases we are far from perfect, and this can be hard to face. To accept that how we look matters, when we have so little control over our appearance, is difficult. But it is necessary. Perhaps more worrying is the suggestion that perhaps some gender stereotypes have a basis in biology. At some level it seems that men will in general have a tendency to value the bodies of young women, and women will tend to value high status over moral virtue or character. Neither of these characteristics would win much approval in most ethical courts – but they seem to ring true when we look around the world we know.

Of course, this is no vindication of such unattractive qualities. We do not have to indulge every appetite. 'I do not know any scientist who seriously thinks you can look to nature for moral guidance,' says Thornhill. Even if these ideas are 100 per cent correct, the really interesting moral questions are still out there. ∎

An international survey has revealed the ideal painting and what is universally disliked,
by Christina Lamb, *The Sunday Times* (December, 1996)

What the whole world likes best

Picasso, van Gogh and Turner have their admirers. But if the general public, from Versailles to Vladivostok, Peking to Perth, could choose the painting they would most like to see hanging over their fireplace, it would be a mainly blue landscape, preferably with a mountain, lake and a few wild animals, and perhaps the odd historical figure wandering around.

The Kenyan Most Wanted Picture by Komar and Melamid

This is the surprise discovery made by two Russian artists, who now live in New York, in a worldwide poll they have commissioned. Impressed by the reliance on market research both by politicians and manufacturers in their adopted homeland, 51-year-old Alexander Melamid and 53-year-old Vitaly Komar decided the principle could be applied to art. Two years ago they began the monumental task of polling the entire world for what people would most like – and dislike – to see in a painting. With more than a third of the planet now surveyed, the pair believe they have a good idea of what would be the world's most wanted – and unwanted – paintings.

The astonishing thing is the similarity in results. Fifteen nations have been polled so far, including China, France, Russia, Kenya, Iceland and Turkey, and there is a continuing poll on the Internet (see www.diacenter.org/km/index.html). In every country people have voted overwhelmingly for a predominance of blue and a pastoral scene with a stretch of water. The greatest dislike in each case has been modern abstract paintings with a preponderance of red.

'What this shows is that there is no such thing as a national culture,' says Melamid. 'There's no big difference between Kenya and Iceland, China and France.' A small wiry man, buzzing with energy, whose latest enthusiasm is for painting elephants, he has been collaborating with the larger more sedate Komar for 33 years, since they met as art students sketching dead bodies in a Moscow morgue.

The American Least Wanted Picture by Komar and Melamid

Anyone who was shocked by the idea of selling art in the same way as tins of baked beans will almost certainly be horrified by the work of these two former dissidents. In the attempt to compute scientifically what people want to see in a painting, they contract professional pollsters to carry out nationwide surveys for about £12,000 a time. They then use the responses to more than 100 questions to paint pictures in which every detail is determined by 'viewer demand' and place them on exhibition in that country. The resulting paintings rank high, frankly, on the kitsch scale.

The first survey was carried out in America, their home since 1978. 'It was a complete shock,' Melamid says. 'We had expected that there would be many different choices broken down into different classes, ethnic groups and ages. Instead, whites, blacks, Hispanics, Jews, rich and poor, all wanted the same thing. We were in panic, because we had organised a huge space for the exhibition and ended up with only two paintings – the favourite and least favourite.'

It was no easy task. 'Painting that first Most Wanted picture was the hardest thing I've ever done,' says Melamid. 'It was real torture.' They painted more than 100 versions before completing one they felt was right.

The French Least Wanted Picture by Komar and Melamid

They were even more amazed when surveys carried out in very different countries revealed the same choices. 'We had thought America was an anomaly,' says Melamid, 'but we got the same results again and again'. Without exception, people want blue landscapes with water and mountains. The Danes wanted a ballet dance by the lake and a national flag; the Portuguese wanted their lake to have a small village on a far bank, and the Kenyans wanted a hippo as well as the two

deer grazing by the lake favoured by other nations, but such differences were slight.

The French Most Wanted Picture by Komar and Melamid

The latest results, for Germany and Holland, are no exception. 'It shows that countries shouldn't try to define themselves by culture, as culturally we're much more similar than we want to admit,' says Melamid. 'People won't want to hear this, but perhaps McDonalds has the right idea.'

Once they have raised the money to do the poll, the next country on their list is Britain. 'The British like to think they're different,' Melamid grins, 'but it will be interesting to see what we turn up.'

Having now painted 15 Most Wanted and Most Unwanted paintings, Melamid and Komar turn them out quickly, in a few days, rather than the weeks needed the first time around. Once every country has been done, they plan a huge touring exhibition as well as a book, from which, they say, 'people can draw their own conclusions'.

Some of the many messages they have received over the Internet are less than polite about the exercise, but Melamid shrugs off criticism. 'If they want to think this is just a global intellectual joke, that's up to them.'

Some critics argue that many different paintings could have resulted from the poll data. But surprisingly, when an American television show invited different artists to do a painting from survey results, they came up with similar pictures.

Melamid claims the exercise was inspired by the western world's reliance on polls: 'If majority will is seen as good enough for determining a country's political set-up, ☞

RESOURCE FILE RESOURCE FILE RESOURCE FILE RESOURCE FILE RESOURCE FILE RESOURCE FILE RESOURCE FILE RESOURCE FILE RESOURCE FILE then why not for art?' But he admits: 'I'm not sure if it's great art or if it's the right path to art – we're just mediums.'

Not surprisingly, many in the art world are less enthusiastic about the idea. Melamid and Komar do not care: 'We're used to being unpopular.' Outraged by the political nature of their work, the Soviet authorities once bulldozed one of their exhibitions, and they won few friends with their 1978 exhibition of World Leaders with Right Ear Cut Off, which showed Brezhnev, Mao, Begin and Sadat with their right ears covered in bandages.

When an exhibition was held last month in Lisbon to show Portugal's Favourite and Least Favourite Painting, the response was positive. 'I can really imagine having this up at home,' said Maria Gomes, a teacher, looking at the tranquil blue scene with evening light rippling over the lake. 'Picasso and all that is all very well in a gallery, but I'm not sure I'd like to live with them. This I could look at every day without being disturbed.'

This is exactly the kind of reaction Melamid believes to be common from the Clinton-style town-hall meetings they have begun holding across America. 'The results of our polls show what we suspected – that artists paint for themselves rather than what people really want. We don't care what the art community thinks – art belongs to the people. They're our audience, after all. What we're seeing is that people really want art, but we, the elite artists, don't serve them.' That said, he admits he would not like one of the World's Favourite Paintings on his own wall. ■

How Proust Can Change Your Life

An excerpt from *How Proust Can Change Your Life* by Alain de Botton.

Proust once wrote an essay in which he set out to restore a smile to the face of a gloomy, envious and dissatisfied young man. He pictured this young man sitting at a table after lunch one day in his parents' flat, gazing dejectedly at his surroundings: at a knife left lying on the tablecloth, at the remains of an underdone, tasteless cutlet and a half-turned back tablecloth. He would see his mother at the far end of the dining room doing her knitting and the family cat curling up on top of a cupboard next to a bottle of brandy being kept for a special occasion ... the mundanity of the scene would contrast with the young man's taste for beautiful and costly things, which he lacked the money to acquire. Proust imagined the revulsion ... [the young man] ... would feel at this ... interior, and how he would compare it to the splendours he had seen in museums and cathedrals. He would envy those bankers who had enough money to decorate their houses properly, so that everything in them was beautiful, was a work of art, right down to the coal tongs in the fireplace and the knobs on the doors.

To escape his domestic gloom ... the young man might leave the flat and go to the Louvre, where at least he could feast his eyes on splendid things: grand palaces painted by Veronese, harbour scenes by Claude and princely lives by Van Dyck.

Touched by his predicament, Proust proposed to make a radical change to the young man's life by way of a modest alteration to the museum's itinerary. Rather than let him hurry to galleries hung with paintings by Claude and Veronese, Proust suggested leading him to a quite different part of the museum, to those galleries hung with the works of Jean-Baptiste Chardin.

It might have seemed an odd choice, for Chardin hadn't painted many harbours, princes or palaces. He liked to depict bowls of fruit, jugs, coffee pots, loaves of bread, glasses of wine and slabs of meat. He liked painting kitchen utensils, not just pretty chocolate jars but salt cellars and strainers. When it came to people, Chardin's figures were rarely doing anything heroic; one was reading a book, another was building a house of cards, a woman had just come home from the market with a couple of loaves of bread and a mother was showing her daughter some mistakes she had made in her needlework.

Yet, in spite of the ordinary nature of their subjects, Chardin's paintings succeeded in being extraordinarily beguiling and evocative.

After an encounter with Chardin, Proust had high

hopes for the spiritual transformation of his sad young man ... Why? Because Chardin had shown him that the kind of environment in which he lived could, for a fraction of the cost, have many of the charms he had previously associated only with the palaces and the princely life. No longer would he feel painfully excluded from the aesthetic realm, no longer would he be so envious of smart bankers with gold-plated coal tongs and diamond-studded door handles. He would learn that metal and earthenware could also be enchanting, and common crockery as beautiful as precious stones. After looking at Chardin's work, even the humblest rooms in his parents' flat would have the power to delight him, Proust promised:
When you walk around a kitchen, you will say to yourself, this is interesting, this is grand, this is beautiful like a Chardin.

Having started on his essay, Proust tried to interest Pierre Mainguet, the editor of the arts magazine the *Revue Hebdomadaire*, in its contents. *I have just written a little study in the philosophy of art, if I may use that slightly pretenious phrase, in which I have tried to show how the great painters initiate us into a knowledge and love of the external world, how they are the ones 'by whom our eyes are opened', opened, that is, on the world ... Do you think this sort of study would interest the readers of the* Revue Hebdomadaire?

Perhaps, but since its editor was sure it wouldn't they had no chance to find out. Turning down the piece was an understandable oversight: this was 1895, and Mainguet didn't know Proust would one day be *Proust*. What is more, the moral of the essay lay not too far from the ridiculous. It was only a step away from suggesting that everything

down to the last lemon was beautiful, that there was no good reason to be envious of any condition beside our own, that a hovel was as nice as a villa, and an emerald no better than a chipped plate.

However, instead of urging us to place the same value on all things, Proust might more interestingly have been encouraging us to ascribe them their correct value, and hence to revise certain notions of the good life, which risked inspiring an unfair neglect of some settings, and a misguided enthusiasm for others. If it hadn't been for Pierre Mainguet's rejection, the readers of the *Revue Hebdomadaire* would have benefited from a chance to reappraise their conceptions of beauty, and enter into a new and possibly more rewarding relationship with salt cellars, crockery and apples.

Why would they previously have lacked such a relationship? Why wouldn't they have appreciated their tableware and fruit? At one level, such questions seem superfluous; it just appears *natural* to be struck by the beauty of some things and to be left cold by others, there is no conscious rumination or decision behind our choice of what appeals to us visually, we simply know we are moved by palaces but not by kitchens, by porcelain but not by china, by guavas but not by apples.

However, the immediacy with which aesthetic judgements arise should not fool us into assuming that their origins are entirely natural or their verdicts unalterable. Proust's letter to Monsieur Mainguet hinted as much. By saying that great painters were the ones by whom our eyes were opened, Proust was at the same time implying that our sense of beauty was not immobile, and could be sensitised by painters, who would, through their canvases, educate us into an

appreciation of once neglected aesthetic qualities. If the dissatisfied young man had failed to consider the family tableware or fruit, it was in part out of a lack of acquaintance with images which would have shown him the key to their attractions.

The happiness which may emerge from taking a second look is central; it reveals the extent to which our dissatisfactions may be the result of failing to look properly at our lives rather than the result of anything inherently deficient about them. The gap between what the dissatisfied youth could see in his flat, and what Chardin noticed in very similar interiors, places the emphasis on a certain way of looking, as opposed to a mere process of acquiring or possessing.

... The incident emphasises once more that beauty is something to be found, rather than passively encountered, that it requires us to pick up on certain details, to identify the whiteness of a cotton dress, the reflection of the sea on the hull of a yacht or the contrast between the colour of a jockey's coat and his face. It also emphasises how vulnerable we are to depression when ... the pre-prepared images run out, when our knowledge of art does not stretch any later than Carpaccio (1450–1525) and Veronese (1528–1588) and we see a two-hundred-horsepower Sunseeker accelerating out of the marine. It may genuinely be an unattractive example of aquatic transport; then again our objection to the speedboat may stem from nothing other than a stubborn adherence to ancient images of beauty, and a resistance to a process of active appreciation which even Veronese and Carpaccio would have undertaken had they been in our place. ∎

As far as the laws of mathematics refer to reality, they are not certain; and as far as they are certain, they do not refer to reality.
Albert Einstein

MATHEMATICS IS THE SUBJECT WHERE WE NEVER KNOW WHAT WE ARE TALKING ABOUT, NOR WHETHER WHAT WE ARE SAYING IS TRUE.
Bertrand Russell

WHEN YOU HAVE SATISFIED YOURSELF THAT THE THEOREM IS TRUE, YOU START PROVING IT.
Arthur Koestler

... it is certain that the real function of art is to increase our self-consciousness; to make us more aware of what we are, and therefore of what the Universe in which we live really is. And since mathematics, in its own way, also performs this function, it is not only aesthetically charming but profoundly significant. It is an art, and a great art.
John W. N. Sullivan

Mathematics transfigures the fortuitous concourse of atoms into the tracery of the finger of God.
Herbert Westren Turnbull

There is nothing that can be said by mathematical symbols and relations which cannot also be said by words. The converse, however, is false. Much that can be and is said by words cannot successfully be put into equations, because it is nonsense.
C. Truesdell

Mathematicians are like Frenchmen: whatever you say to them they translate into their own language and forthwith it is something entirely different.
Johann Wolfgang von Goethe

Mathematics is created in the self-alienation of the human spirit. The spirit cannot discover itself in mathematics; the human spirit lives in human institutions.
Giovanni Vico

You can not apply mathematics as long as words still becloud reality.
Hermann Weyl

On each decision, the mathematical analysis only got me to the point where my intuition had to take over.
Robert Jensen

Nobody untrained in geometry may enter my house.
Plato

Aims

By the end of this chapter you should:

- **understand the axiom-theorem structure of mathematics**
- **understand the implications of this structure for mathematical truth**
- **understand the role of logic in mathematics and the link to rationalism**
- **be able to discuss possible links between mathematics, science, art and language**
- **understand why mathematics may be regarded as an extremely creative discipline**
- **have some insight into the process of attempting to establish a theorem to describe a situation**
- **understand that the initial promise of the axiomatic approach has been undermined by Gödel, and be able to mention possible implications of his ideas.**

Introduction

It may not be obvious immediately why a book with a philosophical leaning contains a chapter on mathematics. What could be less ambiguous, more clearly defined and less open to interpretation than a mathematical problem? A maths problem may not be resolved easily, but there is a right answer, and little room for debate – we are probably all too familiar with the rather tedious and long-winded exercises which are marked right or wrong. So why would we include such a dry topic in a course such as this?

The answer is two-fold. Firstly, the relative certainty of mathematics is exactly the reason we need to include it – if it presents us with indubitable knowledge then we need to learn precisely how it does that and see if we can apply the technique elsewhere. The techniques of mathematics may provide us with a tool that will be central to our search for reliable knowledge. Secondly, we will argue below that the stereotypical image presented above, is just that – a stereotype. There is far more to mathematics than the rigid application of formal rules to meaningless systems of symbols (although this may, arguably, be the end result). It is creative, imaginative, deeply satisfying and in some ways similar to those disciplines sometimes considered diametrically opposed to mathematics – the arts.

Mathematics is a subject which everyone finds difficult at some stage. There are often negative attitudes to the subject, and these arguably stem from the past and present requirements to learn a large body of knowledge that seems to have few relevant applications. However, maths is also an immensely powerful tool in its application to science (at least) as witnessed by cars, telephones, computers, moon landings, aeroplanes and atomic bombs. It plays a central role in any technology, and is increasingly finding its way into apparently unrelated fields such as history, medicine, psychology, art and music. To some, maths is pointless and irrelevant and they will not bother with it if they can avoid it. To others it is fascinating and a source of never-ending delight. That a topic can appear in such diverse contexts, and in such different ways to different people – this alone makes it well worth studying.

Mathematics: invention or discovery?

When you solve a mathematical problem, you probably feel like you are **finding** the solution. You may feel that mathematical truths are always true. $2 + 2 = 4$; no argument there. And 242,324 is an even number, whether we like it or not. We would be foolish to look for a triangle with seven sides. Consider 345×53. You probably can't do it in your head, but you could work it out given a pencil and paper and a little time. Certainly with a calculator the answer could be found quickly. The correct answer doesn't depend on who does it, when they do it or how they do it. They may get it wrong, of course, but the answer itself is always 18,285. We have no choice as to what the answer is. We have to find it.

Imagine we contact alien life forms and try to communicate. Will we find that they believe in different mathematical results? Will they have calculated different mathematical answers to us? If they have calculated π, for example, will they have found the same value as us? Will they believe that $2 + 2 = 4$?

The view that 'maths is out there waiting to be discovered' is called the Platonic view of maths, after Plato, who thought that mathematical truths are eternal and unchanging. At first sight, this seems very appealing, as we have seen from the examples just given. However, there are some difficult questions for Plato to answer:

- Where does mathematics exist?
- How do we 'discover' maths?
- Why does the 'real world' obey mathematical laws?
- If we discover mathematics, where do we look for it?

These are quite profound problems, because many find that the only reasonable answers tend to suggest that, contrary to what we initially suggested, mathematics is purely in the mind. Now Plato would not have minded this (he argued that we are just 'remembering' things we already knew but had forgotten) but this sort of answer doesn't carry much weight today. If we find that mathematics is really in the mind then isn't it an invention? This may answer the problems mentioned above (how?), but it raises its own difficulties.

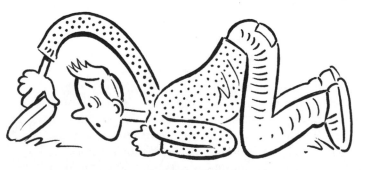

Looking for $\sqrt{2}$

- Surely we can't have invented the fact that $2+2=4$? That goes against all common sense! If maths is invented, why don't different mathematicians invent different mathematics?
- If maths is invented, in the same way that artists invent art, how can answers to mathematical questions be right or wrong?

It has been suggested that mathematicians would like maths to be discovered – that is how they feel emotionally towards their work. They talk about 'discovering' theorems and this attitude pervades their working life from Monday to Friday. However, if pressed hard on the matter, when philosophising at the weekend, most will retreat away from 'discovery' to 'invention' as they cannot logically justify 'discovery' to their satisfaction. One mathematician who refused to retreat in this manner was G. H. Hardy, one of the great number theorists of the twentieth century. In *A Mathematician's Apology* he wrote:

I began by saying that there is probably less difference between the positions of a mathematician and of a physicist than is generally supposed, and that the most important seems to me to be this, that the mathematician is in much more direct contact with reality. This may seem a paradox, since it is the physicist who deals with the subject matter usually described as 'real'; but a little reflection is enough to show that the physicist's reality, whatever it may be, has few or none of the attributes which common sense ascribes instinctively to reality. A chair may be a collection of whirling electrons, or an idea in the mind of God: each of these accounts of it may have its merits, but neither conforms at all closely to the suggestions of common sense.

I went on to say that neither physicists nor philosophers have ever given any convincing account of what 'physical reality' is, or of how the physicist passes, from the confused mass of fact or sensation with which he starts, to the construction of the objects which he calls 'real'. Thus we cannot be said to know what the subject matter of physics is; but this need not prevent us from understanding roughly what a physicist is trying to do. It is plain that he is trying to correlate the incoherent body of crude fact confronting him with some definite and orderly scheme of abstract relations, the kind of scheme which he can borrow only from mathematics.

A mathematician, on the other hand, is working with his own mathematical reality.

Of this reality, I take a 'realistic' and not an 'idealistic' view ... This realistic view is much more plausible of mathematical than of physical reality, because mathematical objects are so much more what they seem. A chair or a star is not in the least like what it seems to be; the more we think of it, the fuzzier its outlines become in the haze of sensation which surrounds it; but '2' or '317' has nothing to do with sensation, and its properties stand out the more clearly the more closely we scrutinise it. It may be that modern physics fits best into some framework of idealistic philosophy – I do not believe it, but there are eminent physicists who say so. Pure mathematics, on the other hand, seems to me a rock on which all idealism flounders: 317 is a prime, not because we think so, or because our minds are shaped in one way rather than another, but because it is so, because mathematical reality is built that way.

Although this is eloquently put, many other mathematicians have disagreed. To begin to derive some insight into this difficult question, we should examine the nature of mathematics itself more carefully. If we can see exactly why maths differs from the sciences and other disciplines, then we might be able to make some progress.

The nature of mathematics

Philosophy is a game with objectives and no rules. Mathematics is a game with rules and no objectives.

Anon

What is the average of this set of numbers?

1, 1, 1, 1, 3, 4, 4, 4, 5, 5, 1027

The answer, of course, depends on what we mean by 'average'.

- If we mean 'add them up and divide by the number of items' then the answer is 96.
- If we mean 'the most common number in the list' then the answer is 1.
- If we mean 'the number in the middle of the list' then the answer is 4.

So which is correct? Which is true? Mathematicians use all three meanings – they are called the 'mean', 'mode' and 'median' respectively. This may seem like a trivial matter, but it is actually central to the nature of mathematics. It doesn't really matter which definition of 'average' we use but, once we have decided, there is only one correct answer. Now some definitions may be more useful than others – we may have good reasons for picking one definition over another (under many circumstances we may well reject the first method) but until we have decided where to start from we can make no mathematical progress.

Mathematics always works this way. We start from certain assumptions and definitions, which we call **axioms**. We take these without question. From these we can use the rules of logic to work out problems and to find other results, which we call **theorems** and which are known with complete certainty. Beyond the school level, proving theorems is largely what mathematics is all about.

As a simple example of the mathematical process, imagine a child learning about odd and even numbers. She starts by being given a list of odd numbers 1, 3, 5, 7, 9, 11, 13 . . . and even numbers 2, 4, 6, 8, 10, 12, 14 . . . Her first job is to tell whether other numbers, say 34, 77 and 66 are odd or even. Once competent in this, she may notice a few patterns. It seems that adding 1 to an odd number gives an even number, and adding 1 to an even number always gives an odd number. It also seems that it's only the last digit that makes a number odd or even; the other digits don't make any difference. She may also spot that adding two odd numbers always gives an even number, or that multiplying two even numbers always gives another even number.

Well, we need to be careful here. We are using the word 'always' a little hastily. After all, there is an infinity of numbers, and the child has only experimented with a few dozen. With several examples, she may have a pretty good idea that the pattern always holds, but this isn't enough. A scientist or historian may have to rest content with 'sufficient evidence' (whatever that may mean), but the mathematician can go one step further. In this case, we can easily prove that the patterns are true for all odd and even numbers. Two examples are given below. They may seem a little pedantic, but the techniques can be generalised to more difficult cases, and they allow us to arrive at certain knowledge. Given the axioms, it is impossible to doubt the conclusion of these steps.

Axioms

- An odd number is a number which can be written as $2n + 1$, where n is a whole number.
- An even number is a number which can be written as $2n$, where n is a whole number.
- The usual laws of arithmetic apply.

Check that the definitions of odd and even numbers make sense to you. Experiment with them until you are happy that they are correct definitions. Let n be 5, 7, 50, 100 or anything else you like and see what you get in the two definitions (this 'playing' is a vital part of maths).

Theorem 1: An odd number and an even number add together to give an odd number.

Proof: Let the odd number be o and the even number be e.
Then $o = 2n + 1$ and $e = 2m$ for some whole numbers n and m, by definition.

$$
\begin{aligned}
\text{So } o + e &= 2n + 1 + 2m \\
&= 2m + 2n + 1 \\
&= 2(m + n) + 1 \\
&= 2p + 1 \text{ where } p \text{ is a whole number} \\
&\text{but this is of the form } 2n + 1 \text{ and hence odd.} \quad \text{QED}
\end{aligned}
$$

Theorem 2: Two odd numbers add together to give an even number.

Proof: Let the odd numbers be a and b.
Then $a = 2n + 1$ and $b = 2m + 1$ for some whole numbers n and m.

$$
\begin{aligned}
\text{So } a + b &= 2n + 1 + 2m + 1 \\
&= 2m + 2n + 2 \\
&= 2(m + n + 1) \\
&= 2p \text{ where } p \text{ is a whole number} \\
&\text{but this is of the form } 2n \text{ and hence even.} \quad \text{QED}
\end{aligned}
$$

These are hopefully straightforward examples, and the results hardly need formal proof – we 'knew' they were true beforehand. However, more complex problems are only really understood once the proofs have been developed, or counter-examples found, and formal proof is what mathematics (beyond the school level) is all about. New mathematics happens in precisely this way – there is a result which may be believed to be true, but not accepted until the proof has been found. The proof is everything, and this is the defining characteristic of mathematics.

> **A** Prove the following theorems:
>   Theorem 3: Trebling an even number results in another even number.
>   Theorem 4: Two even numbers multiplied together give an even number.
>   Theorem 5: Trebling an odd number gives another odd number.
>   Theorem 6: An odd number and an even number multiplied together give an even number.
>   Theorem 7: Two odd numbers multiplied together give an odd number.

You have probably noticed that the claim was made for 'certainty' but not for 'truth'. This is an important distinction and we can see that the 'truth' of mathematics will depend on the axioms. We may apply all the logic we want, but if the axioms we start with aren't any good then we won't get anywhere (this is the 'garbage-in, garbage-out' principle). In the example above, we took as axiomatic, 'An odd number is a number which can be written as $2n + 1$, where n is a whole number.' Is this true? In a way, it is hard to see how it could be true or false – there are numbers of the form $2n + 1$, and we can call them odd if we want to. In a way, all we are doing is giving certain things certain names. Does a pentagon really have five sides? Well, yes, but only because we define pentagons to be five-sided shapes! If we want to take these as certain truths then it has to be said they seem rather empty of content.

The plus side of this method is that if we accept the axioms as true then we do not have to worry about the truth of the conclusion – if we have done our maths right then the conclusion is guaranteed. In this sense, all maths is implicit in the axioms. H. A. Simon writes:

All mathematics exhibits in its conclusions only what is already implicit in its premises. Hence all mathematical derivation can be viewed simply as change in representation, making evident what was previously true, but obscure. This view can be extended to all of problem solving – solving a problem simply means representing it so as to make the solution transparent.

> **A** What is the relationship between truth and mathematics? Why has it been said that maths is a **formal game** or a **closed system**?
> **B** Is all mathematics really just a change in representation? Might the same be said of any other forms of knowledge, or even all forms of knowledge?

So the relationship between truth and mathematics is a difficult one. For our purposes, we can merely note that maths may be certain, but it is far from obvious that it is true, in the usual sense of the word, because the truth of the axioms is not clear. This might suggest that if we could somehow find more definite axioms, the mathematical method of logical deduction might provide a wonderful method for acquiring knowledge. All we need to do is find some certain axioms from which to start. René Descartes had the same idea several hundred years ago. This form of approach to knowledge is called rationalism, and is still hugely influential in many spheres of intellectual life today.

Maths as a creative art

So far we have concentrated on the logical side of maths. Certainly, logic plays a very central role! But there is more to maths than that, and in particular, there is a great deal of creativity and imagination. You may not have seen much evidence of that in the proofs of theorems 1 and 2 (page 57), where each step followed logically and there seemed to be little room for originality or inspiration. But we can easily find problems where a 'logical' approach (what does that mean anyway?) doesn't get us very far.

Recall that we say that a positive whole number is a *prime* number if it has exactly two factors. That is,

> 2 is prime because $2 = 1 \times 2$ so 1 and 2 are the only factors of 2

and 17 is prime because $17 = 1 \times 17$ so 1 and 17 are the only factors of 17

but 21 is not prime because although $21 = 1 \times 21$ (so 1 and 21 are factors of 21) we also have $21 = 7 \times 3$ (so 1 and 21 are not the *only* factors).

With this in mind, we can see that the first few primes are 2, 3, 5, 7, 11, 13, 17, 19, 23, 29, 31, 37, 41, 43, 47, 53, 59, 61, 67, 71, 73, 79, 83, 89, 97...

Now these numbers prove to be very interesting to mathematicians, because they are to arithmetic what the elements are to chemistry. In chemistry, you study the elements so that you understand how more complex substances (which are made up of elements) behave. So, too, in maths we can study prime numbers with a view towards generating insights which work for 'more complex' numbers. So, let us ask ourselves a few questions about primes:

- Are there any more even prime numbers after 2?
- How many prime numbers are there?
- Do the gaps between the primes keep getting bigger?

Can you answer these questions? Can you prove them? Things are getting a little more complex here. There is no immediately obvious way to start trying to prove these – you may have a pretty good idea about the answer (your intuition may be quite well developed) but the formal, logical proof is far from straightforward. And, of course, until the proof is there, mathematicians are going to look at intuition with a fairly sceptical eye. And what about these questions:

- Is there a prime between n and $2n$ for any value of n?
- Is there a prime number between successive square numbers?
- How many prime numbers are exactly 1 more than a square number?
- How many pairs of prime numbers are there which differ by 2 (for example, 11 and 13 or 10,006,427 and 10,006,429)?
- Is every even number greater than 2 the sum of two prime numbers?

How to start these proofs? It is not at all obvious; the definitions of 'prime', 'square' and 'even' do not really seem to help; and there is no clear way to begin. In fact, if you can answer, and prove your answer, to either of the last two questions then you will be a very, very famous mathematician. (The last question was set by Goldbach, 1690–1764, who notoriously conjectured that there is an infinite number of such pairs. It remains one of the outstanding problems of number theory.)

Of course, we are less interested in the actual problems themselves than we are in what they tell us about the nature of the discipline. You must not imagine that your experience of some of these problems is all that different to that of the professional. You may both look at a problem, understand what it is that you want to do, but be unable to see a way of doing it. The difference is that in school maths you can ask your teacher or look up a text, but for the professional, there may be no-one to ask and no books to consult. He is on his own, and he has to come up with something new, something that nobody else has ever thought of.

> **A** Have you ever solved a maths problem when no-one had told you a method or a way of doing it? Have you ever found a solution all by yourself?
> **B** How is this process similar to or different from the scientist, the historian, the novelist or the musician at work?
> **C** So how do mathematicians do it? How do they come up with new ideas?

Of course, part C of this question is impossible to answer. If we could answer it, then we would be back to the stage of reducing maths to a recipe, and mathematicians would merely be following the instructions. We can point to factors that may help creativity – relevant experience, love of subject or whatever – but these are not, in themselves, enough. Plenty of people may be trying to create (discover?) something new, and they may all have 'the right background', but only one actually manages it. The key to their insight is often as obscure to the mathematician as it is to anyone else. Creativity cannot be quantified easily. Recognising this is perhaps the key to understanding why some mathematicians see themselves as artists, and certainly key to understanding why some maths is considered 'great' and other maths not. Great maths, like any great art, does not follow well-trodden paths, nor does it apply tried and tested techniques. Instead it does something genuinely new, deep or profound. Like any great art, great maths is beautiful. The idea of beauty in maths has never been better expressed than by G. H. Hardy:

A mathematician, like a painter or a poet, is a maker of patterns. If his patterns are more permanent than theirs, it is because they are made with ideas. A painter makes patterns with shapes and colours, a poet with words . . . A mathematician, on the other hand, has no material to work with but ideas, and so his patterns are likely to last longer, since ideas wear less than words.

The mathematician's patterns, like the painter's or the poet's, must be beautiful; the ideas, like the colours or the words, must fit together in a harmonious way. Beauty is the first test: there is no permanent place for ugly mathematics.

He goes on to say:

I have never done anything 'useful'. No discovery of mine has made, or is likely to make, directly or indirectly, for good or for ill, the least difference to the amenity of the world. Judged by all practical standards, the value of my mathematical life is nil. I have just one chance of escaping a verdict of complete triviality, that I may be judged to have created something worth creating. And that I have created something is undeniable: the question is about its value. The case for my life ... is that I have added something to knowledge ... and that this has a value which differs in degree only, and not in kind, from the creations of the great mathematicians, or any of the other artists, great or small, who have left some kind of memorial behind them.

A Is mathematical creativity the same as other types of creativity? If not, what are the differences?

B Although Pythagoras' theorem is named after Pythagoras, anyone could have 'found' the theorem. Contrast this to literature. Could anyone else have written Shakespeare's or Dostoyevsky's works? How about music, poetry or architecture?

C It is unfortunate that so much mathematics remains inaccessible to so many. However, we can see where aesthetic appeal comes in from a few simple examples. Consider the following mathematical statements:

$$\sqrt{16} = \pm 4$$

$$\frac{\pi^2}{6} = \frac{1}{1^2} + \frac{1}{2^2} + \frac{1}{3^2} + \frac{1}{4^2} + \ldots$$

$$1 + 3 = 4$$

$$\frac{\pi}{2} = \frac{2 \times 2 \times 4 \times 4 \times 6 \times 6 \times 8 \times 8 \times \ldots}{1 \times 1 \times 3 \times 3 \times 5 \times 5 \times 7 \times 7 \times \ldots}$$

$$2764/23 \approx 116.26$$

$$5 + 9 = 2$$

$$a^2 = b^2 + c^2$$

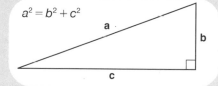

$$e^{i\pi} + 1 = 0$$

$$\frac{1}{2} = \frac{2}{4} = \frac{3}{6} = \ldots = \frac{n}{2n}$$

$$35^2 - 25^2 = (35 + 25)(35 - 25)$$
$$= 60 \times 10$$
$$= 600$$

Could any of these statements be considered beautiful in any way? You may find it helpful to consider notions of brevity, simplicity, truth, utility, elegance and surprise.

D Is there any difference between the beauty in maths and the beauty in, say, music?

A little more about axioms

You have seen that the choice of axioms is central to mathematics. So how do we choose our axioms? It may seem at first that we have no choice over our axioms, at least in certain fields. After all, isn't it true that $5 + 9 = 14$ no matter what our axioms are? Well, in fact no! We can easily change our axioms so that $5 + 9 = 2$; all you have to do is think about clock arithmetic. Moving the hour hand five hours ahead followed by nine hours ahead is the same as moving it two hours ahead. We then generate a whole lot of other 'truths', such as $11 + 1 = 0$, $7 \times 2 = 2$ and so on. These are mathematically correct in the axiomatic system described. We can choose that system and then it follows that $5 + 9 = 14$ will no longer be true!

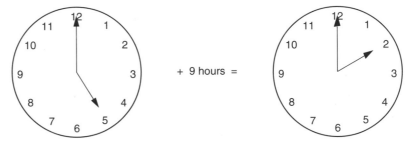

+ 9 hours =

So $5 + 9 = 2$ after all!

So why do we use the number system that we do? The answer is simply that we use it when it is convenient to do so. In the physical world, when we add five things to nine things, we end up with fourteen things, so we say $5 + 9 = 14$. But on a clock face that doesn't work, so we use another system. Similarly, you may see chapters in a book numbered 1.1, 1.2, 1.3 . . . all the way up to 1.9 and then 1.10, 1.11, 1.12. This is incorrect in our normal numbering system, but it is convenient to use in this context. In quantum mechanics, physicists use a system whereby it is possible for one particle and another particle to add up to no particles, simply because it works. So this is the first way we choose our axioms – we see what is useful.

Of course, after reading the last section you know that not all mathematicians are mathematicians because they want to do something useful! They are far more interested in finding insights, elegance and surprises. This affects the choice of axiom, too. Sometimes an axiom can be chosen which seems at odds with anything useful at all. For example, it is possible to construct versions of mathematics where the order of multiplication is important, that is, where $a \times b$ is not the same as $b \times a$. Now our ordinary numbers don't work that way, but we can get some very interesting maths like this. The surprising thing is that, if we construct this maths, it often turns out, later on, that a use can be found for it, even though it was designed purely with aesthetic properties in mind. This seems to indicate a profound truth about the Universe, and reminds us of Hardy's comment: *'Beauty is the first test: there is no permanent place for ugly mathematics.'* It would be a wonderful thing indeed, if, as the physicists Dirac and Einstein hoped, the mathematics describing the world is, at a deep level, profoundly satisfying aesthetically. Perhaps the two methods of choosing axioms, utility and elegance, are not so different after all.

So we are perfectly at liberty to choose any axioms we want, and to work with them to see what develops. Some sets of axioms (the vast majority) will be sterile and uninteresting. Others will generate rich areas with seemingly endless practical and/or aesthetic possibilities. Versions of mathematics that are at first sight bizarre are easy to dismiss, but like the genius artist who starts a new style of painting or music, the genius mathematician is the one who chooses the axioms nobody else even suspected.

A In clock arithmetic, calculate the following:

$5 + 8$ 3×2

$2 - 4$ 5×10

$8 - 12$ $11 + 12$

B What are the right axioms for arithmetic? Is everyday arithmetic 'true'?

These insights may offer a resolution of the discovery/invention dilemma. We are free to invent whatever axioms we choose, and we then discover the consequences of our choices. What we are saying here is in a sense, blindingly obvious – that we must start our argument from somewhere, and even if we don't like the starting points we can develop an argument from them. Any lawyer knows this!

In mathematical terms, this realisation was only fully appreciated at the beginning of the twentieth century, and the possibilities for this approach seemed enormously exciting. The German mathematician David Hilbert started a search for the perfect mathematical tool – a method of telling for sure whether a theorem could be deduced from the axioms or not. He wanted to find a step-by-step recipe which would determine mechanically whether or not any theorem was true or false in the given axiomatic system. Recalling that mathematics is about proving theorems from axioms, and that the theorems follow by the rigid application of logic to the axioms, this does not seem like too much to ask; we want an algorithm (or computer program) into which we can feed the axioms, and the suggested theorem, and then be told if the theorem is correct. All we need to do is find a way to formalise the process of logical deduction into a set of formal rules. This would then provide an incredible shortcut to the mathematical process. In the early parts of the last century, this seemed very exciting.

But alas, this dream was proven impossible in 1931 by the Austrian Kurt Gödel, at the remarkably young age of 25. In two breathtakingly ingenious theorems he proved that Hilbert's dream was impossible; that in all interesting mathematical systems **there will always be mathematical theorems which are true, but which cannot be proven right or wrong from the axioms** no matter how clever or inventive we are.

Gödel's proofs may not sound particularly revolutionary at first, but some of the consequences of this innocent-sounding statement are still hotly debated and it is not an exaggeration to say that the two theorems permanently destroyed a dream of mathematicians just at the time when they seemed to be on the verge of providing us with a complete picture of the mathematical universe. For mathematicians, the consequences are either depressing or delightful, depending on their point of view. The pessimists lament that mathematics can never be completely reduced to a set of rules which can be rigidly applied and guaranteed to determine truth. The optimists rejoice that the grand game will never end, and that there will always be a place for human ingenuity.

If Gödel's results applied only to mathematics they would be of limited interest, but they may well extend further. It has been argued that, since much physics is based on mathematics, if maths is incomplete in principle then so is physics. This means that there are true scientific results which we will never be able to establish. This might mean that we can never reach the end of science – that certain things will be forever beyond us. Gödel's ideas may also prove that humans will always have more powers of logical insight than computers! The details of this argument are too complex to discuss fully, but briefly, one controversial interpretation of it is that Gödel proved that given *any* complex computer program a human mathematician could always find a mathematical truth, which the program could not decide was true or false. In addition, the human could also prove that this statement is true! Re-read these last statements; the implications may be vitally important for our view of ourselves as humans. If humans can do something that no computer can do, then this might mean that there is something about human intelligence that can never be attained by any computer, even in principle. If this controversial interpretation is correct, it has dramatic implications for scientific research into computing techniques. It might prove, once and for all, that it is impossible to have a computer which can think like us!

Many thinkers feel sheer astonishment that a purely logical result can offer such insight into human cognitive processes, though the insight is hotly disputed. On a more general philosophical note, some have interpreted Gödel as sounding a death-knell for the whole possibility of certainty, arguing that if complete certainty cannot be found in mathematics, of all places, then it cannot be found anywhere at all. To consider this more carefully, you will have to look in detail at precisely when Gödel's results hold, and precisely what they say. For our purposes, we simply note that, even if we could apply the mathematical method to other systems of knowledge, we would by no means have the perfect truth-generating machine. We can see that no such thing exists, even in the world of mathematics.

A Do you think it is a shame or a great thing that mathematics cannot be axiomatised?

B Do you like the controversial implications of Gödel's theorem?

Where do we go from here?

In our quest for truth, we looked to mathematics to provide certainty, and to a certain extent we have been successful, but perhaps not as successful as we might have hoped. We have learned that mathematical reasoning based on assumed axioms can generate certain, proven knowledge, and what is more, there even seems to be the possibility of an aesthetic element. Despite Gödel's theorems, this seems to be very promising, and we are immediately led to ask if the mathematical method can be generalised to things other than mathematical objects. If so, then perhaps we have made a significant step in our quest for truth. Traditionally, the application of mathematical principles (logic) to the world has been called rationalism, and it is the subject of the next chapter.

Further reading

It is difficult for the non-specialist to get to grips with much of the mathematical literature, but G. H. Hardy's *A Mathematician's Apology* (Cambridge University Press, 1940 repr. 1994) is a brilliant and engaging description for the lay person. If you would like to get a first-hand, totally non-algebraic experience of mathematical imagination, then Edwin Abbott's classic *Flatland* (Penguin, 1952) and its more readable descendent, Rudy Rucker's *The Fourth Dimension (and how to get there)* (Rider and Company, 1985) are unsurpassed for expanding conceptions of mathematics. Two very readable accounts of humans at the centre of mathematics are David Blatner's *The Joy of Pi* (Penguin, 1997) and Simon Singh's *Fermat's Enigma* (Walker & Co., 1997).

Getting slightly more technical, an outstanding description of what mathematicians actually do can be found in Philip Davis and Reuben Hersh's *The Mathematical Experience* (Houghton Mifflin, 1981). The creative and very human side of the notion of proof is brilliantly explored in play form in Imre Lakato's *Proofs and Refutations* (Cambridge University Press, 1977). If you want an extraordinary introduction to the extraordinary findings of Gödel, then Douglas Hofdstadter's rich, enormously wide-ranging (and simply enormous) *Gödel, Escher and Bach* (Vintage, 1989) remains more a literary experience than simply a book. The same ground is also covered in the excellent Ernest Nagel, James R. Newman and Douglas R. Hofdstader's *Gödel's Proof* (New York University Press, 2001). For two rather lighter but equally worthwhile books, try John Allen Paulo's *Mathematics and Humour* (University of Chicago Press, 1980), which is a short and funny book, or, as previously mentioned, David Blatner's *The Joy of Pi* (Walker & Co., 1999).

■ *Resource file*

IT AIN'T WHAT YOU PROVE, IT'S THE WAY THAT YOU PROVE IT

A play by Chris Binge.

Act 1: Lesson 1

Teacher: Good afternoon class. For homework I asked you to investigate triangles and to try and find some of their properties. Can anyone tell me what they have discovered?

Alpha: Yes. I have found that the angles of a triangle always add up to 180°.

Teacher: Perhaps you could explain how you came to this conclusion.

Alpha: Well, I drew a great many triangles of varying shapes and sizes and found that in nearly every case the angle sum was 180°.

Beta: Just a moment, did I hear you say 'nearly' every case?

Alpha: Yes – I admit there were a few that seemed to come to 181° or even 179°.

Beta: So your result should say that 'The angles of a triangle nearly always add up to 180°.'

Alpha: No, the evidence was so strong that I can explain the few that didn't by inaccuracies of measurement.

Beta: What you are trying to say is that you cling to your hypothesis despite evidence to the contrary. These are clearly counter-examples to your theory and it is most unmathematical to dismiss them so quickly.

Alpha: There is always experimental error when measurement is involved – it must be expected, not considered as a counter-example.

Beta: Teacher I protest. Alpha is using language that is more at home in a science laboratory where vague concepts such as 'strength of evidence' and 'experimental error' may be good enough, but this is a maths class. We are concerned with exactness and absolute truth.

Alpha: Even if I remeasured my triangles more accurately and got 180° every time, I expect you are such a sceptic that you would always say there may be a counter-example I haven't yet found.

Beta: For once you are absolutely correct. No amount of so called 'evidence' will convince me that your hypothesis, however likely, must be true. You are using an *inductive* argument which I cannot accept. I will only believe that when I have a vigorous *deductive* proof that it is the case.

Teacher: I am sure we are all agreed that such a proof would be desirable. Can anybody provide one?

Gamma: Yes. I have a proof that will satisfy Beta. May I demonstrate?

Teacher: Please do.

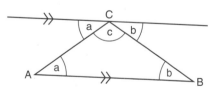

Gamma: You can see the triangle ABC. It contains angles of size a, b, and c. I have drawn a line passing through C which is parallel to AB. Due to the well-known properties of parallel lines, the angles at point C are also a and b as I have indicated. So now a, b and c are on a straight line, so a + b + c = 180°. So Alpha's theorem is proven since this process will work for all triangles.

Teacher: Are there any questions about Gamma's proof, or does this satisfy even Beta?

Delta: Just one small point. You have asserted a 'well-known' result about parallel lines. Could you just prove it for me please.

Gamma: OK . . . it's due to this property. Since (*pointing*) $a + b = 180°$, and $b + d = 180°$ then $a = d$.

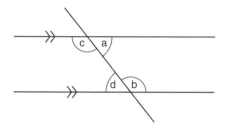

Delta: Ah yes, but just one further question, why do $a + b = 180°$?

Gamma: Well clearly $a + c = 180°$ due to the definition of 180° as the angle (*pointing*) on a straight line. Similarly $d + b = 180°$. Now, that means $a + b + c + d = 360°$. Clearly $a + b$ must be equal to $c + d$ otherwise the lines would not be parallel hence $a + b = 180°$.

Delta: I see. Are you sure there are not other hidden assumptions in your proof?

Gamma: Er yes (*tentatively*).

Delta: In which case may I suggest a couple. Firstly you have assumed that it is always possible to draw a parallel line through a given point. Secondly, you have assumed that it is possible to draw only one such line, that is the one with the angle properties you desire. Can you prove these?

Gamma: You are going to question everything aren't you? Look, a proof is merely an argument from what we already know to be true to a new result. In any proof we must start from assumptions. If you continually question the assumptions we will never be able to reach a new truth. If I use the term 'straight line' there is no point in asking me to prove that it is straight. The same is true with parallel lines. What you are doing is asking for a proof that parallel lines are in fact parallel. All I am saying is, *if* we start with a straight line, *then* we can deduce certain things. I am not, quite

frankly, interested in arguing whether or not it is *really* straight. I am assuming it is – if it isn't then we are talking about a different problem.

Phi: To save all this fuss, why not build the angle property into the definition of a triangle and define a triangle as a shape whose angles add up to 180°?

Gamma: You are being facetious. We define a triangle in terms of a few basic concepts, and from these concepts we prove its properties.

Phi: Perhaps you could give us such a definition.

Gamma: Happily. A triangle is a shape formed by joining three points with three straight lines.

Phi: Now perhaps you will define a straight line.

Gamma: (*wearily*) A straight line is the shortest path that you can draw between two points.

Phi: I will not go on to ask for a definition of points because I already have a counter-example to your theorem, based entirely on the definitions you have given. I have found a triangle whose angles add up to 270°.

Teacher: Please demonstrate.

Phi: (*holds up football*) As you can see, this line gives the shortest path between A and B, the same for BC and CA. All angles are right angles, hence the total is 270°.

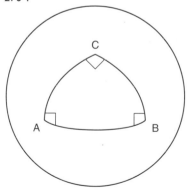

Delta: He's right, you cannot deny that this triangle fits your definitions, but it clearly doesn't follow the result of the theorem. ☞

Gamma: This is ridiculous, that is not a triangle. A triangle is a shape drawn on a flat plane, not on a curved surface.

Delta: I'm sorry Gamma but you never put that in your definition. By your definition there are three straight lines joining three points hence this is a triangle, hence a counter-example.

Gamma: The concept of a triangle being a plane figure is implicit in the definition even if it's not explicit.

Alpha: Even I have to disagree here. If I were to go from Singapore to Tokyo to Sydney and back to Singapore by the shortest routes you would all call my path triangular, yet as Phi has shown the angles do not add up to 180°.

Gamma: Clearly I must make the implicit explicit. I will rephrase the theorem. The angles of a triangle in a plane surface add up to 180°.

Teacher: Before we discuss this any further may I draw your attention to the proof of the theorem? We were happy with the proof and surprised by the counter-example. Should we not examine the proof to see where it breaks down? Then perhaps we will see if there are any other implicit assumptions that must be made explicit.

Alpha: It is the parallel line bit that breaks down.

Phi: I never liked that bit.

Alpha: If we follow the proof like before then you can see that you get three right angles on the line at C! But that's impossible! So the proof doesn't make sense in this case – and you assumed that it would.

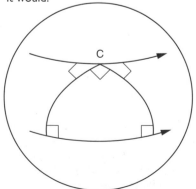

Phi: Mmmm . . . yes. And you know I'm not even sure that the two lines are parallel. Can you be certain that parallel lines can be drawn on a plane? I suggest that any two lines you draw will meet somewhere, if we have a long enough piece of paper. I challenge you to provide an infinitely long piece of paper to prove me wrong.

Alpha: Any lines I draw will be subject to error in measurement and inaccuracy in construction.

Beta: Oh don't start that again, we have had enough science for one day. There is a better way round the problem.

Alpha: Which is?

Beta: Which is to state clearly all assumptions that we are going to call on, and make our definitions subject to those assumptions. I shall call the assumptions 'axioms' and from then we can deduce 'theorems'.

Phi: But what if your assumptions are false?

Beta: Truth or falsehood doesn't enter into it. We assume our assumptions, obviously. That's why they are called assumptions. Therefore anything that follows from them is true in any world where they hold. If you can't find a world where they hold then it doesn't invalidate the theorems or the argument used to deduce them.

Phi: Let us hear your axioms.

Beta: Certainly.
1) There is one and only one straight line between two points.
2) Any finite straight line can be produced indefinitely.
3) All right angles are equal.
4) A circle can be drawn with any point as centre to pass through a given point.
5) Through any point one and only one line can be drawn parallel to a given line.

Teacher: (*an aside to audience*) The axioms were first suggested by the Greek mathematician Euclid over 2000 years ago. They were accepted as the basis for geometry until the nineteenth century when new systems of axioms were considered and new geometries were explored, including that of the sphere.

Gamma: So if we consider these axioms as our starting point, they define what we might call two-dimensional Euclidean space and it is not necessary or meaningful to question their truth since they are the starting point.

Phi: Surely we should define the terms that we use! We must be able to say what we mean by point and line or the axioms themselves are meaningless.

Delta: No, that would be too restrictive, even if it were possible.

Teacher: I think you should explain that statement – how are definitions restrictive?

Delta: Well the axioms that Beta gave us were envisaged in a flat plane, and our points and lines would be so defined.

Phi: Indeed, it is flat plane geometry we are talking about.

Delta: But if we can find another system which obeys the same again then all the theorems which are true for the flat plane are true for the other system.

Phi: I am a bit worried about the direction in which we seem to be moving. We seem to have lost our grip on reality.

Teacher: Perhaps you could elaborate on your fears.

Phi: I shall try. When Alpha first suggested the theorem about triangles, he was, quite rightly, criticised for using what one can only call a scientific method. I mean no insult by this. He allowed experimental evidence to guide his thinking and his conclusion was not an accurate deduction from his results. In maths we are not concerned with measurement of angles and the accuracies and inaccuracies that go with it. We are concerned with the theory of angles and triangles, with provable deductions that have a universal truth.

Teacher: Surely that means you must applaud the move towards an axiomatic structure and clearly defined rules of inference.

Phi: Only to a certain extent. It seems to me that we have gone too far. By suggesting that our initial concepts need have no definitions we have lost any relevance that our results may have to a real situation.

Teacher: Alpha, are you in broad agreement with Phi?

Alpha: I agree with him about going too far and leaving reality behind. It seems to me that maths has no value unless it informs us more about the world we live in and Delta's deduction from axioms and undefined terms seems to be little more than a game. I do however still defend the experimental approach as a starting point, because unless I had found the hypothesis by drawing then we would have had nothing to prove and hence no work to do. The correct procedure must be to find a result by experiment and then, using agreed definitions, we must prove the result true. The important thing is that the definitions characterise the objects of discussion.

Delta: I am sorry, but I disagree. The picturing of any reality is irrelevant, and to look for such a picture is not the purpose of mathematics. The job of a mathematician is to set up axiomatic systems and to deduce from them theorems. Our conceptions of the real are not fixed, they vary from person to person and they change, within each person from time to time. One only has to look at the confusion caused when Einstein asked scientists to drop their Newtonian ideas of physics or the continuing debate over quantum theory and wave theory to see how any supposed picture of reality is inadequate. Whether or not an axiomatic system is of any value to scientists does not affect its validity as a piece of mathematics. We are not concerned with perceptions of an external reality, we are concerned with objects created by the mind, and rules we use to govern these objects. As such the objects cannot and should not be defined in terms of the real world, since the real world, or at least ☞ our view of it, will change.

RESOURCE FILE RESOURCE FILE RESOURCE FILE RESOURCE FILE RESOURCE FILE RESOURCE FILE RESOURCE FILE RESOURCE FILE RESOURCE FILE

69

Beta: I agree with Delta. I also noticed Alpha's attempt to slander axiomatic systems by calling them games. He is probably so upset at being called a scientist that he wanted to throw a few insults of his own. However, he has failed miserably as I do not consider the word 'game' an insult at all. The game of chess is a very good analogy. In chess the pieces have names and their rules for movement are the axioms. A position is allowable only if it can be reached by using the rules. But the pieces are not defined in terms of anything outside chess. We call a bishop a bishop and a knight a knight but their rules of movement bear no relation to any bishops or knights outside the game of chess (if they did then the phrase 'queen mates with bishop on back row' would have a completely different meaning). No attempt is made to use the game as a picture of reality. The pieces are purely man-made concepts and the game is a formal logical structure. Mathematics is a formal logical structure derived from rules in the same way – and the greatest game of all.

A What is the role of experiment in mathematics? How does this differ from the role of experiment in science?

B Once mathematicians believe that they have found a result (or theorem), what is the next step? How does this differ from science?

C What is an axiom? Can an axiom be true or false?

D In your own words, summarise Delta's position on mathematics. How does he differ from Alpha regarding the status of axioms?

E So are the results of mathematics true? What do we mean by mathematical truth?

RESOURCE FILE   RESOURCE FILE   RESOURCE FILE   RESOURCE FILE   RESOURCE FILE   RESOURCE FILE   RESOURCE FILE   RESOURCE FILE   RESOURCE FILE   RESOURCE FILE   RESOURCE FILE

70

'The number system is like human life...'

An extract from *Miss Smilla's Feeling for Snow* by Peter Høeg.

'I'm afraid of being locked up,' I say.

He puts the crabs in the pot. He lets them boil for no more than five minutes.

In a way I'm relieved that he doesn't say anything, doesn't yell at me. He's the only other person who knows how much we know. It seems necessary to explain my claustrophobia to him.

'Do you know what the foundation of mathematics is?' I ask. 'The foundation of mathematics is numbers. If anyone asked me what makes me truly happy, I would say: numbers. Snow and ice numbers. And do you know why?'

He splits the claws with a nutcracker and pulls out the meat with curved tweezers.

'Because the number system is like human life. First you have the natural numbers. The ones that are whole and positive. The numbers of a small child. But human consciousness expands. The child discovers a sense of longing, and do you know what the mathematical expression is for longing?'

He adds cream and several drops of orange juice to the soup.

'The negative numbers. The formalisation of the feeling that you are missing something. And human consciousness expands and grows even more, and the child discovers the in-between spaces. Between stones, between pieces of moss on the stone, between people. And between numbers. And do you know what that leads to? It leads to fractions. Whole numbers plus fractions produces the rational numbers. And human consciousness doesn't stop there. It wants to go beyond reason. It adds an operation as absurd as the extraction of roots. And produces irrational numbers.'

He warms the French bread in the oven and fills the pepper mill.

'It's a form of madness. Because the irrational numbers are infinite. They can't be written down. They force human consciousness out beyond the limits. And by adding the irrational numbers to the rational numbers you get the real numbers.'

I've stepped out into the middle of the room to have more space. It's rare that you have a chance to explain yourself to a fellow human being. Usually you have to fight for the floor. And this is important to me.

'It doesn't stop. It never stops. Because now, on the spot, we expand the real numbers with imaginary square roots of negative numbers. These are numbers we can't picture, pictures that normal human consciousness cannot comprehend. And when we add the imaginary system to the real numbers, we have the complex number system. The first number system in which it's possible to explain satisfactorily the crystal formation of ice. It's like a vast, open landscape. The horizons. You head towards them and they keep receding. That is Greenland, and that's what I can't be without. That's why I don't want to be locked up.'

I wind up standing in front of him.

'Smilla,' he says, 'can I kiss you?'

A Smilla says, 'the foundation of mathematics is numbers'. Is this really the foundation? Are there any other contenders for the foundation of mathematics?

B Smilla describes some operations as 'absurd', and some numbers as 'madness'. What are her grounds for doing so? Are these reasonable grounds?

C Why does Smilla liken maths to human consciousness? Does this analogy tell you anything? Do any of your experiences suggest anything similar?

5

He that will not reason is a bigot; he that cannot reason is a fool; and he that dares not reason is a slave.
William Drummond

We should take care not to make the intellect our god; it has, of course, powerful muscles, but no personality. It cannot lead; it can only serve.
Albert Einstein

I do not feel obliged to believe that the same God who has endowed us with sense, reason, and intellect has intended us to forgo their use.
Galileo Galilei

The further the spiritual evolution of mankind advances, the more certain it seems to me that the path to genuine religiosity does not lie through the fear of life, and the fear of death, and blind faith, but through striving after rational knowledge.
Albert Einstein

The reasonable man adapts himself to the world; the unreasonable man persists in trying to adapt the world to himself. Therefore all progress depends on the unreasonable man.
George Bernard Shaw

MAN IS A RATIONAL ANIMAL WHO ALWAYS LOSES HIS TEMPER WHEN HE IS CALLED UPON TO ACT IN ACCORDANCE WITH THE DICTATES OF REASON.
Oscar Wilde

Fantasy, abandoned by reason, produces impossible monsters; united with it, she is the mother of the arts and the origin of marvels.
Goya

If you want to make someone hate you, explain to them, logically and politely, why they are wrong.
J. Baylock

People generally quarrel because they cannot argue.
G. K. Chesterton

THE BEST WAY I KNOW OF TO WIN AN ARGUMENT IS TO START BY BEING IN THE RIGHT.
Lord Hailsham

Arguments are to be avoided: they are always vulgar and often convincing.
Oscar Wilde

Aims

By the end of this chapter you should:

- understand that the use of reason is a way to extend our knowledge from known facts
- be able to distinguish between inductive and deductive arguments – in both cases to evaluate the strengths and weaknesses of the arguments
- understand the premises/conclusion nature of an argument
- be very clear about the relationship between a valid argument and a true conclusion
- be aware of the need to be rigorous when using logic, the difficulties associated with choice of premises, the dangers of hidden assumptions and the problems with definitions
- be familiar with some elementary fallacies
- be able to apply these ideas to everyday examples
- appreciate that real-life problem solving requires imagination and creativity, and more than simple logic.

Introduction

There is a scene in a Broadway play where a guest at a party meets a Catholic priest. The guest asks, 'Don't you hear some terrible things in confession?' The priest replies, 'Oh yes. In fact when I was just starting out as a priest, the first person who came to me for confession told me they had committed a murder.' Later on in the play, a newcomer joins the party, and on being introduced to the priest says, 'I met you long ago Father. In fact I was the first person to come to you for confession.'

Aha! You immediately realise the connection here. The two pieces of information you have are combined to produce a third piece, and it seems as if you have generated new knowledge just by thinking about it! This seems rather useful – and what's more it is certainly correct! If it is true that the first person who saw the priest for confession was a murderer, and that particular person was the first person to see the priest for confession, then the conclusion is inescapable – we just use logic! Like in maths, we seem to have hit upon a great method for getting new knowledge. If this is true, then we can forget all those messy science experiments ... or is this beginning to sound too good to be true? Can we really get very far just using logic? If we think that we can, then we are embracing what is called the **rationalist** approach – we are saying that reason is the primary source of truth. But is rationalism correct?

Deductive and inductive logic

There are two distinct branches of logic. **Deductive** logic involves examples like the one above, where given the truth of some information, the conclusion must also be true. If the priest and the newcomer were telling the truth then the newcomer must be a murderer. Another very simple example might be:

A: All humans are mortal.

B: I am human.

therefore

C: I am mortal.

If statements A and B are true, then there can be no doubt that C is true. It would be ludicrous to assert A and B but deny C, and we can immediately see that this is as compelling a conclusion as we are likely to find. Of course, A and/or B may be false, but if they are true then there is no way that C can be false. So, if this is anything to go by, logic seems like it might play a prominent role in a search for reliable knowledge. Could certain knowledge be found by a study of precisely why these logical laws are so certain? Consider:

A: I am either a schnoodlepopper or a birshteinwaller, or both.

B: I am not a schnoodlepopper.

therefore

C: I am a birshteinwaller.

Once more, if A and B are true, then we are somehow compelled to accept C. Notice that it is the structure of the argument rather than the content that is important (what is a schnoodlepopper anyway?) and this means that deductive logic can be applied to any subject. When the initial statements (A, B, etc.) are more complex, applying logical analysis can be a very powerful tool.

A Make up some other absolutely convincing arguments.
B Make up some arguments which seem convincing, but in fact are not.

There is, however, another type of logic. **Inductive** logic does not involve certainty in the same way. The classic example involves the European naturalist observing European swans. He sees one swan – it is white. He sees another – it also is white. The third, fourth, fifth . . . they are all white. After many years he has seen thousands of white swans, and he therefore says that the logical conclusion is that all swans are white. This is inductive logic. The naturalist has gone from several specific instances to a general conclusion. The question is, was he correct in doing so? We now know that there are black swans in Australia and New Zealand, so his conclusion was incorrect. The problem of generalising like this is called the 'problem of induction'.

It may seem that this is a million miles away from 'real-life' problems. (When do you ever hypothesise about the colours of animals?) But in fact, it is very common. If you think of the problem of induction as 'drawing general conclusions from specific examples', then you should see that we all do it all the time. A friend buys a car from a dealer, and it turns out to be a bad buy. On the basis of this one case, I will almost certainly not use the same car dealer! We all know that it takes a teacher to be unpleasant only a few times, or a student to miss a deadline a few times, before general conclusions are drawn. In both these cases, the conclusion may or may not be true, but it would be very hard to say that the conclusion is arrived at in an unreasonable way. It is not simply a matter of the number of times that something has happened. Think of the thousands of white swans! We need to realise that drawing general conclusions from specific examples is a very tricky business.

Depending on your approach, the fact that a developing child learns most of what she knows about the world in this manner is either reassuring (since it seems to work a lot of the time) or deeply disturbing (does that mean all our ideas are rather dubious?). In any case, the problem of induction is a very serious one for anyone looking for reliable knowledge.

The problem of induction

We all use induction all the time. I have always enjoyed going for a run, so I assume that when I run today I will enjoy that, too. Day has always followed night in my experience, so I assume that it will continue to do so. It might be suggested that this is just the way the world works – if something has happened often in the past, there is a good chance it will do so again. This is, it might seem, only reasonable. But consider the times you have seen someone on a lucky day, perhaps playing cards, or a sports person having a good day. People talk about 'being on a roll' or 'having a hot streak'. For that person, it seems that nothing can go wrong, and nobody wants to bet against them. Is this another valid application of induction?

Interestingly, the answer, certainly in sports, is a resounding 'no'. Careful research has shown that the idea of a lucky streak is an illusion. A basketball player has a one in five chance of shooting a basket, and she has just shot five in a row. Will she make her sixth shot? Is she 'on a roll'? It turns out that the probability is still one in five – or in other words, the 'past successes' have no bearing on 'future successes'. This is the problem of induction.

So why does the idea of the 'hot hand' still linger? Well, partly because it means that when the player has shot five baskets in a row, one time in five she will shoot six! These freak occurrences will happen by the laws of probability (and when untold quantities of data are available to computers to look for freak occurrences, you can bet they will be reported every time). But more importantly, the idea of a 'hot hand' still lingers because humans have a great tendency to see what they want to see and to remember selectively bits of data that stand out as significant (we shall see this again and again). Induction is about the human need to look for patterns in observations over time, but we need to be careful that our need to categorise and classify doesn't lead us to seeing what isn't really there.

Of course, we don't want to go too far down this road and reject all inductive reasoning; we want to be able to distinguish the good from the bad. Sometimes induction seems to work, and sometimes it doesn't. But how do we tell the difference?

A What do we 'know' about the world by the process of induction?
B Have you ever drawn an inductive conclusion and been surprised?
C Identify some examples where inductive reasoning seems reasonable to you, and some where it seems unreasonable.

Consider the chicken who is fed every day by the farmer. Being a philosophical sort of chicken, after a few weeks it applies induction and comes out to greet the farmer each morning, expecting food. One day, the farmer wrings its neck. Bertrand Russell, the philosopher, remarked that perhaps *'more refined views as to the ... [problem of induction] ... would have been useful to the chicken.'*

A How 'refined' are our views on induction?
B What would the world be like if induction ceased to be reliable?
C Are we going to have a shock one day if we rely on induction?
D How can we justify the use of induction? Here are two possibilities:

'It has always worked before.'
'It is probably correct.'

Neither of these are good justifications, because they are **circular arguments**. What do you think this means?

Of course, in practice we often draw conclusions from limited evidence because we have no choice but to do so. Sometimes this seems reasonable (the sun has risen every day, so it will do so tomorrow), but sometimes not (shares have risen for the last few years, so they will always do so). In this exercise, we consider when evidence supports a conclusion and when it does not. In particular, we will see if we can find some general principles which might indicate when inductive logic is likely to be reliable and when it is likely to lead us astray.

A An investor has purchased one hundred shares of oil stock every December for the last five years. In every case the value of the stock has appreciated every year by around 15 per cent, and it has paid dividends of about 8 per cent. This December she intends to buy another hundred shares of oil stock, reasoning that she will probably receive modest earnings while watching the value of the stock increase over the years.
In each of the following scenarios decide:
a) whether the additional fact makes the inductive conclusion more or less likely to be true
b) what principle governed your decision in the above.

- Suppose in the last five years she had always bought shares of one particular company, and she intends to purchase shares in the same company.
- Suppose that she had been buying oil stocks every December for fifteen years, not five.
- Suppose that oil stocks previously purchased had gone up by 30 per cent each year instead of by only 15 per cent.
- Suppose that her previous purchases of oil stock had been in six different companies, and that she intended to buy stock in a different, seventh one.
- Suppose she learnt that major oil-exporting countries have decided to meet every month instead of every six months.
- Suppose she discovers that tobacco stocks have just raised or lowered their dividend payments.

You should now have a set of principles to guide you in your use of inductive logic.

A Bill has taken four philosophy courses and has found them all extremely stimulating and worthwhile. He therefore signs up for another one, expecting it, too, to be worthwhile. On the basis of the principles you have just found, would the following statements, if true, make the conclusion more or less likely?

- His previous philosophy courses were in ethics, science, logic and language.
- The previous courses had all been taught by the same teacher, and the same teacher is scheduled to teach the present one.
- Professor Abacus taught all the previous courses, but Professor Calculator is scheduled to teach the present one.
- Bill found the previous philosophy courses to be the most exciting intellectual, personal and spiritual experiences of his entire life, and indeed were the only things that gave his life any meaning.
- All previous courses met at 6.50p.m. on Tuesday, but the present one is scheduled for 6.50p.m. on Friday.
- In addition to enjoying philosophy, Bill also enjoys anthropology, economics and political science.

More about deductive logic – arguments

Although we use induction all the time, it seems that if it is certainty we are seeking then we ought to stick with deduction. The examples in the introduction to this chapter showed clearly that deduction allows us to deduce a conclusion with **absolute certainty**. That is, if I am human and if all humans are mortal then it is absolutely certain that I am mortal. It is difficult to say, absolutely precisely, why the conclusion is so compelling, but it is. In this case, the logic of the situation strikes us with some force – which is a very promising start!

Here are a couple of more painful examples. In the following two cases, suppose that A and B are true. Must C also be true?

1 A: No monkeys are soldiers.
  B: All monkeys are smelly.
  C: Some smelly creatures aren't soldiers.
2 A: No emperors are dentists.
  B: All children fear dentists.
  C: No children fear emperors.

These are examples where it's quite hard to get your head around the relationships between the monkeys and the soldiers, and the emperors and the children. Whatever you think about the conclusion, it is clearly less obvious than in simpler examples. Perhaps this is the first problem of rationalism – applying logic can be difficult just because it is!

A useful tool for considering these types of problems is the Venn diagram. Imagine all the things in the problems to be in sets. So for question 1 above, we have the sets of monkeys, soldiers and smelly things. We represent these as three overlapping ovals:

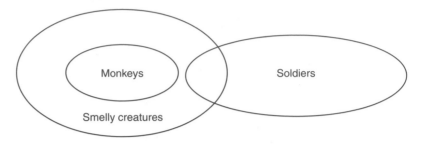

Think carefully about how to arrange the ovals in these diagrams – there is one little problem here, can you see it? Once you have drawn the diagram, you should be able to see that the argument is valid. Try drawing Venn diagrams for the question below.

A Identify the valid and invalid arguments here, using Venn diagrams if you like.

1 If my house is bombed it will be reduced to rubble.
My house is not bombed.
therefore: My house will not be reduced to rubble.

2 If my house is bombed it will be reduced to rubble.
My house is reduced to rubble.
therefore: My house must have been bombed.

3 If my house is bombed it will be reduced to rubble.
My house is not reduced to rubble.
therefore: My house cannot have been bombed.

4 All monetarists control the money supply.
Margaret Thatcher controlled the money supply.
therefore: Margaret Thatcher was a monetarist.

5 All accountants are tennis players.
All youngsters are tennis players.
therefore: All accountants are youngsters.

6 All poets are imaginative.
No poets have business acumen.
therefore: No one with good business acumen is imaginative.

7 All Buddhists are vegetarians.
Peter is a vegetarian.
therefore: Peter is a Buddhist.

8 Some Muslims don't drink alcohol.
All Arabs are Muslims.
therefore: Some Arabs don't drink alcohol.

9 All women are either singers or criminals (but not both).
All women in jail are criminals.
therefore: No woman in jail is a singer.

10 All of my Theory of Knowledge students are male dwarves.
No dwarf can resist giving his teacher large gifts.
therefore: All of my Theory of Knowledge students will give me large gifts.

More about deductive logic – truth and validity

You have probably noticed that so far we have been a little careless with our terms in discussing the use of deduction. We need to make a vital distinction in what we are doing. Consider the following argument:

> A: All students are lazy.
> B: I am a student.
> therefore C: I am lazy.

You can see that this is a perfectly **valid** logical argument. If A and B are true then C must be true. However **the conclusion** is obviously dubious because at least one of the **premises** of the argument (A or B) is incorrect (that is, it is not true that all students are lazy). There are two completely separate issues here – the truth of the premises themselves and the correctness of the method used to draw a conclusion from the premises (the logical argument). This is an extremely important point. For the conclusion of a logical argument to be true, the logic must be correct **and** the premises must be true. If you want to undermine an argument, you can try to fault the logic or you can dispute the premises of the argument.

We can summarise this in the following table:

Validity of logic		Truth of premises	
		True	False
	Valid	Conclusion must be T	Conclusion may be T or F
	Invalid	Conclusion may be T or F	Conclusion may be T or F

A Here are some arguments. Decide whether the premises are true or false, whether the logic is valid or invalid and hence whether or not the conclusion must be true.

1. All Australian cities are in the southern hemisphere.
   Sydney is not an Australian city.
   therefore: Sydney is not in the southern hemisphere.
2. All Australian states are in the southern hemisphere.
   Queensland is an Australian state.
   therefore: Queensland is in the southern hemisphere.
3. All American states have beaches.
   Hawaii is an American state.
   therefore: Hawaii has beaches.
4. All politicians are exceptionally honest people.
   I am a politician.
   therefore: I am an exceptionally honest person.
5. Most people in England speak English.
   Most people in New Zealand speak English.
   therefore: Most people in China speak English. (What sort of logic is this?)

B Make up an argument for each of the categories in the table above.

The importance of premises

The last section alerts us to a crucial problem about knowledge – that the validity of the logic is one thing, but the truth of the conclusion is something entirely different. If the truth of the conclusion depends on the truth of the premises, then we need to take a close look at what we use as premises.

To make the point here we shall try to apply logic to a set of facts (given in story form) to test the truth of certain conclusions.

A First, read the story below.

The dangers of crossing the road
The old lady had just finished her shopping and was starting to cross the road when a car sped around the corner. The cyclist, fearing an accident, shouted 'Watch out', and the car driver slammed on the brakes – but it was too late. A collision was unavoidable. Shopping bags were scattered all over the road, but fortunately no-one was seriously injured.

The police appeared soon afterwards and interviewed all the relevant witnesses. The lady's poor vision had contributed to the accident and the car had been speeding.

Look at the statements below.

If the statement is definitely true (based on **only the information in the story**) mark 'T'.

If the statement is definitely false (based on **only the information in the story**) mark 'F'.

If there is not enough information, and you cannot decide, then mark '?'.

There is, however, one catch. Once you have answered a question, **you should not go back and change any of your earlier answers**. Doing so will invalidate the exercise.

1 There was a car travelling faster than the speed limit.
2 The old lady in the story had been shopping.
3 A vehicle came round the corner just after a lady had stepped off the pavement.
4 The car driver was unable to avoid a collision.
5 The police came to investigate the incident.
6 Although the old lady was struck by the car, she was not seriously injured.
7 Shopping was scattered over the road.
8 The driver slammed on his brakes.
9 The police interviewed the car driver.
10 The old lady had poor eyesight.
11 The car's speeding contributed to the accident.
12 The old lady was riding a bicycle.
13 The cyclist was seriously injured.
14 There was at least one car driver involved in the accident.
15 The lady crossed the road near a corner.

→

B Now follow the same procedure for the story and set of statements below.

Incident in the store
The old man had just turned off the lights in the store and was preparing to lock up and go home when a youth appeared and demanded money. The owner opened the cash register; the contents were grabbed, and the man ran away. The police were informed immediately.

1   A young man appeared after the lights had been turned off.
2   The old man was preparing to go home.
3   The robber demanded money.
4   Someone opened the cash register.
5   The robber demanded money from the owner.
6   The person who opened the cash register was a man.
7   The cash register contained money, but we are not told *how much* money.
8   The gender of the owner was not revealed in the story.
9   The robber did not demand money.
10 After the man grabbed the contents of the cash register, he ran away.
11 The young man appeared after the lights had been turned off.
12 The robber was a man.
13 The owner was a man.
14 The owner appeared and demanded money.
15 The man ran away after he had demanded money.

C Go back and look again. The majority of your answers should be '?'. What do you learn from these stories?

D Make up a situation, like the two stories above, where the reader naturally makes all sorts of assumptions.

In the cases above, few people manage to follow the instructions remotely accurately. You should discuss these stories and see exactly what you assumed and why the stories are so easy to misinterpret. As a matter of fact, it seems that humans find it very difficult indeed to make deductions strictly on the basis of evidence. Instead, we seem to tell ourselves a story, to make assumptions and to embroider events according to our own personal prejudices. The full story here will have to wait until Chapter 9 – for now we should note merely that strict deduction is very difficult to achieve!

Logic in the real world: arguments, axioms and assumptions

We now turn to examining the use of reason in everyday life. For example, consider the following:

If inflation is allowed to continue, the unions will demand a steep rise in wages. And that is what is going to happen, because inflation is going to be allowed to continue.

To see if this is a valid logical argument, we can rewrite it as:

Premise 1: Inflation will imply wage rises.
Premise 2: There will be inflation.
Conclusion: There will be wage rises.

Hopefully, you can now see that this is a valid argument. That is, if the premises are true then the conclusion will also be true. In this case, we can't really be sure about the truth of the premises, although an economist might be inclined to agree with the first one in general terms.

A Evaluate the logic in the following arguments.

1 The alternatives seem to be that either the US government weakens its NATO commitment by withdrawing troops from Europe or that it meets increasing criticism at home for the enormous funds spent in maintaining these troops abroad. The government will never weaken its NATO commitment, so we can expect criticism to increase.

2 The streets are no safer today than they were five years ago, yet if the Crime Control Act was effective we would expect the streets to be safer. Hence the act was not effective.

3 Granted, if there were no problems on Earth, humankind should explore the moon. But there are plenty of problems on Earth, so we should not be spending money to explore the moon.

4 Maybe the President did accept bribes from business interests to pass certain laws. On the other hand, these might be vicious rumours spread by his political enemies. This I cannot believe, so I conclude that the President did accept the bribes.

5 By 2005, either we will institute far-reaching procedures to recycle our waste, or by then we will have to find room for 900 million tons of waste paper, plastic and other junk produced by our affluent society. However, we believe that somehow such room will be found. Hence there will be no need for large-scale recycling.

6 If the French tend to eat, drink and smoke more than people in other European countries then we might expect their life expectancy to be lower than people in, say, Great Britain or Italy, and this is exactly what we find. French men live for an average of 67.1 years and French women for 70.2 years, as opposed to the European male average of 70.3 years and female average of 74.3 years. Hence the French must eat, drink and smoke too much.

B Now that you have had a look at the sorts of problems we encounter in 'real-world' logic, we can try something a little more involved. In questions 7–10 below, all the arguments are valid; they are good deductive logic. But they arrive at opposite conclusions. Examine each one and decide which argument in each pair you find most compelling.

7 • Welfare systems discourage people from working. Having lots of people unemployed is bad for the economy. Therefore, if we want a healthy economy we should look for ways to abandon the welfare system.　　➜

- The more very poor people you have in a generally rich country, the higher the crime rate. A high level of welfare stops people from being very poor, so to keep crime low we should maintain this high level of welfare.

8 • Minorities suffer from increasing racism in a certain country. An increase of foreigners will lead, in practice, to more people suffering from racism. Therefore existing minorities are actually helped by tough immigration laws.

- Minorities suffer from increasing racism in a certain country. An increase of foreigners will, over time, lead to greater acceptance of all minorities. Therefore existing minorities are disadvantaged by tough immigration laws.

9 • Killing someone, unless in self-defence, is wrong. Abortion kills unborn babies. Therefore abortion is wrong.

- What happens to a person's body is ultimately their decision. To prevent a person deciding about their own body is wrong. Having an abortion involves a woman deciding about her body, so to prevent her doing that would be wrong. Hence preventing abortion is wrong.

10 • A race that places itself above all others is despicable. Humans place themselves above all other animals. Therefore humans are despicable.

- A race that did not place itself above all others would not have survived for very long. Hence placing one's race above all others is a natural survival trait. Hence it is perfectly acceptable to place one's race above all others.

Questions 7–10 reinforce the crucial distinction between validity and truth. In particular, it is interesting to see that **logic is of no help in choosing between arguments**. This is perhaps rather surprising, especially since we were hoping to use reason as a tool in our search for truth and certainty. It seems not to be living up to our initial hopes.

C Our final set of exercises illustrates once more the problem of choosing correct premises. In each of the following arguments, there is an unstated assumption required to make the argument valid. Identify that assumption.

11 Property prices are bound to drop soon since they have been rising for a long time now.

12 It must be a good school – the fees are so high.

13 I'm not doing maths homework today because I need to work on my history.

14 Female office workers work just as hard as male office workers and are just as productive. Therefore female office workers doing the same job as men should receive the same pay.

15 Marijuana should be legalised because it is no more dangerous than alcohol, and less dangerous than tobacco, both of which are already legal.

16 Marijuana should not be legalised because it leads to the use of harder drugs such as heroin.

A little more about being careful in arguments: definitions

You may have participated in, or listened to, an argument which seems to go around and around in circles, with neither side able to progress towards a conclusion. This is sometimes inevitable – agreement on certain topics may never happen. But sometimes arguments are particularly frustrating because one or both sides seem unable to see what the other is saying. This can sometimes be due to problems relating to the language we use and, in particular, to problems relating to **meaning** and **definition** (in Chapter 10 we shall see that *meaning* is a very complex and subtle concept; for now we take it at face value).

You have already seen that if we attempt to define terms such as 'art' or 'life' or 'science', then what initially seemed obvious becomes fraught with confusion and ambiguity very quickly. It's not so much that we don't know what we mean when we use these terms, but pinning them down precisely can be difficult, and often other people will hold to slightly different definitions.

Even if we pick a very precisely defined word, we can see that difficulties arise. A 'bachelor' is defined as an adult human male who has never been married. It seems clear enough, but now ask yourself if these people are bachelors.

- Anthony is seventeen years old. He attends school and lives with his parents.
- Bertrand is seventeen years old. He left home at fourteen to start his own company and is now a millionaire. When not abroad attending business meetings, he lives in his own house and has a playboy lifestyle.
- Charlie and Chris are homosexual lovers who have been together happily for twenty years.
- David has been living with Daphne for the last ten years. They have three children. He has never been married, and has no intention of ever getting married.
- Edward is married to a woman who paid him $25,000 so that she could become a citizen of his country. He has met her once, and they have never lived together. They will divorce as soon as it is possible for the woman to retain citizenship. Meanwhile, Edward is seeing other women.
- Father Francis is a Catholic priest.

If you were to argue about any of these, then it would be clear that your argument has nothing to do with the facts of the situation. If I think that David is a bachelor but you don't, then there are no new pieces of information that would help solve the problem. It would be fair to characterise our disagreement as being more about the word 'bachelor' than about David's status.

This sort of disagreement can happen frequently unless we are careful. Most often it happens when terms are vague or emotionally loaded, but it can happen with seemingly 'well-defined' terms like 'bachelor'. We might therefore distinguish between two different types of disagreement:

1 **The factual dispute.** If I think that Singapore is south of the equator, and you maintain that it is just north of the equator, then our disagreement is easily resolved by reference to an atlas. We almost certainly agree on the meanings of 'Singapore' and 'equator' and we have a genuine disagreement.

2 **The merely verbal dispute.** This is where the presence of an ambiguous term conceals the fact that there is no real disagreement. Disputes like these are not always easy to spot, but once we recognise them we can usually resolve the problem by clearing up the ambiguity. As shown in the bachelor example, the ambiguity can arise even with words in common use.

Notice that it is quite possible for both of these types of dispute to be present in an argument! If two people are arguing about a film with explicit sex/violence in it, then there may be a disagreement of type 2 over the term 'explicit' and/or differences of type 1 about whether or not children should see these films (whatever the meaning of the word 'explicit').

A What sort of disputes are these? If merely verbal, resolve the dispute by explaining the ambiguity.

1 **A:** Dave is the best tennis player in the club. His serve is faster than anyone else's.
B: No, Nick is much better! His volleying is amazing.

2 **A:** I read in their annual report that General Industrial's earnings have increased again this year.
B: No they haven't. They may say that they have, but they are currently being investigated for false reporting. Their earnings are actually lower.

3 **A:** National Conglomerate are doing well. Their sales so far this year are 15 per cent up on last year.
B: No, they aren't doing very well. Profits so far this year are 30 per cent lower than they were this time last year.

4 **A:** Jenny is a great student. Although her assignments are always late, she always asks perceptive and intelligent questions in class.
B: Jenny is one of the worst students I've ever met. Her smart answers in class don't make up for never getting assignments in on time.

5 **A:** Even though they are several hundred years old, Shakespeare's plays are enormously relevant. Love, death, duty, sacrifice and honour . . . these themes are as important today as they were when the plays were written.
B: I don't agree. What does Shakespeare have to say about over-population, environmental degradation and unemployment? Nothing. His plays are irrelevant today.

6 **A:** Alice finally got rid of that old computer of hers and bought herself a new one. She uses a Mac now.
B: No, Alice didn't buy herself a new computer. That Mac is a good three years old.

7 **A:** Jim finally got rid of that old computer of his and bought himself a new one. He's using a Mac now.
B: No, Jim didn't buy himself a new computer. It's his roommate's new Mac that he's using.

→

8 **A:** George lives a long way from here. I walked out to see him the other day, and it took me nearly two hours to get there.

B: No, he doesn't live such a long way from campus. I drove over there and we reached his place in less than ten minutes.

9 **A:** It was in very bad taste to serve roast pork at the banquet. There were Muslims present, and it is against their religion to eat pork.

B: Bad taste! No way! That was the tastiest meal I've had in a long time. Lovely!

10 **A:** Our daughter is a wonderful mother to our grandchildren. She lets them want for nothing; they have a beautiful home, wonderful toys and are sent to a fantastic school.

B: I don't think she is a good mother at all. She is so busy working that her children hardly know her. They know their childminders better; she is just someone who pays the bills.

11 **A:** A tree falling in a wilderness with nobody around to hear will produce no sound. There can be no auditory sensation unless someone actually senses it.

B: No, whether anyone is there to hear it or not, the crash of a falling tree will set up vibrations in the air and will therefore produce a sound in any event.

12 **A:** Mr Zebedee is a real Christian. He's such a nice guy and is always helping out in community projects.

B: I wouldn't call Zebedee a Christian. He only goes to church at Christmas.

13 **A:** Don't ask your wife about it. You should use your own judgement.

B: I will use my own judgement, and in my judgement, I should ask my wife.

14 **A:** Tom committed the murder of his own free will. Nobody told him, made him, or even suggested to him that he should do it. It was his own freely made decision.

B: That is impossible. Either it was something in his nature that made him do it, or something in the environment, or maybe some combination. And Tom is not responsible for his own nature (that's his parents' genes) nor his environment (that's society). So he has no free will.

15 **A:** Professor Dogsbreath is one of the most productive scholars here. He has written more than any other staff member.

B: He's not productive! He may have written a lot, but none of it is original or interesting. He is actually completely unproductive.

16 **A:** Unemployment here is only one million according to government statistics.

B: Oh no, there are far more people unemployed! The President's Economic Report states that there are 35 million employed in this country, and the Census Bureau reports a total population of over 55 million. So the government's figures reveal that there are over 20 million unemployed persons in this country.

17 **A:** That man just broke the law by driving like that.

B: No he didn't – that was perfectly legal.

B From the local newspaper, identify three disagreements in current political or social controversy that exhibit the features described in this section.

Common fallacies and errors of reasoning

So far we have looked at the rules for getting an argument right, but in practice they are often broken. When an argument is not valid, we say that it is 'fallacious'. A **fallacy** is an argument which, however appealing it may be, is not logically valid. There are a great many reasons why an argument may seem convincing when it should not. Here are some examples of the most common ones.

> **A** Make sure you understand the principle behind each fallacy listed below and write a definition as to what each one means.
> **B** Find some examples of fallacies in everyday conversation and in the editorials and adverts of newspapers.

■ Ad misericordiam

- We hope you'll accept our recommendations. We spent the last twelve weeks working extra time on them and we are quite exhausted.
- Please give me a good assessment – my parents will be furious if you don't!
- You *always* win these arguments we have. Can't you let me win just this one?

■ Ad hominem

- You may argue that God doesn't exist, but that's just because you are so bigoted.
- Jim's argument about his ex-wife should be ignored because he is very bitter towards her.
- You claim that Tim is innocent, but why should we listen to you? You are a criminal, too.

■ Hasty generalisation

- Fred the Australian stole my wallet. All Australians are thieves.
- Six of my friends like the new school uniform – it will be really popular.
- All the new-born babies I've seen are so cute! Our child is going to be absolutely adorable!

■ Appeal to authority

- One of the world's top economists states that interest rates will fall soon.
- The Prime Minister says that traditional educational methods are in dire need of reform.
- It must be true – our Theory of Knowledge teacher says so!

■ Unpalatable consequences

- Evolution cannot be true because, if it were, then we would be no better than the apes.
- You must believe in God, otherwise life would have no meaning.
- I don't believe a nuclear war will happen because I could never sleep at night if I did.

■ Loaded language

- Clear thinkers will agree with me that we should have another free vote on abortion.
- The Minister *claims* that the new tax rate will benefit the poor.
- The proposal is likely to be resisted by the bureaucrats in the Government.

■ Appeal to common practice

- Some people say that cheating in tests is wrong, but everyone does it, so it's okay.
- Political corruption is just a way of life; there's no point in complaining.
- You shouldn't pick on me for not doing my homework when others haven't done it either.

■ Red herring

- Air bags in cars do not really increase safety, and besides, most cars with air bags are Japanese.
- Women should be able to decide about abortion – men getting involved is just another example of the long history of male oppression of women.
- This may be a meat-importing company, but I happen to like the taste of red herrings.

■ Straw man

- I can't understand anyone wanting to cut military expenditure. Why would anyone want to leave our country defenceless?
- Evolutionists say that life came about by chance – how ridiculous!
- To be anti-abortion is wrong since pro-lifers believe a woman should bring her fetus to term even if it means she dies in the process.

■ False dilemma

- Either you're for me or against me.
- America: love it or leave it.
- Either we cut welfare benefits or we raise income tax: that is the choice we face.

■ Ad ignorantiam

- You can't explain where God is, so God doesn't exist.
- Scientists have not proven that global warming will occur, so let's not worry about it.
- God must exist because it is impossible to prove that he doesn't.

■ Ad bacculam

- You had better agree that the new policy is a good one if you expect to keep your job.

- The defendent is innocent because, if he isn't, there will be a very violent riot.
- If you don't turn to religion you will face eternal damnation.

■ Contradiction in terms

- There are no absolutely true statements.
- It is impossible for written words to communicate anything.
- I do not exist.

■ Begging the question, or circular arguments

- Whatever is denser than water will sink, because such objects cannot float.
- God exists because the Bible says that he does; and the Bible is God's own truth.
- The stock market fell yesterday due to profit-taking by investors.

■ False cause, or post hoc ergo propter hoc

- Smokers get bad grades; to improve yours you had better give up!
- College-educated people earn more money than those who haven't been to college; if I want to earn a lot of money I had better get a good education!
- Both times I have had a car accident I was wearing that shirt. I'll never wear it again.

Vertical and lateral thinking

We have seen that valid logic allows us to construct a chain of reasoning that can extend our knowledge. In some cases, notably mathematics and science, logic allows us to construct incredibly long and complex chains of reasoning. These chains can bring surprising results from 'obvious' premises and the deduction of new knowledge. So the role of logic in deriving knowledge is clear. We are aware of the problems that we may encounter (they are largely the subject of this chapter) but, even so, we can use the methods of logic in a straightforward way. Or can we?

Sometimes logic does not help us find what we want to know, and there are many puzzles which make entertaining use of this fact. Try this problem: a man went to a party and drank some of the punch. He then left early. Everyone else at the party who drank the punch subsequently died of poisoning. Why did the man not die (he did not put the poison in the punch himself!)?

It is interesting that the answer to this problem is logical and yet quite difficult to see. There are no random or bizarre events going on – this is a straightforward application of reasoning. So why is it difficult? Why is the solution (that the poison in the punch came from the ice cubes, so when the man drank the punch the ice was fully frozen, but gradually it melted, poisoning the punch) far from obvious?

A Think of some other problems where the solution seemed very difficult, but was 'obvious' once you knew it.

B Explain why a solution can be both difficult and obvious.

There is a useful metaphor here, which was put forward by the writer Edward be Bono. He described logic as the tool that is used to dig holes deeper and bigger, but he pointed out that, if a hole is in the wrong place, then no amount of digging will get you to your intended destination. He argues that sometimes logic simply isn't enough and you need to think again – that is, you need to dig your hole elsewhere. This process of digging elsewhere, of abandoning the familiar and 'obvious' ways of thinking, has been called 'lateral thinking'. Lateral thinking describes a way of thinking that is supposed to be less constrained and more creative than 'normal' logical thinking. However, we have already looked at 'normal' logical thinking in enough detail to understand that lateral thinking may not be so completely different after all.

A What are the problems associated with 'hidden assumptions' in regular thinking? Why do we make these assumptions?

B Would it usually be desirable to make no assumptions at all?

C How does lateral thinking fit into this way of analysing the issue?

The concept of lateral thinking is a useful way of alerting us to all the things that we assume without realising that we have assumed them. In this respect, it is a crucial part of any form of critical analysis. But this also means that there is not much else that can be said – if there was a formula or a sure-fire method for identifying hidden assumptions then they would not be so hidden, and lateral thinking would be less lateral and more straightforward!

A Explain this: a man walks into a bar and asks the barman for a glass of water. The barman pulls out a gun and points it at the man. The man says 'thank you' and walks out.

Where do we go from here?

We turned to rationalism hoping to generalise the mathematical method. Did we succeed? Well, only partly. We have seen that it is often possible to construct compelling arguments, but only when we are certain about the starting points, or premises, and that this certainty is difficult to find for a number of reasons, not least the problems of meaning in the words we use. (We should also mention that we have not really inquired too closely into exactly *why* a valid argument is compelling – this would take us a little too far afield and into the specialist area of logic.)

In the introduction to this chapter, we asked if using the approach of rationalism was 'correct'. We have seen that it has its strengths and weaknesses, but we will leave a full answer to that question until we have considered the concept of paradigms in

Chapter 9, by which time we will be in a better position to see the complete picture.

Even if the rational approach has its problems, focusing on reasoning in an abstract context should make it easier when we come to apply it to everyday situations, and perhaps it is to these we should now turn. We have been in the abstract world of maths and logic for a while; let us see if we can apply what we have learned to something far more tangible and immediate, something to do with humans. We found that the natural sciences somehow bypassed the human condition, and the arts were centred on them, but in a non-rational way. Can we combine the two, and consider human, or social, sciences? Let us at least try.

Further reading

A very gentle introduction to informal logic can be found in S. Morris Engel's *Fallacies and Pitfalls of Language* (Prentice Hall, 1994) and Neil Browne and Stuart Keeley's *Asking the Right Questions* (Prentice Hall, 1994). A sparkling, accessible, but at the same time profound, approach to reasoning and the possibility of paradox can be found in Raymond Smullyan's brilliant *What Is The Name Of This Book?* (Prentice Hall, 1978). Equally informative is Edward de Bono's classic *Lateral Thinking* (Ward Lock Education, 1970).

More analytical approaches to the use of reason in general can be found in A. J. Ayer's *The Problem of Knowledge* (Open University Press, 1956) and Bertrand Russell's *The Problems of Philosophy* (Oxford University Press, 1998). An overview of what we mean by rationality and different possible conceptions of the notion is found in Mikael Stenmark's *Rationality in Science, Religion, and Everyday Life: A Critical Evaluation of Four Models of Rationality* (University of Notre-Dame Press, 1995).

Some more about the laws of logic...

You have have probably come across arguments such as these:

A All humans are mortal
B I am human
therefore : **C** I am mortal.

or

A Elvis is either dead or alive
B Elvis is not alive
therefore : **C** Elvis is dead.

The commentary that usually goes with these suggests that they are *valid* arguments. That is, it is usually argued that, if A and B are true, then C must be true too. The two important words are *if* (because logic says nothing about the truth of the premises) and *must* (because logic appears to be absolutely certain). And if you agree with this then that's just great for you – you have a powerful tool to use in your search for truth.

But what if I do not agree that that these are valid arguments? Suppose I, a skeptic, concede that A and B are true, but think that C is false. How could you, a believer, convince me that C *must* be true? We can imagine a rather frustrating conversation.

Believer: Are you seriously saying that you agree that (A) All humans are mortal, and (B) I am human, but do not agree that it *must* then be true that (C) I am mortal?
Skeptic: Yes.
Believer: But that's idiotic! Do you really think that I am immortal?
Skeptic: Of course not – that's not what I am suggesting at all. I am just saying that even though A and B are true, C still *could* be false – you still *could* be immortal. I know that you aren't, as you are just like the rest of us, but I maintain that even though A and B are true, it does not mean that you *must* be mortal.
Believer: OK so we agree that I am mortal – but what you say still doesn't make any sense. How can you deny that I have to be mortal? All humans are mortal, I am a human . . .
Skeptic: Yes we agree on this.
Believer: . . . and so I *must* be mortal. It simply *must* be true!
Skeptic: Why? I don't see it.

Believer: Well, when we say *all* humans are mortal, then I come under the *all* bit – that's what it means when we use the words like this.
Skeptic: I understand the words, I just do not see the logic. It seems to me that it is perfectly possible for A and B to be true, but for C to be false.
Believer: How?
Skeptic: Easy – it would be true that (A) All humans are mortal (B) I am a human and also true that (C) I am immortal.
Believer: But that's impossible!
Skeptic: Why? All you are doing is showing a lack of imagination.
Believer: I can show you a thousand people who would agree with me! Would that convince you?
Skeptic: Are you really saying that the so called laws of logic are decided democratically? What happens if those thousand people change their mind? In any case, it is not hard to think of cases where a lot of people believe something which has turned out to be false. Public opinion is hardly an argument – can you find no better way to persuade me?
Believer: All I am saying is that some things are so obvious that they need no reasons and this is one of those things.
Skeptic: What may be obvious to you may not be so obvious to everyone else.

This conversation could go on for a long time, but you can see that, to whatever the believer says, the skeptic can just disagree. And irritating though it is, if the skeptic really cannot see the validity of the argument (it is valid isn't it?) and the believer cannot provide a good reason, then isn't the skeptic right to doubt the validity of the argument?

A Do you think the argument under debate is a valid argument? If so, why? If not, why not?
B How would you convince the skeptic that the argument is valid?
C How would you persuade the believer to doubt the validity of the argument?
D Can you see why many philosophers have thought that there is such a close link between logic and language?

Essentially the skeptic and the believer are arguing about what is 'obvious', but ironically, it seems to be that what is 'obvious' is far from obvious. Many philosophers have shared the skeptic's distrust of the fact that nearly everyone seems to find an argument valid, and looked for a way to base arguments on laws that don't just seem right, but that it is impossible to dispute without talking nonsense. They have traditionally started with far more basic things than the one we have so far discussed, and if you look up 'Laws of Logic' in a dictionary of philosophy then you will find three laws. Here are the first two:

1 The law of *identity*: A thing is what it is. For example, a book is a book and a leaf is a leaf.
2 The law of *non-contradiction*: A statement cannot be both true and false at the same time. For example, if it is true that I always tell the truth, it cannot be true that I am a liar, and if I am dead then I cannot be alive.

Many people think that these are almost too obvious to state – but bearing in mind the skeptic's words above, perhaps this is no bad thing. And if you are worried that these statements are simplistic, you are right – that is why they are axioms and not deductive results.

So the natural question to ask is 'Are these obvious and undeniable?' Could even the skeptic still refuse to believe them? Let's consider the first law:

Skeptic: I refuse to accept the law of identity. I can't see why it has to be true.
Believer: You call that a refusal do you?
Skeptic: I do.
Believer: Well then, in admitting that your refusal is a refusal, you have used the law of identity haven't you? So you must think it is true after all.
Skeptic: Err... well, then it is not a refusal.
Believer: Then you have no refusal. So you do not refuse to accept it, and so you must think it is true after all.
Skeptic: Well, I still deny it.
Believer: But now you are really making no sense at all.
Skeptic: Maybe not to you, but I make perfect sense to me.

A Make up a dialogue between the skeptic and the believer where they debate the second law.
B Explain in your own words the position of the skeptic. Why does he not accept the laws?

C Is the skeptic's position a reasonable one? That is, do you think it is possible to reasonably deny the two laws of logic given?

There is a third law of logic, but it is not so universally accepted:

3 The law of the excluded middle: A statement is either true or false (that is, there is no middle ground between true and false). So, for example, it is either true or false that I am alive, and it is either true or false that I am holding a book.

It has been suggested that there are two other possibilities:

3a There are many other possibilities other than true and false. If true corresponds to the number 'one' and false to 'zero' then these other possibilities refer to numbers between zero and one.
3b In addition to 'true' and 'false' there is one other possibility which is neither true nor false.

A In what subjects that you study might you want to accept either 3, or the modified 3a or 3b? Give some examples, thinking carefully – this is a complex issue (e.g. perhaps surprisingly, there is a branch of mathematics (intuitionism) which holds 3 to be invalid, and uses 3b in its workings).

There has been a great deal of disagreement over laws which are meant to be obvious! And we have not yet begun to look at constructing more complex arguments – so you can see that logical analysis can be a tricky business. To look into this in any more detail would very quickly get very technical and difficult, so perhaps we can end by reiterating two questions that need answering if we are to use logic as a reliable tool.

A What are the 'correct' basic laws of logic?
B Once we have the 'basic' laws, how do we construct more complex ones?

ASK FIVE ECONOMISTS AND YOU'LL GET FIVE DIFFERENT ANSWERS (SIX IF ONE WENT TO HARVARD).
Edgar R. Fiedler

The social sciences are good at accounting for disasters once they have taken place.
Claude T. Bissell

A large part of the popularity and persuasiveness of psychology comes from its being a sublimate spiritualism: a secular, ostensibly scientific way of affirming the primacy of 'spirit' over matter.
Susan Sontag

Capitalism is the astounding belief that the most wickedest of men will do the most wickedest of things for the greatest good of everyone.
J. M. Keynes

Wall Street indices predicted nine out of the last five recessions!
Paul A. Samuelson

To say that a farm boy knows how to milk a cow is to say that we can send him out to the barn with an empty pail and expect him to return with milk. To say that a criminologist understands crime is not to say that we can send him out with a grant or a law and expect him to return with a lower crime rate. He is more likely to return with a report on why he has not succeeded yet, and including the inevitable need for more money, a larger staff, more sweeping powers, etc.
Thomas Sowell

Trying to define yourself is like trying to bite your own teeth.
Alan Watts

Physicists have a subject matter, but sociologists study only methods.
Henri Poincaré

Those who have knowledge, don't predict. Those who predict, don't have knowledge.
Lao Tzu

ECONOMICS IS EXTREMELY USEFUL AS A FORM OF EMPLOYMENT FOR ECONOMISTS.
John Kenneth Galbraith

Psychiatry's chief contribution to philosophy is the discovery that the toilet is the seat of the soul.
Alexander Chase

An economist is an expert who will know tomorrow why the things he predicted yesterday didn't happen today.
Laurence J. Peter

Aims   **By the end of this chapter you should:**

- **understand how the social sciences differ from and resemble other areas of knowledge, especially the natural sciences**
- **understand the role played by reasoning in the social sciences**
- **understand some of the experimental issues which arise in the social sciences**
- **understand the position of ethics within the context of the social sciences**
- **appreciate the difficulties with concepts such as explanation and cause and effect in the humanities**
- **understand some of the underlying dilemmas in dealing with humans, such as the issues of free will, reductionism and the nature/nurture debate.**

Introduction

To some, the idea of a science about humans seems like a contradiction in terms. Arguing that humans are the ultimate variables – we behave in incredible, bizarre and unpredictable ways – the critics suggest that science can never explain basic human nature; that there is something about humans which will forever escape theories and laws. Observing that the human world is based in feeling, emotion and values, they point to this as evidence that there can be no sciences of human behaviour. And they have a point. Certainly it cannot be denied that the study of humans has a fundamental element that is not present in the natural sciences; the study of humans involves the study of conscious creatures.

Despite this, fields of study which might once have called themselves humanities are increasingly going by the name of social sciences, and we might ask why this is. Perhaps it is because, in the early twenty-first century, the natural sciences set the standards for certainty and reliable knowledge, and so modelling psychology, linguistics, sociology, anthropology, economics and political theory on them may not be such a bad idea. Just as the goal of natural scientists is a deep understanding of nature, so social scientists seek explanation, order and underlying pattern in aspects of human behaviour. Since humans are, after all, a part of nature, we might not be too surprised to see that both natural and social sciences can share a common approach, but we must be alert to possible differences, too.

A Here are some statements of the kind made by social scientists. Identify why we might be suspicious of the hypotheses and potential problems with determining the truth.

- First-born children tend to be more successful in their careers.
- Hierarchical relationships are inevitable in human societies.
- High inflation causes unemployment.
- There is more social mobility in the USA than in the UK.
- The concept of 'social status' underlies different greeting rituals in different cultures.
- Most boys have a subconscious sexual attraction to their mothers and feel jealous of their fathers.

- Distinct patterns can be observed in urban land use.
- The higher the price of a good, the lower the demand for that good.
- In any country, the second biggest city will be half the size of the biggest one; the third biggest city will be one-third of the size of the biggest one, and so on.
- Class is the determining factor in educational success.

B With what degree of certainty can these claims ever be known?
C Are they suitable for testing to determine their validity? If so, how?
D What is the difference between these 'laws' of social science and physical 'laws', such as 'water boils at 100°C' or '$e = mc^2$'?
E Is it possible that the social sciences will ever produce statements of the same mathematical accuracy as the natural sciences? If so, give a possible example. If not, explain carefully why not.
F Individuals behave very strangely at times, and no scientist can accurately and reliably predict an individual's behaviour. However, in large numbers, humans seem to behave fairly predictably, which is why we can say that more people will go to the beach in warm weather than in cold. Although no scientist can predict quite who will be involved in car accidents in any given year, they can come very close to predicting the total number of accidents. Is there an analogy here with molecules within a gas and the pressure exerted by the gas?

Positive and normative statements

In my opinion, we don't devote nearly enough scientific research to finding a cure for jerks.

Bill Larson in
Calvin and Hobbes

Many thinkers have argued that there is a fundamental difference between studying the objects of the natural world and the constructs of humans. When we investigate physics, chemistry and biology we seek to understand and to explain *how* things work. We wouldn't dream of suggesting how they *should* work – indeed such a claim would be pointless. This is in marked contrast to the social sciences where we study *how* things work in order to make them work better – or to make them work *as we think they should*. Why else study population movement, urban land use, crime, capitalism, socialism, communism or work efficiency unless to improve the situations that we have? As such, the social sciences have a prescriptive or **normative** aspect to them, as well as a descriptive or **positive** aspect. This is an important distinction: **positive** statements are statements of **fact**; **normative** statements go beyond this and are statements of **value**. For example:

Appraising staff takes around 60 hours a year.	POSITIVE
This is an important task for middle managers.	NORMATIVE
Men are generally more aggressive than women.	POSITIVE
Aggression is a good trait in business.	NORMATIVE
Crime costs insurance companies $12 billion a year.	POSITIVE
We should always lock up criminals after one offence.	NORMATIVE
Increasing the money supply leads to short-term unemployment.	POSITIVE
Medium levels of unemployment are a price worth paying for a growing economy.	NORMATIVE

The positive statements are either right or wrong. They can be tested, and like all good theories can potentially be falsified by looking at the evidence. Social scientists can do this sort of study if they can be precise enough about what they mean. The normative statements, on the other hand, cannot be tested in the same way. No evidence will tell you whether or not something is important or worth it because you cannot measure importance or worth by looking at evidence. A value judgement must be made, and this cannot be done from within the framework of the social sciences. The values come from outside the disciplines, and in many cases they boil down to ethics. Is it right to foster a very competitive environment in a workplace if it leads to unhappiness but greater profits? Is it right to sack people while the managing director gets a huge pay rise if the analysis shows that such action will push the share price up? If men and women are equal, is it right to have different retirement ages?

These questions cannot be answered by sticking to a purely positive footing. Any social science finding must be combined with an ethical attitude before it can be turned into a decision or policy. Conversely, any ethical or political decision must be based in the evidence provided by the social sciences before it can be said to be an informed decision. So we begin to see that the social sciences are an essential and vital part of modern society, but they must be complemented by a broader philosophical position on social justice and individual rights.

A Examine some economic policy from a recent issue of *The Economist* or *Newsweek*. Identify the positive and normative aspects of the policy.

B Do the natural sciences contain both positive and normative statements, or does one type of statement dominate? Why might the natural sciences be different to the social sciences in this respect?

Some experimental issues

It's hard to imagine anything more difficult to study than human sexuality, on every level from the technical to the political. One has only to picture monitoring orgasm in the lab to begin to grasp the challenge of developing testing techniques that are thorough and precise, yet respectful.

Winnifred Gallagher

Any science must have a good body of empirical evidence on which to base study, but accurate and informative experimentation is always difficult, and the social sciences present their own particular problems. Not least among these is the sheer breadth of the scope of the social sciences – the techniques and problems found in psychology are very different to those found in economics, which themselves differ from those found in human geography. We cannot fully cover all the issues here, but the following examples show that experimentation in the social sciences can raise additional difficulties of a different nature to those found in the natural sciences.

For example, in two similar surveys during the Second World War people were asked about their opinion regarding post-war planning. The following results were obtained:

		In favour of planning for peace	Opposed to planning for peace	No opinion
Survey 1	Do you think we ought to start thinking now about the kind of peace we want after the war?	81% (yes)	14% (no)	4%
Survey 2	Which of these seems better to you: for us to win the war first and then think about the peace, or to start thinking now about the kind of peace we want after the war?	41% (start thinking about peace)	55% (win the war first)	4%

Source: National Opinion Research Centre, September 1942

The difference in results between the two surveys is clearly related to the nature of the questions asked. We might think that it would be easy to fix this – just ask the same question all the time. But which question is better? Perhaps the surveys were not really about eliciting opinions, but more about creating them. The people interviewed may never have thought about the issue before, but the nature of the questions made one of the answers very much more likely than the other. So we might conclude that we should stick to neutral questions, but which question is more neutral? In another case, a house-to-house survey was carried out with the aim of studying magazine readership. One of the questions was: 'What magazines does your household read?' This question seems neutral enough, but when the results were analysed most people seemed to read 'intelligent' magazines and very few seemed to read 'common' magazines. These findings were totally at odds with the publishers' data, which indicated the reverse. The most obvious explanation was that the surveys had been concentrated in a particular part of one town – for example, beside a university. But in fact the survey had been nationwide and had a very broad sample. The only conclusion is that people lied about their habits, and perhaps, in hindsight, this was not surprising. We all want to appear intelligent and sophisticated, especially in front of strangers asking questions about our personal lives.

Still more bizarre is the famous Hawthorne effect, named after a study at the Hawthorne plant of the Western Electric Company in 1927–29. The experiment involved monitoring the effect of changes in lighting on the rate of work of women assembling items. The experimenters measured a base rate, and then dimmed the lighting. They were pleased to find that efficiency improved, so they dimmed it some more, and efficiency improved again.

More dimming yielded still further improvements, even though it was actually getting dark in the test room! Wondering what was going on, the experimenters began to turn the lights back up again, and incredibly, the efficiency of the workers continued to rise! It appears that the overriding factor was the fact that the workers were the subject of an experiment; that someone was taking an interest in what they were doing had very positive effects on their level of production.

There is also a famous experiment where a team of industrial social psychologists went into an organisation to provide free 'counselling'. They were instructed to listen to whatever the workers wanted to say and to respond only by repeating whatever they were told, prefixed by phrases such as 'Am I correct in understanding that you are saying...'. The response to the experiment was overwhelmingly positive, with employees saying things like '[this is the] best thing the company has ever done' despite the fact that the 'counsellors' offered no real counselling.

These results serve as a vivid reminder that we are dealing with humans, not robots.

A How would you find an answer to the post-war planning issue in the example above?

B How would you find out what magazines people read? What would you do if you wanted to know, accurately, how many people in each house read each magazine?

C Take a controversial issue, such as abortion or euthanasia.

- Design a questionnaire which would 'persuade' most people to respond positively (e.g. pro-euthanasia).
- Design a questionnaire which would 'persuade' most people to respond negatively (e.g. anti-euthanasia).
- Design a neutral questionnaire which will elicit people's 'true' opinion.

Despite the problems that can be encountered in the social sciences, it is also worth mentioning the tremendous ingenuity which has gone into designing meaningful experiments. Pscyhology, in particular, is full of such examples, often because psychologists are trying to measure things like thoughts!

Imagine that in a criminal case the defendant says that he can't read, and that the whole case rests on finding out whether or not he is telling the truth. Remember that the defendant may be a very ingenious and convincing liar, capable of excellent bluffing, so you can't just give a reading test. Perhaps the best approach is to use a technique which has been developed over the last 65 years – the so-called Stroop technique, whereby the subject is shown the word 'red' written in purple, the word 'yellow' written in blue and the word 'purple' written in orange. The subject is required to state the colour of the words. Now if the subject cannot read then the task is very easy – he just sees colours and says what he sees. But if he can read then the task is a little more difficult, as the meaning of the words contradicts the colours in which they are written, and the task takes a significantly longer time. Only those who can read suffer the interference between meaning and colour, and so it is easy to distinguish between the two cases.

Still more ingenious is a series of experiments from developmental psychology, which aims to show what a baby understands. Given that the baby cannot speak, this might seem like an impossible task, but it has been done. The basis of many of the experiments is a simple one – that babies look for longer at things in which they are interested. Suppose, for example, we wish to see if a baby has the concept of number and simple addition. A baby is shown a marble dropped into a box with no bottom. The box is lifted, and the baby sees the marble on the floor. The box is replaced and another marble is dropped in. Again, the box is lifted, and the baby can again see what is there. Now this is the clever bit – sometimes the psychologists have a trick whereby the second marble stays in the box, leaving only one marble on the floor when the box is lifted. In these cases, the baby consistently looks far longer at the remaining marble. The study has been duplicated many times, and the best interpretation seems to be that the baby knows that something is strange and worthy of attention. For similar reasons, infants stare for a long time at an object which seems to be hovering in mid-air, though the same object on the floor warrants hardly a second glance.

A whole range of similar experiments have shown that even very young babies are sensitive to an enormous range of events, perhaps rather surprising those philosophers who believed in the infant as a *tabula rasa* or blank slate, waiting to be filled by a myriad of experiences. It appears that infants come into the world with a well developed sense of how things should behave.

We should perhaps remember that experimental difficulties may appear to be overwhelming, but that in fact they are not always insurmountable. Creativity, imagination and a willingness to try new ideas all play a large part in successful experimentation.

> **A** Would it be possible to design an experiment to see whether blind babies have a similar feel for numbers?
>
> **B** How might you determine whether or not new-born babies are more sensitive to the language that their parents spoke during pregnancy than to other languages?
>
> **C** Would the same techniques work for telling if a child could recognise music that the mother heard often during pregnancy?

The reduction of social data to numerical form

If it can't be expressed in figures, it is not science; it is opinion.

Lazarus Long

In the search for accurate theories and predictions, the social sciences are increasingly turning to the language of the natural sciences – mathematics. However, we can quickly run into problems when we generate statistical data, especially when it relates to human activity. We may be aware of the famous phrase 'lies, damned lies and statistics', but it is not always clear exactly how devious statistics can be. Of course, unscrupulous tricksters can 'fiddle' information, and there may be little we can do about that – if we are told that GDP grew by two per cent then it may be hard for us, as non-experts, to know if this is true or not. We shall not be concerned with simple falsehoods here. Rather we shall show that sometimes even honest and well-meaning reporting of 'facts' can contain some very questionable assumptions, and indeed suggest results which, while not objectively 'false', are certainly not objectively 'true'.

Let us look back to the Olympic Games in Atlanta, 1996. This far after the event one might imagine that there is nothing of interest to debate – the races have been run, the medals awarded, the athletes have long gone and we know who won each event and who broke which record. But which country did best? Here are some selected results from those Olympics.

Country and ranking	G	S	B	Total
1 USA	44	32	25	221
2 Russia	26	21	16	136
3 Germany	20	18	27	123
4 China	16	22	12	104
5 France	15	7	15	74
6 Italy	13	10	12	71
7 Australia	9	9	23	68
23 Japan	3	6	5	26
33 North Korea	2	1	2	10
41 Indonesia	1	1	2	7
48 Thailand	1	0	1	4
52 Hong Kong	1	0	0	3
58 Malaysia	0	1	1	3
62 Taiwan	0	1	0	2
64 Philippines	0	1	0	2
71 India	0	0	1	1

A Which country did best? How do you know? Do you have any reasons to doubt the truth of your answer?

B The table was calculated on the basis of three points for a gold, two for a silver and one for a bronze. So three silvers = two golds (both worth six points) and three bronzes = one gold (both worth three points).
Would you prefer three silvers or two golds? What do you think an Olympic athlete would say?

C Most Olympic athletes would rather have one gold to five silvers, or ten bronzes. So how should we allocate points? How many silvers should equal one gold? How do you know?

There are other factors to consider, too. In the Olympics, some countries have a natural advantage. In China, the size of population provides a huge pool of talent. In other tiny states, even sending a team to the Olympics can seem fanciful! So here is an adjusted table; the points have been scaled to reflect different population sizes. In other words, the points have been adjusted to allow for the fact that some countries have bigger populations than others (the points have been divided by the population and multiplied by a hundred million for clarity's sake).

Country and ranking	Points according to old calculation	Points according to new calculation
1 Tonga	2	1894
2 Bahamas	2	725
3 Cuba	51	464
4 Jamaica	11	437
5 New Zealand	14	389
6 Hungary	39	381
7 Australia	68	372
11 Ireland	10	279
12 Switzerland	18	254
13 Namibia	4	242
29 Italy	71	124
34 Russia	136	91
38 USA	221	83
46 Great Britain	46	43
47 North Korea	10	42
49 Mongolia	1	40

A Which country did best? How do you know?
B Do you have any reasons to doubt the truth of your answer?
C Is this a better method of calculating points than the first one? How do you know?

There might be other factors we should also take into account. Some countries are obviously wealthier than others, and so the population of these countries can devote more time to sports. Perhaps we should therefore measure the GDP of each country and then scale the results in a similar way to the population scaling.

A What other factors might you need to consider when calculating points?
B Which factors are the important ones? How do you know?

C What can you say about the language used in a claim such as 'Country X did best'?

D So which country did best at the 1996 Atlanta Olympics?

E Identify another example where language or data presentation hides values and judgements behind a facade of fact.

F Look at the results from the recent Olympics and see what they tell you.

Of course, the Olympics provide us with data which is almost as simple as it could be. In any given event, we end up with an ordered list of names, and we are merely trying to aggregate the scores. But even so, we still come across some rather difficult problems – imagine the problems in trying to describe human behaviour when we have more complex data! It is not difficult to see why many have declared that the whole notion is nonsense and that human behaviour cannot be reduced to underlying laws and structures.

However, the physical world also seems irreducibly complex to the untrained eye. It has taken thousands of years to discover that everything is made up of some hundred-odd elements, and that they, in turn, are all made up of identical protons, neutrons and electrons. We should not assume without good evidence that the same might not be true of the social sciences. When we look at the evidence, we find that the jury is very much out. In some areas – for example, sociology – there seems to be little consensus of opinion, and the discipline is largely descriptive; it may look scientific but in fact the theories have, as yet, little explanatory power. In other areas, however, such as linguistics, the progress made since the 1950s has been explosive and questions that once seemed to be total mysteries are now being investigated in highly focused, analytical and predictive ways. In a manner reminiscent of the convergence of thermodynamics and mechanics (where the former turned out to be the latter when looked at in the right way), linguistics is finding that it is consistent with dominant paradigms in other areas such as molecular genetics, information theory, neuroscience and Darwinian evolution. The story is a truly fascinating one, and seems to suggest that certain areas in the social sciences may be amenable to rigorous mathematical analysis. Regarding the humanities topic of the inflection of words, the linguist Stephen Pinker writes:

[This has] long been mulled over by novelists and poets, dictionary writers and editors, philologists and linguists. Now this topic straight out of the humanities is being probed with the cutting-edge tools of molecular genetics and imaging of the brain. Some people fear this kind of development as crass 'reductionism' that will marginalise the humanities and plough under the richness of their subject matter, but it is far from that. Without an understanding of the contents of the mind from psychology, linguistics, and all the other disciplines that they touch, neuroscientists would not know where to begin studying the human brain, and their technologies would all be expensive toys. Ultimately all knowledge is connected, and an insight into a phenomenon can come from any direction.

This is not to say that numerical analysis will be, in the final instance, the ultimate arbiter of human truth. There is a big difference between information and wisdom, and some argue that while mathematical tools of analysis may take us far, they will not really tell us about ourselves in any concrete and immediate way. Noam Chomsky writes:

It is quite possible – overwhelmingly probable, one might guess – that we will always learn more about human life and human personality from novels than from scientific psychology.

A What does Pinker mean when he speaks of a 'crass reductionism'?
B Does reductionism have to be cross?
C Do you think a rigorous mathematisation of the social sciences is possible? If not, why not? If so, is it desirable?
D Chomsky suggests that the arts may provide a vehicle for certain types of knowledge which the sciences (social or natural) cannot match. What types of knowledge do you think he means? Do you agree?

Causation in the social sciences

It would be enormously useful if we could positively identify the causes of our social problems. We might then be able to tackle them effectively and efficiently. Take crime as an example. Suppose we find that crimes are generally committed by poor people. Do we then say that poverty causes crime? Even this step is difficult to take (why?). Should we then say that to tackle crime we must attack poverty? So what are the causes of poverty? Again, we can't be sure of them and, even if we could, we could ask what caused them, and so on.

A One can imagine that crime is caused by poverty, poverty by unemployment, unemployment by high wage costs, high wage costs by crime . . . So what is the cause of crime?
B Are there any equivalent problems in the natural sciences?
C A man has a heart attack while jogging. The following pieces of information are available. Which would you accept as a cause of his heart attack?

- He was given a new pair of jogging shoes for his birthday and wanted to try them.
- He had eaten far, far too much the previous week.
- He had always loved chocolate cake and had been unable to resist it for years.
- As a child he had associated his mother's chocolate cake with approval, since she rewarded him with extra pieces if he had done well.
- He loved his mother.
- Poor jogging shoes had, in the past, made his shins ache.
- He liked a sporty image.
- He would have liked his wife to think of him as a thwarted athlete.

- He was pleased that his wife gave him a sporty present.
- The road on which he was jogging was hilly.
- He is over 60 years old.
- Although basically fit, he hadn't been jogging for six weeks.
- His mother admired athletic prowess.
- He was born.
- He had jogged 15 km when he had the heart attack.
- He decided to go jogging at that moment because his wife and son were arguing.

Without any one of these factors, the man would not have had a heart attack. So what do we mean by **cause** in this case?

Of course, in this example we are asking an extremely difficult question – what is the cause of an event which is related to one single person? Normally the social sciences do not attempt such a difficult task – they look at much larger quantities of data and derive their theories from more statistically valid samples. However, there is another extremely easy mistake to make, which is especially common when the sample is larger. Consider these (made up, but representative) statistics, describing average lifetime earnings of people with different levels of education.

Educational level	Average lifetime earnings ($)
Left school at 16	750,000
Left school at 18	1,200,000
Bachelors degree	2,025,000
Masters degree	2,640,000
Doctorate	2,000,000

The obvious conclusion, or at least the one often drawn by colleges in their recruitment drives, is that if you get a bachelors or masters degree then you are more likely to earn far more than if you don't. Of course, we can find numerous exceptions – after all, it's not an exact science – but the general rule is clear. Education up to a masters degree results in higher earnings.

But this is wrong, all wrong! We need to look carefully to see a huge danger in dealing with this sort of data. There is a hidden assumption here that college-educated people earn more money, therefore it must be because they went to college. But that is far from clear – the high earners may have made just as much money, or even more, had they left the education system earlier. The type of students who enter academic education tend to be either bright or rich, and having either of these characteristics is often enough to command a high income in later life. So **correlation does not prove cause.** The belief that because things occur together, one must cause the other is such a common error, or logical fallacy, that it has actually been given a name – *post hoc ergo propter hoc* – meaning 'after this, therefore because of this' (see also Chapter 5, page 89).

In the social sciences, there are several alternatives to simple causation. Sometimes it is very difficult to tell which is the cause and which is the effect (the more shares you own, the richer you tend to be). Sometimes there is genuine chance involved (and where computers can rapidly examine huge amounts of data spurious correlations will be found – apparently Scottish Highland rainfall levels have been very closely correlated to stock market levels). Sometimes there is a genuine correlation which, on inspection, appears to be the result of some underlying variable (in the college education example, the underlying variable is the type of student who goes to college).

Of course, just because the correlation does not prove the cause does not mean that there cannot be a causal relationship, but you have to look fairly hard to be sure. In the college education example, an alternative explanation may be, for example, that getting a qualification, which most people do at college, is the reason that many people earn a lot of money over their lifetimes. Or it may not. This is an empirical question which cannot be resolved from the correlation alone.

In some cases, a true causal link is denied! That there is a very good correlation between smoking and lung cancer is beyond dispute, but the tobacco companies' claim in years gone by that there is no causal link (often citing this very fallacy) is cynical and manipulative. There is a causal link – doctors have shown that the chemicals in cigarette smoke cause cancerous cells to develop. So do not always reject correlations as meaningless, but do treat them with caution.

A Here are some data which have been found to be closely correlated. For each case, find at least two explanations for the correlation. Explain whether or not you think it is likely that there is a genuine causal relationship. If there is, suggest the nature of the causal link. If not, explain why the correlation occurs.

- The number of cigarettes smoked is well correlated with poor school grades.
- Increases in UFO sightings are well correlated with increases in confectionery prices.
- The distance you run is well correlated with the time you spend running.
- Cancers are increasingly frequent in Switzerland, where a lot of milk is consumed, but relatively low in Sri Lanka, where very little milk is consumed.
- Profits of casinos are well correlated with teachers' salaries in Macau, China.
- Rises in profits of a particular company are well correlated with rises in workers' salaries.

B Find some examples from newspapers or magazines of correlations, and decide if there is any genuine causal relationship. Is a causal relationship suggested? Are the problems acknowledged?

C Are there problems of causation in the natural sciences? Give examples to illustrate your answer.

Determinism and free will

Whence and how do [my musical ideas] come? I do not know and I have nothing to do with it.

Mozart

The aim of the social sciences is to give us knowledge about individual humans and how these humans interact in their societies. They also aim to tell us what influences us, how we make our decisions and what factors might be important in doing so. Of course, the task is not easy, and there are always problems when looking for reliable knowledge. As we have seen in the last few sections, the social sciences present us with some unique difficulties. There is, however, an issue which seems to be either the greatest problem of all or the solution to all other problems, depending on how you look at it. The issue is that of free will. Does it exist? Do we really have the freedom to do what we want, or are we just responding to some combination of our nature and our nurture? This is a philosophical problem which has been examined for literally thousands of years. It is one which many great philosophers claim to have solved, sometimes in radically different ways. But somehow, the solutions do not seem to answer the nagging doubts that many people feel when they think hard about it. To see why the problem is such a thorny one, we will build up to it with a few examples.

The destruction of the space shuttle *Challenger* was an event that will live forever in the memories of anyone who saw it. Instead of a triumphant ascent into space, the craft dissolved into a fiery ball of burning fuel and oxygen. What should have been a great moment in the exploration of space turned into a national disaster and a human tragedy. The subsequent investigation found the cause of the explosion: a component of the fuel delivery system had cracked due to the low temperatures on the day of the launch and the rocket fuel had leaked and ignited. The faulty component had been manufactured years prior to the shuttle launch and, on a cold day, was always going to fail. No matter how expert the astronauts, how rigorous the training procedure, how brilliant the engineers, if it launched on a cold day, that shuttle was going to blow up. The physical state of the damaged component was such that there was no way the shuttle could have survived. Thus the disaster was, in some sense, inevitable.

Consider now the man who decides to commit suicide, and who throws himself from a very high building, but who changes his mind on the way down. Imagine him flailing his arms, and shouting. It is all to no avail; he will hit the ground. There is nothing in the situation which gives him any freedom to do anything except fall. The force of gravity acts on every particle in his body and, irrespective of his wishes, he cannot do anything but fall. Again, the position is one of unavoidable forces doing what they do. Once the man has jumped, the outcome is preordained, and all the man's protests to the contrary are meaningless.

Once the shuttle had launched, and once the man was falling, the final outcomes were fixed. The principle seems to be that once certain conditions are met, the laws of the physical world take over and the outcome is determined. Now let's imagine ourselves making some decision. It is made in the brain, which operates according to physical laws just like everything else. Our memories/experiences/preferences are physically encoded in synaptic structures, our senses pass information in electrochemical signals, and the brain processes these signals in an extraordinarily complex way, but one which is fully grounded in chemistry and biology. Just as gravity operates independently of our wishes, so too do the laws of chemistry and biology. So how does the decision get made? Presumably by the laws of the physical world. If this is the case, there is simply no room for us to have any say in the matter. If you believe this then you are said to be a **determinist**, in that you believe that all choices are determined by the physical conditions that come before them.

A computer analogy may be helpful here (although some philosophers have not thought so). Why does a word-processor refuse to print a document? Is it because it finds it offensive, because it is tired, because it has exercised a free choice? These seem ridiculous suggestions. Of course, a word-processor may refuse to print (we have all been there!), but if so it is for a physical reason, not because the word-processor has made a choice. A state of affairs has prevented printing, and once that state has been identified it can be altered – thus allowing or, more precisely, forcing the printing to occur. Determinists would suggest that we are exactly the same; we want to eat when something in our brain says so – maybe due to blood sugar levels, whether we are on a diet, etc. – but there is no choice involved. If someone could reach into our brain and somehow 'tweak' the right bit, we would decide to eat now, or in one hour's time, or whatever.

If we take this view as essentially correct, the consequences seem severe. If all our choices are determined by the events that came before them, and those events by those that came before them, and so on, then all the choices we make today can, in theory, be traced back as far as we like – right back to the start of the Universe! In other words, the whole of reality is totally determined. In 1820, Pierre Laplace imagined the situation where a being of sufficient intelligence, who knew for just one instant the position and velocity of every particle that exists, could work out the whole subsequent course of the Universe. For this being, nothing would be uncertain and the future, as the past, would be present to its eyes.

Of course, this may seem ludicrous after a little reflection – we think carefully about our actions, we weigh up pros and cons, we balance all sorts of factors and we certainly feel that we are free to decide for ourselves. The feeling of self-determination is absolutely overwhelming. We seem (at least to ourselves) to be free agents capable of doing what we will, and other people seem to have the same capabilities. We might think that we are not like the falling man, or the doomed shuttle, because we can avoid our ending; unlike these examples we do not have to break the laws of physics to avoid our fate. We just make a decision and exercise our free will. Like many of the best philosophical problems, the arguments for and against determinism both seem very powerful.

A Do you choose your favourite colour of your own free will? That is, could you decide that your favourite colour is something else? You can certainly say the words, 'Now I no longer like blue best; green is my favourite' and stop wearing blue clothes in favour of green. But can you really make yourself prefer green to blue?

B If there is an omniscient God then he already knows your actions and choices before you do. Does this generate a problem for the concept of free will?

C When we say that we have free will, we mean that in any given situation we could have done something other than what we actually did. Let us examine that a little more carefully. Is there any actual evidence that we could have done something other than the thing that we actually did? Explain your answer carefully.

D There are at least two factors that influence decisions we make – our inherent nature and the environmental nurture we have experienced. Are there any other factors which do not fall into one of these two categories? Do we have any choice over these categories?

E The brain appears to operate according to scientific laws. Does this leave any room for free will? If so, how?

F Camus wrote: *'In a universe divested of illusions and lights, man feels an alien, a stranger. His exile is without remedy since he is deprived of the memory of a lost home and the hope of a promised land.'* Suppose it were to be discovered that we do, indeed, have no free will at all, that we are robot-like and all our choices are pure illusions. What impact would this have on your life? Think particularly about your ethical and religious beliefs.

The philosopher Wittgenstein once invited his audience to consider themselves as autumn leaves floating to the ground, saying to themselves, 'Now I'll go this way . . . now I'll go that way.' Think about yourself as a leaf blowing in the wind. The philosopher Spinoza said that if a falling stone could talk, it would say that it was falling of its own free will.

Most people find these illustrations depressing. To say that we have no free will would put us on the same level as puppets, with physical laws pulling the strings. The implications for our lives are frightening, and it is not hard to understand why determinism is sometimes seen as more than a little terrifying. Daniel Dennett writes that if determinism is true then:

one is falling, falling and watching, horrified; one's deliberative machinery is disengaged, wheels spinning futilely as the relentless inexorable drama plays itself out.

This might have deep implications for our views on ethics and justice, and for our paradigm of the place of humans in the Universe. However, many philosophers have felt that there are powerful arguments against determinism. Some say that it is at least compatible with free will. They concede that everything has physical causes, but argue that this does not mean that we do not have free will (this view is called **compatibilism**). Others have suggested that determinism is either unimportant or wrong. The feeling that we are free is an overpowering one and if this is the case then there must be a fault with determinism, even if we can't find it.

A Recent physical theories suggest that some events on the tiniest (quantum-mechanical) scales are truly random, and are thus in some sense uncaused. If our brain works in this non-deterministic way, might that offer an avenue whereby free will can arise?

B Maybe the whole problem of determinism is a pseudo-problem. Robert Nozick wrote: *'No one has ever announced that because determinism is true thermostats do not control temperature.'* Daniel Dennett echoed this, suggesting that, *'determinism does not, in itself, erode control'*. If we are controlled by physical events, but those events are happening within our own brain, does that really matter? Doesn't that amount to free will anyway?

C If determinism is true, then we have no choice as to what happens. So why worry about it? Watching a film does not become pointless when we know the ending because we can enjoy the experience. We should sit back and enjoy the ride. Is this a possible solution to the problem or would a determined life be deeply unsatisfying?

In terms of our quest for reliable knowledge, whatever we think about determinism has implications. The issue underlies the whole of the social sciences – if determinism is true, then arguably the whole concept of choice and action requires a fairly radical change of perspective. For the most part, we certainly live our lives as if we have free will, though we always acknowledge that we have to take into account in-built factors (which we now know are genetic in basis) and environmental factors (such as our education, background and circumstances). This leads us to the (in)famous issue of nature/nurture.

The nature/nurture debate

If the misery of the poor be caused not by the laws of nature, but by our institutions, great is our sin.

Charles Darwin

Nowhere do the links between social sciences, natural sciences, paradigms, language, ethics and politics become more obvious than in the nature/nurture debate, and over few other issues do tempers run as hot. The issue is easily stated: is my intelligence/personality/whatever due to my intrinsic biological nature or due to my upbringing and environment? **Genetic determinism** and **environmental determinism** are the two extreme responses, whereby nature or nurture respectively is said to be completely dominant.

Many books and articles have been written supporting both extremes and all intermediate positions. Of course, debates in scientific circles are hardly rare – indeed they are the very lifeblood of any academic subject – so why is this particular one worthy of special consideration? The reason is that the nature/nurture debate is central to social policy, especially with regard to race. For example, if characteristics are genetically determined, then racial group A may be less intelligent than average, group B more lazy, and group C downright immoral. If one or all of these groups is at the bottom of the socio-economic ladder, it could then be said that is where they deserve to be – they are naturally less able! Why waste money trying to fight nature? Perhaps all those social welfare programmes are a waste of time and the money should be redirected elsewhere. (It is not hard to guess which social group would benefit from this line of thinking.) In other words, emphasis on 'nature' rather than 'nurture' can reinforce and serve as a justification for racism.

Others argue that genetic determinism is nonsense; that all humans are created equal in ability, and that with similar experiences of family, education, healthcare and opportunity, all racial groups can succeed in any walk of life. Therefore, the racial divisions in most societies are the legacy of past and ongoing prejudices and they can be fought by social programmes. In 1925, James Watson wrote:

Give me a dozen healthy infants, well-formed, and my own specified world to bring them up in, and I'll guarantee to take anyone at random and train him to become any type of specialist I might select – doctor, lawyer, artist, merchant-chief, and yes, even beggar-man and thief, regardless of his talents, penchants, tendencies, abilities, vocations and race of his ancestors.

However, we should note that if, like many physical characteristics, those in the brain are genetically determined, it may be that some characteristics are inherited. Therefore there may be racial characteristics. The linguist Noam Chomsky writes:

No one would take seriously the proposal that the human organism learns through experience to have arms rather than wings, or that the basic structure of practical organs results from accidental exposure. Rather it is taken for granted that the physical structure of the organism is genetically determined, though of course variation . . . will depend in part on external factors.

The development of personality, behaviour patterns and cognitive structures in higher organisms has often been approached in a very different way. It is generally assumed that in these domains, social environment is the dominant factor. The structures of mind that develop over time are taken to be arbitrary and accidental; there is no 'human nature' apart from what develops as a specific historical product.

But human cognitive systems, when seriously investigated, turn out to be no less marvellous and intricate than the physical structures that develop in the life of an organism. Why, then, should we not study the acquisition of a cognitive structure such as language more or less as we study some complex bodily organ?

A Choose any personality trait – intelligence, friendliness, aggression, happiness. Do you think it is nature or nurture that forms this characteristic in people? Justify your answer carefully. Are the reasons you give based in evidence, reason or faith?

The idea that there is a fixed biological hierarchy smacks of Hitler's master race. It is a view which is unlikely to be favourable to anybody who isn't near the top of the pecking order, and the belief that some people or races are superior to others has been, and is being, put to violent and ugly use all over the world. Small wonder that many feel moral outrage at the idea that our capacities are innate and fixed genetically. However, at this point we should feel a little uneasy for at least two reasons.

■ We might feel moral outrage at a theory, but we need to distinguish very carefully between our moral beliefs and our beliefs about facts. We may be morally outraged at the American intervention in Vietnam, or by the destruction of the World Trade Center, but we cannot therefore deny that these things actually happened. Similarly, we may be morally outraged if we find that our capacities are innate, but as seekers of reliable knowledge we should not shy away from the search. If it is true, then we may be left with difficult ethical issues, but burying our heads in the sand and ignoring the problem is not a responsible way forward.

■ Even if all our traits are genetically determined, that does not mean that we can draw any moral conclusion whatsoever. We do not make moral judgements about tall people as opposed to short people, although height is, to be sure, strongly determined by genetics. Why should we feel differently about intelligence? Even if it turns out that one race is less intelligent than another, that would be no justification for treating one race as better than another. The distinction between positive and normative social science is absolutely clear here.

> **A** Would you want to know if there was a biological hierarchy of intelligence?
> **B** Do you think it would be good for society to know if there was such a hierarchy?
> **C** Suppose some group in such a hierarchy turns out to be the least intelligent. Construct arguments to suggest that the group gets more, less and the same amount of education. Which argument is 'best'? On what principles do you base your argument? Are they positive or normative principles?

You have probably already thought that nature and nurture interact, and that both extremes are obviously wrong. Perhaps the way forward is to determine the relative importance of each factor? Is it 40 per cent nature and 60 per cent nurture? Or precisely equal at 50:50?

Although this approach might seem appealing, it is ultimately futile. One can imagine few things more foolish than two pianists arguing about how a piano makes sounds; one says that it is because of the impact of the hammer on the strings inside the piano (the natural qualities of a piano); the other says that it is because the player presses the keys down (the environment of the piano). Unable to agree, they decide that it is some combination of the player and the strings and resolve to investigate whether the relative proportions are 60:40 or 80:20. Clearly, this is totally meaningless. Without either, nothing happens. Similarly nature and nurture in humans are not opposites. They do not lie at opposite ends of a spectrum as competing forces. Nature is 100 per cent important and nurture is 100 per cent important. To contrast them is an artificial and outdated notion.

The linguist Stephen Pinker asks us to imagine the most sophisticated computer available – it has the fastest processor, gigabytes of RAM, terabytes of disc storage, a 3D virtual reality display, speech recognition and output, wireless internet access, and hundreds of built-in software modules. In other words, it has a very, very complex nature. Does that mean that, whatever we type into it, it will always respond in the same way, that the environment is unimportant? Of course not! In fact, the very reverse is true – the built-in complexity allows the machine to respond in complex ways, and the more complex the built-in machinery, the more complex the reaction to inputs.

The analogy with humans could not be clearer. Nature and nurture cannot be separated in any meaningful way. Without at least the innate capacity to learn, the environment could not have any effect. If we had no innate capacities we would be inanimate. Let's leave the last words to another scientist, Stephen Jay Gould, who has written extensively on the subject.

Of all the baleful false dichotomies that stymie our understanding of the world's complexity, nature vs. nurture must rank among the top two or three (a phoney division only enhanced by the euphony of these names).

Can we use a scientific approach with humans?

As soon as questions of will or decision or reason or choice of action arise, human science is at a loss.

Noam Chomsky

Now that we have seen several of the issues and problems, let us list and summarise the objections to the application of the 'scientific method' in the social sciences, and see whether or not they are good grounds for making vital distinctions.

1 **All humans are unique individuals; there can be no laws that apply to them all.** This is a common objection, but a little thought shows that it is far from certain. For example, in everyday life we tend to find that men and women behave differently and we treat people differently according to their sex. We can discuss whether or not it is right to make gender distinctions, and argue about nature or nurture (as we have done), but the brute fact remains that there are characteristics common to large classes of humans. This is not a dehumanising thing – underlying unities do not necessarily conflict with our uniqueness as individuals. We can study photosynthesis without demanding that all plants are the same. Why then should laws describing human behaviour require that all humans are identical?

It is certainly at least possible that humans share deep underlying patterns of behaviour. We cannot dismiss this out of hand without looking at the evidence carefully and without prejudice – that is, it is a matter for scientific enquiry, not armchair philosophy.

2 **Social sciences can never make accurate predictions with which to test theories.** It is certainly true that predictions in social sciences are extremely difficult to make, whereas physicists can sometimes predict results to ten decimal places. However, this is a difference of degree and not kind; no sociologist would hesitate to predict that an openly homosexual man will not be elected to be governor of the

American state of Kansas, and no physicist would care to predict the path of a cork floating down a river. It may be that the social sciences are in their infancy, and that we will see extremely accurate predictions in the future. Again, this is a matter for open-minded scientific investigation.

3 **In the social sciences you cannot generate laws because the objects are always moving – there are no constants.** This is in marked contrast to the natural sciences where there are universal and unchanging (as far as we know) constants of nature (such as the speed of light in vacuum). It is true that social scientists have no such bedrock of stability, but as explained in point 1, that is not to say that there are no constants in human nature. Cultures and traditions may differ, but there may be deep underlying features. In the same way as rocks, trees, the sea and the air are superficially different, but are all made of molecules, all cultures and traditions might exhibit structural similarities, and it is the job of the social scientist to look for them.

4 **You cannot measure social data in numerical form as you can in the natural sciences.** This is certainly true at the moment – it is not possible to quantify things such as 'respect for elders' and 'social harmony'. Even numerical quantities, such as IQ and economic data, are often rather dubious measures. But again, even if this turns out to be a fundamental limitation of the social sciences, we cannot assume it from the start. Before the concepts of energy, force and work were clarified, the physical sciences were largely descriptive, and not readily amenable to quantification as they are now. The social sciences may one day find their Newton, and all may change.

5 **In the social sciences, an experimenter can change the thing he is trying to investigate; there is an unavoidable interaction between subject and scientist.** There are clearly cases where this is true – imagine an expert economist predicting a massive fall in the stock market, or that certain social groups are less likely to be successful at work. In both cases, the statements may become self-fulfilling (it is also possible to imagine self-defeating predictions). The problem is that of a conscious and freely-acting subject who can decide to do exactly what he is not supposed to. This is in marked contrast to all the natural sciences – an astronomer's prediction of the next sighting of Halley's comet will hardly speed or delay its return! So there is some truth in this problem, but there are similar issues in the natural sciences – for example, to measure the speed of a particle requires interaction of some sort, and hence a change in the speed of the particle. In quantum mechanics, this principle is fundamentally limiting. In any case, in sophisticated social theory we can imagine taking all these interactions into account – so again, this is no reason to assume that social sciences will fail.

6 **Social issues cannot be studied like sciences because you can't control variables or repeat experiments; whole areas are inherently irreducible.** There certainly are problems here. If we want to investigate inflation and its link to

unemployment, we cannot hold manufacturing output, exchange rates, wage increases, money supply and other relevant variables constant while we carry out our investigation. In fact, we probably couldn't even identify all the relevant variables in many cases, and even if we could control them that would (arguably) invalidate the whole experiment! So the *ceteris paribus* assumption in economics is simply unrealistic, and things in, say, psychology are still more complicated! But this is also a little unfair. Experiments in meteorology, geology and astronomy can also be difficult or in many cases impossible – scientists have to make simplifying models and to deduce what they can, recognising that the model is just that, and extrapolating its results with great care. There may or may not be ways to overcome experimental problems, but we won't find solutions by assuming that there are none.

7 **The social sciences are permeated with values in a way that the natural sciences are not; they are normative as well as positive.** That the social sciences can be normative is indisputable, but surely the same can be said of the physical sciences as well, though perhaps to a lesser degree. In studying the reaction of organic acids with plastics, there may be few obvious questions of value, but that is not to say that all natural sciences are purely objective and value free. When a new drug is being developed we must ask what risks we are prepared to put up with, and for what benefit. A drug that cures cancer but induces early arthritis would be very popular; one which cures headaches but with the same side-effect would never reach the market. In building a bridge, it may be possible to spend a hundred times as much money to ensure that the risk of collapse falls from one in a million to one in ten million. Should the extra expense be laid out? There are issues of the value of human life involved here, in addition to the science. In the big picture we can see that, for example, Darwin's science of evolution is changing our values radically.

So the social sciences are not alone in dealing with issues of value, and we can make a case that natural scientists have a long history of abdication from responsibility. Along with all their benefits, scientific advances have been partially responsible for physical, chemical, biological and nuclear weapons; the depletion of the ozone layer; Chernobyl; global warming; loss of rainforest and natural diversity and so on. Perhaps natural scientists should take a more active interest in the application of their advances, and in the implication of their work for the general good of humankind.

A Examine the objections above and the responses. Find an example for each of the objections and discuss whether or not the objection raises a fundamental distinction between social and natural sciences.

B Are there any other objections to the application of the scientific method to the study of humans? Evaluate them carefully.

There is a natural tendency to believe that the study of our behaviour should be somehow different in principle to that of chemicals, and that no scientist will ever fathom our motives, thoughts and interactions. Our paradigm of self-worth and individuality is threatened by a science that 'explains' humans. However, paradigms sometimes come to an end and must be replaced if they can be shown to be based on error. In any case, as will be suggested below, even if humans can be 'explained' right down to the 'last detail' (whatever that might mean), our dignity and value as humans cannot be explained away, and we should not fear to look at ourselves for fear of what we might find.

Of course, it may be that the social sciences are doomed to failure; maybe we are incapable of understanding ourselves and our societies. This is a possibility which may also arise in the natural sciences, but there we are studying objects which are external to us. In the social sciences, there is an additional factor **– we are studying the thing which is doing the studying –** and this raises an interesting possibility. The more complex we are, the better equipped we are to study ourselves, but the more difficult a job we have. Conversely, the less complex we are, the easier we are to investigate, but the less able we are to comprehend ourselves! We can (arguably) understand some animals' social behaviour, but they (presumably) can't. So are we intelligent enough to understand ourselves? Emerson Pugh once quipped, *'If the human mind was simple enough to understand, we'd be too simple to understand it.'* There may well be truth in that.

But we are getting ahead of ourselves. If there are practical limits to our understanding of ourselves, then so be it. We cannot be sure about that purely by engaging in this sort of abstract speculation. The scientific method is the best tool we have for discovery; we would be foolish to dismiss it out of hand. Social science may not be quite the same as natural science, but whoever said that it had to be? As good philosophers, the theoretical objections should inform and guide our inquiries, but as good scientists, we should go ahead and do the experiments which will confirm or falsify our best theories as to the nature of (social) reality.

How much can the social sciences tell us?

You cannot acquire experience by making experiments. You cannot create experience. You must undergo it.

Albert Camus

Imagine a world where the social sciences reign supreme, where new concepts and theories have been elucidated, developed, refined and perfected. Crime, poverty and all manner of social ills have been eradicated by the development of social technologies based on these theories. The social world is a happy, peaceful and totally managed one, and no citizen of the future would wish it otherwise – indeed they cannot imagine how bad it must have been before the incredible breakthroughs of the twenty-second century! When a problem arises in their world, the social scientists set up the mathematical models, run some computer simulations and perform a few validating experiments. They then give a practical and efficient solution which accurately predicts how to set up situations such that the general population will, of their own free choice, behave in such a way as to rectify the problem.

> Let us ignore, for a moment, whether or not this society is a 'good' thing. Consider instead the implications of this scenario coming to pass.
>
> **A** Would our lives then be 'described' or 'explained' in some way?
> **B** So do these theories tell us everything about us that is important?
> **C** Is there anything about us that escapes explanation? Or are we, in this scenario, just parts of a social scientific theory and nothing more?

Here we might reflect a little on the limitations of the scientific approach. Reading any scientific textbook it is clear that science necessarily deals in types – 'a **sample** of phosphorus'; 'a **specimen** of e coli'. Science is not, and cannot be, interested in individual cases except in so far as they conform to given types. That is the whole point of science – to make generalisations about classes of objects and to see beyond the differences to the underlying shared characteristics. Thus, as far as science is concerned, specific characteristics are of no interest – it cannot deal with them and they have no place in the scientific canon. But it is precisely our individuality and uniqueness that make us who we are as humans, regardless of our shared general characteristics. In a *New York Times* obituary, Eudora Welty writes of author Victor Pritchett:

The characters that fill [his stories] – erratic, unsure, unsafe, devious, stubborn, restless and desirous, absurd and passionate, all peculiar unto themselves – hold a claim on us that cannot be denied. They demand and get our rapt attention, for in the revelation of their lives, the secrets of our own lives come into view. How much the eccentric has to tell us of what is central.

Most of our bodies are pretty similar as far as science is concerned (which is just as well if you are a surgeon), but to us as human beings, living and experiencing our lives every day, some bodies seem very different to others. Why is it that I love watching sunsets? Maybe science can find the circuits of the brain that are involved in appreciating colourful scenes, but surely no scientist can ever describe in scientific language what it is actually like for me to sit on the beach and bask in the final rays of the day. This extends to all of our experiences. What is it like for you, now, to be reading this page? What was it like for Neil Armstrong to set foot on the moon? What is it like to parachute? What is it like to think that you are going to die? What is it like to sneeze? What is it like to have sex? What is it like to fall asleep?

Thus any type of science, natural or human, will always fall short of some types of knowledge. No matter what wonderful theories and technologies are invented or discovered, some central and vital parts of our lives cannot, by their very nature, be explained by science in a meaningful way. Therefore we should never fear scientific explanation – if it misses such a central part of our being, if it has nothing to say about us as individuals, then it will never impinge on human dignity and human life.

A Try to answer some of the 'What is it like to . . .' questions above. What does this tell you about the limits of sciences and languages?

B Consider the future world described at the beginning of this section. Given what has been said, do you think the people in this world are in any way impoverished by the scientific knowledge that they have?

Where do we go from here?

So do the social sciences offer us a reliable and coherent way of knowing? It should be clear that this really depends on what type of 'knowledge' we are looking for. It is possible that the social sciences are converging with the natural sciences, so perhaps we should stick our necks out (hoping that the future will not chop them off!) and suggest that one day the social sciences will hold the same hope for qualified certainty as the natural sciences. However, the qualification is an important one. As we have seen, the natural sciences provide no sure route to absolute certainty and, even if they did, there are still aspects of human existence which seem to be beyond the scientific approach in principle. If we are to find ourselves with knowledge about ourselves, then perhaps we need to look at lived human life and actual human experience. Perhaps it is time we turned to history.

Further reading

For the problems in representing human information in meaningful form, Stephen Jay Gould's handling of IQ in *The Mismeasure of Man* (W. W. Norton, 1981) is lengthy but brilliant. Philip Davis and Reuben Hersh tackle the issue more generally in *Descartes' Dream* (Harvester Books, 1986). A reasonably technical but readable and rich account of the emerging discipline of decision theory (which attempts to model how humans actually make decisions) can be found in Stephen Watson's *Decision Synthesis* (Cambridge University Press, 1977).

The issue of free will is brilliantly introduced in chapter 6 of Donald Palmer's *Does the Centre Hold?* (Mayfield, 1991) and is further explored in Daniel Dennett's *Elbow Room* (MIT Press, 1984). For a case study on psychology, try Adrian Furnham's *All in the Mind* (Whurr Publishers, 1996). General reflections on human nature, with an emphasis on language, can be found in the early chapters of Noam Chomsky's *Powers and Prospects* (Pluto, 1996). The links with the natural sciences are superbly and controversially explained in Edward Wilson's *Consilience* (Vintage, 1999), Matt Ridley's *The Red Queen* (Penguin, 1993) and Stephen Pinker's *How the Mind Works* (Penguin, 1998). A broader, far more philosophical (and far more difficult) approach is taken by John Searle in *The Construction of Social Reality* (Penguin, 1995).

■ *Resource file*

RESOURCE FILE RESOURCE FILE RESOURCE FILE RESOURCE FILE RESOURCE FILE RESOURCE FILE RESOURCE FILE RESOURCE FILE RESOURCE FILE RESOURCE FILE RESOURCE FILE RESOURCE FILE

Testing: a case study of a problem in the social sciences

An extract from *Descartes' Dream* by Philip Davis and Reuben Hersh.

In order to 'mathematise' society – to convert it to a form where it can be processed by a digital computer – it is first of all necessary to mathematise society's principal components – people. To mathematise people means to encode them, or to represent them, by sequences of zeros and ones.

In many respects, we are already encoded. Our medical records are essentially lists of numbers: blood pressure and pulse at various times, blood counts (note the arithmetical turn of phrase) and so forth and so on. Our school records, or 'transcripts' as they are called, are also lists of numbers, denoted by the special term of 'grades'. You realise that 'letter' grades are also arithmetical. One need only decode from A, B, C, D, E to 1, 2, 3, 4, 5. And then there are our tax records at the IRS. Numerical indeed!

But these numbers don't suffice for the purpose of mathematising society. The principal social function of each of us is not as a pupil or a patient. It is, as an employee or worker, to participate in the economy. So our places and positions in the economic system have to be mathematised or digitised.

How do we do this? We take a test! The nation's grand central test-maker, the Educational Testing Service of Princeton, NJ., sells test to the CIA, the Defence Department, the National Security Council, the government of Trinidad and Tobago, the Institute for Nuclear Power Operations, the National Contact Lens Examiners, the International Council for Shopping Centres, the American Society of Heating, Refrigerating and Air-Conditioning Engineers, the Commission on Graduates of Foreign Nursing Schools, the Malaysian Ministry of Education, the National Board of Podiatry Examiners, and the Institute for the Advancement of Philosophy for Children. In some parts of the country you cannot become a golf pro, a real-estate salesman, a certified consultant, a certified auto mechanic, a merchant marine officer, a fireman, a travel agent, a certified business-form consultant, or, in Pennsylvania, a beautician or a barber, without passing an ETS test. And we have not even mentioned the great vortex and centre of testing; the schools – from kindergarten through graduate school. The tests we take in K-12 are a major part of our work file, the raw material for the computation that will determine what kind of work we get to do and how much we get paid for doing it.

In June 1985, an unexpected and tragic death occurred in Jakarta. The Indonesian Minister of Education and Culture, Professor Nugroko Notosusanto, suffered a brain haemorrhage, at the age of only 54 years. He was buried at the Heroes Cemetery, Kalibata, with full military honours. According to the Jakarta press, Dr. Notosusanto brought about a major reform in Indonesian education. He established a uniform nation-wide test for completion of secondary school. Unfortunately, almost all the candidates failed the test. To correct this calamity, he decreed that the test results should be 'curved' – that is, fitted to a normal bell curve. When this was done, the result was that almost everyone passed the test. This, it seems, was a second calamity. Dr. Notosusanto was quoted as saying, 'It seems no matter what I do people are angry at me.' (Rough translation from Indonesian.)

At any rate, he had been in good health so far as his friends and family knew. This double calamity of testing was the only source of stress in his life mentioned in the press. Dr. Notosusanto's most notable accomplishment (again according to the Jakarta press) was ☞

an increased emphasis on religion (Islam) and history (Indonesian history as a tool in 'nation-building'). He was regarded as a sensitive, conscientious man, very faithful to duty. In view of that description, it seems possible that he was actually killed by the stress due to the problem of testing.

It's worth giving a moment's thought to this sad story. It casts in sharp focus the issue of what testing is really all about.

In particular, it is not just a matter of examining the students (i.e., in the simple literal sense of the word, looking them over), deciding which are OK, by some clear cut, 'objective' standard, and which are not OK and then labelling them as such. If that were the case, it would be inconceivable that the same set of high-school graduates taking the same exam would nearly all pass on one day and nearly all fail on another day. Rather, a test, as it is used nowadays in modern societies such as the U.S.A. or Indonesia, is a partition device, a method for sorting a population into two sub-populations. The first sub-population will be admitted to some desired status. The second will be excluded.

Testing is also a way of putting people into computable form. Such and such a score means such and such a rank in the bureaucratic hierarchy. The decision can be automatic (capable of being carried out by machine) and objective (no human being appears openly to whose prejudices the decision can be attributed). Being automatic and objective, it may appear to its recipients or victims as something God-given; that is, inevitable, eternal, and unquestionable. In truth, of course, it is the opposite; it is temporal and questionable and avoidable.

There are two crucial questions about testing: is it accurate? and is it harmful? In other words, does it fulfil its intended purpose? and does it do harm in other respects? On the first point, the answer is that, when properly done, testing does carry out a certain task accurately. This task, however, is related to, but not identical to, that originally envisioned. Take intelligence testing, for example. Does an IQ test measure intelligence? It measures something; for it does have, within reasonable tolerance, the statistical attribute called 'reliability'. Reliability tells us that a statistical

measure (i.e., IQ score) is meaningful. The question is, what meaning? Are we measuring intelligence or something else?

The IQ is exact. It is a number. Intelligence, on the other hand, is an amorphous, verbally-defined quality. How could they be the same? IQ purports to be in some sense an approximation or equivalent to intelligence. How could we justify or prove this claim for IQ? In order to do so, we would have to analyse 'intelligence' into its various manifestations: ability to solve problems, to succeed in difficult situations, to behave in the most appropriate manner. But, *what kind* of problems or situations? A quick glance at an IQ test will show that the only problems and situations for which the IQ questions are pertinent are classroom or academic ones. The IQ test is really just an instrument for predicting success in school. (And far from infallible, even at that!) It has little bearing on occupational or professional success or success in business, in love, or in the other testing grounds of life. There is a dramatic meaning-shift in passing from the 'intelligence' of ordinary language to the 'I' of IQ.

While IQ is a reasonable predictor of success in school, it is of course not the same as success in school. Some people with a relatively low IQ do well in school, and some people with a high IQ do badly. What then, really, is IQ? The only honest answer is, it is what it is. More wordily, the IQ score is a measure of one's ability on the IQ test. If someone chooses to use it with another meaning than that, he does so at his (and his victims') risk.

The same argument applies to any other 'objective' test of some 'aptitude' or 'ability'. The test does not measure exactly the aptitude or ability we are interested in, but, rather, some artefact brought into being by the invention of the test. As a consequence, test-taking ability becomes a new and crucial 'aptitude' for getting ahead in the world. This is no joke. The coaching for various tests (Medical School Aptitude Tests, Law School Aptitude Tests) has become a substantial industry in itself. In many medical schools, whose students must pass the nationwide 'Board' exams after two years, the faculty supply their students with substantial, systematic coaching on exam-taking strategy. Would not those students' future patients be better served if the exam were cancelled and the extra time spent on pharmacology or anatomy?

This leads into our second issue: aside from its accuracy or inaccuracy in its intended measurement, does 'objective testing' do any positive harm? On this issue tremendous controversies are raging. For instance, it is claimed that IQ tests and other 'objective' tests are culturally biased. There is no question that results of these tests are being used to justify claims of inferiority of the non-white part of our population.

It is obvious that tests could be written which consistently demonstrate Black superiority. As it happens, no one is seriously interested in writing and administering pro-Black IQ tests, whereas the present tests, which give Blacks, on the average, slightly lower scores, continue to be used. One rationale for these results is to say that many Black people are educationally and culturally deprived, and the test merely reflects this deprivation. There is nothing wrong with the test, only with the reality it reports. Although this defence may seem plausible, it is fallacious insofar as it treats the IQ as an objective, God-given measurement; we know the IQ is man-made and arbitrary.

A more serious defect in this defence of IQ is that it treats IQ as a purely passive intuition, something which merely reflects what is. On the contrary, the IQ also affects what is. IQ and other culturally biased tests are part of the apparatus which restricts and makes more difficult the attempts of many Blacks and other non-whites to rise in our socio-economic order. Naturally, these tests are attacked by the political organisations of Black people and their supporters.

For example, Arthur R. Jensen (*Straight Talk About Mental Tests*, 1981) has gained international fame by reiterating the claim that the average difference of 15 points between IQs of Blacks and Whites is genetic in origin. A strong attack on Jensen's view is contained in *The Mismeasure of Man* by Stephen J. Gould, 1981. Related in spirit to Gould's is *The Science and Politics of IQ*, by Leon J. Kamin, which details the connection of IQ tests with racism and anti-semitism ever since

they were first brought to the U.S.

Most readers will choose sides according to their political and philosophical preferences. There are many citizens who are quite comfortable with the belief that objective tests have demonstrated that some folks are just superior to other folks. This kind of thinking is sometimes called 'conservative'. On the other side, people with a belief in social betterment or racial equality (liberals, Lefts, or what you will) are more likely to be convinced by Kamin's and Gould's arguments that IQ testing (and other similar 'objective' testing) are not merely objective measurements of reality, but are also instruments of social control for maintaining the status quo.

Since these remarks are, unavoidably, weighted on the liberal side, let us try to restore the balance by referring to a review in *Policy Review* (well-known as a 'conservative' journal) by Michael Levin, a well known 'conservative' professor of philosophy. Levin reviews both Jensen and Gould, praising Jensen and condemning Gould, as one might expect in view of his political orientation. Most of the review deals with the specific arguments of these two books, but, at the end, the political animus becomes overt: 'Peering out from between [Gould's] lines are our friends Marx and Lenin and ... the new Left.' Thus does the mathematical element become politicised.

Race and politics aside, the effect of objective testing is to devalue those qualities which cannot be so tested. For example, in high-school English classes, multiple-choice tests have become very common, while essay tests have become less common. Consequently, the importance of learning to write has been greatly diminished both for teachers and for students.

As we mathematise the world, we proceed to lose or to throw away those parts of the world that cannot be mathematised. What isn't mathematised seems not to exist, even never to have existed.

We should never forget that a stroll in the woods or a deep conversation with a new or old friend are beyond mathematics. And then, when we go back to our jobs, as administrators, teachers, or whatever, let us still remember that numbers are only the shadow, that life is the reality.

Is economics a science

Two views

An account from a chemist's point of view by Arthur Williamson, First Vice President, New Zealand Institute of Chemistry.

R ecently I have noticed that economists have begun to draw on some of the jargon and concepts of physical chemistry and are using ideas of thermodynamics to support their assertions about the possibility of continued economic growth. I guess this gives a thermodynamicist some reciprocal right to expound on the method of economics.

An aspect of economics which interests me is the relationship between theory and real behaviour. In both fields it appears that one can devise theories about the behaviour of a system and then use them to make predictions about the future behaviour of the system, which can then be compared with the actual behaviour. At this point physical science and economics seem to diverge. When actual and predicted behaviour differ, the physical scientist generally concludes that either the observations or the theory are in error. If the observations are trustworthy, then the theory has to be wrong. In economics there seems to be a third possibility which is illustrated by the current 'free-market' approach. In this case disagreement between prediction and actuality is often ascribed to 'market failure'. I imagine that the equivalent in physical science would be to say that a disagreement between theory and experiment is due to 'reality failure'. Perhaps even more mystifying to the physical scientist is the fact that the economist will then sometimes go one step further and propose a measure to 'correct' this 'failure'. This is equivalent to the physical scientist attempting to do something to bring reality more into line with the existing theory.

One must conclude that the relationship between theory and reality is indeed different in these two fields. Physical science aims at elucidating characteristics assumed to be inherent in the system and expressed in its behaviour, while economics seems to be about the construction of models and attempts to impose these models on the system. To my mind the ability that the economist has to 'interfere' with the object of his theory adds a dimension of subjectivity that is not present in physical science and suggests that there can be no inherent rightness in any particular economic theory.

A reply from an economist by Seamus Hogan, Department of Economics, McGill University, Montreal.

T **here are a number of similarities in the methodologies of physical science and economics. Unfortunately, the similarities in substance are not as great as the similarities in the language used to express the substance. A lot of our technical language is borrowed from the physical sciences (principally physics, since many of the economists who first brought mathematical rigour to the subject earlier this century had received their original training in physics). Naturally, the borrowed language has taken on its own meaning in economics, adapting to the differences in the disciplines. This can lead to misunderstanding if professionals from one area try to read material from the other.**

One similarity between the physical sciences and economics is that both involve the systematic investigation of complex

phenomena. The human brain has only a limited capacity to comprehend complex systems of interacting forces without an organising framework. One way of providing such a framework is to invest ideal worlds that contain many of the interactions that we wish to comprehend but are still relatively simple and can be used as benchmarks against which to test the real world.

For instance, a physicist might consider the dynamics of a body on a frictionless surface attached to an ideal spring (i.e. a spring that has no mass and gives rise to a restoring force that is proportional to the distance the body is displaced from rest). Obviously, ideal springs or frictionless surfaces do not exist, but it is easier to comprehend the observed behaviour of a spring by considering how the presence of friction or spring mass distort the dynamics that it is trying to model. Similarly, modern economic theory is built on a mathematical structure that can analyse the simultaneous interaction of all decision-making agents in an economy (consumers, firms, governments, etc.). This structure makes a number of simplifying assumptions that are palpably false, but, as with the ideal spring, it provides a benchmark, exceptions from which generate our comprehension of the real economic world.

One reason for calling the simplified worlds 'ideal' is that they often contain a number of desirable properties that one would like to approximate in practice (e.g. minimising friction can reduce the amount of energy that one needs to supply in order to achieve a particular amount of work). Since the economic benchmark also has some desirable properties, one set of real-world deviations from this benchmark are termed 'market failures'. To continue with the analogy, an economist's recommendation that economic policy be used to remove a market failure would be equivalent to a physicist's recommendation that lubricant be used to reduce friction.

Professor Williamson's final point is that 'the ability that an economist has to "interfere" with the object of his theory adds a dimension of subjectivity which is not present in physical science'. There is an important difference between physical sciences and economics in the methodology of connecting theory (in the physical-science use of the term) and reality. The most important of these is that economists can almost never use controlled experiments. One can think of a controlled experiment as being an attempt to create the conditions of an imagined 'ideal' world in order to isolate a small number of phenomena from the distractions of real world interactions. Economics certainly does have a 'dimension of subjectivity which is not present in physical science', but this is precisely because the economist cannot 'interfere' with the object of his theory in the way that a physical scientist can through the use of controlled experiments.

THOSE WHO CANNOT REMEMBER THE PAST ARE CONDEMNED TO REPEAT IT.
Santayana

Historians are dangerous people. They are capable of upsetting everything.
Nikita Khrushchev

It is surprising that history should be so dull considering that so much of it is invented.
Jane Austen

The charm of history and its enigmatic lesson consists in the fact that, from age to age, nothing changes and yet everything is completely different.
Aldous Huxley

The quickest and surest way to find the present in the past, but hardly the soundest, is to put it there.
C. H. McIlwain

The historian makes a distinction between what may be called the outside and the inside of an event. The outside means everything belonging to it which can be described in terms of bodies and their movements (e.g. Caesar's crossing of the Rubicon or his assassination in Rome). The inside means that which can only be described in terms of thought. When a scientist says, 'Why did that piece of litmus paper turn pink?', he is investigating the outside of the event. By contrast, when a historian asks 'Why did Brutus stab Caesar?', he means, 'What did Brutus think that made him decide to stab Caesar?' – he is investigating the inside of the event. The cause of the event means the thought in the mind of the person by whose agency the event came about . . . All history is then the history of thought.
R. G. Collingwood

Hardly a pure science, history is closer to animal husbandry than it is to mathematics, in that it involves selective breeding. The principal difference between the husbandryman and the historian is that the former breeds sheep or cows or such, and the latter breeds (assumed) facts. The husbandryman uses his skills to enrich the future; the historian uses his to enrich the past. Both are usually up to their ankles in bullshit.
Tom Robbins

EVEN GOD CANNOT CHANGE THE PAST.
Agathon

What is history but a fable agreed upon?
Napoleon Bonaparte

Introduction

In our search for certainty, looking to the past is very appealing. The past is fixed; immutable and absolutely certain. Nothing we do can change it, and so as the historian G. R. Elton put it:

In a very real sense the study of history is concerned with a subject matter more objective and independent than that of the natural sciences. Just because historical matter is in the past, is gone, irrecoverable, its objective reality is guaranteed; it is beyond being altered for any purpose whatsoever.

It would certainly seem difficult to deny this, and therefore we can, it seems, hold up history as the model for truth and certainty. Or can we? Look carefully at what Elton has written and you will see that he has been very careful in his choice of words – . . . *the study of history . . . subject matter . . . historical matter* . . . He does not actually say anything about history itself. So what does he mean?

We might make an important distinction here, and one that will be familiar to all historians. In English the word 'history' is used in two very different senses; there is history as the series of all past events, and there is history as the academic inquiry carried out by historians. It is only in this first sense that history is fixed in the way that Elton suggests. History in the second sense is all about how we know history in the first sense, and we would do well not to confuse the two. Once this distinction is made, the hope for certainty begins to fade rather rapidly – we can be certain that something happened (history in the first sense), but finding out about it (history in the second sense) may be a completely different matter! Historians sometimes use the term **historiography** to refer to the study of the writings of historians (that is, history in the second sense); the term **history** itself may be used in either sense. In fact, as any historian knows, what we know about the past may be incomplete, inaccurate or even completely wrong, and because the past is gone it may be extremely difficult to ever find out. What Elton portrays as a strength may turn out to be a weakness!

So history presents unique problems, but we shall also see that it shares some features with other forms of knowledge. History is important in a very human sense – our communities are shaped by their histories, and in many cases around the world sadly bound and limited by them in terms of hatred and violence. To understand the past, and to attempt to find the truth about it, may be a factor in rising above the social and cultural norms caused by the actions of people now dead. To understand the past must be an important step to understanding the present, and maybe even shaping the future.

The facts of history

If the historian attempts to find out about the past then the first step is surely to find out as many facts as possible. In what might be thought to be a truly objective, scientific spirit, she should collect all the facts, and then analyse them. In this way, the historian might attempt first to establish a 'hard core' of indisputable facts and, on the basis of these, and only these, to theorise.

Let us imagine some 'historical facts' such as 'Hong Kong was returned to China in 1997'; 'The Battle of Bosworth Field took place in 1485, on Bosworth Hill'; 'Caesar crossed the Rubicon in 49BC'. We should acknowledge that many such facts are beyond dispute (though not all of them – many 'certain' historical facts have been shown to be false!) and to determine them accurately is important. But as Alfred Housman once quipped, *'Accuracy is a duty, not a virtue.'* These are all very tedious facts! Just as we look to a mathematician for getting more than his arithmetic right, so we expect more than the 'basic facts' from the historian. Such facts are not history itself, but the building blocks from which history is made. No-one really cares much about them, and historians hope to answer far more interesting and important questions such as, 'What effect did reunification of Hong Kong and China have on fledgling political parties within China?'; 'Was social inequality the main factor behind the tensions in England in the fifteenth century?'; 'Why was the crossing of the Rubicon an important step?' Once we have acknowledged this, it is also clear that the desire to establish the answers to these questions immediately tells us about the wishes and interests of the historian. He, and not the basic facts, has decided that the fledgling political parties in China are of interest and are worthy of historical inclusion.

Of course, the historian is not always freely choosing from reams of information. Just as geologists know little about animals which were too soft to leave an imprint in the fossil record, so there may be little for the historian to go on. Historians in the Central and South American ruins of the Mayans, Aztecs and Incas marvel at the wonders of the architecture and the beauty of the cities, but they also find it rather frustrating. What were the buildings for? How were the societies formed? What were the people interested in? What were their beliefs? What were the dramas, hopes, loves and fears of the people? Of course, there is some information on these questions but the data is woefully incomplete and there is much we do not know. Even written sources often do not help us answer the questions we have.

In recent history, of course, the opposite problem arises – there is far too much information. It has, for example, been estimated that the administration of each recent US President produced upward of five million pieces of paper a year, which works out at 14,000 pieces of paper each day! This flow of information/policy/spin may be beyond the grasp of any one individual, but it will be the job of the historian to provide structure and to separate the trivial from the momentous. This data is meaningless in historical terms until it has been sorted and sifted. But as that happens it ceases to be mere data – the categorisation employed to do the sorting and sifting comes from the theories of the historian, not the original data. Once the material is sifted and sorted, theory is inextricably tied up with the data, and there is no longer any 'hard core' of fact. In this age of information, the job of the historian is undoubtedly more difficult, but more important than ever. Unless the historian makes sense of the data then it is non-sense. Contrary to popular belief, facts never speak for themselves.

On top of this is the enormous problem of source reliability. Even official records of diplomatic meetings often portray one side's arguments as powerful and compelling statements of clarity and eloquence, and the other side's as feeble-minded. It comes as no surprise that the records of the other side portray exactly the opposite story. The point is that documents are written by humans – they have already been processed. No document can tell us more than the author of the document thought happened, thought would happen, thought ought to happen, would like to have happened or even would like others to think he thought would happen. Historical 'facts' are never pure, as Winston Churchill knew when he said, *'History will be kind to me for I intend to write it.'*

So the whole idea of a 'hard core' of evidence is a difficult one to maintain. The view that all the historian has to do is to collect the facts and let, as Mach said, *'the bare data confront us'* is naïve and untenable.

A What are the two meanings of the term 'history'? Are there any other possible meanings?

B Think of some part of history about which little is known. Is there any chance that much will ever be known, or is it totally wiped from human knowledge?

C Take a copy of a quality daily newspaper. Estimate the number of 'facts' in it. Then, allowing for the number of newspapers in your country, estimate the number of 'facts' reported every year. (Remember that different newspapers may report the 'same event' in different ways.)

D Think of some part of history for which the information is totally overwhelming (recent world events seem most obvious here). Will historians ever be able to sort through the information to arrive at the 'truth' about what happened?

E Why is the notion of establishing certain facts before theorising an appealing one? Why might it be a very difficult thing to do?

F How does this concept of mixing theory and observation apply to other disciplines?

G What did Reuben Abel mean when he wrote: *'The patterns said to be found in past events are selected by the historian; like the hypotheses of the scientist, they may be suggested, but are neither imposed nor dictated, by "the facts".'*?

At this stage, we should mention the term **bias** and contrast it with the concept of **selection**. It is often said that bias is an important problem facing the historian. In modern history this is undoubtedly true, at least on occasion. It is a difficult task for historians to transcend their own paradigms when writing about, for example, their own countries – and it is easy to find histories of troubled areas which show the historian's country coming out very well indeed. However, we should not be too ready to dismiss modern history as a result. It is also possible to find historians who are very critical of their own countries, and in most countries historical debate is alive and well. Even if individuals are biased, the international historical community as a whole may well be able to come to reasoned conclusions about particular theories. Thus the problem of bias may not be as serious as it first appears. Arguably, it may hardly apply to medieval or ancient history at all, where far fewer people will feel the same levels of personal involvement. Bias almost implies some sort of dishonesty, and to this extent a biased historian is a bad historian, and the problem of bias is similar to the problem of a scientist fixing his experimental data – in all likelihood he will be found out. But the biased historian is not the same as the selective historian. Selectivity is not an option – it is a requirement for the meaningful study of the past (and the present for that matter) and this contrast starkly with bias; a non-selective historian is a bad one. All historians are selective and they select on the basis of their own paradigms – this is what makes them worth reading.

A What fallacy are you committing if you dismiss an historian's views because she happens to paint her country in a positive light? (You may need to refer to the section on common fallacies in Chapter 5 on page 87.)

B What is the difference between bias and selection?

C Are bias and selection 'crimes' for an historian? If so, which is the more serious?

D Are they both inevitable? What are the alternatives?

The selection of the facts of history

The facts are like fish swimming in a vast and murky ocean, and what the historian catches will depend partly on chance but mainly on what part of the ocean he chooses to fish in and what bait he chooses – these two facts of course being determined by the type of fish he wants to catch. By and large the historian will get the facts he wants.

E. H. Carr

Recognising that we cannot 'show it as it really was', that selection inevitably occurs, and that history has been called 'an act of creation', we need to see what factors might make up the historian's overall paradigm, and understand, in general terms, the basis on which any selection is made.

The first point is an obvious but important one – any historian is an individual human, and his history will be based on his particular interests, which are, in turn, partially dependent on his culture. There was a time when English schoolchildren studied the kings and queens of England almost exclusively, reflecting the interests of teachers and academic historians (because the English education system is international, this was also true for children all over the world; the same has been true in other disciplines, so sometimes people living on the equator have had to study glaciation!). This time has passed, and the lives of 'average' or 'typical' people seem to be far more important than they once were, but what aspect of their lives do we look at? We deem education, gender roles and social equality to be very important, and we naturally focus on them. But the people living at the time may not have shared our priorities. Things cannot be important *per se* – they can only be important to someone, and that someone is the historian. Carr writes:

Study the historian before you begin to study the facts. Find out what bee he has in his bonnet. When you read a work of history, always listen out for the buzzing. If you can detect none either you are tone deaf or the historian is a dull dog.

Reading an eighteenth-century history about the thirteenth century will tell you as much about the eighteenth century as it will about the thirteenth century, quite possibly more. The same is true of more recent histories. Making the point entertainingly in a well-known paragraph, the historian A. J. P. Taylor writes the complete biography of King George V:

George V (1865–1936), second son of Edward VII; married Princess Mary of Teck, 1893; King, 1910–1936; changed name of royal family from Saxe-Coburg to Windsor, 1917; his trousers were creased at the sides, not front and back.

The problem is compounded as soon as we acknowledge that historians do not write in a social and cultural vacuum. Possibly more than any other discipline, history is fundamentally and unavoidably a social construct. Consider this history of a nation:

Our forefathers had occupied the land from time immemorial. When the invaders first came they were only in small numbers and pretended to be friendly. We were friendly to them and even helped them to survive. However, without our knowledge or consent they invited other invaders to join them. Soon they began moving into more of our territory. With their superior weapons they defeated us repeatedly. Sometimes they signed treaties with us allowing us a certain portion of our own land – but these were later broken or revised.

Finally, the whole land was occupied by the invaders. We were deprived of our livelihood and way of life and reduced to a few tiny areas. The invaders now claimed that all the land was rightfully theirs. The invasion and occupation was complete.

This extract is, of course, about the USA. History is written by the winners – sometimes because the losers are dead. There were once millions of thriving native Native Americans. Where are they today? The 'facts' are out there, and some say that they indicate that genocide has occurred. But it isn't known 'history' in the same way as the genocide against the Jews in the Second World War. It often seems to happen that the victors of a conflict turn out to have been noble and humane fighters, respecting human dignity and life. If, somehow, after the use of atomic weapons in 1945, the course of the Second World War had turned and the Allies had lost, what would now be the 'historical truth' about the bombings of the civilian populations of Hiroshima and Nagasaki? Perhaps the term 'Holocaust' would have a more general meaning, or perhaps not.

Related to this is the availability of analytical and conceptual apparatus. For example, the Marxist view of class conflict gave us a whole new mental structure through which to view historical events. In a similar way, new psychological theories may offer novel and unforeseen insights. Thus history will change as the theoretical frameworks of inquiry advance. Once again, we see that history is as much a product of the present as it is a fixed entity in the past.

This issue operates on both the macro and the micro scale. We choose how we describe events and what is important according to the level of analysis we are:

- capable of and have available to us
- 'given' by our paradigms, context and culture.

Consider events whereby a group of people plant bombs in certain places in an attempt to force a government to make social change. We call the explosions which are killing people 'terrorism' in one set of circumstances and 'resistance' or even 'freedom-fighting' in another, largely depending on what we think about the government in question. This issue is related to, but not limited by, the language we use. Consider these points:

- Was the dropping of the atom bombs on Japan the final act of the Second World War or the first act of the Cold War? Or both? Or something else entirely? Or just the explosion of extremely powerful bombs?
- Henry VIII failed to seduce Anne Boleyn and married her instead. Was this a rather sordid business, or the start of the fall of the Catholic Church in England?
- Was the fall of the Berlin Wall the nail in the coffin of communism? Was it a triumph of western democracy? Was it any of these things at the time? Or was it just a lot of people smashing a wall?
- Many people at a particular time and place are running around killing each other. Later on this is seen as a decisive battle. Was it a decisive battle at the time?

We impose a useful structure on certain 'facts'. But the structure must, of necessity, go beyond these facts if it is to be useful. And, of course, utility is not necessarily a good indicator of truth anyway. We have seen that the structure is, inevitably, *our* structure. The facts suggest that many years ago men were sailing on boats, dying of scurvy and petrified that they would be eaten by sea monsters or fall off the ends of the Earth. Historians later called these torrid journeys the 'Voyages of Discovery'. One might argue that this goes well beyond selection, and that relabelling in this way is as close to creation as it is to selection!

> **A** Find an account of any significant event in a history textbook. Look at:
>
>   ■ the language that is used
>   ■ what information has been included/omitted
>   ■ what details are stressed
>   ■ what analytic concepts have been used
>   ■ the extent to which selection, interpretation and packaging have been used to create historical 'truth'.
>
> **B** Find another history text which gives an account of the same event. Compare and contrast the two and determine which is more accurate. On what basis do you make your decision?
> **C** What will our own age be called far in the future? The Age of Democracy? The Age of Hypocrisy? The Age of Disaster? How do you sum up an age in one phrase?
> **D** For what reasons might future historians have a name for our age which we are totally unable to predict?
> **E** It has been said that the historian is like a painter rather than a photographer. By examining the nature of painting and photography, explain to what extent you agree with this analogy.

Jorge Luis Borges has written entertainingly and illuminatingly on similar issues in literature. In *Kafka and his Precursors*, he tells how he found echoes of Kafka's writings in a number of earlier authors, but how these authors share no other similarity. It is only in light of Kafka that we can identify these shared aspects of these 'precursors', of which he writes:

In each of these texts we find Kafka's idiosyncrasy to a greater or lesser degree, but if Kafka had never written a line, we would not perceive this quality; in other words, it would not exist. The poem 'Fears and Scruples' by Browning foretells Kafka's work, but our reading of Kafka perceptibly sharpens and deflects our reading of the poem. Browning did not read it as we do now ... The fact is that every writer creates his own precursors. His work modifies our conception of the past, as it will modify the future.

> **A** When Browning wrote his poem, was he a precursor of Kafka, or did he only become so when Kafka started writing?
> **B** Consider the line, '... *if Kafka had never written a line, we would not perceive this quality; in other words, it would not exist*'. If we regard Kafka as a modern historian, and the other authors as sources, what does this analogy suggest about history? Is it a helpful analogy?
> **C** John Dewey famously described the past as the 'past-of-the-present'. In the light of what you have read in this section, what do you think he meant?

History and people

The history of the world is but the biography of great men.

Thomas Carlyle

Let us consider what might, at first, seem to be real but unimportant features of dealing with people in history. As people, we all know that our decisions and actions are affected by such things as physical and mental health, but we also recognise that historians will often have very little access to these feelings. In *War and Peace*, Tolstoy suggests that Napoleon's poor performance in a key battle was due to his having a bad head cold, but we do not know if this is true. It has also been suggested that the deep unhappiness of Luther, one of the key figures in the Reformation, was directly attributable to his own private agony caused by acute constipation. Two hundred years ago, the majority of the population suffered from toothache, and it is certainly conceivable that the ill health of many major historical figures played a role in their decisions, but these facts are rarely recorded. These seem like rather pedestrian points for an historian to worry about, but if we are trying to understand behaviour, then state of mind must be a crucial factor. If this is the case, it means that important, maybe vital, historical factors will be forever beyond our reach.

Of course, we can generalise this idea beyond the concept of health. In any humanities subject, we are investigating an incredibly complex, multi-faceted and dynamic subject – humankind. The state of the art in most areas is such that the current aim is to explain group rather than individual behaviour. In history, this is often not the case, and while A. J. P. Taylor's claim that, *'the history of modern Europe can be written in terms of three titans: Napoleon, Bismark and Lenin'*, may be overstating the case, it is certainly a reminder that the behaviour of individuals plays a crucial role in history. This makes the job of the historian extremely difficult. The historian Barbara Tuchman writes:

Each man is a package of variables impossible to duplicate. His birth, his parents, his siblings, his food, his home, his school, his economic and social status, his first job, his first girl, and the variables inherent in all of these, make up that mysterious compendium, personality – which then combines with another set of variables: country, climate, time and historical circumstance. The range of factors available make interpretation very difficult.

Her point is a good one, and seems to strongly limit the possible scope of history. The historian R. G. Collingwood reinforced this when he said, *'All history is the history of thought.'* This stark comment cuts deep and leaves historians slightly nervous. If it is thought we are after, then we are going to struggle! Arguably, even the 'perfect source' – a private diary – is one step removed from 'thought'; it may well be written with an eye to posterity, even if it is private. Thus even the perfect source may be an interpretation, which we then interpret ourselves. We are then already two steps away from thought and possibly liable to find serious distortion. Of course, when we move to sources further removed, we face many difficulties. If we read a public diary or official record then we read what the author wanted us to think he thought; or possibly even what he wanted us to think he wanted us to think he thought!

Some historians attempt to play down the problem with individuals by arguing that history is really less to do with individuals than the interplay of titanic social and economic factors. There does seem to be some sense in this – could any leader stop, for example, the impact of information technology? Could any chancellor stop the flow of capital around the world? Recent history might suggest not. Perhaps we should regard societies as unstoppable monsters, headed in a particular direction; the best any leader can do is to ride the beast in the same direction, perhaps speeding it up or slowing it down. This **social determinism** does not exactly make the historian's job simple. Analysing individuals may be difficult, but are these mysterious 'social forces' any easier to understand? Or are we just using the words 'social forces' to label the problem rather than solve it (like explaining that a pigeon finds its way home via its 'homing instinct')?

A What are the problems in trying to analyse an event when you are part of it?

B What are the problems in trying to analyse an event by standing back and getting an overview of the whole event?

C What problems are raised by regarding history as the plaything of individual figures?

D What are the alternatives to this point of view? Do they solve the problems or do they raise more?

E Do you think that history is about individuals or social forces? Is this even a valid distinction? Justify your answer with concrete examples.

We can see that the human factor makes historical explanation very difficult because it muddies the waters of causation. If things happen on a leader's whim, then what hope is there for us to explain why he or she did something? But we shall find that these waters are hardly crystal clear at the best of times, and even if we could solve this problem, there are other difficulties which might stop us reaching a full understanding.

Causation in history

Any event, once it has occurred, can be made to appear inevitable by a competent historian.

Lee Simonson

When we let go of an unsupported object it falls. We may not know why this happens, but we may invoke some phenomenon like 'gravity', or we may say that things have a tendency to fall. That is perfectly acceptable, but it hardly qualifies us as scientists. Similarly we can read or even write about the past and be content. We can say that the Cold War was due to tension between the superpowers, but we may have to remind ourselves that this is a long way from studying history. History, like science, is all about finding out the causes and effects of events, and the greatest historians, like the greatest scientists, are those who manage to find a new way of explaining why things happen. An historian's approach to cause and effect will largely determine the sort of historian he will be.

In our search for causes, we immediately run into problems when we ask a question as apparently basic as 'Why did the Second World War happen?'. Any student will quickly realise that there are a number of causes, and to offer merely one would be ridiculous. However, to offer a long list of ten causes would not be much better. What we want is an ordered list with some indication as to the 'most important' cause, and an indication as to why that cause is central in a way that the others are not. (If we are extraordinarily fortunate then maybe we can even see a contemporary situation where we can try to 'test' our theory.)

So how might we go about establishing such a hierarchy of causes? The interlinking nature of history causes problems. How far back should one go when looking for a cause and how far forward when looking for an effect? There is the old tale of the country that was lost because a war was lost; the war was lost because the battle was lost; the battle was lost because a general didn't receive orders; the general didn't receive orders because a message was delayed; the message was delayed because a messenger stopped *en route*; the messenger stopped *en route* because his horse's shoe came off; the shoe came off because of a sharp rock in the road . . . and we are very quickly into absurdity. Does this mean that history is one continuous stream of cause and effect, with accident and chance events playing major roles? This theory goes by the name of Cleopatra's Nose, based as it is on the idea that had Cleopatra's nose been slightly longer, Mark Antony would not have fallen in love with her, and the subsequent history of the Roman Empire and the world would have been completely different. This has been a popular view: King Alexander of Greece died from a monkey bite in 1920 and this event started a tragic series of events, about which Winston Churchill later remarked *'a quarter of a million persons died of this monkey's bite'*. If this view is correct, then we may as well give up looking for causes before we start.

Of course, most events are multi-causal, and the simple chain of event stories like those above may not be realistic. However, this just makes the problem far more difficult! You can imagine a huge web of cause and effect that soon becomes impossible to grasp. If we have to take every little thing into account then history will become nigh-on impossible and certainly lose all its explanatory power.

There are other views of causation, but they seem equally difficult. In *War and Peace*, Tolstoy vividly portrays the bewilderment of the millions of people caught up in the crises and upheavals of the Napoleonic Wars. On the cause of the war, he writes:

The causes of this war seem innumerable in their multiplicity. The more deeply we search out the causes the more of them we discover; and every cause, and even a whole class of causes taken separately, strikes us as being equally true in itself, and equally deceptive through its insignificance in comparison with the immensity of the result, and its inability to produce (without all the other causes that concurred with it) the effect that followed . . . And consequently nothing was exclusively the cause of the war, and the war was bound to happen, simply because it was bound to happen.

Few historians today would agree with this historical determinism, but it is really no different from social determinism, genetic determinism, or plain determinism. The issue is related to that of free will and perhaps here we need do no more than point out that the idea is barren. Even if the course of events is fixed, we should still try to determine what that fixed course is. So historical determinism adds nothing of any interest. It does not take us anywhere, and so maybe purely on pragmatic grounds we should leave it there.

Another idea is that history is cyclical, and that the same things happen over and over again in different guises. If we believe that history can teach us anything about the future then we must, to a greater or lesser degree, subscribe to this notion. Other paradigms have stressed the primacy of race, climate, class struggle, psychology, progress, *zeitgeist* (spirit of the age) and pure chance or luck as central to historical causation. We shall not discuss these all now – for present purposes we merely note that it is only once we have selected our paradigm that we can select our data. Once we have the data, we should attempt to be open-minded enough to change our paradigm if the need arises. Any good historian will have a number of approaches available – the key is deciding which is most productive under any given set of circumstances, and not to have a closed mind. (Ever original, A. J. P. Taylor suggested that railway timetables were a key cause of the First World War!) The best we can hope for is that we generate a dynamic relationship between our beliefs and the evidence we have – but that extends far beyond knowledge in the historical domain.

A Identify an historic event which you believe has a single cause. What was the cause of that cause? Trace the sequence back as far as you feel is meaningful, and explain your choice of where to stop.

B Do you think that all events have causes which are identifiable by historians?

C What do we mean by historical cause?

Selecting the right selection: which is the right version of history?

There is no Archimedean point of view; and neither the bird's eye view nor the worm's eye view is infallible.

Reuben Abel

We have come a long way from Elton's insistence that the past is fixed and unchangeable. He is right, but not in a useful sense, and in distinguishing between the past and what we can know of it, we must be wary of glib claims of truth. History, like science, aims for objectivity, but history, like science, is a human endeavour with all that entails. Given all the problems we face in history, how close can we come to the truth? If all versions are selective, how do we select the right version?

Since selective knowledge is, by definition, incomplete knowledge, there is a temptation to fall into empty statements such as, 'history is constructed by biased historians working with biased sources which were written by biased people; therefore there is no such thing as historical truth.' But just because it is selective and written by people does not mean that history has to be hopelessly twisted, subjective or fabricated. It does mean that it is very difficult to attain certainty, and that the historian will never know all there is to be known about an event. But the historian openly accepts this, and the problem is hardly unique to history. We can have three accounts of an event in Roman times – one from a twentieth-century African, one from a fifteenth-century Scot and another from a tenth-century Turk, and while no single account will be entirely true, they will all contain elements of truth and it does not always help to ask which is the right one.

So the historian recognises the problems, and looks to solve them. The historian seeks a convergence of evidence, and hopes that the explanations developed are reasonable, and consistent with as much of the evidence as possible. Theories will be scrutinised, arguments examined and accounts questioned. In this respect history, like science, is self-correcting. The alternative to absolutism does not have to be nihilism; just because we don't have certainty about the past, it does not follow that anything goes.

In addition to the intellectual argument, there is a pressing moral need for us to acknowledge the reality of the past and not accept the 'anything goes' version of history. The revisionist historian David Irving suggests that Hitler did not attempt to exterminate the Jews in the concentration camps. Others have said that the number of victims was far less than the generally accepted six million. However, mainstream historians, and the vast majority of those who have investigated the evidence in any depth, feel that the evidence is overwhelming, and to deny what happened in the concentration camps is to do more than merely cite another historical perspective. There is often an ethical dimension to history, and that makes either complete relativism or complete scepticism as dangerous as certainty and prejudice. We may not like the uncertainty we face in dealing with the past, but if we want to predict the future where else can we look? Santayana's remark does not imply that we can use the past reliably, but reminds us that we have little choice but to try:

Those who cannot remember the past are condemned to repeat it.

A Some historians claim that they are not even seeking the truth. Why do you think they say that? Do they mean that they are simply telling stories? What is the value of their study?

B Does the open admission of many historians that the truth is unattainable in any way devalue the discipline?

C What is the most important or serious problem an historian faces?

Where do we go from here?

We turned to history hoping that the fact that it was fixed would offer us the opportunity to find certainty and truth. What we failed to take account of was that we live in the present, and that current attitudes and values always shape how we interpret the evidence of our senses. In this, history has something in common with social sciences, natural sciences, and even, come to think of it, the arts. What is more, evidence often forms the premises of our reasoning, and so the problems of evidence seem to play a central role in all the areas we have looked at. Perhaps it is an underlying theme, like rationalism, worthy of attention in its own right. Let us turn, then, to empiricism.

Further reading

A very brief overview of some ideas is given in chapter 15 of Reuben Abel's *Man is the Measure* (The Free Press, 1976), but perhaps the classic introduction is E. H. Carr's very accessible *What is History?* (Random House, 1967). A useful overview of the post-modern criticisms of historical truth is found in K. Jenkins (ed.) *The Post-Modern History Reader* (Routledge, 1997); a response to these claims has been mounted in R. J. Evans' *In Defence of History* (W.W. Norton and Co., 1999). Other excellent books are A. Marwick's *The Nature of History* (Lyceum Books, 1989) and Barbara Tuchman's engaging collection of essays called *Practicing History* (Ballantine Books, 1991).

To look at current controversies and some lesser-known views, you will not find better themes than in Ward Churchill's *A Little Matter of Genocide* (City Light Books, 1997) and James Peck (ed.) *The Chomsky Reader* (Random House, 1987).

Is history a guide to the future?

An extract from
Practicing History by
Barbara Tuchman.

The commonest question asked of historians by laymen is whether history serves a purpose. Is it useful? Can we learn from the lessons of history?

When people want history to be utilitarian and teach us lessons, that means they also want to be sure that it meets scientific standards. This, in my opinion, it cannot do, for reasons which I will come to in a moment. To practise history as a science is sociology, an altogether different discipline which I personally find antipathetic – although I suppose the sociologists would consider that my deficiency rather than theirs. The sociologists plod along with their noses to the ground assembling masses of statistics in order to arrive at some obvious conclusion which a reasonably perceptive historian, not to mention a large part of the general public, knows anyway, simply from observation – that social mobility is increasing, for instance, or that women have different problems from men. One wishes they would just cut loose some day, lift up their heads, and look at the world around them.

If history were a science, we should be able to get a grip on her, learn her ways, establish her patterns, know what will happen tomorrow. Why is it that we cannot? The answer lies in what I call the *Unknowable Variable* – namely, man. Human beings are always and finally the subject of history. History is the record of human behaviour, the most fascinating subject of all, but illogical and so crammed with an unlimited number of variables that it is not susceptible of the scientific method.

I say this bravely, even in the midst of the electronic age when computers are already chewing at the skirts of history in the process called quantification. Applied to history, quantification, I believe, has its limits. It depends on a method called 'data manipulation', which means that the facts, or data, of the historical past – that is, of human behaviour – are manipulated into named categories so that they can be programmed into computers. Out comes – hopefully – a pattern. I can only tell you that for history 'data manipulation' is a built-in invalidator, because to the degree that you manipulate your data to suit some extraneous requirement, in this case the requirement of the machine, to that degree your results will be suspect – and run the risk of being invalid. Everything depends on the naming of the categories and the assigning of facts to them, and this depends on the quantifier's individual judgment at the very base of the process. The categories are not revealed doctrine nor are the results scientific truth.

The hope for quantification, presumably, is that by processing a vast quantity of material far beyond the capacity of the individual to encompass, it can bring to light and establish reliable patterns. That remains to be seen, but I am not optimistic. History has a way of escaping attempts to imprison it in patterns. Moreover, one of its basic data is the human soul. The conventional historian, at least the one concerned with truth, not propaganda, will try honestly to let his 'data' speak for themselves, but data which are shut up in prearranged boxes are helpless. Their nuances have no voice. They must carry one fixed meaning or another and weight the result accordingly. For instance, in a quantification study of the origins of World War I which I have seen, the operators have divided all the diplomatic documents, messages, and utterances of the July crisis into categories labelled 'hostility', 'friendship', 'frustration', 'satisfaction', and so on, with each statement rated for intensity on a scale from one to nine, including fractions. But no preestablished categories could match all the private character traits and public pressure variously operating on the nervous monarchs and ministers who were involved. The massive effort that went into this study brought forth a mouse – the less than startling conclusion that the likelihood of war increased in proportion to the rise in hostility of the messages.

Quantification is really only a new approach to the old persistent effort to make history fit a pattern, but reliable patterns, or what are otherwise called the lessons of history, remain elusive ...

To me it is comforting rather than otherwise to feel that history is determined by the illogical human record and not by large immutable scientific laws beyond our power to deflect.

I know very little (a euphemism for 'nothing') about laboratory science, but I have the impression that conclusions are supposed to be logical; that is, from a given set of circumstances a predictable result should follow. The trouble is that in human behaviour and history it is impossible to isolate or repeat a given set of circumstances. Complex human acts cannot be either reproduced or deliberately initiated – or counted upon like the phenomena of nature. The sun comes up every day. Tides are so obedient to schedule that a timetable for them can be printed like that for trains, though more reliable. In fact, tides and trains sharply illustrate my point. One depends on the moon and is certain, the other depends on man and is uncertain.

In the absence of dependable recurring circumstance, too much confidence cannot be placed on the lessons of history.

There are lessons, of course, and when people speak of learning from them, they have in mind, I think, two ways of applying past experience. One is to enable us to avoid past mistakes and to manage better in similar circumstances next time; the other is to enable us to anticipate a future course of events. (History could tell us something about Vietnam, I think, if we would only listen.) To manage better next time is within our means; to anticipate does not seem to be beyond us.

Theories of history go in vogues which, as is the nature of vogues, soon fade and give place to new ones. Yet this fails to discourage the systematisers. They believe as firmly in this year's as last year's, for, as Isaiah Berlin says, the 'obstinate craving for unity and symmetry at the expense of experience' is always with us.

I do not know what the new explanation is, but I am sure there must be some thesis, for as one academic historian recently ruled, the writing of history requires a 'large organising idea'.

I visualise the 'large organising idea' as one of those iron chain mats pulled behind by a tractor to smooth over a ploughed field. I see the professor climbing up on the tractor seat and away he goes, pulling behind his large organising idea over the bumps and furrows of history until he has smoothed it out to a nice, neat, organised surface – in other words, into a system.

The human being – you, I, or Napoleon – is unreliable as a scientific factor. In combination of personality, circumstance, and historical moment, each man is a package of variables impossible to duplicate. His birth, his parents, his siblings, his food, his home, his school, his economic and social status, his first job, his first girl, and the variable inherent in all of these, make up that mysterious compendium, personality – which then combines with another set of variables: country, climate, time, and historical circumstance. Is it likely, then, that all these elements will meet again in their exact proportions to reproduce a Moses, or Hitler, or De Gaulle, or for that matter Lee Harvey Oswald, the man who killed Kennedy?

So long as man remains the *Unknowable Variable* – and I see no immediate prospect of his ever being pinned down in every facet of his infinite variety – I do not see how his actions can be usefully programmed and quantified. The eager electronic optimists will go on chopping up man's past behaviour into thousands of little definable segments which they call *Input*, and the machine will whirr and buzz and flash its lights and in no time at all give back *Output*. But will *Output* be dependable? I would lay ten to one that history will pay no more attention to *Output* than it did to Karl Marx. It will still need historians. Electronics will have its uses, but it will not, I am confident, transform historians into button-pushers or history into a system.

Pearl Harbor is the classic example of failure to learn from history. From hindsight we now know that what we should have anticipated was a surprise attack by Japan in the midst of negotiations. Merely because this was dishonourable, did that make it unthinkable? Hardly. It was exactly the procedure Japan had adopted in 1904 when she opened the Russo-Japanese War by a surprise attack on the Russian fleet at Port Arthur.

In addition we had every possible physical indication. We had broken the Japanese code, we had warnings on radar, we had a constant flow of accurate intelligence. What failed? Not information by judgment. We had all the evidence and refused to interpret it correctly, just as the Germans in 1944 refused to believe the evidence of a landing in Normandy. Men will not believe what does not fit in with their plans or suit their prearrangements. The flaw in all military intelligence, whether twenty or fifty or one hundred per cent accurate, is that it is not better than the judgment of its interpreter, and this judgment is the product of a mass of individual, social, and political biases, prejudgments, and wishful thinkings; in short, it is human and therefore fallible. If man can break the Japanese code and yet not believe what it tells him, how can he be expected to learn from the lessons of history?

Why did the chicken cross the road?

The problem of historical causation in a different context...

Many, many thinkers have attempted to explain why things happen as they do. The following list is based on real theories, and knowingly misapplied. Can we learn anything from this?

Freud: It was an unconscious drive.

Chomsky: Because it had innate road-crossing capacity.

Karl Marx: It was an historical inevitability.

Machiavelli: So that its subjects will view it with admiration, as a chicken which has the daring and courage to boldly cross the road, but also with fear, for whom among them has the strength to contend with such a paragon of avian virtue? In such a manner is the princely chicken's dominion maintained.

Hippocrates: Because of an excess of light pink gooey stuff in its pancreas.

Jacques Derrida: Any number of contending discourses may be discovered with the act of the chicken crossing the road, and each interpretation is equally valid. Authorial intent can never be discovered because structuralism is dead.

Thomas de Torquemada: Give me ten minutes with the chicken and I'll find out.

Darwin: It was the next logical step after coming down from the trees.

Epicurus: For fun.

Goethe: The eternal hen principle made it do it.

Hemingway: To die. In the rain.

Heisenberg: We are not sure which side of the road the chicken was on, but we know that it was moving pretty fast.

Hume: Out of custom and habit.

Plato: For the greater good.

Pyrrho the Sceptic: What road?

Thoreau: To live deliberately ... and to suck all the marrow out of life.

Mark Twain: The news of its crossing has been greatly exaggerated.

Zeno: To prove it could never reach the other side.

Edmund Hillary: Because it's there.

Douglas Adams: Forty-two.

Germaine Greer: Who said it was a chicken? It might have been a hen.

Nietzsche: The chicken is dead.

Skinner: Because external influence which had from birth pervaded its sensorium had caused it to develop in such a fashion that it would tend to cross roads, even while believing these actions to be of its own free will.

Jung: The confluence of events in the cultural gestalt necessitated that individual chickens cross roads at this historical juncture, and therefore synchronicitously brought such occurrences into being.

Sartre: In order to act in good faith and to be true to itself.

Wittgenstein: The possibility of 'crossing' was encoded into the objects 'chicken' and 'road' and circumstances came into being which caused the actualisation of this potential occurrence.

Einstein: Whether or not the chicken crossed the road or the road crossed the chicken depends on your frame of reference.

Aristotle: To actualise its potential.

Buddha: If you meet the chicken on the road then kill it.

Dali: The Fish.

Schrödinger: There is a finite probability of the chicken still being in the middle of the road.

Lao-Tze: Whether or not the chicken crossed the road, the way goes on forever.

Confucius: The chicken was crossing the road to dutifully visit its parents. It is therefore to be honoured as a paragon of filial piety.

Hegel: The delight from the dialectic generated by the question outweighs the illusion of certainty that may be gained from answering it.

Darth Vader: Because it could not resist the power of the Dark Side of the Road.

Baldrick: It had a cunning plan.

Martin Luther King: It had a dream.

James T. Kirk: To boldly go where no chicken has gone before.

Ronald Reagan: I forget.

Descartes: *Cluckito ergo sum.*

Fox Mulder: You saw it cross the road with your own eyes. How many more chickens have to cross the road before you believe it?

Is history a science?

An extract from *The Nature of History* by Arthur Marwick.

The great value of the 'Is history a science?' debate is the manner in which it helps clarify the nature of history and to delimit what history can, and cannot do. To the ordinary common-sense mortal ... the most striking difference between history and natural science is the degree to which proof can be established of the various contentions made by the scientist and the historian respectively. I say 'degree', though the more self-regarding historians would probably join with history's severest critics in saying there is little or no similarity between the scientist's methods and the historian's 'intuition', between the scientist's empirical expertise and the historian's creative flights. Yet neither 'intuition' nor 'creation' need represent a fundamental divide between history and science. The gifted scientist will usually develop a 'feel' for his subject which may not be greatly different from the intuition of which some historians boast. The scientist of course will attempt empirically to demonstrate the validity of any hunch he may have; his 'feel' will take him in the direction of trying one kind of experiment rather than another, not towards stating untested assumptions. But again this is not terribly different from the way the professional historian (as distinct from the inspired charlatan) sets to work; intuition may suggest certain causal connections but the historian will do his best from the material at his disposal to establish at least the probability of such a casual relationship; better still he may be stimulated to seek for entirely new source materials (rather as a scientist might devise an entirely new type of experiment). On the matter of 'creativity', it is surely not to be contested that Einstein's theory of relativity is one of the great monuments to human creative thinking. Of course most practising scientists are engaged on much more basic tasks; but then a large number of historians are engaged on pretty mundane work as well.

Rather cunningly, a few sentences ago, I introduced the word 'probability'. The historian can only show from his sources that it was likely or at most, probable, that something happened in the way he says it did. But natural science today also deals in probabilities rather than in the certainties of nineteenth-century days. Many of those who so vehemently deny that history can have any resemblance to a natural science reveal appalling ignorance of the direction natural sciences are currently taking ... With the 'Relativity Revolution', the Newtonian absolutes were dethroned. The discovery of 'quanta' contradicted the conception of the continuity of the infinitesimal calculus. The theory of mutations pointed to change coming through leaps, not by a gradual process. Today, scientists can, from time to time, be heard calling for a revision of scientific laws: in October 1968 Professor Fred Hoyle challenged the Royal Astronomical Society with the need for a radical change of the laws of physics; only thus, he said, would it be possible to account for the 'funny things which are going on' in the universe. Let us therefore agree that, save on the most banal level, there are no absolutes in the natural word. So when the historian fails to establish conclusive proofs for his version of past events he may not necessarily be exposing himself as thoroughly unscientific.

However, there is a difference, and we all know there is a difference. The physical scientist cannot call for a repeat performance of the past. The scientist, it may be argued further, can preserve an ☞

objectivity towards the phenomena he is studying, whereas the historian can never be completely objective. On the whole this distinction must be allowed to stand, though again as one of degree rather than as an absolute. After all, as has often been pointed out, the man who assembles the apparatus for a particular experiment effectively becomes a part of the experiment: even in physical science the human, subjective element can never be entirely excluded.

The other central problems in the 'Is history a science?' debate are these: the ultimate (often remote) objective in scientific exploration is the formulation of a scientific law, but there are no general laws in history (attempts in this direction having commended themselves neither to historians nor to non-historians); scientific knowledge provides the power of prediction; the historian cannot predict. The latter point is in some ways a bit of a red herring: the historian's concern, by definition, is with the past; he may well, as a result of his expertise, make some intelligent predictions about the present and future, but that is not strictly his business. The historian E. H. Carr has given an example of the kind of prediction the historian might indulge in:

'People do not expect the historian to predict that revolution will break out in Ruritania next month. The kind of conclusion which they will seek to draw, partly from specific knowledge of Ruritanian affairs and partly from a study of history, is that conditions in Ruritania are such that a revolution is likely to occur in the near future if somebody touches it off, or unless somebody on the government side does something to stop it; and this conclusion might be accompanied by estimates, based partly in the analogy of other revolutions, of the attitude which different sectors of the population may be expected to adopt. The prediction, if such it can be called, can be realised only through the occurrence of unique events, which cannot themselves be predicted; but this does not mean that inferences drawn from history about the future are worthless, or that they do not possess a conditional validity which serves both as a guide to action and key to our understanding of how things happen.'

An overwhelming majority of historians in fact will probably have no knowledge whatever of Ruritania and little knowledge of revolutions. Non-historians do have a right to expect intelligent and informed comment on current events from their historical friends; statesmen, civil servants, television commentators may reasonably be presumed to react more intelligently to current crises if they have a historical training. But this is really to move away from the kind of 'prediction' continuously practised by the professional historian in the normal line of business, a type of 'prediction' which in a small way is analogous to the prediction of the physical scientist. This comes about when the historian, using the evidence he has painfully accumulated, together with the feel for the way things happen in certain circumstances which he has developed over the years, makes an inference about something for which he does not in fact have full and sufficient evidence. He is 'predicting' what will be seen to have happened once the full evidence is forthcoming. This, in the end, is certainly not the same as the scientist's prediction (indeed the special word 'retrodiction' has been coined to capture the difference) but again, one might argue that it is a difference of degree rather than of kind.

Much time, most fruitfully, has been spent over the issue of general laws. It has now become something of a platitude that . . . whenever the historian speaks of a 'war', of a 'revolution', of 'feudalism', of 'representative government', he is using a generalisation. In each of these cases he is suggesting that there are certain general features which characterise a 'war', 'feudalism', etc. However, the use of such generalisation still leaves us a long way from the formulation of general laws. Given all the qualifications that must now be made about the nature of scientific laws, that they are working hypotheses, expressions of tendencies and probabilities, not iron-hard certainties, it still does seem that in the physical sciences there are laws which differ in scale from any generalisation which the historian might feel competent to make. Again the distinction is not an absolute one; after all, the formulation of scientific laws only exercises the physical scientist operating at the highest level: most scientists are just as immersed in detail as are most historians.

There is one further point which is sometimes thrown into the argument, notably ... by Trevelyan. This is the one about science having use, while history, of course, is 'useless'. What is meant, of course ... is immediate tangible use: television sets, pasteurised beer, nuclear bombs. The natural scientist working as a scientist (and not as an industrial chemist or scientific adviser to some government or corporation) would however deny that his researches are directed towards such utilitarian products. The scientist seeks knowledge of the phenomena of the physical universe as the historian seeks knowledge of the human past. If the scientist is anything more than a crusty misanthropist he will believe that somewhere sometime his discoveries in 'pure' science will have practical application; that belief is not fundamentally different from that of historians ...

All this would suggest that while there is no fundamental distinction between the main aims and methods of the historian and of the physical scientist, nonetheless there are good reasons for the common-sense assumption that differences do exist. The final point which highlights this sense of difference springs from the manner in which, in one form or another, history becomes implicated in the making of value judgments. Most historians would accept Professor Knowles' neat statement: 'The historian is not a judge, still less a hanging judge.' But they also rejoice at the delicate come-uppance which the late Professor Alfred Cobban administered to Professor Michael Oakeshott's pleas for complete moral neutrality (in papers read to the second and fourth Irish Conferences of Historians):

'It is admittedly difficult', says Professor Cobban, 'to avoid "the description of conduct in, generally speaking, moral terms". This I take to mean that, for example, we cannot help describing the September massacres as massacres. The important thing is to avoid any suggestion that massacres are a bad thing, because this would be a moral judgment and therefore non-historical.'

The historian cannot help but make moral judgments, if only by implication or by virtue of his selection of the facts: these judgments are of a type not encountered in the natural sciences. Finally, to recall a point already made ... if the historian's activities truly are necessary to society, he must communicate the fruits of his labours to that society. There falls upon the historian a duty to write serviceable prose which does not fall on the scientist, whose labours may best be summed up in a few pages of equations.

The most apposite words of all are those of Professor E. E. Evans-Pritchard, the anthropologist: 'When will people get it into their heads that the conscientious historian ... is no less systematic, exacting and critical in his research than a chemist or biologist, that it is not in method that social science differs from physical science but in the nature of the phenomena they study.' Here surely is the crucial point: the historian is concerned with a different kind of material, human experience in the past, from that with which the natural scientist is concerned.

Introduction to *Memoirs found in a Bathtub*

An extract from *Memoirs found in a Bathtub* by Stanislaw Lem.

It is the third millennium, and a set of memoirs has been found in an archaeological dig. Historians have named the memoirs 'Notes from the Neogene' and published them. This is the introduction.

'Notes from the Neogene' is unquestionably one of the most precious relics of Earth's ancient past, dating from the very close of the Prechaotic, that period of decline which directly preceded the Great Collapse. It is indeed a paradox that we know much more of the civilisations of the Early Neogene, the protocultures of Assyria, Egypt and Greece, than we do of the days of paleoatomics and rudimentary astronavigation. While those archaic cultures left behind permanent monuments in bone, stone, slate and bronze, almost the only means of recording and preserving knowledge during the Middle and Late Neogene was a substance called papyr.

Papyr was whitish, flaccid, a derivative of cellulose, rolled out on cylinders and cut into rectangular sheets. Information of all kinds was impressed on it with a dark tint, after which the sheets were collated and sewn in a special way.

In order to understand what brought about the Great Collapse, that catastrophic event which in a matter of weeks totally demolished the cultural achievement of centuries, we must go back three thousand years. Metamnestics and data crystallisation did not exist in those days. Papyr performed all the functions now served by our mnemonitrons and gnostors. True, there were the beginnings of artificial memory; but these were large, bulky machines, troublesome to operate and maintain, and used only in the most limited, narrow way. They were called 'electronic brains', an exaggeration comprehensible only in the historical perspective, much like the boast of the builders of Asia Minor, that their sacred temple Baa-Bel was 'sky-reaching'.

No-one knows exactly when and where the paprlysis epidemic broke out. Most likely, it happened in the desert regions of a land called Ammer-Kam where the first space-port was built. The people of that time did not immediately realise the scope of the impending danger. And yet we cannot accept the harsh judgement delivered by so many subsequent historians, that these were a frivolous people. To be sure, papyr was not distinguished by is durability; but one should not hold a Prechaotic civilisation responsible for failing to foresee the existence of the RV catalyst, also known as the Hartian Agent. The true properties of this agent, after all, were discovered only in the Galactic Period by one Prodoctor Six Folses, who established RV's origin as the third moon of Uranus. Unwittingly brought back to Earth by an early expedition (the eighth Malaldic, according to Prognostor Phaa-Vaak), the Hartian Agent set off a chain reaction and papyr disintegrated around the globe.

The details of the cataclysm are not known. According to verbal reports crystallised only in the Fourth Galactium, the focal points of the epidemic were enormous data storage centres called li-brees. The reaction was practically instantaneous. In place of those great treasuries, those reservoirs of society's memory, lay mounds of grey, powdery ash.

The Prechaotic scientists thought they were dealing with some papyrophagous microbe, and wasted valuable time in the attempt to isolate it. One can hardly deny the justice of Histognostor Four Tauridus's bitter remark, that humanity would have been better served had that time been spent engraving the disintegrating words onto stone.

Gravitronics, cybereconomics and synthephysics were all unknown in the Late Neogene, when the catastrophe occurred. The economic systems of various ethnic groups called nashens were relatively autonomous, and wholly dependent upon the circulation of papyr, as was the flow of supplies to the Syrtic Tiberis colony on Mars.

Papyralysis ruined a great deal more than the economy. That entire period is rightly named the Era of Papyrocracy, for not only did papyr regulate and coordinate all group activities, but it determined, in some obscure way, the fate of individuals (for example, the 'identity papyrs'). The functional and ritual roles of papyr in the folklore of that time (the catastrophe took place when Prechaotic Neogene was at its height) have yet to be fully catalogued. While we do know the meaning of some expressions, others remain empty phrases (cheks, do-ments, ree-seets, etc.). In that era one could not be born, grow up, obtain an education, work, travel, marry or die except through the aid and mediation of papyr.

Only in the light of these facts can one appreciate the full extent of the disaster which struck Earth. The quarantine of whole cities and continents, the construction of hermetically sealed shelters – all such measures failed. The science of the day was helpless against the catalyst's subatomic structure, the product of a most unusual anabiotic evolution. For the first time in history society was threatened with total dissolution. To quote an inscription carved upon the wall of a urinal in the Fris-Ko excavations by an anonymous bard of the cataclysm: 'And the heavens above the cities grew dark with clouds of blighted papyr and it rained for forty days and forty nights a dirty rain, and thus with wind and streams of mud was the tale of man washed from the face of the earth forever.'

It must have been a cruel blow indeed to the pride of Late Neogene man, who saw himself already reaching the stars. The papyralysis nightmare pervaded all walks of life. Panic hit the cities; people, deprived of their identity, lost their reason; the supply of goods broke down; there were incidents of violence; technology, research and development, schools – all crumbled into nonexistence; power plants could not be repaired for lack of blueprints. The lights went out, and the ensuing darkness was illumined only by the glow of bonfires...

Desperate measures were employed. Certain branches of the   . amusement industry (such as feelms) mobilised their entire production to record incoming information on the positions of spaceships and satellites, for collisions were multiplying rapidly. Circuit diagrams were printed, from memory, on fabrics. All available plastic writing materials were distributed among the schools. Physics professors personally had to tend atomic piles. Emergency teams of

scientists flitted from one point of the globe to another. But these were merely tiny particles of order, atoms of organisation that quickly dissolved in an ocean of spreading chaos. Shaken as it was by endless upheavals, engaged in a constant struggle against the tide of superstition, illiteracy and ignorance, the stagnant culture of the Chaotic should be judged not by what it lost of the heritage of centuries, but by what it was able to salvage, against all odds...

Most of the Neogene, we fear, will forever remain shrouded in mystery, for even chronotraction methods have failed to provide the most fundamental details of the social life at that age. Any systematic presentation of those few moments of history which we have been able to recreate goes well beyond the limits of this introduction. So we will limit ourselves to a few remarks in the way of background...

The evolution of ancient beliefs underwent a curious bifurcation. In the first period, the Archeocredonic, various religions were founded upon the recognition of a supernatural, nonmaterial principle, causative with respect to everything in existence. The Archeocredonic left behind permanent monuments – the pyramids of the Early Neogene, the excavations of the Mesogene (the Gothic cathedrals of Lafranss).

In the second period, the Neocredonic, faith assumed

a different aspect. The metaphysical principle somehow merged with the materialistic, the earthly. Worship of the deity Kap-Eh-Taahl (or, in the Cremonic palimpsests, Kapp-Taah) became one of the dominant cults of the time. This deity was revered throughout Ammer-Ka and the faith quickly spread to Australindia and parts of the European Peninsula. Any connection, however, between the cult of Kap-Eh-Taahl and the graven images of the elephant and the ass found here and there throughout Ammer-Ka does seem somewhat doubtful. It was forbidden to utter the name itself, 'Kap-Eh-Taahl' (analogous to the Hebrew interdiction); in Ammer-Ka the deity was generally called 'Almighty Da'Laahr'. But there were many other liturgical names, and special monastic orders devoted themselves entirely to an appraisal of their changing status (the Mer-L-Finches for example). Indeed, the fluctuation in the accepted value of each of the many names (or were they attributes) of Kap-Eh-Taahl remains an enigma to this day. The difficulty in understanding the true nature of that last of the Prechaotic religions lies in the fact that Kap-Eh-Taahl was denied any supernatural existence, was therefore not a spirit, nor was he even considered a being (which would help explain the totemistic features of that cult, so unusual in an age of science) – he was, to all extents and purposes,

equated with assets, liquid, fixed, and hidden, and had no existence beyond that. However, it has been shown that in times of economic decline, sacrifices of sugarcane, coffee, and grain were made to placate the angry god. This contradiction is deepened by the fact that the cult of Kap-Eh-Taahl did possess some elements of the doctrine of incarnation, according to which, the world owed its continuing existence to 'sacred property'. Any violation of that doctrine met with the most severe punishment...

Up to the very end – that is, to the formation of the Earth Federation – the centre of the most fanatic devotion to Kap-Eh-Taahl was Ammer-Ka, a land governed by a series of dynasties of Prez-tendz. These were not high priests of Kap-Eh-Taahl in the strict sense of the word. It was during the Nineteenth Dynasty that the Prez-tendz (or Prexy-dents, in the nomenclature of the Thyrric School) built the Pentagon. What was it, that first of many granite leviathans, that stern edifice which ushered in the twilight of the Neogene? Prehistorians of the Aquillian School considered the Pentagon's tombs for Prez-tendz, analogous to the Egyptian pyramids. This hypothesis was discarded in the light of subsequent discoveries, as was the theory that these were shrines to Kap-Eh-Taahl, where crusades were planned against the Heathen Dog, or strategies devised to ensure his successful conversion.

We hear and apprehend only what we
already half know.
Henry David Thoreau

We sometimes get all the
information, but we refuse to get
the message.
Cullen Hightower

WE SHALL SEE BUT A
LITTLE WAY IF WE
REQUIRE TO
UNDERSTAND WHAT WE
SEE.
Henry David Thoreau

There's more to
seeing than meets
the eye.
K. T. Cole

Everyone hears only what he
understands.
Johann Wolfgang von Goethe

The eye sees only what the mind is prepared to
comprehend.
Henri Bergson

Aims

By the end of this chapter you should:

■ be able to notice, in everyday life, those times where your senses are not reliable

■ understand why perception is an active not a passive process, and the implications of this

■ be aware of the often unnoticed role that reason plays in interpreting our sensory information

■ understand and be able to discuss the basic philosophical problems with empirical knowledge

■ understand and be able to discuss the meaning of the phrase 'the mental construction of reality'.

Introduction

If we are on a search for certain knowledge, then perhaps the obvious starting point should be our senses. What could be more certain than the fact that I can see that the sea is blue today, or that a rose smells sweet and fresh? We learn in nursery school that we have five senses – sight, sound, touch, taste, and smell – and we rarely question them. Indeed, trusting our senses is so natural that we have sayings that tell us how reliable they are, such as 'I'll believe it when I see it' and 'Seeing is believing'. We even have a word for something which is ridiculous – we call it 'non-sense'.

So are our senses really the bedrock of certainty and reliability that they may appear to be? You may well have guessed that we shall suggest that the answer is 'no'. It only takes a little thought to see some of the problems. Have your senses ever let you down? Have you ever thought you saw or heard something when, in fact, you did not, or what was there was actually different to what you thought it was? There are dramatic cases where a witness in a murder trial swears that he saw the suspect enter a house, but where it is later proven beyond all doubt that the suspect was not even in the same country at the time! We probably do not need to go to these extremes to find that we cannot rely 100 per cent on our senses – our everyday experience is almost certainly full of good reasons to doubt that certainty can be found here.

A Think of occasions where your senses have led you astray. Can you explain why they did so?

There are a class of problems in this area which are rather more abstract in nature. The sea may be blue, but is it still blue on a cloudy day, or to a person who is colour blind? What about someone who has just had a bright light shining in their eyes, or someone who is wearing strange-coloured glasses? These factors have nothing to do with the sea, but they all make the sea look different. So what is the real colour of the sea? Does the answer have to be confined to what a 'normal person' sees on a bright and sunny day?

You may think these questions are foolish – after all, don't we all know what we perceive? To say that the colour of the sea depends on the observer seems strange – surely the colour of the sea is the colour of the sea, irrespective of any observer! The point is that the relationship between what we perceive and what is 'really there' is far from clear.

This is just the first of many problems. Science has demonstrated that there are plenty of examples where the information our senses give us seems to conflict with the real world. Psychology tells us that our visual perception is actually more like a series of photographs than like a film, but our brain 'joins the photos together' to present a seamless and unbroken picture to our minds. Arthur Eddington uses another example to make the point powerfully:

As a conscious being I am involved in a story. The perceiving part of my mind tells me a story of a world around me. The story tells of familiar objects. It tells of colours, sound, scents belonging to these objects; of boundless space in which they have their existence, and of an ever-rolling stream of time bringing change and incident. It tells of life other than mine busy about its own purpose.

As a scientist I have become mistrustful of this story. In many instances it has become clear that things are not what they seem to be. According to the story teller I am sitting at a substantial desk; but I have learned from physics that the desk is not at all the continuous substance that it is supposed to be in the story. It is a host of tiny electric charges darting hither and thither with inconceivable velocity. Instead of being solid substance my desk is more like a swarm of gnats.

So I have come to realise that I must not put overmuch confidence in the story teller who lives in my mind.

We can find plenty of other difficulties in literature and from everyday experience – mirages, illusions, fake sensations, imagined perceptions and so on. The plain fact of the matter is that we have plenty of reason to doubt the information of our senses, and it is our purpose here to begin to consider why this may be. Notice that we do not intend to suggest that the whole world is an illusion and we are being deceived by an evil demon (as imagined by René Descartes) or an evil computer (as imagined in the film *The Matrix*). Rather we shall assume that our senses tell us something about the world – the only question is, is what they tell us correct?

The study of our sensory, or empirical, knowledge, goes by the name of **empiricism**, and it is a broad and deep topic. The questions raised will prove to spill out into other areas and raise more general questions, and because of this, you should read this chapter in close conjunction with Chapter 9 (on paradigms). In this chapter, we will look at the more abstract issues; in the next, we will consider the more practical and immediate difficulties.

The limitations of our senses

The traditional idea of 'five senses' is a woefully inadequate way of describing our perceptions. We have several other senses, including the senses of balance, pain and temperature, and the so-called kinesthetic sense (whereby we know where our arm is without having to look at it). There is also evidence that it may be possible, through feedback, to extend this last sense to monitor internal states such as heart rate and blood pressure. Our sensory inputs are based on many variables.

For now though, we shall consider the two senses we probably rely on the most: sight and sound. Both light and sound can be represented as waves with particular frequencies (we ignore, for these purposes, the fact that light and sound are fundamentally different quantities). Broadly speaking, we see light between frequencies of $4 \times 10^{14}\,\text{Hz}$ and $9 \times 10^{14}\,\text{Hz}$, and we hear sounds between 20 Hz and 20,000 Hz. However, sound and light exist at many other frequencies.

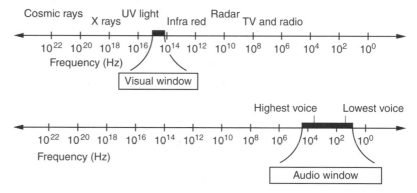

Notice that these scales are not linear – in fact, the distance between 10^{22} and 10^{16} is 99.9999 per cent of the entire scale from 0 to 10^{22}, so the audio and visual windows are actually far, far smaller than they appear in the diagrams!

A Why do you think we are able to see and hear in the regions shown on the scales?

B Some animals can hear/see other frequencies of sound/light. What do you think life must be like for them?

C How do you think this idea translates to the senses of touch, smell and taste?

D What implications does this kind of thinking have for what we know about the world?

If we are looking for 'objective' knowledge, we should remember that there are several other senses in the animal kingdom that we do not possess. Recent research shows that sharks have lateral lines which are sensitive to the electric fields around them. They can sense the electric fields of prey that are totally motionless and hidden under the sand. Given that much of the electric activity is generated by the brain, this is almost telepathy! Ants and other insects are believed to have great chemical sensitivity (combining touch, taste and smell in some unimaginable way); birds are believed to find their way home by following the Earth's magnetic field; Sargasso eels return by an unknown sense to the St Lawrence and other rivers which their ancestors knew, but which they themselves have never seen. We can only imagine what impression of the world these animals must have, but surely it is rather different to our own.

> **A** Imagine you possessed a chemical sense. You can sense in nearby people hundreds of aromas in their clothes, levels of adrenaline and other hormones in their sweat. You are, in fact, a walking forensics lab. What would the world be like for you?
>
> **B** Can you think of any other senses which animals (or aliens) might have?
>
> **C** What implications does this sort of thinking have for how we acquire knowledge through our senses?
>
> **D** What is it like to be a bat?

What is in the mind and what is in the world?

Reality is merely an illusion, albeit a very persistent one.

Albert Einstein

The psychologist Richard Cytowic has written about a man named Michael who, when he puts different things in his mouth, has the sensation of different shapes. In the following extract, Cytowic is talking to Michael at a dinner party while he is cooking and has just tasted the sauce that he has made for the chicken. Michael seems displeased:

'O dear, there aren't enough points on the chicken.'

'Aren't enough what?' I asked.

His face turned red. 'You'll think I am crazy,' he stammered. 'I hope nobody else heard,' he said, glancing at the other guests nearby.

'Why not?' I asked.

'Sometimes I just blurt these things out,' he whispered, leaning towards me. 'I know it sounds crazy, but I have this thing, see, where I taste by shape.'

'What do you mean?' I asked.

'Flavours have shapes,' he said, staring at the roasting pan. 'I wanted the shape of this chicken to be pointed, but it came out all round.' He looked up at me, blushing. 'I mean, it's nearly spherical,' he emphasised, trying to keep the volume down so the others couldn't hear him. 'I can't serve this if it doesn't have points.'

Later on, the conversation continues:

'People think I'm on drugs or making it up. That's why I keep it to myself. But it's so perfectly logical that I thought everybody felt shapes when they eat. If there aren't shapes then there's no flavour.'

I tried not to sound surprised. 'Where do you feel these shapes?' I asked.

'All over,' he replied, 'but mostly I feel things rubbed against my face or sitting in my hands.'

I kept my poker face and said nothing.

'When I taste something with an intense flavour,' Michael continued, *'the feeling sweeps down my arm into my fingertips. I feel it – its weight, its texture, whether it's warm or cold, everything. I feel it – like I'm actually grasping something.'*

Later on, Cytowic reflects:

. . . taste, touch, movement and colour meshed together seamlessly in his brain. For Michael, sensation was simultaneous, like a jumbalaya instead of neat, separate courses.

Cytowic's book also describes people who see colours when music is played. They literally see blotches of colour appear in front of their eyes when they hear music. Or does that mean that they see music?

It isn't a hoax – several people around the world have reported exactly the same thing. This sounds crazy, and one immediate reaction is to suggest that these people have some wires crossed in their brains, but this may be a premature judgement. How do you know that you are 'right' and that they are 'wrong'? All you know is that you, and everybody you know, have always seen colours when you look at things. That suggests that your brain is wired one way. Michael has his brain wired another way. We know which is more common, but which is more 'correct'?

A Suppose that you woke up tomorrow and everybody except you saw colours when music was played. Would you say that you are the only person who has got it right?

B Suppose every single human saw colours when music was played. Would we then see music?

C Why should light be associated with the experience of colour, and noise with the experience of sound?

This may seem a rather offbeat point, of interest only to psychologists, but let's develop these ideas further. Imagine taking a bucket of boiling water and placing your hand in it. Clearly, you would experience pain. But where is the pain? It seems obvious that the pain is in your mind, not the water. The energy of the water molecules is passed to your hand by contact – at this stage, there is no pain (as proven by lepers who cannot feel pain in their hands). This energy is converted to impulses in your arm – still no pain – and sent to your brain. Here we enter the realm of speculation, but let us observe one thing – that the brain needs to decode the messages from the hand before it 'realises' what is happening. After all, the impulses might say 'lovely and warm'. So there is no pain until the brain has decoded the signal. Then there is a great deal of pain!

We can conclude the following, uncontroversial (I hope), points:

■ Pain is an experience in our minds. It is the finale to a complicated process, involving sensory inputs (such as heat) being converted to electrical impulses, which are sent to the brain and decoded into messages, which we interpret as pain.

151

- If pain is in our minds, then there is no pain in the world of things and objects. The water only appears painful to me – it is not, objectively speaking, painful.

Let us now apply this model of sensory perception to the sense of sight. You have a big, bright green apple. When you look at it you see the colour. But let us ask again, where is the colour? On the basis of the hot water example, you can probably see where we are going with this. The energy of the light is passed to your eye by contact when the light enters through the lens – at this stage there is no colour (as proven by those sighted people who have suffered accidents where their optic nerves have been cut). This energy is converted to impulses in your eye – still no colour – and sent to your brain. Here we enter the realm of speculation, but let us observe one thing – that the brain needs to decode the messages from the eye before it 'realises' what is happening. After all, the impulses might say 'red'. So there is no colour until the brain has decoded the signal. Then there is plenty of colour!

We can conclude the following, rather more controversial, points:

- Colour is an experience in our minds. It is the finale to a complicated process, involving optical inputs being converted to electrical impulses, which are sent to the brain and decoded into messages, which we interpret as colour.
- If colour is in our minds, then there is no colour in the world of things and objects. The apple only appears green to me – it is not, objectively speaking, green.

These are deeply disturbing findings. Notice that this does not mean that the world is black and white. It means that there are no colours, black and white included, in the world. We immediately find that this is almost incomprehensible, but we must remember that perceiving colour, like pain, is 'just' a conversion of energy from light to electrical energy in the brain. Similarly, our sensation of smell is the result of a chemical reaction in the lining of our nose.

A common objection to this is to point out that different types of light do have different colours: red light vibrates at a particular frequency, blue light at a different frequency, etc. So light is coloured after all, and there is colour in the world. But this objection is misplaced – we can happily concede that there are different frequencies of light, just as there are different degrees of hot water (tepid, warm, hot, scalding). The different temperatures will cause mild irritation, sharp pain, or intense agony, but this doesn't alter the argument; all these sensations are in the mind, and not the water. Similarly the different frequencies of light will cause red, blue and green sensations, but let us be clear that the sensations are not the same thing as the light.

A Follow the examples of pain and colour closely to explain where sounds are to be found.

B How do you answer the objection that sound must be in the world outside us as it is carried by air molecules from the source of the sound to our ears? (Hint: look again at the colour example.)

C How far can we extend this argument? What about smell, taste, and even the sensation of touch? What are the implications for what we know about the world? How much of it is in our minds?

Notice that our **language** is a part of the problem. When we say, 'The apple is green,' the subject of the sentence is the noun 'apple', the adjective 'green' modifies the noun, and the 'is' clearly attaches the quality of greenness to the subject 'apple'. It is perhaps to be expected that our language reflects the messages from our senses. Language crystallises the deception, as it were, and reflects it back to us, reinforcing our belief that the quality 'green' does, in fact, belong to the object. Such is the 'tyranny of language'.

So the result of all this is that we have to question radically the information from our senses. How much of the 'real' world is in our minds? The philosopher Plato would have said that we see only shadows of reality, which may be very different to the real thing. We can wonder what the reality is, but to say that we are being deceived may be an overly suspicious conclusion. After all, none of our senses intend to deceive us! The truth is, of course, that our senses have evolved with us, and they allow us to make sense of the environment. Notice here the phrase 'make sense' rather than 'find sense'. We literally 'make sense' of the world – it does not come prepackaged in sensible parts. There are many possible senses, and our view of the world is at least partly constrained and limited by the particular ones we have. Using these senses, the mind manufactures experience, with our senses giving us the kind of information we need to survive. What else could we ask of them?

A There is an old riddle that asks, 'does a tree in a forest make a noise when it falls if there is nobody there to hear it?' How does this relate to the senses?

B Given what we have seen about our senses, what can we say about the objects themselves? How can we find out about the 'real apple' rather than the shiny green and almost spherical object that appears to our senses?

It is difficult to know how to proceed from here. The notion that the world has no colours, sounds, smells, tastes or sensations is a profoundly scary one, and one that seemingly casts everything into doubt. Of the eerie 'real world', Lincoln Barnett writes:

... paradoxically what the scientist and the philosopher call the world of appearance – the world of light and colour, of blue skies and green leaves, of sighing wind and murmuring water, the world designed by the physiology of the human sense organs – is the world in which we are imprisoned by our essentially limited nature. And what the scientist, and the philosopher call the world of reality – the colourless, soundless, impalpable cosmos which lies like an iceberg beneath the palace of man's perceptions – is a skeleton structure of symbols.

This ghostly 'iceberg' is, of course, nothing but a challenge to any philosopher with any spirit. But a word of warning – the next section is tough going. It's well worth it if you can follow, but not vital for our purposes if you can't.

Is there a solution? The thoughts of some philosophers

Donald E. Carr points out that the sense impressions of one-celled animals are not edited for the brain: 'This is philosophically interesting in a rather mournful way, since it means that only the simplest animals perceive the Universe as it is.'

Annie Dillard

These problems have, throughout the ages, been extensively examined by philosophers in search of a rock-solid foundation for knowledge (and I really do mean extensively). While we can't even summarise what has been said, it will be helpful to sketch a few important ideas.

A famous approach was taken by the French philosopher and mathematician René Descartes in 1641, when he determined never to make an error by trusting unreliable data, at least for philosophical purposes. He imagined the admittedly unlikely possibility that all his senses were being deceived by an 'evil genius' (in this, Descartes anticipated the 1999 movie *The Matrix* by over 350 years) and wondered how he could ever find out if this logical possibility was true. He reasoned that there would be no sensory evidence that could persuade him, as no matter what evidence he found, he wouldn't be able to trust it as it might have come from the demon. So what could he do? If he had to reject all empirical knowledge, what would be left?

Descartes' famous suggestion that we use *reason* to find the truth should sound familiar to you – we said much the same thing in an earlier chapter. In studying rationalism we were following Descartes, even if we didn't know it at the time, and we saw that reason is a powerful tool but that it needs some starting points, or premises, if it is to get anywhere. So what did Descartes use if he could assume absolutely nothing at all about the material world? Well, the details need not concern us here, but he suggested that he could not possibly doubt that he was doubting – because to do so would be to doubt anyway! And if he doubted, he was thinking. And if he was thinking, he existed. And so he arrived at *cogito ergo sum* – I think therefore I exist. We have to admire Descartes' thoroughness in his willingness to doubt everything!

Having proved to his own satisfaction that he existed (an often neglected first step in many arguments), he went on to demonstrate, again to his own satisfaction, the existence of God. We will consider his proof elsewhere, but for now we merely note that God is a benevolent being, and decent enough to prevent us always being deceived by our senses. So finally, we can be sure that the real world is not always deceiving us, because God ensures it.

For many today, Descartes' explanation is unsatisfactory. Even if we believe in God, we are probably reluctant to invoke him to explain the world in this way. In 1689, the English philosopher John Locke proposed another solution to the problem of colours (and the rest of sensory data) existing in the mind rather than the 'real' world. His solution is completely opposed to Descartes – he suggests that all our ideas come from experience, not reason; that a new-born baby is, in another famous phrase, a *tabula rasa*, or blank slate, on which all ideas and concepts are subsequently written.

Still, the problem remains – what parts of the world are in our minds and what parts are outside? Locke's answer is that objects possess 'qualities' which give rise to ideas of colour, smell, hardness, etc. Some of these qualities – 'primary qualities' – really do exist in the bodies themselves (for example, length and hardness) while 'secondary qualities' produce ideas which are only in the mind and not in the bodies themselves (for example, colour and taste). So when we look at our apple, the colour may be in our minds, but that's okay because we can be sure that the 'real' apple (that is, the atoms of the apple) are 'out there'. In this scheme, the 'truth' will be the facts about the primary qualities, and those are reachable through mathematical physics.

A Which of the two theories do you find more appealing – Descartes' or Locke's?

B Can you prove that either you or God exists without appealing to any sensory evidence whatsoever, like Descartes thought? Even if you can, what can you deduce from these facts?

C What are the problems with Locke's method? Does it explain how some of our senses seem to tell us about things which only exist in our minds (for example, colours, sounds)? What do you think of his distinction between primary and secondary qualities?

The primary and secondary distinction is rather dubious and soon came under attack, notably from Bishop George Berkeley. Essentially, Berkeley says, 'Okay granted, colours and sounds and tastes are only in the mind. But exactly the same argument can be applied to anything – even your so-called primary qualities. How do you know that they are there at all?' He points out that the way we know the 'primary quality' of length is by noting differences in secondary qualities (for example, the brown colour of the table against the white colour of the wall, or the difference between the feel of the table and the feel of the air) and argues that the notion of a primary/secondary distinction is nonsense – everything is secondary and thus everything is in the mind! If everything is in the mind, there cannot be anything which is not in someone's mind, and so if people do not have something in mind then it does not exist! This is the reasoning behind the infamous *esse est percipi* – to be is to be perceived – which is a far more subtle argument than is sometimes acknowledged.

That is not to say that we would necessarily want to accept this argument! Even Berkeley himself would not have said that our apple vanishes when we stop looking at it, only to appear again miraculously just as we opened our eyes. But he seems to have committed himself to this unless, like Descartes, he is prepared to trust God to watch everything for us! That means that God is perceiving everything, so everything stays in existence! Ronald Knox has expressed the idea entertainingly:

There was a young man who said 'God
Must think it exceedingly odd,
If he finds that this tree
Continues to be
When there's no one around in the Quad.'

Dear Sir:
Your astonishment's odd.
I am always about in the Quad.
And that's why the tree
Will continue to be
Since observed by
>*Yours faithfully*
>>*God.*

A Explain how Berkeley's ideas follow naturally from Locke's. Consider their consequences for what we know.

B Read 'Ghosts' in the Resource file for Chapter 1 (pages 12–13). How do the ideas in this article relate to this chapter?

C Dr Johnson, a contemporary of Berkeley, thought that Berkeley's **idealism** (that is, the theory that the 'real' world is linked to mental states) was ridiculous, saying 'I refute it thus' and kicking a stone. This might be our first reaction, too – the existence of stones does refute idealism, doesn't it? Or does it? Do you suppose that Berkeley was unaware of the existence of stones? What would he say to the objection?

You might think that Berkeley's scepticism is about as far as you can go, but you would be wrong. The Scottish philosopher David Hume took the ideas even further, with devastating critiques of concepts as basic as causality and self, but for these, you will have to go to the philosophy books (see further reading on page 162)!

To follow this tale of intellectual intrigue a little further, we turn to the great German philosopher Kant. Writing well before the scientific discoveries which would verify some of his ideas, he suggested that there are some things which we can know without any experience at all (we call these things 'a priori' meaning known 'from before' experience). These are things like the categories of time and space. Kant then suggests that a new-born infant uses these and other categories (colour, substance, mind, etc.) to put all its sensations into some sort of order. But these categories are, to some extent, arbitrary. So we come back to the idea that we impose our thinking on the world, rather than the reverse. As for the question that started this all off – 'what can we learn about the real world through our senses?' – Kant said that we can know precisely nothing. You might feel that this is an unsatisfactory answer to 100 years of effort!

In retrospect, the extremes of rationalism and empiricism seem a little strange. We have two marvellous tools for finding out about the world – our minds and our senses. We would be foolish to handicap ourselves by pretending that one tool is useless, as both empiricists and rationalists did. What we need is a coherent method for combining both strands of knowing, so that the weaknesses of each tool will be compensated for by the strengths of the other. Maybe we cannot get to the 'skeleton structure of symbols', but is that such a disappointment?

> **A** Consider the fields of knowledge you are studying. Identify issues or areas where rational or empirical ways of knowing occur. To what extent is it possible to have purely rational or purely empirical knowledge?
>
> **B** In light of these philosophers, to what extent do you think reality is only in the mind?

The mental construction of reality

Let us leave the search for ultimate reality, and ask some more everyday questions. If we have seen that we make sense of the sensory data we receive, then perhaps we should ask precisely how we do that, and attempt to explain the nature of interpretation. In this section therefore we will examine the claim that we make sense of the world in a little more detail, with the emphasis on our visual senses. It is perhaps easy to think that there is only one way to interpret light arriving in our eyes – after all, we all see the same things don't we? The aim of this section is to show you that what you see is affected by a large number of factors, and the light arriving in your eyes is only one of them.

It is comforting to see that we can follow up the difficult ideas of the last section with some simple and familiar examples, which sometimes go by the name of optical illusions. When philosophical theories can be tested, or at least explored via simple examples, it is a great help! Do not dismiss the simple examples as simplistic.

In the figure on the left, you will probably find grey dots appearing at whatever intersections you don't watch. It can be an amusing task to chase them around – they always seem to be one step ahead. So where are the grey dots? You don't need to be Berkeley or Hume to realise that they aren't on the paper!

This isn't the only case where the brain invents things which aren't there. Consider these three cases of non-existent shapes:

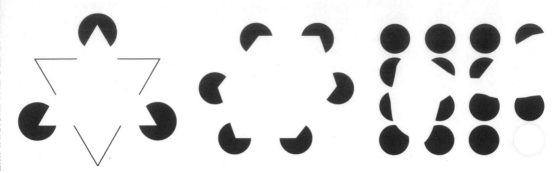

So what is happening here? Taking a few liberties with detail and blurring a few distinctions, we might say that your brain is taking the sense data from your eyes and trying to see what is the best story it can tell your mind. In the cases above, the best story, given the exact alignment of certain edge-pieces, is that there is an object. So you do not see what is 'really there'; you see what your perceptual system thinks *should* be there! In this case, they are different things.

There are plenty of illusions which clearly demonstrate that your brain is very, very ingenious in finding ways to interpret evidence. What do you think is happening here?

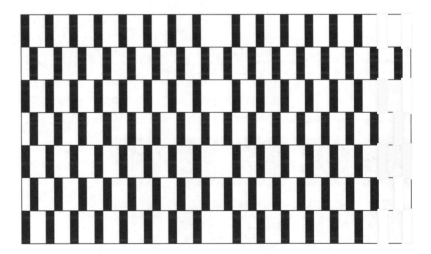

The horizontal lines seem curved, though they are in fact straight, and we might speculate that we can account for this by assuming that the picture is three-dimensional. Your brain has assumed that the vertical lines are continuous (not a bad assumption – where do you get lines as closely and regularly aligned like this in nature, except when they are in fact related to each other?), and they are offset because some are closer to you than others. That is, some rows have been pulled out of the plane of the paper, and the middle of each strip has been stretched a little to arch the strip towards you. Now once the brain has that decided, it knows that the vertical lines at the edge of each strip are further away, and so if they look same size as those in the middle, they must be bigger (just as an elephant in the distance may actually look the same size as a dog which is close up). And if they are bigger the horizontal strips must be getting narrower in the middle, and if that is the case then the horizontal lines must be curved.

This explanation is speculative; but something like this must happen to explain why the straight lines seem bent. The brain is constantly doing a detective's job; what is surprising is not that we can catch it out every now and then, but that it happens so rarely!

You should be able to find a 3D explanation for the following striking image, which makes the paper seem creased. Certainly any artist will immediately see the technique.

The tricks certainly don't all rely on the third dimension for their power. Are these balls stacked vertically?

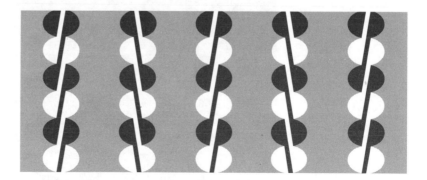

A very ingenious set of images has been created by the Japanese psychologist Akiyosho Kitaoka. They play cleverly on complex cognitive devices, creating powerful illusions. To explain the next two visuals fully, I imagine you will need to know a fair bit of psychology!

Of course, the brain is not foolproof. If you give it too many options, it may get a little confused. Try staring at the last two images for a minute or two, in the same way as you look at a 'magic-eye' picture. Things start to get a little strange, and you get to observe a process that is normally well hidden – that of the brain trying to weigh the options, figure out the best interpretation, and tell the most convincing story.

The following example is especially good. As you look at it, you must remember to ask, what is the real pattern?

A In the example above you should flip between 'diamonds' and 'rectilinear' patterns. Where is the pattern – is it secondary or primary?

B Imagine you are in a noisy room with lots of people talking, including you. You can't hear the other conversations, but suddenly you hear your name mentioned across the room. This seems very strange . . . you couldn't hear the conversation, but you heard your name. Explain.

C In each eye there is a blind spot. The blind spot is a small area near the centre of the visual field where the optic nerve leaves the eye to go to the brain. There are no light receptors in this area (hence the name blind spot), so why don't we see small dark spots there?

D Professional tea tasters can distinguish between literally thousands of brands of tea. Wine tasters can tell you the grape, year, country, region, vineyard and even which side of the valley a particular bottle of wine has come from. But these professionals have no more taste buds than you or I do. They have no more nerves in the tongue, and those that they do have are not any more sensitive than the norm. How can this be?

E Like most people, you probably have an excellent sense of balance. This sense comes from the tubes in your ear, where fluid in certain canals causes small hairs to lean one way or another. You have absolutely no experience or awareness of these small hairs, but you are very conscious of the angle of your head. What's going on here, and how does it relate to perception in general?

Back to sight for the final examples! These are very famous examples because it is so difficult to see both aspects of the pictures. Many people can only see what is there when they have been told. Once they can see 'the other' picture, they can no longer see the first! So is seeing believing or is believing seeing?

Where do we go from here?

We were initially attracted to the idea of sense perception because it seemed to be an issue which appeared again and again. Indeed, it has proved to be important, but perhaps in unexpected ways. Rather than finding a bedrock of certainty on which to build, we have actually been forced to question things that seemed intuitively absolutely certain, such as the existence of the material world! We seem to be forced to accept that much of what we thought went on in the world seems to be going on in our heads and that what we know is as much about how we interpret the world as it is about the world itself. This seems to suggest that paradigms, the basis of our interpretation, should be the next topic in our quest for truth.

Further reading

The phenomenon whereby senses get 'mixed up' (technically, 'synesthesia') and its implications are described in detail in Richard Cytowic's *The Man who Tasted Shapes* (Abacus, 1993). An overview of the philosophical ideas may be found in any introduction to philosophy; I recommend chapter 3 of Donald Palmer's *Does the Centre Hold?* (Mayfield, 1991) or chapter 3 of John Hosper's *An Introduction to Philosophical Analysis* (Prentice Hall, 1953).

For a defence that the world really is there (do you need one?), chapter 1 of Martin Gardner's *The Whys of a Philosophical Scrivener* (Oxford University Press, 1983) is delightful. A more controversial (maybe extreme, but still important and interesting, if rather difficult) defence of empiricism may be found in A. J. Ayer's *Language, Truth and Logic* (Dover Books, 1946). *Empiricists [Abridged] Locke, Berkeley and Hume* (Anchor Books/Doubleday, 1961) is a good primary source.

As far as the practical problems go, a powerful book based on a legal perspective is psychologist Elizabeth Loftus' *Eyewitness Testimony* (Harvard University Press, 1979).

Bats: sight and sound

An extract from
The Blind Watchmaker by
Richard Dawkins.

These bats are like miniature spy planes, bristling with sophisticated instrumentation. Their brains are delicately tuned packages of miniaturised electronic wizardry, programmed with the elaborate software necessary to decode a world of echoes in real time. Their faces are often distorted into gargoyle shapes that appear hideous to us until we see them for what they are, exquisitely fashioned instruments for beaming ultrasound in desired directions.

Although we can't hear the ultrasound pulses of these bats directly, we can get some idea of what is going on by means of a translating machine or 'bat-detector'. This receives the pulses through a special ultrasonic microphone, and turns each pulse into an audible click or tone which we can hear through headphones. If we take such a 'bat-detector' out to a clearing where a bat is feeding, we shall hear when each bat pulse is emitted, although we cannot hear what the pulses really 'sound' like. If our bat is *Myotis*, one of the common little brown bats, we shall hear a chuntering of clicks at a rate of about 10 per second as the bat cruises about on a routine mission. This is about the rate of a standard teleprinter, or a Bren machine gun.

Presumably the bat's image of the world in which it is cruising is being updated 10 times per second. Our own visual image appears to be continuously updated as long as our eyes are open. We can see what it might be like to have an intermittently updated world image, by using a stroboscope at night. This is sometimes done at discotheques, and it produces some dramatic effects. A dancing person appears as a succession of frozen statuesque attitudes. Obviously, the faster we set the strobe, the more the image corresponds to normal 'continuous' vision. Stroboscopic vision 'sampling' at the bat's cruising rate of about 10 samples per second would be nearly as good as normal 'continuous' vision for some ordinary purposes, though not for catching a ball or an insect.

This is just the sampling rate of a bat on a routine cruising flight. When a little brown bat detects an insect and starts to move in on an interception course, its click rate goes up. Faster than a machine gun, it can reach peak rates of 200 pulses per second as the bat finally closes in on the moving target. To mimic this, we should have to speed up our stroboscope so that its flashes came twice as fast as the cycles of mains electricity, which are not noticed in a fluorescent strip light. Obviously, we have no trouble in performing all our normal visual functions, even playing squash or ping-pong, in a visual world 'pulsed' at such a high frequency. If we may imagine bat brains as building up an image of the world analogous to our visual images, the pulse rate alone seems to suggest that the bat's echo image might be at least as detailed and 'continuous' as our visual image. Of course, there may be other reasons why it is not so detailed as our visual image.

Indeed, if I were forced to try the impossible, to imagine what it is like to be a bat, I would guess that echo-location for them might be rather like seeing for us. We are such thoroughly visual animals that we hardly realise what a complicated business seeing is. Objects are out there, and we think that we 'see' them out there. But I suspect that really our percept is an elaborate computer model in the brain, constructed on the basis of information coming from out there, but transformed in the head into a form in which that information can be used. Wavelength differences in the light out there become coded as 'colour' differences in the computer model in the head. Shape and other attributes are encoded in the same kind of way, encoded into a form that is convenient to handle. The sensation of seeing is, for us, very different from the sensation of hearing, but this cannot be directly due to the physical differences between light and sound. Both light and sound are, after all, translated by the ☞

respective sense organs into the same kind of nerve impulses. It is impossible to tell, from the physical attributes of a nerve impulse, whether it is conveying information about light, about sound or about smell. The reason the sensation of seeing is so different from the sensation of hearing or the sensation of smelling is that the brain finds it convenient to use different kinds of internal model for representing the visual world, the world of sound and the world of smell. It is because we internally use our visual information and our sound information in different ways and for different purposes that the sensations of seeing and hearing are so different. It is not directly because of the physical differences between light and sound.

But a bat uses its sound information for very much the same kind of purpose as we use our visual information. It uses sound to perceive, and continuously update its perception of the position of objects in three-dimensional space, just as we use light. The type of internal computer model that it needs, therefore, is one suitable for the internal representation of the changing positions of objects in three-dimensional space. My point is that the form that an animal's subjective experience takes will be a property of the internal computer model. That model will be designed, in evolution, for its suitability for useful internal representation, irrespective of the physical stimuli that come to it from outside. Bats and humans need the same kind of internal model for representing the position of objects in three-dimensional space. The fact that bats construct their internal model with the aid of echoes, while we construct ours with the aid of light, is irrelevant. That outside information is, in any case, translated into the same kind of nerve impulses on its way to the brain.

My conjecture, therefore, is that bats 'see' in much the same way as we do, even though the physical medium by which the world 'out there' is translated into nerve impulses is so different – ultrasound rather than light. Bats may even use the sensations that we call colour for their own purposes, to represent differences in the world out there that have nothing to do with the physics of wavelength, but which play a functional role for the bat, similar to the role that colours play to us. Perhaps male bats have body surfaces that are subtly textured so that the echoes that bounce off them are perceived by females as gorgeously coloured, the sound equivalent of the nuptial plumage of a bird of paradise. I don't mean this just as some vague metaphor. It is possible that the subjective sensation experienced by a female bat when she perceives a male really is, say, bright red: the same sensation as I experience when I see a flamingo or, at least, the bat's sensation of her mate may be no more different from my visual sensation of a flamingo, than my visual sensation of a flamingo is different from a flamingo's visual sensation of a flamingo.

I can imagine some other world in which a conference of learned, and totally blind, bat-like creatures is flabbergasted to be told of animals called humans that are actually capable of using the newly discovered inaudible rays called 'light', still the subject of top-secret military development, for finding their way about. These otherwise humble humans are almost totally deaf (well, they can hear after a fashion and even utter a few ponderously slow, deep drawling growls, but they only use these sounds for rudimentary purposes like communicating with each other; they don't seem capable of using them to detect even the most massive objects). They have, instead, highly specialised organs called 'eyes' for exploiting 'light' rays. The sun is the main source of light rays, and humans, remarkably, manage to exploit the complex echoes that bounce off objects when light rays from the sun hit them. They have an ingenious device called a 'lens', whose shape appears to be mathematically calculated so that it bends these silent rays in such a way that there is an exact one-to-one mapping between objects in the world and an 'image' on a sheet of cells called the 'retina'. These retinal cells are capable, in some mysterious way, of rendering the light 'audible' (one might say), and they relay their information to the brain. Bat mathematicians have shown that it is theoretically possible, by doing highly complex calculations, to navigate safely through the world using these light rays, just as effectively as bats can in the ordinary way using ultrasound – in some respects even more effectively! But who would have thought that humble humans could do these calculations?

How do we know anything?

An extract from *What Does It All Mean?* by Thomas Nagel.

If you think about it, the inside of your own mind is the only thing you can be sure of.

Whatever you believe – whether it's about the sun, moon, and stars, the house and neighbourhood in which you live, history, science, other people, even the existence of your own body – is based on your experiences and thoughts, feelings and sense impressions. That's all you have to go on directly, whether you see the book in your hands, or feel the floor under your feet, or remember that George Washington was the first president of the United States, or that water is H_2O. Everything else is farther away from you than your inner experiences and thoughts, and reaches you only through them.

Ordinarily you have no doubts about the existence of the floor under your feet, or the tree outside the window, or your own teeth. In fact most of the time you don't even think about the mental states that make you aware of those things: you seem to be aware of them directly. But how do you know they really exist?

If you try to argue that there must be an external physical world, because you wouldn't see buildings, people or stars unless there were things out there that reflected or shed light into your eyes and caused your visual experiences, the reply is obvious: How do you know *that*? It's just another claim about the external world and your relation to it, and has to be based on the evidence of your senses. *But you can rely on that specific evidence about how visual experiences are caused only if you can already rely in general on the contents of your mind to tell you about the external world. And that is exactly what has been called into question.* If you try to prove the reliability of your impressions by appealing to your impressions, you're arguing in a circle and won't get anywhere.

Would things seem any different to you if in fact all these things existed only in your mind – if everything you took to be the real world outside was just a giant dream or hallucination, from which you will never wake up? If it were like that, then of course you couldn't wake up, as you can from a dream, because it would mean there was no 'real' world to wake up into. So it wouldn't be exactly like a normal dream or hallucination. As we usually think of dreams, they go on in the minds of people who are actually lying in a real bed in a real house, even if in the dream they are running away from a homicidal lawn mower through the streets of Kansas City. We also assume that normal dreams depend on what is happening in the dreamer's brain while he sleeps.

But couldn't all your experiences be like a giant dream with no external world outside it? How can you know that isn't what's going on? If all your experience were a dream with nothing outside, then any evidence you tried to use to prove to yourself that there was an outside world would just be part of the dream. If you knocked on the table or pinched yourself, you would hear the knock and feel the pinch, but that would be just one more thing going on inside your mind like everything else. It's no use: if you want to find out whether what's inside your mind is any guide to what's outside your mind, you can't depend on how things seem – from inside your mind – to give you the answer.

But what else is there to depend on? All your evidence about anything has to come through your mind – whether in the form of perception, the testimony of books and other people, or memory – and it is entirely consistent with everything you're aware of that nothing at all exists except the inside of your mind.

It's even possible that you don't have a body or a brain – since your beliefs about that come only through the evidence of your senses. You've never seen your brain – you just assume that everybody has one – but even if you had seen it, or thought you had, that would have been just another visual experience. Maybe you, the subject of experience, are the only thing that exists, and there is no physical world at all – no stars, no earth, no human bodies. Maybe there isn't even any space.

The most radical conclusion to draw from this would be that your mind is the only thing that exists. This view is called solipsism. It is a very lonely view, and not too many people have held it. As you can tell from that remark, ☞

I don't hold it myself. If I were a solipsist I probably wouldn't be writing this book, since I wouldn't believe there was anybody else to read it. On the other hand, perhaps I would write it to make my inner life more interesting, by including the impression of the appearance of the book in print, of other people reading it and telling me their reactions, and so forth. I might even get the impression of royalties, if I'm lucky.

Perhaps you are a solipsist: in that case you will regard this book as a product of your own mind, coming into existence in your experience as you read it. Obviously nothing I can say can prove to you that I really exist, or that the book as a physical object exists.

On the other hand, to conclude that you are the only thing that exists is more than the evidence warrants. You can't know on the basis of what's in your mind that there's no world outside it. Perhaps the right conclusion is the more modest one that you don't know anything beyond your impressions and experiences. There may or may not be an external world, and if there is it may or may not be completely different from how it seems to you – there's no way for you to tell. This view is called scepticism about the external world.

An even stronger form of scepticism is possible. Similar arguments seem to show that you don't know anything even about your own past existence and experiences, since all you have to go on are the present contents of your mind, including memory impressions. If you can't be sure that the world outside your mind exists now, how can you be sure that you yourself existed before now? How do you know you didn't just come into existence a few minutes ago, complete with all your present memories? The only evidence that you couldn't have come into existence a few minutes ago depends on beliefs about how people and their memories are produced, which rely in turn on beliefs about what has happened in the past. But to rely on those beliefs to prove that you existed in the past would again be to argue in a circle. You would be assuming the reality of the past to prove the reality of the past.

It seems that you are stuck with nothing you can be sure of except the contents of your own mind at the present moment. And it seems that anything you try to do to argue your way out of this predicament will fail, because the argument will have to assume what you are

trying to prove – the existence of the external world beyond your mind.

Suppose, for instance, you argue that there must be an external world, because it is incredible that you should be having all these experiences without there being some explanation in terms of external causes. The sceptic can make two replies. First, even if there are external causes, how can you tell from the contents of your experience what those causes are like? You've never observed any of them directly. Second, what is the basis of your idea that everything has to have an explanation? It's true that in your normal, non-philosophical conception of the world, processes like those which go on in your mind are caused, at least in part, by other things outside them. But you can't assume that this is true if what you're trying to figure out is how you know anything about the world outside your mind. And there is no way to prove such a principle just by looking at what's inside your mind. However plausible the principle may seem to you, what reason do you have to believe that it applies to the world?

Science won't help us with this problem either, though it might seem to. In ordinary scientific thinking, we rely on general principles of explanation to pass from the way the world first seems to us to a different conception of what it is really like. We try to explain the appearances in terms of a theory that describes the reality behind them, a reality that we can't observe directly. That is how physics and chemistry conclude that all the things we see around us are composed of invisibly small atoms. Could we argue that the general belief in the external world has the same kind of scientific backing as the belief in atoms?

The sceptic's answer is that the process of scientific reasoning raises the same sceptical problem we have been considering all along: science is just as vulnerable as perception. How can we know that the world outside our minds corresponds to our ideas of what would be a good theoretical explanation of our observations? If we can't establish the reliability of our sense experiences in relation to the external world, there's no reason to think we can rely on our scientific theories either.

There is another very different response to the problem. Some would argue that radical scepticism of the kind I have been talking about is meaningless, because the idea of an external reality that no one could ever discover is meaningless. The argument is that a dream, for instance, has to be something from which you can wake up to discover that you have been asleep; a hallucination has to be something which others (or you later) can see is not really there. Impressions and appearances that do not correspond to reality must be contrasted with others that do correspond to reality, or else the contrast between appearance and reality is meaningless.

According to this view, the idea of a dream from which you can never wake up is not the idea of a dream at all: it is the idea of reality – the real world in which you live. Our idea of the things that exist is just our idea of what we can observe. (This view is sometimes called verificationism.) Sometimes our observations are mistaken, but that means they can be corrected by other observations – as when you wake up from a dream or discover that what you thought was a snake was just a shadow on the grass. But without some possibility of a correct view of how things are (either yours or someone else's), the thought that your impressions of the world are not true is meaningless.

If this is right, then the sceptic is kidding himself if he thinks he can imagine that the only thing that exists is his own mind. He is kidding himself, because it couldn't be true that the physical world doesn't really exist, unless somebody could observe that it doesn't exist. And what the sceptic is trying to imagine is precisely that there is no one to observe that or anything else – except of course the sceptic himself, and all he can observe is the inside of his own mind. So solipsism is meaningless. It tries to subtract the external world from the totality of my impressions; but it fails, because if the external world is subtracted, they stop being mere impressions, and become instead perceptions of reality.

Is this argument against solipsism and scepticism any good? Not unless reality can be defined as what we can observe. But are we really unable to understand the idea of a real world, or a fact about reality, that can't be observed by anyone, human or otherwise?

The sceptic will claim that if there is an external world, the things in it are observable because they exist, and not the other way around: that existence isn't the same thing as observability. And although we get the idea of

dreams and hallucinations from cases where we think we can observe the contrast between our experiences and reality, it certainly seems as if the same idea can be extended to cases where the reality is not observable.

If that is right, it seems to follow that it is not meaningless to think that the world might consist of nothing but the inside of your mind, though neither you nor anyone else could find out that this was true. And if this is not meaningless, but is a possibility you must consider, there seems no way to prove that it is false, without arguing in a circle. So there may be no way out of the cage of your own mind. This is sometimes called the egocentric predicament.

And yet, after all this has been said, I have to admit it is practically impossible to believe seriously that all the things in the world around you might not really exist. Our acceptance of the external world is instinctive and powerful: we cannot just get rid of it by philosophical arguments. Not only do we go on acting as if other people and things exist: we believe that they do, even after we've gone through the arguments which appear to show we have no grounds for this belief. (We may have grounds, within the overall system of our beliefs about the world, for more particular beliefs about the existence of particular things: like a mouse in the breadbox, for example. But that is different. It assumes the existence of the external world.)

If a belief in the world outside our minds comes so naturally to us, perhaps we don't need grounds for it. We can just let it be and hope that we're right. And that in fact is what most people do after giving up the attempt to prove it: even if they can't give reasons against scepticism, they can't live with it either. But this means that we hold on to most of our ordinary beliefs about the world in face of the fact that (a) they might be completely false, and (b) we have no basis for ruling out that possibility.

We are left then with three questions:

- Is it a meaningful possibility that the inside of your mind is the only thing that exists – or that even if there is a world outside your mind, it is totally unlike what you believe it to be?
- If these things are possible, do you have any way of proving to yourself that they are not actually true?
- If you can't prove that anything exists outside your own mind, is it all right to go on believing in the external world anyway?

The test of a first-rate intelligence is the ability to hold two opposed ideas in the mind at the same time, and still retain the ability to function.
F. Scott Fitzgerald

NEVER SOLVE A PROBLEM FROM ITS ORIGINAL PERSPECTIVE.
Charles Thompson

Man's mind, once stretched by a new idea, never regains its original dimensions.
Oliver Wendell Holmes

In seeking truth you have to get both sides of a story.
Walter Cronkite

I am quite sure now that often, very often, in matters concerning religion and politics a man's reasoning powers are not above the monkey's.
Mark Twain

If everybody is thinking alike, then somebody isn't thinking.
General George S. Patton, Jr

Discovery consists of seeing what everybody has seen and thinking what nobody has thought.
Albert von Szent-Gyorgy

MAN THE BATTLE STATIONS! SOMEONE'S COMING WHO WANTS TO REASON WITH US.
Ashleigh Brilliant

Sometimes I think we're alone. Sometimes I think we're not. In either case, the thought is staggering.
Buckminster Fuller

Great spirits have always found violent opposition from mediocrities. The latter cannot understand it when a man does not thoughtlessly submit to hereditary prejudices but honestly and courageously uses his intelligence.
Albert Einstein

In science it often happens that scientists say, 'You know that's a really good argument; my position is mistaken', and then they would actually change their minds and you never hear that old view from them again. They really do it. It doesn't happen as often as it should, because scientists are human and change is sometimes painful. But it happens every day. I cannot recall the last time something like that happened in politics or religion.
Carl Sagan

Aims

By the end of this chapter you should:

- understand the meaning of the term 'paradigm' and recognise how paradigms shape our reason and our perception
- understand why paradigms naturally and inevitably affect both rational and empirical approaches to knowledge
- appreciate the strengths and weaknesses of holding a paradigm
- be able to give and discuss examples of paradigms at several levels (the 'grand' paradigms and the 'everyday' paradigms)
- appreciate the role of culture as an important paradigm
- reflect on the nature of your own culture and its conventions.

Introduction

The notion of a paradigm is in one sense quite trivial – paradigms mean that different people interpret things in different ways. But in another sense, the notion is profound because we often forget that we are operating under our own paradigms and we think that we have some special channel to 'the truth'. In the sense that we shall use the term here, a paradigm is a mental construction by which we organise our reasoning and classify our knowledge. People holding different paradigms may see exactly the same scene, but interpret it completely differently.

A In each of the following cases, identify the differing paradigms held by each of the two people and think of a third paradigm.

- Two people look at a vast, beautiful mountain. One sees evidence of a good God; the other sees a geological formation.
- Two people visit an extremely harsh prison, where facilities are minimal, prisoners do manual labour for eight hours a day in silence, and life is very unpleasant. One says that it seems barbaric; the other that it is an excellent prison.
- Lights are present in the sky. One person sees UFOs; the other sees a freak weather phenomenon.
- A Brazilian minister and a tribal Indian survey the felling of Amazonian trees. The minister watches with pride whilst the tribal Indian views the scene with dismay.
- Two people are in downtown New York during rush hour. One feels an exciting 'buzz' from the city; the other merely feels depressed.

Case study: paradigms of the riverboat pilot

The steam boat was once a common form of transport in America. These huge boats would sail the great rivers, but the sailing was not as safe as it is today. Unmanaged and unmonitored, the rivers were dangerous places. There were no signs or warnings, and a shallow fallen tree or a sharp rock could spell grave danger to an unwary pilot, whose job it was to learn to 'read' the river and navigate the dangers.

In *Life on the Mississippi*, Mark Twain recounts a scene where the novice riverboat pilot and his friend (who had not been trained in the same way) were watching the sunset. The friend found it beautiful, but the pilot was able to see something else.

The face of the water, in time, became a wonderful book – a book that was a dead language to the uneducated passenger, but which told its mind to me without reserve, delivering its most cherished secrets as clearly as if it uttered them with a voice. In truth, the passenger who could not read this book saw nothing but all manner of pretty pictures in it, painted by the sun and shaded by the clouds, whereas to the trained eye these were not pictures at all, but the grimmest and most dead-earnest of reading matter.

Now when I had mastered the language of this water and had come to know every trifling feature that bordered the great river as familiarly as I knew the letters of the alphabet, I had made a valuable acquisition. But I had lost something too. I had lost that which could never be restored to me while I lived. All the grace, the beauty, the poetry had gone out of the majestic river. I still kept in mind a certain wonderful sunset which I witnessed when steam-boating was new to me. A broad expanse of the river was turned to blood; in the middle distance the red hue brightened into gold, through which a solitary log came flowing, black and conspicuous; in one place a long slanting mark lay sparkling on the water; in another the surface was broken by boiling rings, that were as many tinted as an opal; where the ruddy flush was faintest, was a smooth spot that was covered with graceful circles and radiating lines, ever so delicately traced; the shore on our left was densely wooded and the sombre shadow that fell from this forest was broken in one place by a long ruffled trail that shone like silver; and high above the forest wall a clean-stemmed dead tree waved a single leafy bough that glowed like a flame in the unobstructed splendour that was flowing from the sun. There were graceful curves, reflected images, woody heights, soft distances; and over the whole scene, far and near, the dissolving lights drifted steadily, enriching it, every passing moment with some new marvel of colouring.

I stood like one bewitched. I drank it in, in a speechless rapture. But as I have said, there came a day when . . . if that sunset scene had been repeated, I should have looked upon it without rapture, and should have commented inwardly, after this fashion: The sun means that we are going to have wind tomorrow; that floating log means that the river is rising; that slanting mark on the river reflects a bluff reef which is going to kill somebody's steamboat one of these nights if it keeps on stretching out like that; those tumbling 'boils' show a dissolving bar and a changing channel there; that tall dead tree, with a single living branch is not going to last long, and then how is a body ever going to get through this blind place at night without the friendly old landmark?

No, the romance and the beauty were all gone from the river. Since those days I have pitied doctors from my heart. What does the lovely flush in a beauty's cheek mean but a 'break' that ripples above some deadly disease? Does he ever see her beauty at all, or doesn't he simply comment on her unwholesome condition all to himself? And doesn't he sometimes wonder whether he has gained most or lost most by learning his trade?

Twain suggests that he and his friends see different things when they look at the river. This says far more about the watchers than it says about the thing being watched, and it shows how paradigms affect our perception. But the impact of paradigms goes much further than perception – they impact on our reasoning, too. Paradigms are important because they play a central role in both our ways of acquiring knowledge.

A In what sense are the two friends seeing the same thing? In what sense are they seeing different things?

B Twain suggests that there are two ways of perceiving the river. How would you characterise the two paradigms? Are there any others?

C Might someone be able to see the river in both ways? What about the example of doctors – are they unable to see beauty in patients?

D Which of the two paradigms leads to a more realistic understanding of the river?

E Has the riverboat pilot 'gained most' or 'lost most' by mastering the language of the river?

How do paradigms affect how we think?

Recall the section on 'The importance of premises' in Chapter 5 (page 80). You were asked about logical deductions based on a story. To refresh your memory, here is one of the stories again:

The old man had just turned off the lights in the store and was preparing to lock up and go home when a youth appeared and demanded money. The owner opened the cash register, the contents were grabbed, and the man ran away. The police were informed immediately.

In one of the questions you were asked if it is possible to say if the following statement is true, false or cannot be decided: 'The cash register contained money, but we are not told *how much* money.' Most people say that the statement is true. In fact it is undecided, and after a little reflection that is quite obvious. Let us examine why most people make an error in answering this question.

On a simple model of deduction, we start with our premises and we try to build a logically valid tower of truth from them. Socrates' famous syllogism shows us the model, as you have seen.

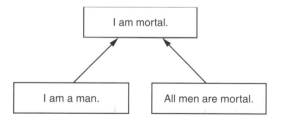

If our premises are true, the correct application of the rules of logic guarantee the truth of the conclusion. This much we know. So let us apply this model to the above story where so many people come unstuck. Why is it that most people initially say that the statement is correct, but when they are told that they are wrong, are quickly able to see that this is not a logically valid derivation?

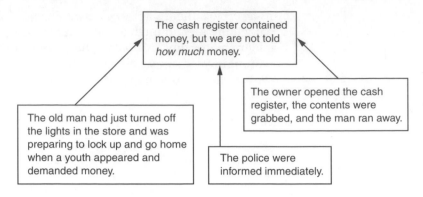

We have already seen that we are likely to assume things that strictly speaking we have should not have assumed. In particular, we probably assumed that this is a simple robbery involving two people, that the robber was male and that cash was stolen. If we show these on the diagram, then the deduction is a good deal more plausible.

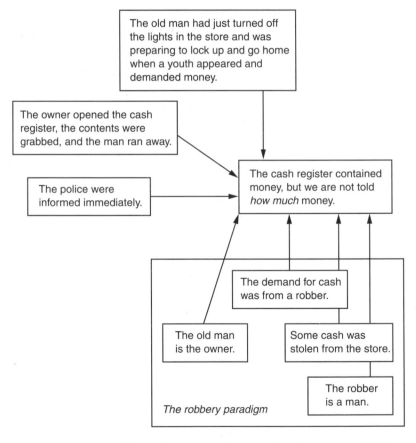

The robbery paradigm

A crucial aspect of the robbery paradigm is that it remains hidden unless we have reason to bring it out into the open. This means that its central influence on what we know can go unnoticed. The stories in 'The importance of premises' were designed to confront you with your automatic assumptions. We can now see that a network of these assumptions formed a filter through which you interpreted the whole story.

Taken together, these hidden assumptions and the hundreds of others that are not included, make up what I have called the robbery paradigm. This paradigm consists of all the expectations that we have about robberies. Other possible aspects of the paradigm relating simply to the man who demanded the money (who said it was a robbery?) might be:

- his age (was he over 70 years old?)
- his race (do you hold stereotypical views of race?)
- his clothing (was he wearing a suit or a balaclava?)
- what he was carrying (do you think he had an umbrella, a gun or a heavy pile of books?).

One can almost imagine the unconscious mind telling itself a story and passing it up to the conscious mind:

'The old man...' *White hair? Glasses? Maybe unsure on his feet?*

'had just turned off the lights in the store...' *Probably a shopkeeper? Probably end of the day about to close up shop?*

'and was preparing to lock up and go home...' *Definitely a shopkeeper closing up at the end of the day – it is probably dark outside.*

'when a youth appeared and demanded money...' *Appeared from where? Didn't just walk in? Why did he 'demand' money and not 'ask' for money? And what is the relationship with the shopkeeper? This seems odd...*

'The owner opened a cash register...' *Who is the owner? Somebody else? The man who appeared? The old man? Best guess is the old man – so the owner is a man. Why did he open the cash register? Probably to give the man who appeared the money. If it is the end of the day then there is probably money in the register, so this seems likely.*

'The contents were grabbed...' *Who did that? The owner or the man who appeared? And it probably is money isn't it?*

'and the man ran away...' *Ah, who ran away? The owner or the man who appeared? And why? Sounds like something bad is happening. Was any money handed over?*

'The police were informed immediately.' *So the police were told; maybe there was a crime involved; so the money must have been stolen. But I know this type of thing – it's a robbery. Now it all makes sense; someone is holding up a store late at night. The robber demands money; the old man/owner opens the cash register, the robber leans over, grabs the cash and runs out.*

This last story is the story that your conscious mind gets. All the other little details that were considered along the way are not available to you – you only get the 'finished' version. We have no direct way of knowing if the unconscious mind really works this way, but we also know that even if this wasn't the precise story you had in mind, you were thinking of some sort of story that went far beyond what you were actually told. The mind fills in the missing details – it assumes certain things and to do this it must rely on certain guiding principles, certain stories about stories (meta-stories). These are our paradigms.

A Look at the other story on page 80. Identify some of the assumptions you made and see if they fit into an overall paradigm.

B Look again at the diagram showing the robbery paradigm on page 172. This is only one of the multitude of everyday paradigms which impinge on our interpretation of a given situation. Most of these paradigms are the built-in common-sense assumptions we make when we are not told anything to the contrary. Identify some of these other paradigms.

C What is the difference between a paradigm and a belief?

D Why do we have these paradigms built in to our cognitive systems? Wouldn't life be much easier if we could get rid of them altogether and avoid making all these unnecessary assumptions?

E Several years ago, I was shopping for apples. At that time South Africa was practising apartheid, and for this reason I did not want to buy South African fruit. I asked the shopkeeper where the fruit was from; he said it was from Europe. 'Oh that's fine then,' I said. 'I'll buy these apples.'

'No, I wouldn't buy South African fruit either,' said the lady in the queue behind me. The natural interpretation was that the lady did not support apartheid either. It was only when I heard the lady muttering 'all those black hands' under her breath that I realised why she had supported me. I had perhaps assumed too much! How is this related to paradigms? Can you think of any similar situations yourself?

How do we choose our paradigms?

If it is reliable knowledge that we seek, and our knowledge is heavily influenced by our paradigms, then we need to be very careful that our paradigms are reliable or we have no hope of making progress. So how do we choose them?

We should perhaps distinguish between how we do choose them, and how we should choose them. It is clear that we have little or no conscious choice over many of our paradigms, and our backgrounds are quite influential (this is explored later on in this chapter when we look at culture). So we sometimes have little choice as to our hidden paradigms. However, once our attention has been drawn to our own, perhaps deeply-held convictions, we should take stock and review. This review will consist of looking reflectively at the paradigm, weighing up the empirical and rational reasons for belief, and making a judgement about it. In short, a critical analysis of the paradigm is called for, using all the tools that you are reading about in his book.

There are two possible cardinal errors. The first is to think that all paradigms are equally valid. They are not. Requirements such as logical consistency and the ability to stand up to available evidence must be stringently applied. If paradigms fail these tests they should be abandoned and rethought. Even in this age of politically correct speech and tolerance, we should not be duped into respecting ridiculous beliefs just because they are part of someone else's paradigm! Having said that, we should beware the second possible error, which is perhaps even less attractive – that of closed-mindedness and bigotry. Other paradigms may be seriously flawed, but so may ours. We have a duty to try honestly to stand back from our own sentiments and prejudices and to attempt to see our views as others see them.

There is no sure-fire method of choosing the 'right' paradigms any more than there is a sure way of finding a 'true' scientific theory or writing a 'beautiful' piece of music. The best we can do is to be aware of where our own beliefs lie, and to test them continually against experience and reason.

A Identify a commonly-held paradigm that you believe is completely wrong, and justify an alternative paradigm.

Everyday paradigms case study: only one can go free

Many years ago, a prince visited the jail in the French city of Toulon. It was well known that the jail was a terrible place, with awful conditions for the prisoners, so when the warden offered to free one of them in honour of the prince, all the inmates were extremely hopeful that they would be chosen. The prince said to the warden, 'Let the prisoners elect the three most deserving of them; I will then select from the three.'

And so the prince came to hear the stories of the three prisoners. The first man said:

'I was in love with the daughter of a rich man, and she loved me, too. But my family was poor, and the father thought I was not good enough for her. So one day when his daughter was not there he gave me a diamond ring, and told me that he would give me a thousand gold coins if he never saw me again. His daughter appeared before I could reply, and I did not tell her. But I also did not accept the offer.

The next day the police came to my home, searched it and found the ring and I was taken to jail. At the trial, the father said that I had stolen the ring – and as he was rich the judge took his word over mine.

My beloved still waits for me; she suspects the truth. Please release me from this unjust imprisonment.'

The warden mentioned that the father had later been arrested and was in jail on charges of corruption. The daughter visited regularly and often told the warden that her father had wrongly had her lover jailed.

The second prisoner had this to say:

'I am here for theft. Alas I have no excuse – I stole from my kind and generous employer when he left me in charge of the house. I could be freed if I could repay him, but I do not have the money to do so. I deserve this sentence – the punishment is just. I do not ask for your leniency.

My trial was fair and my sentence was just. I have begged my employer for forgiveness, but I cannot repay the money I took from him. At least I can repay my debt to society. Thank you for considering to release me, but I am sure there are others who deserve freedom more than I do.'

The warden told the prince that the employer had actually asked the judge to let him go, but that the judge felt that he needed to make an example of a thief.

The last man had this to say:

'I am a farmer from Tanzania. My farm is by the coast, and I have much work to feed my family of six children and five grandchildren. One day I was walking home for food when a group of white men came upon me, attacked me and carried me off to their ship.

They made me work for eight months on the voyage to France, cleaning the decks. When we arrived I had a chance to escape, so I ran, but I was weak and one of the sailors caught me. We fought, and I was crazy for freedom, and my life. I pushed him into a rough sea and he drowned.

In court I was found guilty of murder. My sentence is to be here until I die.'

The warden said that some of the man's children had visited, and that he was a kind and gentle man who was much liked in the prison.

It is recorded that the prince released the second prisoner. But he may have made a bad choice. Before we decide, we should consider some important factors which might influence our conclusion.

Answer the following questions, which are designed to make you aware of your own paradigms in this case.

1　A prison is a place where:
- society takes revenge against criminals.
- criminals are punished so that they do not re-offend.
- society protects itself by locking criminals away.
- criminals are re-educated so that they do not re-offend.
- life is made so unpleasant that potential criminals are deterred from crime.

2　On the basis of your answer to the previous question, would you have released:
- the most deserving prisoner
- the prisoner whose release would serve justice best
- a prisoner who is ready to return to society?

3　How could the prince decide which of the prisoners was telling the truth?
- Is this really important?
- Do you think most prisoners claim they are innocent?
- Could the prince rely upon the information given to him by the warden?

4　Consider the effect of releasing each of the three prisoners on:
- the rich merchant whose ring the court had judged stolen
- the daughter who was waiting for her lover to be released
- the family of the man who waits for his release from a foreign prison
- the community and the judge who convicted the confessed thief.

5　So who would be the correct person to release? For what reasons?

6　How does this case study relate to paradigms?

The grand paradigms

Paradigms affect the ways we filter and interpret evidence. They are common enough, and you are now familiar with the everyday variety. But I want to suggest that there are broader, 'bigger' paradigms of which we may not be aware. We all have a set of beliefs about ourselves, ranging from the trivial (my name is Nick) to the profound (I'm deeply misunderstood). Many of these beliefs refer to our place in the Universe and how we fit into the bigger picture – beliefs such as I am unique, I am more intelligent than a cockroach, humans are the most advanced creatures alive, God loves me, there is no God, we are controlled by fate, and so on. When taken together, these various assumptions, many of which we probably couldn't put into words, make up a belief set, a model of what it is to be a human in this Universe. This model affects the way we think about ourselves, and when something threatens it we feel disorientated and disturbed. You are probably aware that sometimes novel ideas are rejected simply because they are new and new things upset people.

Because we are all unique, we all have different models and different beliefs. But there is a paradigm that is common to many – the paradigm that modern man holds. Modern man, of course, doesn't exist: he is an abstract concept like 'the average taxpayer' or 'the typical 'student' (I obviously intend the term 'man' to include women as well). But in many senses, we all share beliefs, and here we explore the model that characterises the way man currently thinks of himself.

It will surprise no-one to learn that this hidden paradigm – this model of what we are, and where we fit into the Universe – has changed radically over time. Sometimes these changes have been gradual and practically undetectable. The basic Western model of man's place in the Universe that was constructed by the Ancient Greeks around, say, 500BC, changed very little as it was adopted by the Romans, suffered a few setbacks in the Dark Ages after the fall of the western Roman Empire, but was resurrected in the Middle Ages, and was not seriously challenged until 1543. In other words, this paradigm was not overthrown for well over 2000 years. In all this time, man's perception of himself changed very little.

What was this paradigm? It may be broken down roughly like this:

Classical paradigm
Humans are at the centre of the Universe.
Humans were placed there by God(s).
Human purpose is the worship of God(s).
Religion is the path to truth.

It supports a view of humankind roughly like this:

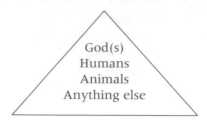

God(s)
Humans
Animals
Anything else

On this 'celestial pyramid', humans are slightly lower down on the ladder than God(s). Certainly they are above lowly animals. This had important implications for the way that holders of this paradigm related to the world. For now, we merely note that man was a privileged creature.

Certain modifications have occurred over time. The vision of many gods – the view of the classical Olympians – was replaced by One God; the pagan augurs and soothsayers were replaced by the Church. This may or may not have been a move from falsehood to truth, but this is not the issue currently at stake. The shadowy Greek Hades was replaced by the Christian Heaven and Hell, and Plato's theory that man exists to contemplate God was replaced by the idea that man exists to worship Him. But these are only minor changes so far as our inquiry is concerned. The basic conception of man as superior to everything except God, and of man as central to God's design, remained unaffected. Until 1543 that is.

A paradigm is a model of how our view of the world should be. When new discoveries come along we try to fit them into this model. Some new ideas can be fitted in easily: exchanging a belief in several gods for a belief in one God makes little difference to the paradigm as a whole. But some discoveries simply cannot fit into the model, and when that occurs, and the new discovery is certain and important enough, then the model itself has to change. We call such a change a **paradigm shift**: when a new piece of knowledge is so fundamentally different to previous ideas that we have to throw all our ideas out and build a new paradigm around this discovery. Such a thing happened in 1543, when a Polish astronomer named Nicolaus Copernicus published a work called *De revolutionibus caelestrium orbium*, or *On the Revolution of the Heavenly Orbs*. What Copernicus questioned in this work was the first belief in the paradigm set: the belief that the Earth was at the centre of the Universe. Up to this time, with one or two notable exceptions, the generally accepted model of the Universe had been the so-called Ptolemaic one: the Earth was at the centre, and all other heavenly bodies orbited at different distances, as if part of a series of concentric spheres. Copernicus rightly contested this view, and argued that the Sun was, in fact, central to the system, and that the Earth revolved around the Sun. The work of Copernicus met violent opposition from the Catholic Church, and both he and his successors, Kepler and Galileo, were persecuted for this discovery. The fact that the Catholic Church was so offended by this discovery had nothing to do with its scientific truth. It is simply the fact that if this was true, then the whole view of man's place in the Universe – the whole paradigm – would have to be rewritten.

Why? Well, up to this point, man had believed that he was at the centre of everything. From this simple belief flowed a host of other beliefs – that he was superior to all other living things, that he was especially loved of God and made in His image, that the Universe was created for him alone, and designed to ensure his well-being. Suddenly Copernicus revealed that the Earth did not rule the Universe; rather, it was only one of many planets subject to the Sun, no more important perhaps than the other planets visible to the naked eye. Suddenly the Universe seemed much bigger, and man seemed much less significant. Of course, in itself this constitutes a simple scientific paradigm shift: the old geocentric or Ptolemaic paradigm was replaced by the heliocentric model. But the effect of this scientific paradigm shift on man's larger conception of himself was enormous: suddenly priorities changed, and man felt a need to reassert himself, to find other reasons for claiming his universal superiority.

You will notice that in the classical and medieval paradigm, the basic belief set is religious: man's divinely chosen centrality to everything secured him an existence in which he had no doubts and no need to question. After Copernicus, the emphasis changed. In the following centuries man was certain of his superiority not through his faith, but through his scientific inquiry. We call this the Enlightenment paradigm, although the

---

Enlightenment paradigm
Man is rationally superior to all things.
Reason is a gift of God.
Man's purpose is to investigate the Universe.
Science is the source of truth.

---

term Enlightenment is more properly applied to the eighteenth century, when the desire for scientific understanding displaced the need for theological dispute. But this is characteristic of the whole period: after Copernicus, man needed a new reason to assert his evident superiority. No longer geographically central to the scheme of things, he seized upon the one faculty that seemed to mark him out from the rest of the living world: his ability to reason. Now man became obsessed with understanding the world around him, and through understanding, controlling it. The new celestial pyramid showing how Enlightenment man typically saw his place in the Universe is thus:

Above all was God, but second only to God was mind, or reason. And mind in this sense is unique to humans. How convenient! With our minds we can explore, understand, control; we can bring order to chaos, and design to order; we can take an ordinary lump of flint and turn it into a tool with a purpose; we can build houses out of brick, we can make weapons out of metal ore; we can plough fields and make them produce crops; we can use steam to drive an engine; we can alter the landscape to make it more beautiful even than nature. This sense of purpose – of adapting nature to our own ends – is characteristic of Enlightenment thought. Although such adaptation had existed for thousands of years, it had never been so central to the way man defined himself; it had never been paradigmatic.

After Copernicus, man had to earn his exalted status on the second rung of the ladder after God – the pattern of the Universe no longer guaranteed it. Now it was possible to doubt the sacred beliefs of the older paradigm, and indeed atheism, the denial even of God's existence, finds its first real apologists in this period. Rather than innocently celebrating man's greatness, people began to doubt that they were as central as they had previously thought.

Copernicus' proof of the heliocentric system was a shattering blow to human confidence in human superiority, but perhaps unfortunately for man, the story did not end there. A succession of great discoveries torpedoed any remnants of the Enlightenment paradigm. Darwin's theory of evolution offered an alternative to Creation, and the reverberations of that theory are still echoing through the intellectual landscape. Whether or not Darwin was right, his alternative to Creation by God, is a psychological blow for many. Sigmund Freud showed that we are not fully in control of our behaviour: below our conscious thoughts lies subconscious thoughts that drive us to do inexplicable things. We are not aware of these urges, but they may nevertheless determine how we feel and act. Man can no longer see himself simply as a rational, self-controlled being. He is, in part at least, subject to uncontrollable mental forces of which he is not aware. Albert Einstein has taught us that our concept of space–time is not fixed or objective, but is subject to the observer's state of motion relative to the objects being observed; in the field of quantum physics, we now know that an event may be uncaused; Werner Heisenberg has taught us that a particle's position and velocity can never be simultaneously known – the so-called Uncertainty Principle; and so on. The Enlightenment search for scientific knowledge has led science to uncover its own problems. Fashionable new theories like Chaos Theory, Superstrings or the Gaia hypothesis create increasingly bizarre (according to a common-sense paradigm) models of the Universe every day. We live in a unique time: in the last few decades we have watched scientists genetically alter living matter; we have seen men walking on the moon, and babies conceived outside the womb. Could it be possible, in these turbulent times, that there is still a paradigm to which we all more or less subscribe? Is there anything left to believe in?

Perhaps after the findings of Copernicus, Darwin, Freud, Einstein, Heisenberg (and others), today's paradigm should look something like this:

Modern paradigm

Humans are random evolutionary accidents.

Humankind is one of a billion biological species.

There is no God.

There is no purpose to life.

There is no path to truth.

This paradigm leaves no room for a celestial pyramid because the Universe just is. There is no hierarchy, and there is no favoured place for man. Possibly for this reason, many will find this a pretty depressing belief set, and few would happily admit that this model underlies their conception of themselves. But such a view seems to be accepted by many in the scientific community. This extract is from the physicist Stephen Hawking in his best-selling book, *A Brief History of Time*:

We have developed from the geocentric cosmologies of Ptolemy and his forebears, through the heliocentric cosmology of Copernicus and Galileo, to the modern picture in which the Earth is a medium-sized planet orbiting around an average star in the outer suburbs of an ordinary spiral galaxy, which is itself only one of about a million million galaxies in the observable universe. Yet [some] . . . would claim that this whole vast construction exists simply for our sake. This is very hard to believe.

At this point, we need to exercise caution. We are dealing with massive generalisations, and in our search to discover how we as a race see ourselves, we may need to forget how we as individuals see ourselves. Clearly the two views are different. From the cosmic point of view, we are all insignificant blips in organic and geological history. From my point of view, I can think of nothing more significant than me. This ability to see the world from the objective and subjective points of view characterises the human way of thinking and creates some interesting dilemmas. This is the basic problem with much of our philosophy, but if we are careful, we should be able to talk about a paradigm that characterises us not as individuals, but as a race at a particular point in time. While billions of people will subscribe to one of the earlier paradigms, the modern paradigm is increasingly influential.

Grand paradigms case study: the harmony of the spheres

An article by Paul Davies, *Time*, 1996.

If we discover extra-terrestrial life, our world will never seem quite the same.

Paul Davies

The discovery of life beyond Earth would transform not only our science but also our religions, our belief systems and our entire world view. For in a sense, the search for extra-terrestrial life is really a search for ourselves – who we are and what our place is in the grand sweep of the cosmos.

Contrary to popular belief, speculation that we are not alone in the Universe is as old as philosophy itself. The essential steps in the reasoning were based on the atomic theory of the ancient Greek philosopher Democritus. First, the laws are universal. Second, there is nothing special or privileged about Earth. Finally, if something is possible, nature tends to make it happen.

Philosophy is one thing; filling in all the physical details is quite another. Although increasingly many astronomers suspect that bio-friendly planets may be abundant in the Universe, the chemical steps leading to life remain largely mysterious.

Traditionally, biologists believed that life is a freak – the result of a zillion-to-one accidental concatenation of molecules. It follows that the likelihood of it happening again elsewhere in the cosmos is infinitesimal. The viewpoint derives from the second law of thermodynamics, which predicts that the Universe is dying – slowly and inexorably degenerating toward a state of total chaos. Life bucks this trend only because it is a statistical fluke.

Similar reasoning applies to evolution. According to the orthodox view, Darwinian selection is utterly blind. Any impression that the transition from microbes to man represents progress is pure chauvinism on our part. The path of evolution is merely a random walk through the realm of possibilities.

If this is right, there can be no directionality, no innate drive forward; in particular, no push toward consciousness and intelligence. Should Earth be struck by an asteroid, destroying all higher life-forms, intelligent beings, still less humanoids, would almost certainly not arise next time around.

There is, however, a contrary view – one that is gaining strength and that directly challenges orthodox biology. It is that complexity can emerge spontaneously through a process of self organisation. If matter and energy have an in-built tendency to amplify and channel organised complexity, the odds against the formation of life and the subsequent evolution of intelligence could be drastically shortened.

The relevance of self-organisation to biology remains hotly debated. It suggests, however, that although the Universe as a whole may be dying, an opposite, progressive trend may also exist as a fundamental property of nature. The emergence of extra-terrestrial life, particularly intelligent life, is a key test for these rival paradigms.

These issues cut right across traditional religious dogma. Many people cling to the belief that the origin of life required a unique divine act. But if life on Earth is not unique, the case for a miraculous origin would be undermined. The discovery of even a humble bacterium on Mars, if it could be shown to have arisen independently from Earth life, would support the view that life emerges naturally.

Historically, the Roman Catholic Church regarded any discussion of alien life as heresy. Speculating about other inhabited worlds was one reason philosopher Giordano Bruno was burned at the stake in 1600. Belief that mankind has a special relationship with God is central to the monotheistic religions. The existence of alien beings, especially if they were more advanced than humans intellectually and spiritually, would disrupt this cosy view.

Christianity faces a peculiar problem in relation to the Incarnation. Was this event unique in the Universe, as doctrine insists, or did God take on alien flesh too? Is Christ the saviour of humans alone, or of all intelligent beings in our galaxy and beyond?

Weighed against these threatening factors is the uplifting picture of the Universe that the ubiquity of life and consciousness implies. A cosmos that starts out in a sterile Big Bang and gradually progresses through complex chemistry to life, intelligence and culture – and sentient beings who can look back and reflect on the meaning of it all – is profoundly inspiring. The fact that this advance can take place entirely naturally, without divine intervention, adds to the wonder.

Bertrand Russell argued that a universe under a death sentence from the second law of thermodynamics rendered human life ultimately futile. All our achievements, all our struggles, 'all the noonday brightness of human genius' as he put it, would, in the final analysis, count for nothing if the very cosmos itself is doomed.

Russell's despairing tone is frequently echoed by contemporary thinkers. Thus the French Nobel Prize-winning biologist Jacques Monod writes, 'Man at last knows that he is alone in the unfeeling immensity of the Universe, out of which he has emerged only by chance.'

But what if, in spite of the second law of thermodynamics, there can be systematic progress alongside decay? For those who hope for a deeper meaning or purpose beneath physical existence, the presence of extra-terrestrial life-forms would provide a spectacular boost, implying that we live in a universe that is in some sense getting better and better rather than worse and worse.

A Imagine we discover intelligent alien life. What questions would we want to ask if we could communicate with the aliens? What answers would most disturb you? Why?

B Are there any questions that you would not want to ask for fear of the answers? If so, what does this tell you about your paradigms?

Culture

It will be no news to you that we do not exist in a social vacuum. Instead we inhabit a complex world where the attitudes and beliefs of our parents, siblings and friends have a massive impact on every aspect of our lives. Consider meeting a stranger – what we say as a greeting, when we say it, how loud we say it, what tone we say it in, who else is present when we say it, whether we bow or offer a handshake or a kiss – all these are factors that we automatically take into account when we meet someone. How we greet is influenced as much by these factors as by our wish to make a greeting. And this is true not just for greeting, but for many aspects of our lives – how we eat, how we dress, our relationships, how we speak to others, how we expect to be treated, and so on.

Culture mediates almost every aspect of our daily lives and experiences. It dictates to us with regard to language, customs, ethics, values, legal systems, eating habits and traditions. Most importantly, for our purposes, these norms can influence what we believe and what we know. Since different cultures hold certain values which may not be shared by other cultures, practices differ around the world. This is an excellent example of the central importance of paradigms to everyday life.

A Consider the following twenty statements. With which of them do you agree:

- People usually shake hands when introduced to each other.
- Blowing your nose in public is okay.
- A woman should not look a man in the eyes when he is talking directly to her.
- Asking someone how much they earn is okay.
- Asking someone about their religious beliefs is okay.
- Promiscuity is okay.
- When invited to a party, bringing a friend is okay.
- When eating dinner at a friend's house, asking for a second helping is okay.
- A woman's primary role in life is to serve her husband and raise his children.
- It's common for students to call teachers by their first names in secondary schools.
- Couples in love should get married.
- It's common to introduce yourself to new neighbours and to buy them a small gift.
- Teachers should strike students who are disobedient or disrespectful.
- Students should always stand up when answering a teacher's question.
- You should always bring a gift when you go to a friend's house for dinner.
- Parents decide who their children will marry.
- Teenagers go out on dates a lot.
- A man usually gives a woman a gift when they go out on a date.
- Young people usually live with their parents after they get married.
- A couple will live together before they get married.

B Which statements, if any, would you say should be true for all cultures?

Of course, our parents, siblings and friends are not immune to the influence of culture either, and their attitudes and values will also be shaped by their contexts. For older children and adults, this will include the media, religious beliefs, academic trends and political movements. We call the whole social, personal, intellectual, spiritual and commercial environment a **culture**. A culture is a paradigm in that it forms a filter for us to interpret the world, and it should be clear that cultures based on national/racial lines are just one type of culture. We can easily distinguish between, say, Italian and British cultures by spoken language, body language, personal space habits, physical intimacy and cuisine (to pick a few of the more obvious traits). But we can also speak of the culture of a corporation or of a school, or even of a family. The point is simply that the culture has certain norms which the members tend to obey, and these norms may appear very strange to outsiders.

Once different cultural viewpoints have been identified, there immediately arises a problem – which viewpoint is better? We have seen this problem before, but the point is worth stressing because it is so central to identifying standards of judgement. We should neither blindly accept nor blindly reject any cultural perspective which differs from ours. Rather we should try to subject the differing view, and our own view on the subject, to an evaluation that is as objective as is possible.

At some levels, this is clear – for example, why do we not accept the values of a racist culture? Well, partly because it 'feels' wrong to us (probably because of our cultural background), but also because when we subject racist values to scrutiny, we find that these values do not have a sound basis in reason or in experience. For this reason, the apartheid regime in South Africa was, by and large, not respected by thinking people, regardless of the fact that the racism was institutionalised as part of the culture. Of course, we need to be careful that we reject other cultural habits for 'good' reasons and not just because they come from other cultures (eating food with one's hands is an interesting example). Otherwise, we are guilty of blind prejudice.

However, it is extremely difficult to judge different perspectives (see questions below). How can we try to do so? Possibly the best we can do is to be aware of our own cultural paradigms, both the 'grand' and the 'everyday' ones, and to understand how reason and experience can be brought to bear on a problem, while being aware of the pervasive influence of language. This is, of course, part of the nature of this course.

A Reflect on your own experiences and identify times when you have had different cultural expectations of a situation from somebody else. These situations often arise when a newcomer meets/joins an established group. If possible, find examples where the cultural paradigms are:

- national/racial in nature
- based on gender
- based on family situations
- based on friendship groups.

Can you identify aspects of the cultures that are in conflict? Which aspect is 'right'?

B All of the twenty examples given on page 185 were/are the norm in some cultures at some point in time. Some of them are now considered barbaric by many cultures, but the obvious question which arises is, how do we know that what we consider acceptable will not be considered barbaric at some point in the future? Or more generally, how can we be sure that our cultural paradigm is a good one?

C What do we mean by 'good' in the last line of the previous question?

D 'We should neither blindly accept nor blindly reject any cultural perspective which differs from ours. Rather we try to subject the differing view, and our own view on the subject, to an objective evaluation.' This was offered as a recipe for choosing the 'best' cultural perspective. What are the problems with 'an objective evaluation' of any cultural view?

Culture case study: Japanese politeness

The interplay of language, culture, and thought
by Eileen Dombrowski.

Inscrutable, evasive, insincere. Saying 'yes' when they really mean 'no', and smiling politely all the while. The image of the Japanese in the west is often of an incomprehensible culture, whose smooth and polished surface cannot be penetrated. It is perhaps through examining the Japanese language, though, that English speakers might gain a glimpse into the culture, as the language and culture are so reciprocally interconnected. The Japanese language shows some of the substance behind the polished surface, as it reveals a culture of politeness, of respectful treatment of others, and of highly tuned social awareness.

In Japanese, one can scarcely speak to another person, and certainly not correctly, without a highly developed sensitivity to relative social position, based on a fusion of factors such as age, gender, or importance in a company. The language provides different levels of politeness, so that the speaker must recognise whether to speak 'up' to a superior, 'level' to an equal – though never 'down' to an inferior! 'We can't say exactly what form for what occasion,' writes Misa Tanaka, 'but we have to use our sensitivity.'

This sense of relative position permeates the forms of the language. 'If I want to say something very polite,' comments Junko Sagara, 'I have three ways. One is to put the verb or sentence in the polite form. The second is to use the verb which is used only for a respected person for the action of the person I am talking to. The third is to put the verb which shows my own action into the modest form.'

To complicate matters, modesty and humility are so much part of speech that one would refer indirectly to one's own group – one's family, for example – using a humble form which pushes them downward, and to the group of the person to whom one is speaking in an honorific form, raising them upward in comparison, in order to be respectful toward the other person.

The words for 'I' and 'you' likewise vary according to the relationship between people, to the point that Japanese students in an English-speaking college describe responding quite differently toward bilingual teachers depending on whether they are speaking with them in English or Japanese. Izumi Sasaki describes her feeling that English gives her different possibilities from Japanese in forming relationships with families where she was a guest:

I would like to give an example from my experience here. When I was in Japan, I went to stay at my friend's house for the weekend. Of course, I was talking to my friend using the informal form of 'you', and I was using polite forms (for which the exact translation in English does not exist, as far as I know) for her parents and her grandparents. Although I had known all those people for quite a long time, I never got to talk to her parents and her grandparents about their private life as I do to her, because those polite forms that I was using would not go together with those questions that I wanted to ask them about their private life. I would never ask those questions in those polite forms unless I was their lawyer or something like that. If I actually did ask them, I might have been considered as being such a nagging teenage girl. Therefore, I never got to know how her parents met each other, or even about their childhood or adolescence at all. No matter how close the friend might have been to me, the relationship with her family was always like this.

But when I stayed at my host's family's place for the first time in Canada, the condition was totally different. First of all the feeling that I had when I was asking them on the phone if I could stay or not, was the one that I had never experienced when I was talking to someone who I had met (or talked to) for the first time. Although we were talking to each other without even knowing the other person's face, we were talking to each other in such a way that people who overheard our conversation might have thought that I was talking to my friend. Actually, I myself couldn't believe that I was talking to my host family rather than my friend. It seems to me that this was because we were both using the same word 'you'.

Male and female speech also varies, with 'I' and 'you' in different forms and particular endings added to other words. The possibility for subtlety and innuendo, though, is not eliminated by such structure. Saeko Hagihara comments, 'If I, as a woman, use "ore", the word for guys, that means I'm wild or I don't feel feminine.'

Japanese politeness, however, is not confined to this sense of relative social position. It also affects the openness or frankness of speech. Makiko Oyama describes the way in which indirectness can soften potential conflict in order to preserve a social harmony:

When talking in English, usually one can get the other's opinion as soon as that person starts talking, whereas in Japanese, one may have to wait for a longer time to hear the other's opinion since the verb which states the final conclusion is at the end. Therefore, in Japanese, since it is difficult when one has to respond negatively, one can start speaking a little bit in an affirmative way by stating one's reasons politely and, through explaining, one can reach the negative conclusion at the end. The Japanese are used to this kind of situation. However, it could cause a problem when English speakers have to deal with this, since it is thought to be polite to answer straightforwardly for them.

This indirectness – a sidestepping of the confrontational or the too naked assertion – also characterises the content of what is appropriate to say. Akiko Koyama tells a story in one of her essays of a romance which floundered on language:

Once my Dad told me a funny story about his 'miai'. An arranged marriage starts not with love between the young man and woman but with an introduction, a 'miai', set up by a go-between who thinks they would make a good couple. If they finally find that they hit it off, the go-between sees them through to marriage. Anyway, he had a 'miai' with a lady who had been in USA for a long time, before he got married to my mom.

This is what he said to me. The lady to whom he was introduced seemed graceful and nice. This is a part of their conversation at the 'miai' which is a very common and typical question at any 'miai':

Dad: Do you have any pastimes?

Lady: Oh, yes! I have lots. Especially I am really good at playing the piano. All my friends love me playing it. I'm sure you'll love it, too.

He was quite shocked by her words, and he found that there was no way to marry her, because he thought that she lacked modesty, which means for Japanese that she had no common sense. I wonder if non-Japanese can see what is wrong with this part of conversation. Probably not. But if the lady had been a typical Japanese, what would the conversation be like?

Dad: Do you have any pastimes?

Lady: Yes I play the piano only a little bit. But I am too shy to play it in front of you.

These words were expected to be said even if she was an amazing pianist. At the same time people would know for sure that she is a good pianist if she says that she plays it 'only a little bit'.

Clearly, Japanese, both in the content of what is spoken and in the linguistic forms of the language, reflects and reinforces a culture in which group harmony is more important than individual self-expression, and in which politeness is a supreme value. Sylvia Cousineau emphasises that the politeness is much more than a veneer or a false mask, and that the linguistic forms are an integral part of the Japanese way of thinking:

I was a grown individual, aged 21, when I learned Japanese, but even acquiring the language at that point of relative maturity, as an outsider, I found that it mediated my thinking. Perhaps it has not changed the filters through which I see reality, but it has modified them.

In Japan one is never determined by the self as an individual, but always as a member of a group, and the language is shaped by that. In learning Japanese, I had to come to a new understanding of myself, and of hierarchy and group, and the language forced me to internalise this new understanding, partly intellectually, partly organically.

I had previously assumed that sincerity was something that one saw on someone's face. Not anymore. In Japan, the language is such that personal expression makes one feel quirky. It is rough, confrontational. In Japanese society, feelings are not displayed but intimated; it is not a culture of representation of the self but of representation by consent. In Japan, one generally deals with people completely in their social roles, where everything is codified, and smooth, with the support of the expected: one always knows what to do or to say.

The Japanese are thought of as hypocritical, but they are less hypocritical than people in the west, because no one is fooling anyone else. I find this more honest. The mask is a lie – but it is a socially true lie. In the west we also wear masks, but we pretend that it is our real self. In fact, we have a 'representational neurosis' – enhanced by television, with its emphasis on faces – whereby people are acting their own lives. 'I feel joy. I feel anger. Can't you see it on my face?'

She comments, too, on the way that Japanese manners penetrated her own Canadian conduct. 'When I returned from

Japan, I found that at first I was very formal with everyone – and when I talked on the telephone, I found that as I spoke I kept bowing to the phone!'

Language, culture, and thought can scarcely be disentangled. Perhaps it is easier to recognise the union in a language which is not our own, as our own ways are so often invisible to us, simply assumed as the way things are and therefore must be. For English speakers, then, a consideration of Japanese might illuminate these interconnections and help us to raise some questions about our own invisible norms.

Where do we go from here?

We have learnt that paradigms are an unavoidable part of the human condition, and that they, and culture in particular as the paradigm *par excellence*, play a large part in the way we interpret the world. Awareness of this cannot be anything but a step in the right direction. If we are sensitive to the fact that all we have is interpretation, then we will be sensitive to the interpretations of others. Of course, that does not mean that we never have the 'best' interpretation – we wouldn't want to say that we can *never* get it right – but this sensitivity allows or makes us experience the world in a different way.

An issue which has arisen several times throughout the course, but which seems to be central to our understanding of paradigms and interpretations, is that of language. As language is the means by which we communicate anything, perhaps we should take a closer look at it.

Further reading

The term 'paradigm' was made common by Thomas Kuhn's *The Copernican Revolution* (Random House, 1959) and the more abstract *The Structure of Scientific Revolutions* (University of Chicago Press, 1970), both of which are very readable and extremely interesting. There are few books which deal directly with the issue (most are written in a particular paradigm), but Paul Davies' *Are We Alone?* (Penguin, 1995) deals with the implications of finding alien life.

Few other books that I am aware of deal with the topic of directly, but a great read is Peter Suber's *The Case of the Speluncean Explorers* (Routledge, 1998), which takes a legal/ethical problem (involving cannibalism, murder and so on) and approaches it from several difficult judicial perspectives. That opposing paradigms can come to a similar conclusion, and similar paradigms arrive at opposing conclusions, gives a fascinating insight into the issue.

Perhaps most helpful would be a list of books dealing with the great paradigm shift we are currently in. With the topic of evolution so controversial, why take anyone's word for it? Read the following and make your own mind up! Richard Dawkins' *The Blind Watchmaker* (repr. W.W. Norton and Co, 1996) and *The Selfish Gene* (repr. Oxford University Press, 1990) were the first popular books to spread evolutionary arguments to the general public in a detailed way. Robert Wright's *The Moral Animal* (Vintage, 1994) applies the theory to see if it can explain our sense of right and wrong, and Stephen Pinker in *How The Mind Works* (Penguin, 1998) argues that most aspects of what we know about the brain support evolutionary theory. Daniel Dennett's *Darwin's Dangerous Idea* (Touchstone, 1996) takes an overview.

Anti-evolution writers who argue that the scientific evidence is simply not good enough to support the theory include Micheal Behe, who in *Darwin's Black Box: The Biochemical Challenge to Evolution* (Touchstone, 1998) suggests that irreducible biochemical complexity in nature cannot be explained by evolution. Phillip E. Johnson's *Objections Sustained: Subversive Essays on Evolution, Law and Culture* (Intervarsity Press, 1998) takes a similar line and this is followed up in detail by Lee M. Spetner in *Not By Chance* (Judaica Press, 1998) where many examples are taken which, it is suggested, show that many natural forms of life must have been designed. A. N. Field in *The Evolution Hoax Exposed* (Tan Books, 1971) suggests that believing in evolution leads to many social ills, and Michael Denton, in *Evolution: A Theory in Crisis* (Adler & Adler, 1996) argues that a rational appraisal of the evidence will lead to the jettisoning of Darwinism in due course.

Humans universals

An extract from *Humans Universals* by Donald Brown.

In a course that I teach on the peoples and cultures of Southeast Asia I have often illustrated the cultural elaboration of rank that is found in many Southeast Asian societies – and certainly among the Brunei Malays with whom I did my doctoral research – with the following anecdote. In the course of my research I was once seated with two young men on a wooden bench at the front of the house that my wife and I rented in a ward of the Brunei capital. A third young man was seated just a few feet away on the rung of a ladder but at the same height as the rest of us. There was no one else around. Tiring of sitting on the bench, I slipped down from it to sit on the walkway. I was followed almost instantly by all three of the young men. Just as quickly I realised that they had done it not because they too were uncomfortable on the bench (I had been there longer than they) but because in the Brunei scheme of things it is not polite to sit higher than another person, unless you considerably outrank that other person. So I protested, urging them to please remain seated on the bench. They said it wouldn't look nice. I said there was no one but us around to notice. One of them closed the matter by noting that people across the river – to which he gestured (it was about a quarter mile away) – just might see what was going on. The clear implication was that he and his fellows weren't about to let anyone see them apparently breaking one of the important rules in the etiquette of rank, even though they knew they wouldn't be offending me.

I always told this story to illustrate difference, to show the extremity to

which Bruneis concerned themselves with rank, and it always seemed to be a very effective message. As a teacher of anthropology I knew very well that cultural differences elicit some sort of inherent interest. Ruth Benedict's *Patterns of Culture* (1934) is an all-time anthropological best-seller, and its essential message is the astonishing variability of human customs. No one teaching anthropology can ignore the way students react to revelations about the amazing ways other peoples act and think. And no one teaching anthropology can fail to sense the wheels turning in students' minds when they use these revelations to rethink the ways people act and think in their own society. Teachers of anthropology not only see this in students, they cultivate it. But are the differences all that should be of concern to anthropology? Does an emphasis on differences present a true image of humanity?

I now realise that the story I have told my students is pervaded with evidence of similarities: above all, the young men were concerned with what other people would think about them; they were also concerned with politeness in particular, rules in general; even their concern with rank was only a matter of difference in degree. I could go on, mentioning their use of language and gestures; the smooth conversational turn taking; the concepts of question, answer, explanation; the use of highness/lowness to symbolise rank; and much more.

At a more subtle level, I believe, some amazing things were happening that I took no note of. Without my explaining things in detail, in my broken Malay, the young men had instantly grasped my point: the setting was informal and I wanted them to treat me as they would treat each other (they would not have moved down or up in unison for each other in those circumstances); furthermore, it was 'not my custom' to be offended by people sitting higher than me. I think

that my companions sized up these aspects of the immediate situation just as I had.

But they also saw a wider context in which their behavior could be misinterpreted by others, and with what seemed like a few words and a gesture, they explained their position to me and closed the matter. There were more than a few words and gestures: there were tone of voice, facial expressions, body language, and an enormously complex context of past, present, and future. And there were four human minds, each observing, computing, and reacting to the 'implicature' (Scheff 1986:74) of the bare words so silently and automatically as to occasion no notice. All this – from the conscious concern with what others would think to the unconscious assessments of implications – formed a plainly human background, from which I in my lectures had pulled out a quantitative difference as the focus of attention.

I use the word 'quantitative' because, although it may not be my custom to think that the height of one's seat should match one's rank, the idea is not foreign to western culture. There are some wonderful examples of the equation between seating height and rank, or dominance, in Charlie Chaplin's film 'The Great Dictator'. What distinguishes the Bruneis from us is the greater frequency of day-to-day contexts in which the equation is observed among Bruneis.

[Brown later goes on to argue that the following characteristics are found in all human cultures: prestige and status, inequality of power and wealth, property, inheritance, reciprocity, punishment, sexual modesty, sexual regulation, sexual jealousy, a male preference for young women as sexual partners, a division of labour by sex (including more childcare by women and greater public political dominance by men), hostility by other groups, conflict within the group, including violence, rape and murder.]

The body rituals of the Nacirema

An extract from *Body Ritual Among the Nacirema* by Horace Miner.

The anthropologist has become so familiar with the diversity of ways in which different peoples behave in similar situations that he is not apt to be surprised by even the most exotic customs. In fact, if all of the logically possible combinations of behaviour have not been found somewhere in the world, he is apt to suspect that they must be present in some yet undescribed tribe. This point has, in fact, been expressed with respect to clan organisation by Murdock. In this light, the magical beliefs and practices of the Nacirema present such unusual aspects that it seems desirable to describe them as an example of the extremes to which human behaviour can go.

Professor Linton first brought the ritual of the Nacirema to the attention of anthropologists twenty years ago, but the culture of this people is still very poorly understood. They are a North American group living in the territory between the Canadian Cree, the Yaqui and Tarahumare of Mexico, and the Carib and Arawak of the Antilles. Little is known of their origin, although tradition states that they came from the east. According to Nacirema mythology, their nation was originated by a culture hero, Notgnihsaw, who is otherwise known for two great feats of strength – the throwing of a piece of wampum across the river Pa-To-Mac and the chopping down of a cherry tree in which the Spirit of Truth resided.

Nacirema culture is characterised by a highly developed market economy which has evolved in a rich natural habitat. While much of the people's time is devoted to economic pursuits, a large part of the fruits of these labours and a considerable portion of the day are spent in ritual activity. The focus of this activity is the human body, the appearance and health of which loom as a dominant concern in the ethos of the people. While such a concern is certainly not unusual, its ceremonial aspects and associated philosophy are unique.

The fundamental belief underlying the whole system appears to be that the human body is ugly and that its natural tendency is to debility and disease. Incarcerated in such a body, man's only hope is to avert these characteristics through the use of the powerful influences of ritual and ceremony. Every household has one or more shrines devoted to this purpose. The more powerful individuals in the society have several shrines in their houses and, in fact, the opulence of a house is often referred to in terms of the number of such ritual centres it possesses. Most houses are of wattle and daub construction, but the shrine rooms of the more wealthy are walled with stone. Poorer families imitate the rich by applying pottery plaques to their shrine walls.

While each family has at least one such shrine, the rituals associated with it are not family ceremonies but are private and secret. The rites are normally only discussed with children, and then only during the period when they are being initiated into these mysteries. I was able, however, to establish sufficient rapport with the natives to examine these shrines and to have the rituals described to me.

The focal point of the shrine is a box or chest which is built into the wall. In this chest are kept the many charms and magical potions without which no native believes he could live. These preparations are secured from a variety of specialised practitioners. The most powerful of these are the medicine men, whose assistance must be rewarded with substantial gifts. However, the medicine men do not provide the curative potions for their clients, but decide what the ingredients should be and then write them down in an ancient and secret language. This writing is understood only by the medicine men and by the herbalists who, for another gift, provide the required charm.

The charm is not disposed of after it has served its purpose, but is placed in the charm-box of the household shrine. As these magical materials are specific for certain ills, and the real or imagined maladies of the people are many, the charm-box is usually full to overflowing. The magical packets are so numerous that people forget what their purposes were and fear to use them ☞

again. While the natives are very vague on this point, we can only assume that the idea in retaining all the old magical materials is that their presence in the charm-box, before which the body rituals are conducted, will in some way protect the worshipper.

Beneath the charm-box is a small font. Each day every member of the family, in succession, enters the shrine room, bows his head before the charm-box, mingles different sorts of holy water in the font, and proceeds with a brief rite of ablution. The holy waters are secured from the Water Temple of the community, where the priests conduct elaborate ceremonies to make the liquid ritually pure.

In the hierarchy of magical practitioners, and below the medicine men in prestige, are specialists whose designation is best translated 'holy-mouth-men'. The Nacirema have an almost pathological horror of and fascination with the mouth, the condition of which is believed to have a supernatural influence on all social relationships. Were it not for the rituals of the mouth, they believe that their teeth would fall out, their gums bleed, their jaws shrink, their friends desert them and their lovers reject them. They also believe that a strong relationship exists between oral and moral characteristics. For example, there is a ritual ablution of the mouth for children which is supposed to improve their moral fibre.

The daily body ritual performed by everyone includes a mouth-rite. Despite the fact that these people are so punctilious about care of the mouth, this rite involves a practice which strikes the uninitiated stranger as revolting. It was reported to me that the ritual consists of inserting a small bundle of hog hairs into the mouth, along with certain magical powders, and them moving the bundle in a highly formalised series of gestures.

In addition to the private mouth-rite, the people seek out a holy-mouth-man once or twice a year. These practitioners have an impressive set of paraphernalia, consisting of a variety of augers, awls, probes and prods. The use of these objects in the exorcism of the evils of the mouth involves almost unbelievable ritual torture of the client. The holy-mouth-man opens the client's mouth and, using the above mentioned tools, enlarges any holes which decay may have created in the teeth. Magical materials are put into these holes. If there are no naturally occurring holes in the teeth, large sections of one or more teeth are gouged out so that the supernatural substance can be applied. In the client's view, the purpose of these ministrations is to arrest decay and to draw friends. The extremely sacred and traditional character of the rite is evidence in the fact that the natives return to the holy-mouth-men year after year, despite the fact that their teeth continue to decay.

It is to be hoped that, when a thorough study of the Nacirema is made, there will be careful inquiry into the personality structure of these people. One has but to watch the gleam in the eye of a holy-mouth-man, as he jabs an awl into an exposed nerve, to suspect that a certain amount of sadism is involved. If this can be established, a very interesting pattern emerges, for most of the population shows definite masochistic tendencies. It was to these that Professor Linton referred in discussing a distinctive part of the daily body ritual which is performed only by men. This part of the rite involves scraping and lacerating the surface of the face with a sharp instrument. Special women's rites are performed only four times during each lunar month, but what they lack in frequency is made up in barbarity. As part of this ceremony, women bake their heads in small ovens for about an hour. The theoretically interesting point is what seems to be a preponderantly masochistic people have developed sadistic specialists.

The medicine men have an imposing temple, or *latipso*, in every community of any size. The more elaborate ceremonies required to treat very sick patients can only be performed at this temple. These ceremonies involve not only the thaumaturgy but a permanent group of vestal maidens who move sedately about the temple chambers in distinctive costume and headdress.

The *latipso* ceremonies are so harsh that it is phenomenal that a fair proportion of the really sick natives who enter the temple ever recover. Small children whose indoctrination is still incomplete have been known to resist attempts to take them to the temple because 'that is where you go to die'. Despite this fact, sick adults are not only willing but eager to undergo the protracted ritual purification, if they can afford to do so. No matter how ill the supplicant or how grave the emergency, the guardians of many temples will not admit a client if he cannot give a rich gift to the custodian. Even after one has gained admission and survived the ceremonies, the guardians will not permit the neophyte to leave until he makes still another gift.

The supplicant entering the temple is first stripped of all his or her clothes. In everyday life the Nacirema avoids exposure of his body and its natural functions. Bathing and excretory acts are performed only in the secrecy of the household shrine, where they are ritualised as part of the body-rites. Psychological shock results from the fact that body secrecy is suddenly lost upon entry into the *latipso*. A man, whose own wife has never seen him in the excretory act, suddenly finds himself naked and assisted by a vestal maiden while he performs his natural functions into a sacred vessel. The sort of ceremonial treatment is necessitated by the fact that the excreta are used by a diviner to ascertain the course and nature of the client's sickness. Female clients, on the other hand, find their naked bodies are subject to the scrutiny, manipulation and prodding of the medicine men.

Few supplicants in the temple are well enough to do anything but lie on their hard beds. The daily ceremonies, like the rites of holy-mouth-men, involve discomfort and torture. With ritual precision, the vestals awaken their miserable charges each dawn and roll them about on their beds of pain while performing ablutions, in the formal movements of which the maidens are highly trained. At other times they insert magic wands into the supplicant's mouth or force him to eat substances which are supposed to be healing. From time to time the medicine men come to their clients and jab magically treated needles into their flesh. The fact that these temple ceremonies may not cure, and may even kill the neophyte, in no way decreases the people's faith in the medicine men.

There remains one other kind of practitioner, known as a 'listener'. This witch-doctor has the power to exorcise the devils that lodge in the heads of the people who have been bewitched. The Nacirema believe that parents bewitch their own children. Mothers are particularly suspected of putting a curse on the children while teaching them the secret body-rituals. The counter-magic of the witch doctor is unusual in its lack of ritual. The patient simply tells the 'listener' all his troubles and fears, beginning with the earliest difficulties he can remember. The memory displayed by the Nacirema in these exorcism ceremonies is truly remarkable. It is not uncommon for the patient to bemoan the rejection he felt upon being weaned as a babe, and a few individuals even see their troubles going back to the traumatic effects of their own birth.

In conclusion, mention must be made of certain practices which have their base in native aesthetics but which depend on the pervasive aversion to the natural body and its functions. There are ritual fasts to make fat people thin and ceremonial feasts to make thin people fat. Still other rites are used to make women's breasts larger if they are small and smaller if they are large. General dissatisfaction with breast shape is symbolised by the fact that the ideal form is virtually outside the range of human variation. A few women afflicted with almost inhuman hypermammary development are so idolised they make a handsome living by simply going from village to village and permitting the natives to stare at them for a fee.

Reference has already been made to the fact that excretory functions are ritualised, routinised and relegated to secrecy. Natural reproductive functions are similarly distorted. Intercourse is taboo as a topic and scheduled as an act. Efforts are made to avoid pregnancy by the use of magical materials or by limiting intercourse to certain phases of the moon. Conception is actually very infrequent. When pregnant, women dress so as to hide their condition. Parturition takes place in secret, often without friends or relatives to assist, and the majority of women do not nurse their infants.

Our review of the ritual life of the Nacirema has certainly shown them to be a magic-ridden people. It is hard to understand how they have managed to exist so long under the burdens which they have imposed upon themselves. But even such exotic customs as these take on real meaning when they are viewed with the insight provided by Malinowski when he wrote:

Looking from afar and from above, from our high place of safety in the developed civilisation, it is easy to see all the crudity and irrelevance of magic. But without its power and guidance early man could not have mastered his practical difficulties as he has done, nor could man have advanced to the higher stages of civilisation.

The loss of the creature

From *Ways of Reading:
An Anthology for Writers* by
Walker Percy.

An American couple, we will say, drive down to Mexico. They see the usual sights and have a fair time of it. Yet they are never without the sense of missing something. Although Taxco and Guernavaca are interesting and picturesque as advertised, they fall short of 'it'. What do the couple have in mind by 'it'? What do they really hope for? What sort of experience could they have in Mexico so that upon their return, they would feel that 'it' had happened? We have a clue: their hope has something to do with their own role as tourists in a foreign country and the way in which they conceive this role. It has something to do with other American tourists. Certainly they feel that they are very far from 'it' when, after travelling five thousand miles, they arrive at the plaza in Guanajuato only to find themselves surrounded by a dozen other couples from the Midwest.

Already we may distinguish authentic and unauthentic elements. First, we see the problem the couple faces and we understand their efforts to surmount it. The problem is to find an 'unspoiled' place. 'Unspoiled' does not mean only that a place is left physically intact; it means also that it is not encrusted by renown and by the familiar (as in Taxco), that it has not been discovered by others. We understand that the couple really want to get at the place and enjoy it. Yet at the same time we wonder if there is not something wrong in their dislike of their compatriots. Does access to the place require the exclusion of others?

Let us see what happens.

The couple decide to drive from Guanajuato to Mexico City. On the way they get lost. After hours on a rocky mountain road, they find themselves in a tiny valley not even marked on the map. There they discover an Indian village. Some sort of religious festival is going on. It is apparently a corn dance in supplication of the rain god.

The couple know at once that this is 'it'. They are entranced. They spend several days in the village, observing the Indians and being themselves observed with friendly curiosity.

Now may we not say that the sightseers have at last come face to face with an authentic sight, a sight which is charming, quaint, picturesque, unspoiled, and that they see the sight and come away rewarded? Possibly this may occur. Yet it is more likely that what happens is a far cry indeed from an immediate encounter with being, that the experience, while masquerading as such, is in truth a rather desperate impersonation. I use the word 'desperate' advisedly, to signify an actual loss of hope.

The clue to the spuriousness of their enjoyment of the village and the festival is a certain restiveness in the sightseers themselves. It is given expression by their repeated exclamations that 'this is too good to be true', and by their anxiety that it may not prove to be so perfect, and finally by their downright relief at leaving the valley and having the experience in the bag, so to speak – that is, safely embalmed in memory and movie film.

What is the source of their anxiety during the visit? Does it not mean that the couple are looking at the place with a certain standard of performance in mind? Are they like Fabre, who gazed at the world about him with wonder, letting it be what it is; or are they not like the overanxious mother who sees her child as one performing, now doing badly, now doing well? The village is their child and their love for it is an anxious love because they are afraid that at any moment it might fail them.

We have another clue in their subsequent remark to an ethnologist friend. 'How we wished you had been there with us! What a perfect gold-mine of folkways! We kept wishing that you were there! You must return with us.' This surely testifies to a generosity of spirit, a willingness to share their experience with others, not at all like their feelings toward their fellow Iowans on the plaza at Guanajuato!

I am afraid this is not the case at all. It is true that they longed for their ethnologist friend, but it was for an entirely different reason. They wanted him, not to share their experience, but to certify their experience as genuine.

'This is it' and 'Now we are really living' do not necessarily refer to the sovereign encounter of the person with the sight that enlivens the mind and gladdens the heart. It means that now at last we are having the acceptable experience. The present experience is always measured by a prototype, the 'it' of their dreams. 'Now I am really living' means that now I am filling the role of sightseer and the sight is living up to the prototype of sights. This quaint and picturesque village is measured by a Platonic ideal of 'The Quaint and the Picturesque'.

Hence their anxiety during the encounter. For at any minute something could go wrong. A fellow Iowan might emerge from a hut: the chief might show them his Sears catalogue. (If the failures are 'wrong' enough as these are, they might still be turned to account as rueful conversation pieces: 'There we were expecting the chief to bring us a *churinga* and he shows up with a Sears catalogue!'). They have snatched victory from disaster but their experience always runs the danger of failure.

They need the ethnologist to certify their experience as genuine. This is borne out by their behaviour when the three of them return for the next corn dance. During the dance, the couple do not watch the goings-on; instead they watch the ethnologist! Their highest hope is that their friend should find the dance interesting. And if he should show signs of true absorption, an interest in the goings-on so powerful that he becomes oblivious of his friends – then their cup is full. 'Didn't we tell you?' they say at last. What they want from him is not ethnological explanations; all they want is his approval.

What has taken place is a radical loss of sovereignty over that which is as much theirs as it is the ethnologist's. The fault does not lie with the ethnologist. He has no wish to stake a claim to the village; in fact, he desires the opposite: he will bore his friends to death by telling them about the village and the meaning of the folkways. A degree of sovereignty has been surrendered by the couple. It is the nature of the loss, moreover, that they are not aware of the loss, beyond a certain uneasiness. (Even if they read this and admitted it, it would be very difficult for them to bridge the gap in their confrontation of the world. Their consciousness of the corn dance cannot escape their consciousness of their consciousness, so that with the onset of the first direct enjoyment, their higher consciousness pounces and certifies: 'Now you are doing it! Now you are really living!' and, in certifying the experience, sets it at nought.)

Their basic placement in the world is such that they recognise a priority of title of the expert over his particular department of being. The whole horizon of being is staked out by 'them', the experts. The highest satisfaction of the sightseer (not merely the tourist but any layman seer of sights) is that his sight should be certified as genuine. The worst of this impoverishment is that there is no sense of impoverishment. The surrender of title is so complete that it never even occurs to one to reassert title. A poor man may envy the rich man, but the sightseer does not envy the expert. When a caste system becomes absolute, envy disappears. Yet the caste of layman expert is not the fault of the expert. It is due altogether to the eager surrender of sovereignty by the layman so that he may take up the role not of the person but of the consumer.

A We are all familiar with the phrases 'This is it' and 'Now we are really living'. At face value, they seem to indicate little more than expressions of excitement. The author of this extract draws a deeper conclusion. Describe what you think he means. Is there anything from your own experience (not necessarily related to travel) which confirms or denies this?

B How is this related to the notion that for the tourists their 'experience always runs the danger of failure'? How can an experience fail? Have any of your experiences ever failed? Have any ever succeeded?

C Why does the author suggest that there is no way of avoiding what he describes as 'impoverishment'? Do you think he is correct?

D In what way, if any, could animals feel 'impoverished' in the same way that we might do? Does this tell us anything about how language and culture relate to the human experience?

What's in a name? That which we call a rose
By another name would smell as sweet.
William Shakespeare

If thought corrupts language, language can also corrupt thought.
George Orwell

WITH A KNOWLEDGE OF THE NAME COMES A DISTINCTER RECOGNITION AND KNOWLEDGE OF THE THING.
Henry David Thoreau

Language is not only the vehicle of thought, it is a great and efficient instrument in thinking.
Humphrey Davy

One of the most powerful aspects of language is the way it is used to make simple classifications: 'animals'; 'courage'; 'blue'. One of the most dangerous aspects of language is the way it is used to make simplistic classifications: 'Third World'; 'fascist'; 'terrorist'; 'communist'.
Anon

The limits of my language stand for the limits of my world.
Ludwig Wittgenstein

Verbosity leads to unclear, inarticulate things. .
Dan Quayle

I know more than I can say.
Michael Polanyi

IF YOU CAN'T SAY IT, YOU DON'T KNOW IT.
Hans Reichenbach

We are getting into semantics again. If we use words, there is a very grave danger they will be misinterpreted.
H. R. Haldeman

How often misused words generate misleading thoughts.
Herbert Spencer

Aims

By the end of this chapter you should:

- appreciate that language is an incredibly rich and complex thing, and that it can be non-spoken
- appreciate the distinction between language as a neutral, transparent tool for communication and language as a value-laden system of persuasion and implication
- understand that language may not map perfectly to the 'real world' and that this can mask a poor understanding of the 'real world'
- understand the arguments for and against the position that language can affect thought
- be informed about some of the issues raised by the existence of several languages
- begin to appreciate the subtleties and difficulties associated with the concept of meaning
- begin to appreciate possible links between language, experience and identity.

Introduction

The whole concept of naming has long and mysterious overtones in mythology, religion, literature and superstition. 'In the beginning was the Word . . .' will be a familiar phrase to many, but it is not only Christians for whom words have a mystic significance. Orthodox Jews do not name a child after any living relative. In some creation myths, the act of naming things brings them into existence and in some religions the name of God is secret and unutterable. In some cultures people are reluctant to tell strangers their names, for fear of giving the strangers power over them. (In some tribes people even had two names – their 'real' one and one for strangers.)

Nor are we immune from this way of treating words with a certain amount of respect. We are offended when people consistently forget our names, even if they remember our faces. We feel that referring to humans by numbers and not names is cold and unfeeling (though of course in some ways a number is a word just like a name). Some people have words they would rather not use for fear of bringing bad luck – this is why we use terms like 'pushing up the daisies' rather than 'dead'. Some even consider it 'tempting fate' to talk too much about a baby before it is born, fearing the words will bring on a difficult or dangerous birth.

Despite these examples, most of us no longer believe that language is important in this way, and can hardly see what all the fuss was ever about. Ever since the story of the Danish King Canute who tried to order the waves back, but who got his feet wet, we have realised that the world does not bend to our language. We have words to describe the world, and we all use them – as long as we all use the same words then everything will work out. Language is rather like money – it has no intrinsic value, but a socially constructed purpose. We need to communicate, and depending on where and in what age we are born, we will learn whatever language we are taught, and use it more or less effectively to do what we need to do. Language may change over the centuries, and older folk may make a little fuss about each new generation taking liberties with grammar, but that applies to most fields of life! What could be more transparent and easy to understand than words and language?

In this chapter we shall see that language, while not having any magical effects, is in fact far from simple and straightforward. Spoken language presents enormous problems and areas of research not only to linguists, but also to philosophers, computational theorists, anthropologists, psychologists, evolutionary biologists and neurobiologists. To us, spoken language appears to be effortless, simple and easy – but if eagles could speak, they would probably describe their aerial manoeuvres in much the same way. The ease with which language comes to us makes it all the more miraculous. If I make up a sentence such as 'Blue Arabian princesses always choose to eat roast pineapple rather than grilled jellyfish, except when dining with the emperor's cousin' then not only have I constructed something unique in the history of the Universe, but I have also managed to convey to you, in the space of a few seconds, a remarkably complex hypothetical situation. Even though I know only a few thousand words, I can convey an unlimited number of ideas about people, places and times; I can create whole worlds of the imagination. Once we begin to look closely at what words actually mean, rather than what dictionaries say they mean, we shall see that anyone who can use everyday language is performing incredible mental feats whenever they utter a single, simple, meaningful sentence.

Humans are unique in their ability to use language. Although other animals have signs and signals for certain biological needs and functions (and arguably even emotions), none lives in the same linguistic world that we do. Every group or tribe of humans ever discovered has had a language of its own; deaf and speechless humans develop sign languages every bit as subtle and nuanced as spoken languages. We shall see that our language capacity is many-faceted, and is intimately related to the human experience.

A Are there any phrases or sayings that you (or someone you know) avoid because they are unlucky in some way, or which 'shouldn't be said' for some reason?

B Think of a situation where language has got in the way of straightforward communication, or where language has been abused to serve some end other than the neutral transfer of information.

Language and values

The point about language and values is best made through some examples.

- What is the difference between a devout believer and a fanatic?
- What is the difference between a black person, a person of colour, a coloured, a non-white, and a nigger?

- When the African National Congress was fighting a guerrilla war in South Africa against the apartheid regime were they freedom fighters or terrorists? Justify your choice.
- Which of the above descriptions would you apply to the PLO or the IRA?
- Look up the words 'black' and 'white' in a detailed dictionary. Is it possible to draw a conclusion about racial characteristics or how they are perceived?

In each of these cases we might distinguish between what object/concept the word refers to and the ideas associated with it. Technically speaking, 'black man' and 'nigger' might refer to the same person, but one is clearly offensive and unacceptable (although it is interesting to note that some black people use the word 'nigger' themselves, and in this context it is not racist). The denotation of the word 'nigger' is a black person, but the word has racist **connotations**. Many words have connotations.

A What is the denotation of the word 'stud' (that is, what does the word stand for)? What is the connotation of the word?

B What is the denotation of the word 'slut'? What is the connotation of the word?

C Here is an extract from the *Encyclopaedia Britannica*:

The famous siege of the Alamo in San Antonio lasted from February 23 to March 6, 1836. The strategic objective of the stand was to delay Mexican forces and thereby permit military organisation of the Texan settlers. As the battle climaxed with a massive attack over the walls, the defenders (about 187) were all killed. Among the dead were the famous frontiersmen Jim Bowie and Davy Crocket. On April 21 Sam Houston led a surprise attack on the Mexican troops at San Jacinto and he succeeded in capturing Santa Anna and in securing victory for the Texans.

The Texan revolution was not simply a fight between the Anglo-American settlers and Mexican troops; it was a revolution of all the people who were living in Texas against what many of them regarded as tyrannical rule from a distant source. Many of the leaders in the revolution and many of the armed settlers who took part were Mexican.

Which side do you think the writer of the piece supported? Why?

Rewrite the piece to give essentially the same information but with the opposite bias. You may find it helpful to refer to 'Mad Dogs and Englishmen' on page 202 and 'Mokusatsu' on page 203.

D Consider the following:

- I am firm; you are stubborn; he is a pig-headed fool.
- I am sparkling and witty; you are talking a lot; he is jabbering on.
- I daydream; you are an escapist; he is totally delusional.

E 'Conjugate' the following in the same way:

- I am ambitious...
- I have a sense of humour...
- I love my country...

The rest of this section consists of extracts that deal with issues such as racism, terrorism, the Gulf War, the dropping of the atomic bomb in the Second World War and a fairy tale. Apart from the fairy tale, you might think that the theme is something to do with war, or maybe morality. It is easy enough to link the articles to these themes. But the real point of looking at these extracts now is to consider how the language is used in each case, and how the 'facts' are conveyed in and by language. As you read, think carefully about the way the words are chosen and the way they are put together.

Mad Dogs and Englishmen

These are all expressions used by the British press while covering the Gulf War

We have...

army, navy and air force

reporting guidelines

press briefings

They have...

a war machine

censorship

propaganda

We...

suppress

neutralise

dig in

They...

destroy

kill

cower

We launch...

first strikes

pre-emptively

They launch...

sneak missile attacks

without provocation

Our soldiers are...

boys

lads

cautious

confident

young knights of the skies

loyal

desert rats

resolute

brave

Their soldiers are...

troops

hordes

cowardly

desperate

bastards of Baghdad

blindly obedient

mad dogs

ruthless

fanatical

Our missiles are...

like Luke Skywalker zapping
Darth Vader

causing collateral damage

Their missiles are...

ageing duds (*rhymes
with scuds*)

killing innocent civilians

George Bush is...

at peace with himself

resolute

statesmanlike

assured

Saddam Hussein is...

demented

defiant

an evil tyrant

a crackpot monster

Our planes...

suffer from a high rate of attrition

fail to return from missions

Their planes...

are shot out of the sky

are zapped

Mokusatsu

Asked what he would undertake first,
Were he called upon to rule a nation,
Confucius replied: 'To correct language...
If language is not correct
Then what is said is not what is meant;
Then what ought to be done remains undone;
If this remains undone, morals and art will deteriorate;
If morals and art deteriorate, justice will go astray;
If justice goes astray
The people will stand about in helpless confusion.
Hence there must be no arbitrariness in what is said.
This matters above everything.'

Asked to surrender in World War II,
The Japanese employed the word 'mokusatsu'
In replying to the Potsdam ultimatum.

The word given out by the Dome news agency
Was interpreted in Washington as 'treat with contempt'
Rather than 'withholding comment' – pending a decision –
Its correct meaning.

The American concluded that their ultimatum had been rejected;
The boys in the back-room could play with their new toy.
A hundred and forty thousand people lay around in helpless confusion.

Today 'peace' is mistranslated and means a seething stalemate
Instead of calm;
'Strength' is mistranslated, and means paranoid force
Instead of right-minded confidence;
'Defence' is mistranslated and means the psychotic accumulation of weapons
Instead of the exercise of skill;
'Testing' is mistranslated and means the detonation of a nuclear device and
the release of radioactive clouds
Instead of a tentative experiment;
A 'disarmament treaty' is mistranslated and means dismantling obsolete
weapons in the face of economic constraints,
Ritually attended by a spurious euphoria;
'First strike' is mistranslated
And means last strike;
'Safety' is mistranslated,
and means danger.

by Heathcote Williams

There was Once

by Margaret Atwood

– There was once a poor girl, as beautiful as she was good, who lived with her wicked stepmother in a house in the forest.

– Forest? Forest is passé. I mean, I've had it with this all this wilderness stuff. It's not the right image of our society today. Let's have some urban for a change.

– There was once a poor girl, as beautiful as she was good, who lived with her wicked stepmother in a house in the suburbs.

– That's better. But I have to seriously question this word 'poor'.

– But she was poor!

– Poor is relative. She lived in a house didn't she?

– Yes.

– Then socio-economically speaking, she was not poor.

– But none of the money was hers. The whole point of the story is that the wicked stepmother makes her wear old clothes and sleep in the fireplace.

– Aha! They had a fireplace. With 'poor', let me tell you, there's no fireplace. Come down to the park, come to the subway stations after dark, come down to where they sleep in cardboard boxes, and I'll show you poor!

– There was once a middle-class girl, as beautiful as she was good –

– Stop right there. I think we can cut the 'beautiful' don't you? Women these days have to deal with too many intimidating physical role models as it is, what with all these bimbos in the adverts. Can't you make her, well, more average?

– There was once a girl who was a little overweight and whose front teeth stuck out. Who –

– I don't think it's nice to make fun of people's appearances. Plus you are encouraging anorexia.

– I wasn't making fun! I was just describing.

– Skip the description. Description oppresses. But you can say what colour she was.

– What colour?

– You know. Black. Brown. White. Red. Yellow. Those are the choices. And I'm telling you right now that I've had enough of white. Dominant culture this, dominant culture that...

– I don't know what colour.

– Well it would probably be your colour wouldn't it?

– But this isn't about me! It's about this girl –

– Everything is about you.

– Sounds to me like you don't want to hear this story at all.

– Oh well, go on. You could make her ethnic. That might help.

– There was once a girl of indeterminate descent, as average looking as she was good, who lived with her wicked –

– Another thing. Good and wicked. Don't you think we should transcend these puritanical, judgmental, moralistic epithets? I mean, so much of it is conditioning isn't it?

– There was once a girl, as average-looking as she was well-adjusted, who lived with her stepmother, who was not a very open and loving person, because she herself had been abused in childhood.

– Better. But I am so tired of negative female images. And stepmothers – they always get it in the neck! Change it to stepfather why don't you? That would make more sense anyway, considering the bad behaviour you are about to describe. And throw in some whips and chains. We all know what those twisted, repressed, middle-aged men are like –

– Hey just a minute! I'm a middle-aged –

– Stuff it Mr Nosy Parker. Nobody asked you. Go on.

– There was once a girl –

– How old was she?

– I don't know. She was young.

– This ends with a marriage, right?

– Well, not to blow the plot, but – yes.

– Then you can scratch the condescending paternalistic terminology. It's woman pal. Woman.

– There was once –

– What's this 'was once'? Enough of the dead past. Tell me about now.

– There –

– So?

– So what?

– So, why not here?

A What does this conversation tell us about the opening phrase, 'There was once a poor girl, as beautiful as she was good, who lived with her wicked stepmother in a house in the forest'?
B What sort of things does the second speaker object to?
C What is the principle behind the objections?
D Is the principle reasonable?
E What would happen if the second speaker applied her own principle to her own speech?
F What can we learn about language from his dialogue?
G Take a simple sentence and subject it to the same scrutiny as has been done here.

Language and thought

We dissect nature along lines laid down by our native language. Language is not simply a reporting device for experience but a defining framework for it.

Benjamin Whorf

Developing an awareness that language contains values, and a sensitivity to the possibility of being influenced by these values, is important because it helps us to retain our independence and not be influenced by 'weasel words'. However, some have suggested that the influence of language runs far deeper than values, and that the languages we speak determine what we can think. This might sound silly at first, but **linguistic determinism** is the idea that our thoughts are completely limited by our language and is sometimes called the **Sapir–Whorf hypothesis**, after the two anthropologists who suggested it. Particularly interesting evidence has been found from interviews with bilingual Japanese women living in America. These women were married to Americans and only spoke Japanese when they met each other – they used English the rest of the time. According to the Sapir-Whorf hypothesis, the way these women thought should vary according to which language they were using, and an experiment was conducted to see whether or not this was the case.

The experiment involved a bilingual Japanese interviewer who visited each woman twice. In the first interview, he chatted with them only in Japanese. In the second interview, he asked them exactly the same questions, but only in English. The results are surprising; rather than giving the same answers but in different languages, as one might expect, the answers that were given seemed to depend on the language spoken. Here are two examples where the same woman seemed to change her views completely.

'When my wishes conflict with my family's . . .
. . . it is a time of great unhappiness.' (Japanese)

. . . I do what I want.' (English)

'Real friends should . . .
. . . help each other.' (Japanese)

. . . be very frank.' (English)

Proponents of the Sapir-Whorf hypothesis argue that the bilingual women 'lived in different language worlds' when they spoke English and Japanese, and this accounted for the difference in answers, attitudes and thoughts.

We might also consider the role of language in our everyday lives and skills. Think of, for example, the surgeon specialising in the human hand who has a vast knowledge of every muscle, vein and joint. Much of this knowledge comes from extensive experience and training, but the training is not just a matter of chance. Training is important because in a few years it is possible to pass on what has taken hundreds of years to find out. The medical profession has developed a highly specialised and technical sub-language which has the sole purpose of communicating anatomical structure and form. The training of the surgeon must involve learning this dialect, because without it the anatomical facts could not be passed on to her with any degree of precision. By this argument, we need to develop certain aspects of language before certain skills.

A The argument above suggests that it is unimaginable for us to become experts in certain skills without learning the language developed for them. Is this correct? To what extent might this suggest that language determines thought?

B Can you imagine developing the language of a skill without developing the skills itself? What might this suggest about the relationship between language and skills?

C How do you think the surgeon learned the vocabulary she needed?

D Explain, in words, how to tie your shoelaces. Do the words make it any easier? Do you use the words when you are tying your laces?

E To what extent are your skills and thoughts dependent on language?

There seems to be some merit to the claim that aspects of language need to be developed before certain skills. If we have words for certain things then it makes effective communication and effective action much easier. Since these things (presumably) rely on thought, it seems that words make thought easier. In an extreme case, taking mathematics as a language (debatable, but let that pass for a moment), imagine trying to do maths of any complexity without employing the symbolic language of algebra. Trying to solve complex equations using words seems ridiculous, and certainly far harder than employing algebraic language. It is similarly difficult to imagine a lawyer who is not familiar with legal language, even ignoring the ridicule from fellow professionals (remember language also mediates social inclusion).

So if surgeons, mathematicians and lawyers can use their medical, mathematical and legal languages to think in highly sophisticated ways about their subjects, perhaps, by analogy, different natural languages lend themselves to thinking about nature in completely different ways. Tony Croft once quipped, *'Italian is designed for love; we speak with our friends in French; we use English to talk to our dogs.'*

> **A** The analogy between 'professional languages' and natural languages is used in the quote from Croft to suggest that different natural languages are better suited to certain tasks. Is this a good analogy?
>
> **B** If you are bilingual or trilingual, do you find it easier to think certain things in certain languages? Is it possible to think exactly the same things in different languages?

This idea has been famously extended by George Orwell in *1984*, when he wrote about the government-invented language, Newspeak.

The purpose of Newspeak was not only to provide a medium of expression for the world-view and mental habits proper to devotees of Ingsoc [the ruling political party], *but to make all other modes of thought impossible. It was intended that when Newspeak had been adopted once and for all and Oldspeak forgotten, a heretical thought – that is a thought divergent from the principles of Ingsoc – should be literally unthinkable, at least so far as thought is dependent on words. Its vocabulary was so constructed as to give exact and often very subtle expression to every meaning that a party member could properly wish to express, while excluding all other meanings and also the possibility of arriving at them by indirect methods. This was done partly by the invention of new words but chiefly by eliminating undesirable words and by stripping such words as remained of unorthodox meanings, and so far as possible of all secondary meanings whatever. To give a simple example – the word 'free' still existed in Newspeak, but it could only be used in statements such as 'This dog is free from lice' or 'This field is free from weeds'. It could not be used in its old sense of 'politically free' or 'intellectually free', since political and intellectual freedom no longer existed even as concepts, and were therefore of necessity nameless. Quite apart from the suppression of definitely heretical words, reduction of vocabulary was regarded as an end in itself, and no word that could be dispensed with was allowed to survive. Newspeak was designed not to extend but to diminish the range of thought, and this purpose was indirectly assisted by cutting the choice of words down to a minimum.*

> **A** Orwell notes that 'a heretical thought . . . should be literally unthinkable'. What does he mean?
>
> **B** Do you think that his analysis of the term 'free' is correct? Would people have the concept without the word?
>
> **C** Orwell is writing about a totalitarian society where language is under the direct control of the Government. Is the passage relevant to us in a more general sense?

Compared to the suggestion that language is needed for effective action, Orwell was defending a stronger form of the Sapir-Whorf hypothesis. Stronger still was its original formulation. In a now famous passage, Whorf wrote:

We dissect nature along lines laid down by our native languages. The categories and types that we isolate from the world of phenomena we do not find there because they stare every observer in the face; on the contrary, the world is presented in a kaleidoscopic flux of impressions which has to be organised by our minds – and this means largely by the linguistic systems in our minds. We cut nature up, organise it into concepts, and ascribe significances as we do, largely because we are parties to an agreement to organise it in this way . . . [this agreement is] codified in the patterns of our language.

You can see that Whorf suggested that language is the way humans solve what we have seen is a fundamental problem with our perception – our need to provide a structure to our sensory inputs. He suggests that people literally think in English, or Spanish, or Swahili. When you come across this idea for the first time, it may seem to be a bizarre and extreme position; that language shapes our entire worldview would suggest that native speakers of different languages see the world in a completely different way to each other. We should be clear that this has moved well beyond the vague 'French is the language of love' statement – it is a very precise articulation of the notion that our complete conceptual and intellectual apparatus is intimately linked to the spoken language. This may seem an absurd position, and one that can be instantly dismissed by common sense. After all, if I go on holiday to China and meet someone with whom spoken communication is impossible, we seem to share most concepts (as far as we can tell, which admittedly, may not be much) and deal with the world in the same way. However, common sense is not always a trustworthy guide to what is true and what is not, and some of the evidence we have seen so far might be difficult to explain otherwise (recall the data from bilingual Japanese women) so we should not dismiss Whorf out of hand. We should look at the evidence.

In one sense, we certainly dissect nature along lines laid down by our native languages, at least in the way we speak. We do not have words for every concept or thing, and different languages sometimes have words with no direct translation into other languages. For example, the Portuguese word 'geram' means 'unbearably cute'; the German word 'schaudenfreude' means 'pleasure at the misfortune of others'; the French 'chez' means 'at the home of the family of . . .'; 'mamihlapinatapai' from Tierra del Fuego means 'the state of mind in which two people regard each other, and both want something done, but neither of them wants to be the first to do it.' These and other words of the same type have sometimes been taken to support a strong form of linguistic determinism. 'Who but the Germans would have a word for such an idea – they think differently to us!' is often the rather racist remark that goes along with such ideas. But a little reflection should show that, on the contrary, these words completely undermine strong linguistic determinism! When non-German speakers come across a translation of 'schaudenfreude' they aren't unable to grasp its meaning. They think, 'Aha! there is a word for that feeling that I know so well!' The words are strong evidence that speakers of the two languages share a common mental world – which is, in this case, the world of universal human emotion. We might, of course, ask why it is that the Germans have a word for that particular emotion when others do not, and this is certainly worth exploring, but it hardly seems to indicate that their thoughts are radically different to those of anyone else.

The idea that our mental world is far richer than our vocabulary is the basis of *The Deeper Meaning of Liff* by Douglas Adams, from which some of the following examples are taken.

CORRIEARKLET (n) The moment at which two people approaching from opposite ends of a long passageway, recognise each other and immediately pretend they haven't. This is to avoid the ghastly embarrassment of having to continue recognising each other the whole length of the corridor.

ELBONICS (n) The actions of two people manoeuvring for an armrest in a cinema.

ELECELLERATION (n) The mistaken notion that the more often, or the harder, you press an elevator button, the faster it will arrive.

OUGHTERBY (n) Someone you don't want to invite to a party but whom you know you have to as a matter of duty.

SCONSER (n) A person who looks around when talking to you, to see if there's anyone more interesting about.

SCAPTOFT (n) The absurd flap of hair a vain and balding man grows long above one ear to comb it to the other ear.

SHOEBURYNESS (n) The vague uncomfortable feeling you get when sitting on a seat which is still warm from somebody else's bottom.

Again, all these words are probably naming things with which you are already familiar, but which are unnamed. It can be interesting to discuss these ideas with speakers of other languages and to find concepts which have no direct translation.

> **A** Identify some more mental concepts for which there should be words. Why is it difficult to do so? What implications does this have for the relationship between language and thought?

There is however, more evidence which Whorf used to support his theory of linguistic determinism:

- The perception of colour. Whorf noted that different languages have different numbers of colour words. Latin has no words for brown or grey; Shona speakers have separate words for greenish-yellow and yellowish-green and so on. He explains this by suggesting that the speakers of these languages cannot tell the difference between these colours, and so do not give names to them. Is this convincing?
- As an amateur linguist, Whorf's translations indicated to him that speakers of Apache and English think entirely differently. Here are some examples (Apache translation in italics);
    It is a dripping spring. → *As water or springs, whiteness moves downward.*
    The boat is grounded on the beach. → *It is on the beach, pointwise as an event of canoe motion.*

He invites people to a feast. → *He, or somebody, goes for eaters of cooked food.*

He cleans a gun with a ramrod. → *He directs a hollow moving dry spot by movement of tool.*

With such different ways of describing the world, the speakers must think differently. Is this convincing?

Many have argued, however, that this evidence for linguistic determinism is not strong. Regarding colour, our visual apparatus is built around rods and cones which are sensitive to certain frequencies of light. Irrespective of the language we speak, all humans share basic physiology. Experiments have shown that speakers of colour-impoverished languages can distinguish between items which have colours outside their vocabulary. And how would babies learn to perceive colour if they needed language to do so? Animals don't need it, so why should we?

Some also remain unconvinced by the issue of translations. On the basis of different ways of speaking. Whorf argues that different ways of speaking suggest different ways of thinking. But surprisingly, he has no evidence of different ways of thinking other than their way of speaking (see the questions below for more analysis of this). It also turns out that Whorf made his claim about the ways Apaches think without meeting any, and was content to merely study their grammar. It is difficult to see how he could really have understood their thoughts!

Perhaps the most famous linguistic story of all relates to this area – it is about Inuit and the number of words they have for snow. Some accounts suggest that they have up to 400 words for different types of snow with meanings such as 'deep, soft snow, making walking difficult'; 'snowdrift formed on the side of a steep hill'; 'snowdrifts formed by a north-east wind'; 'snow with a thin hard crust that gives way underfoot'; 'snow roughened by rain or frost' and so on. Proponents of the Sapir-Whorf hypothesis have taken this as the archetypal example of linguistic determinism, and suggested that Inuit live in a different conceptual world to speakers of other languages, and that if you and an Inuit were to look out over a snowy landscape, you would see entirely different scenes.

Unfortunately (as it seems such a gripping example), the notion that Inuit have hundreds of ideas for snow is a complete myth. Stephen Pinker, in his brilliant *The Language Instinct*, notes that the ideas could not have originated with anyone who has actually studied the Yupik and Inuit-Inuoiaq languages spoken from Siberia to Greenland. Apparently, Whorf's teacher mentioned in 1911 that there were four unrelated root words for 'snow', Whorf exaggerated this to seven and implied that there were more. From there began the legend and its successively inflated exaggerations and misinterpretations. Some experts maintain that there are around a dozen words, but with 'snow', 'slush', 'avalanche', 'hardpack', 'powder', 'drift', 'blizzard' and 'dusting' (and I am sure there are others), English doesn't come too far behind. In *The Great Eskimo Vocabulary Hoax*, the linguist Geoffrey Pullman makes a second point. Even if there were a large number of words for 'snow', so what? Printers have literally thousands of words for different fonts and are probably far more alert and aware of nuances in printed scripts, but that does not mean printers have a different perceptual status. Surely this is another example of the weaker form of linguistic determinism – that related to the language of the surgeon, mathematician and lawyer.

A When you are trying to solve a problem of some sort, to what extent is it useful to think in words? Do you ever find it helpful to read a problem out loud? What does this tell you?

B Consider Whorf's Apache evidence. Let us couch this argument in logical terms:

Premise: Apaches speak differently.

Conclusion: Apaches think differently.

You should be able to see that this is not a valid argument. In fact, there is a missing premise, one which Whorf assumed but did not make explicit. What additional premise is required to make the argument logically valid? Why does this premise, far from bolstering the argument, completely undermine it?

Just because Whorf's argument is invalid does not mean that his conclusion is wrong. So after all the different examples and ideas, and hopefully after some reflective introspection, the big question still remains. To what extent is thought dependent on language?

Language as a means of miscommunication

Distrust of grammar is the first requisite for philosophising.

Ludwig Wittgenstein

There are many puzzles, riddles and jokes which are based around language. Here are some old favourites:

- What happens when an irresistible force meets an immovable object?
- Question: Which is better – eternal happiness or a bar of chocolate?
  Answer: Nothing is better than eternal happiness, but a bar of chocolate is better than nothing. Therefore a bar of chocolate is better than eternal happiness.
- First man: I didn't sleep with my wife before we were married. Did you?
  Second man: I don't know – what was her maiden name?

Before you go any further, try to answer the first question and resolve the ridiculous conclusion of the second example.

Some people, including philosophers, have said that philosophers are more concerned with playing clever games using complicated words than with actually getting to grips with reality. They felt this way because problems in language seemed to be getting in the way of them making any progress with their inquiries. As a result, the twentieth century saw philosophers take a very close look at language, with the result that some very influential thinkers (most notably **the logical positivists**) suggested that much of what we say is completely and utterly without any meaning! While a detailed analysis of these ideas is beyond our scope here, in any search for reliable knowledge it is helpful to consider a few of the ways in which language can get in the way of understanding.

The most obvious difficulty is when a word has several meanings. This is such a persistent problem that logicians talk about the **fallacy of ambiguity**. In the world of physical objects, we are well aware that just because things look the same doesn't necessarily mean that they are the same (we learn this from bitter experience with tomato ketchup and chilli sauce). But this is not always so clear in the world of abstract concepts. A word may appear to be one thing, but turn out to be another.

A In the following sentences, analyse the different ways in which the bold words are used.

- Speeding is against the **law**.
- Things fall according to the **law** of gravity.
- It's an unwritten **law** that to get big business deals you need to bribe officials.
- If you persistently speed, the **law** of averages says that sooner or later you'll be caught.
- The **laws** of grammar dictate that you should not split infinitives.

- It is the **truth** that a triangle has three sides.
- 'There is ice at the North Pole' is the **truth**.
- There is real **truth** in that painting.
- 'Ain't that the **truth**!'

B Things get much worse when we begin to look at the meanings of sentences. Consider 'Time flies like an arrow.' This looks like a simple sentence – it means 'Time proceeds as quickly as an arrow proceeds' doesn't it? Here's another meaning: 'Measure the speed of flies in the same way as you measure the speed of an arrow.' Find three other meanings of the sentence, 'Time flies like an arrow.'

C Consider this sentence: 'We need some new alternative source of energy.' What would it mean if you said this? What would it mean if said by the chairman of an oil company?

D Think of some other phrases with multiple interpretations.

In addition to problems of ambiguity, we can sometimes be led into trouble by the **structure of sentences**. A common form of sentence in some languages is 'This chocolate is nice.' It is the form of the sentence we are interested in here. Similar sentences might be 'I am tired' or 'We are in love' or 'The rose is red.'

This type of sentence may seem innocent enough, but the concept behind the last example came under some scrutiny in previous chapters. When we say 'The rose is red' we mean that looking at this rose gives us the sensation of redness. The redness was not in the rose because red is an experience. Admittedly, the rose has properties which seem to cause most humans to have this experience under certain lighting conditions, but that does not mean the rose possesses some quality of redness. The point is far more obvious with regard to 'The chocolate is nice.' Even though we understand the sentiment, in fact, the chocolate is not nice. Niceness is not a property that can exist outside the mind. When we say 'The chocolate is nice' we are using a shorthand for something like 'When I eat the chocolate, I have a sensation which I find pleasurable.' There is room for debate here, but we must be alert to the fact that language may suggest that properties of the mind are to be found in the material world.

A Each of the following sentences asserts that certain material objects possess certain qualities. In which cases are the qualities properties of the mind, and in which cases are they properties of the objects?

- The drink is sweet.
- This knife is sharp.
- It is a hot day.
- We are in love.
- That is an excellent film.
- This is a hard exam.

- She is so sweet.
- He is as sharp as a knife.
- This curry is hot.
- The drink is fizzy.
- Here is a hard chair.
- He is intelligent.

B If you found any of the qualities to be in the mind, explain the meanings of the sentences.

The final problem we shall consider is that which arises when we rename a problem and think we have solved it. Imagine a little boy and his dad out for a walk. The boy sees some birds swooping around, falling, rising and squawking. The boy asks his dad why the birds are behaving in that way, and the father replies, 'Because they are starlings, and that is what starlings do.' Now children are wonderful in that they might not let Daddy get away with that – and nor should they. The problem of the birds' behaviour has been renamed as 'starling behaviour', but it is still a problem. As we all know, a repeated 'why?' may soon become difficult to answer, but it is better to admit ignorance than just to rename the problem.

The problem can be more or less serious, depending on the context. If I say that I find someone is attractive and you ask me why, I might say it is because they have big eyes. Well, the problem was to explain why a particular face is attractive, and now the problem has become to explain why big eyes are attractive. We may be happy to leave it there, and in this case we have clarified the statement somewhat, but we have made little progress towards understanding the nature of attractive features. We could ask ourselves why we find large eyes attractive, but the chain of 'whys' can go on and on, and quite when we should be satisfied is very difficult to determine. Suffice to say that if you give an answer which is no more general than the question, and is still quite mysterious, then you may have used language to rename the problem, but you have still made no progress towards a solution.

A Identify the problem with the following explanations:

- The bird found its way home by its homing instinct.
- He seems nervous; perhaps he has lost his confidence.
- Everyone listens to her – she has real presence.
- She seems so relaxed, as if she has found a new serenity.
- He fell to the ground, senseless. He must have lost consciousness.
- It fell because of gravity.
- He did well on the test because he has such a high IQ.

Language and meaning

We have seen that, in our search for reliable knowledge, we need to be wary of several pitfalls of language. We have, however, yet to deal with a very profound problem – that of meaning. What does 'meaning' mean?

The most obvious reply seems to be that language means something because it stands for something 'real' – words label things and thus represent the world. 'John' is a symbol which represents a particular person, and 'brown house' is a pair of symbols which represent a building of a particular colour. However, we quickly run into some obvious problems with this theory of meaning as representation. What does 'different' or 'perhaps' or 'wonderful' label? They clearly do not refer to any object at all, even an abstract one. Even simple phrases can turn out to represent far more than a state of affairs in the material world. The complexities of meaning are usually hidden from us because we are all so incredibly sophisticated at analysing everyday language. (Recall 'Time flies like an arrow' from page 212 and its multiple meanings.)

This is a far from obvious point, but it can best be seen when learning a foreign language. One of my German students said that 'Hab dich lieb' means 'I love you' in German. I don't speak German, but I had thought that 'I love you' was translated as 'Ich liebe dich'. When I asked the student if there was a difference, she said at first that they were the same. The conversation went as follows:

'So are there any other ways you could say "I love you" in German?'

'You could say "Ich mag dich", but you wouldn't say that to your best friend.'

'Why not?'

'It's not as strong as "I love you" in English. "Hab dich lieb" is friendlier.'

'So "Ich mag dich" is an unfriendly way of saying "I love you"?'

'No! It's just that "Hab dich lieb" would be something between boyfriend and girlfriend, or maybe mother and child, or best friends. "Ich mag dich" is more like "I like you". You would say it to somebody if you wanted to get together with them.'

'So would a husband say "Hab dich lieb" to his wife?'

'Not really,' (*screws face up*) 'It's kind of a teenager thing. Or maybe between best friends, or a mother and child. You have to really know each other to use it, but adults wouldn't use it. "Hab dich lieb" is kind of a cute or a cool way of saying it. Adults would sound pretty funny saying it. A husband would say "Ich liebe dich" to his wife. That's closest to "I love you" in English.'

'What would you say to a really close friend?'

'As a teenage girl, I would say "Hab dich lieb".'

'So boys couldn't say that?'

'Well that would indicate that they were gay.'

'But it doesn't mean that girls who say it are lesbian?'

'No.'

'So how would straight teenage boys indicate that they liked their best male friend very much?'

' "Ich mag dich" I suppose ... But that sounds pretty weird. Guys just wouldn't say that, or maybe they'd just say something like "Du bist cool" – "You're cool".'

'OK. And what about if you love running, or eating chocolate, or something?'

' "Ich liebe rennen" is "I love running". "Ich liebe ..." can be about things or people, but when it's about people it must be about boyfriend/girlfriend.'

'And what about "Hab dich lieb"?'

'That can only be about people.'

'How about "I love my pet dog"?'

'No. That would be either "Ich lieb meinen Hund" or "Ich mag meinen Hund" – either would be OK.'

> **A** The German student who told me all this thought that she knew what 'Hab dich lieb' meant, and indeed she did, though perhaps not consciously until we had discussed it. The sentence meant a lot more than it appeared to, and had more meanings than can be found in a dictionary. Find something that is similar in one of the languages you speak. You are looking for language which appears very simple but in fact has many shades of grey, many hidden rules, and which is doing far more than the simple, straightforward communication of one meaning.

The problems of translating between languages can be a source of great amusement. Apparently, when the Ford motor company introduced the Pinto car in Brazil, sales were almost non-existent, but when the company later learned that 'Pinto' is Brazilian slang for 'tiny male genitals' all became clear. Similar problems got an American chicken merchant into trouble when his advertising campaign featured a picture of him with a chicken. The macho slogan was supposed to say, 'It takes a tough man to make a tender chicken,' but when translated into Spanish it came out as, 'It takes a sexually aroused man to be affectionate with a chicken.' Other howlers include the following:

'Bite the wax tadpole.'
('Coca-Cola' as originally translated into Chinese.)

'Pepsi brings your ancestors back from the grave.'
('Pepsi Comes Alive' as originally translated into Chinese.)

'You are invited to take advantage of the chambermaid.'
(In a Japanese hotel.)

'Drop your trousers here for best results.'
(In a Bangkok dry cleaner's.)

'I am amazingly diverted by your entreaty for a room. I can offer you a commodious chamber with balcony imminent to the romantic gorge, and I hope that you want to drop in. A vivacious stream washes my doorsteps, so do not concern yourself that I am not too good in bath, I am superb in bed.'
(From a response to an inquiry about accommodation.)

'It is forbidden to enter a woman, even a foreigner, if dressed as a man.'
(Sign in a Bangkok temple.)

'Would you like to ride on your own ass?'
(Advertisement for donkey rides in Thailand.)

These examples using foreign languages show that meaning is not at all straightforward, but the same is true of any language. The linguist Noam Chomsky uses the words 'brown house' to illustrate the point in English. We immediately know that a brown house is something with a brown exterior, not necessarily a brown interior. In this sense, we use the word 'house' in the sense of a surface, or a covering. A little thought shows that we use 'mountain', 'igloo', and many other words in much the same way. (To show this, consider the following observation: when you are in a cave inside a mountain you would probably say that you could no longer see the mountain, even though you could see the walls in the cave, so 'mountain' must be the exterior of the object.) The assumption works for incredible and imaginary objects as well – if I say that the castle floating in the air is golden then you immediately understand that it is the outside that is golden, not the inside. (Of course, I could explicitly mention that the inside is golden, too, but this would be an additional piece of information; if I only meant the outside then I would not need to explain that.) So the 'brown house' seems to go beyond a house which is brown; it means something about the geometric surfaces which are brown. This might be slightly surprising, but things go a lot further, because we do not always think of the brown house as the geometric surface. If I am inside a brown house then I would not say that I am near it. Nor, if I were in the middle of the house, would I say that I am further from the house than someone standing at the front door, which would be a logical thing to say if we really thought of the house as a surface. Now the brown house is not a surface, but more like a volume. So what does 'brown house' really mean? Does it have many meanings?

In some contexts the house is a surface, but in others it is not! So much for the meaning of 'house' referring to some physical object in a straightforward way. Like 'I love you' in German, even an apparently simple concept can turn out to be rather more complex when analysed carefully. Examples are legion. Consider 'Tokyo' – we might think that 'Tokyo' is simply the buildings in a certain area, but that can't be the whole story. If it burnt to the ground, it could be rebuilt out of completely different materials, and it will still be Tokyo, even if the rebuilt one is completely different, and possibly even in a different place. (Contrast this with my 'car' – if it is burnt to the ground, then it cannot be rebuilt, even if we somehow use the ashes of the old car to do so it will still be a different car.)

To go any further would take us into semantics and other difficult linguistic areas. For our purposes, we simply note the enormous complexity of the meaning of even simple concepts such as 'brown houses', 'Tokyo' and 'car'. If we come to concepts such as love, energy, gross domestic product, disarmament and justice then we will be in even deeper water. The point is that there are not always objects in the world which correspond exactly to what we are talking about, and so we are left with a very profound problem to do with the meaning of words. When we combine words to create sentences, the problems rapidly multiply. An old joke illustrates the point: a child answers a phone, and the person calling says, 'Hello, is your mummy in?' The child answers 'Yes' and puts the phone down. We laugh (perhaps) because we understand what the child did not – that the meaning of a sentence goes far, far beyond the apparent meaning. Linguists refer to this as 'parole'. The child has understood only the direct meaning of the question, and not all the other social meanings that go with it. Think about a teacher saying 'Good Morning' to a class and you saying 'Good Morning' to your family. These two greetings may mean different things. But how can this be?

One final example of this nature: imagine you are changing a flat tyre on the side of the road on a cold winter's day. Someone approaches and says, 'Got a flat tyre?' What is the **psychological** meaning here? We might suggest something like:

Hello. I can see that you have a flat tyre and that you are changing it. It is not good weather to be doing a job like that – I wouldn't want to be doing it by myself! And so perhaps, even though I do not know you, I can help. But I don't really know you well enough just to offer – and I do not wish to be embarrassed by a rejection. Are you approachable and friendly? This is my voice – you can see I am trustworthy. How about you? Will you give me a sign as to whether or not you wish for help?

It is interesting to see that most meaning is about the social and emotional needs of the speaker or the listener. Very little of it is actually about 'fact' in the way we sometimes think. Quite *how* we manage to communicate such subtleties of meaning by so few words is still something of a mystery!

Despite these problems, most of the time we manage to communicate without actually saying what we mean. Some linguists have even gone so far as to refer to this as a scandal! Chomsky writes:

About all we can say at a general level is that the words of our language provide complex perspectives that offer us highly special ways to think about things – to ask for them, tell people about them etc... People use words to refer to things in complex ways, reflecting interests and circumstances, but the words do not refer; there is no word–thing relation.

In other words, to ask 'What does a word mean?' is like asking 'What does this chess piece mean?' The answer is that it only means something in the context of the rules that govern its use. Of course, this is unhelpful because we are then led to ask about the nature of these rules, and this is the subject matter of semantics. (This is an excellent example of a metaphysical problem being clarified enough to allow empirical enquiry – and what was once philosophy is now becoming science.)

A Find a word or simple phrase and apply the same kind of analysis as Chomsky has done to 'brown house'.

B Look at Chomsky's 'John, Bill, eat' example on page 225. Construct another series of sentences along the same lines which show the same problems of meaning.

C Find other examples of constructions that seem to follow different rules, though they look superficially identical.

D Explain in your own words what Chomsky claims that words 'mean' or 'do'.

E We have not yet touched on metaphorical or artistic meaning. Review the section in Chapter 3 (page 40) called 'The arts, experience, and the nature of artistic truth'. Find a copy of *The Sunlight on The Garden* by Louis MacNeice (do an internet search) and decide what the poem means.

If we turn from specific to general ideas, we soon come across the ideas of Ludwig Wittgenstein, perhaps the most original of the twentieth-century philosophers (although some of his writing reads more like a mystic's guide to life). In his first major work, the rather grandly-named *Tractatus Logico-Philosophicus*, he addressed the relationship between language and the world. He suggested that language gives us a representation of the world, and the nature of this representation is fundamentally limiting. Just as we might use a physical model of cars to represent the situation during a road accident, so meaningful language stands for objects in the world, and nothing else. That is, he argues that words that do not directly correspond to objects do not have any meaning at all.

The correct method in philosophy would really be the following: to say nothing except what can be said, i.e., propositions of natural science – i.e., something that has nothing to do with philosophy – and then, whenever someone else wanted to say something metaphysical to demonstrate to him that he had failed to give a meaning to certain signs in his propositions.

One of the features of this view (that any language which does not stand for anything in the world is literally meaningless and not worthy of attention) is that religion, aesthetics, ethics and indeed philosophy itself are consigned to the dustbin! This rather restricted view of language was very popular in the mid-twentieth century, perhaps because it allowed people to dismiss many traditional ethical problems as meaningless and to think that they were 'solving' the problems by doing so. Since then it is fair to say that ideas have moved on and that hardly anyone today would argue that language alone can solve such a wide range of problems. Nevertheless, that was exactly what Wittgenstein thought. He even suggested that his own work, the *Tractatus*, was meaningless. He thought it should be used like a ladder to apprehend the truth about the language and the world, and then thrown away afterwards, and the whole of philosophy forgotten as a foolish and pointless pastime. This rather dramatic ending to the *Tractatus* may be summarised by its final classic sentence:

Whereof we cannot speak, thereof must we remain silent.

A Chomsky and the early Wittgenstein (he later took a different view)
share a common suspicion about the meaning of words, but they
look for solutions in completely different ways. Describe these
ways, in your own words, and explain which one appeals to you
more.

It's not that Wittgenstein didn't think that, for example, God
exists, but that talking about God was literally meaningless. *'It is
clear that ethics cannot be put into words. Ethics is transcendental.'* Later
on, he was to change his views totally, and in his second major
work, *Philosophical Investigations*, he suggested that far from being
meaningless, the purpose of philosophy is to unravel errors in
thinking which arise through linguistic errors, and thus get a
clearer view of what he earlier thought were meaningless
propositions. He suggested that language is not a picture of the
world (perhaps now more in agreement with Chomsky), but
more like a net that consists of many pieces of interconnected
string. Our understanding becomes knotted when we misuse a
word in a situation to which it does not apply.

*The fundamental fact here is that we lay down rules, a technique, for a
game, and that when we follow the rules, things do not turn out as we
had assumed. That we are therefore, as it were, entangled in our own
rules. The entanglement in our rules is what we want to understand (i.e.,
get a clear view of).*

Thus philosophy appears to have little connection with reality
and seems more concerned with language, in which we are
entangled. A central point here is the suggestion that language
does not provide a good description of the world. If we come
across a paradox or a problem, sometimes we find that it is purely
because we have set up a system with words that does not match
the 'real world'. Often we don't realise that language is the
problem because we naturally assume that it is a transparent and
neutral thing.

Another point which emerges again and again is that of
definition and meaning. If we try to pin down the precise
meaning of art, or science, then we find that we can never quite
do so – something always seems to elude our definition. In fact,
as we have seen, the same can be said of even the most mundane
items – like 'house'. Wittgenstein gave a famous example:

*Consider for example the proceedings we call 'games'. I mean board-games,
card-games, ball-games, Olympic games and so on. What is common to
them all? Don't say there must be something common, or they would not all
be called 'games' – but look and see whether there is anything common at
all. For if you look at them you will not see something that is common to all,
but similarities, relationships, and a whole lot of them at that. To repeat:
don't think, but look! Look, for example, at board-games, with their
multifarious relationships. Now pass to card games; here you will find
many correspondences with the first group, but many common features
drop out and others appear. When we pass to ball games, much that is
common is retained, but much is lost. Are they all 'amusing'? Compare
chess with noughts and crosses. Or is there always winning and losing, or*

competition between players? Think of patience. In ball games there is winning and losing but when a child throws his ball at the wall and catches it again, the feature has disappeared. Look at the parts played by skill and luck; and at the difference between skill in chess and skill in tennis. Think now of games like ring-a-ring-a-roses; here is the element of amusement, but how many other characteristics have disappeared. And we can go through the many, many other groups of games in the same way; we can see how similarities crop up and disappear.

It certainly seems strange that the only things that all 'games' have in common is that we call them 'games', and that we cannot find necessary and sufficient conditions for something to be called a game. However you define 'game', something is either excluded when it should be included, or included when it should be excluded. Wittgenstein suggests that this is true about words generally – they are far more complex than they appear to be.

Some have gone further than Wittgenstein and argued that defining what we mean precisely is totally impossible! Even ignoring the difficulties above, suppose, for example, I try to define 'game' as 'a sort of contest'. You then ask what I mean by 'contest', and I say it is 'an event where there is a winner' (or some such thing). If you ask me what I mean by 'winner' then I may answer, but you can then ask me for a further definition, and ultimately will not really have got anywhere. At some point, we have to make do with undefined terms. In this example, if we do not define 'winner' then 'contest' remains undefined and so does 'game'. So perhaps we should not waste too much time worrying about the exact meanings of words!

However, if we can maintain a sense of clarity (easier said than done), it doesn't necessarily have to be a problem. As long as we recognise that there is not necessarily a direct relationship between language and the real world we can avoid at least some of the difficulties. Here are two quotes which clearly demonstrate that language can set up a system which is completely in accordance with the way the world is, or completely at odds with it.

If we do not succeed, then we run the risk of failure.
Dan Quayle

I believe we are on an irreversible trend toward more freedom and democracy, but that could change.
Dan Quayle

Suppose we were thinking about this second quote seriously, trying to see how something could be moving irreversibly, but with the possibility of change. We would be puzzled. We know that the statement is nonsense, so we don't bother with it. Wittgenstein would have said that this is indicative of most philosophical thinking. We think we have a problem, but really there is no problem at all – language has posed a situation which seems puzzling, but only because we have described it poorly.

We might leave the final word to another American politician. When Abraham Lincoln was asked, 'If the tail of a dog was called a leg then how many legs would a dog have?' he said, 'Four; calling a tail a leg doesn't mean that it is one.' Is he correct?

Language and human experience

In considering issues related to the nature of meaning, we have seen that language is closely tied to ideas about human cognition and interaction with the world. Some thinkers go further and suggest that language is not an optional part of this interaction; that for humans, language shapes and moulds it. In *Men of Ideas*, Bryan Magee interviews John Searle, who is one such thinker.

Magee: Philosophers like yourself regard language as absolutely fundamental to human life ... it would be interesting to hear your reasons.

   Searle: We tend to have the idea that words are ... transparent, and that we can just apply them to reality – we just name our experiences, our social relations and the objects we encounter. But in fact ... what we find is that those forms of experience and those forms of social relations that we regard as characteristically human would be impossible without language; and that language is what distinguishes us more than anything else from other forms of animal life.

   It might seem to us that our experiences come to us independently of any language, but Wittgenstein gives the following very simple example to illustrate the dependence of experience on language.

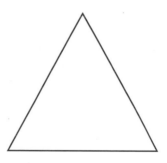

   He draws a triangle and says, 'See this [left-most] point as apex and the [right-hand] side as base.' Then he says, 'Now see [the top] point as apex and [the bottom] side as base.' You find that you have a different experience. One is immediately aware of two different experiences even though the optical conditions are identical ... These are not experiences my dog can have – not because he has not got the optical apparatus, but because he has not got the conceptual apparatus. The words ... are part of the experience. One can give a lot of more grand examples. La Rochefoucald says somewhere that very few people would fall in love if they had never heard about it. I think that there is a profound truth

underlying that remark, and it is that the possession of verbal categories like 'love' and 'hate' themselves help to shape the experiences they name; the concepts are part of the experience; and indeed in many cases it would be impossible to have the experience at all without a mastery of the appropriate vocabulary.

__Magee:__ What you are saying really is that the world does not consist of a lot of entities to which we, as human beings, then attach the labels and names but rather that the objects of experience do not exist independently from the concepts we have. In this way the words enter into the very structure of our experience . . .

__Searle:__ Yes that's the point I am making but it is essential to understand it precisely. I am not saying that language creates reality. Far from it. Rather I am saying that what counts as reality is a matter of the categories that we impose on the world, and those categories are for the most part linguistic. And furthermore, when we experience the world we experience it through linguistic categories that help to shape the experiences themselves. The world does not come to us sliced up into objects and experiences. What counts as an object is already a function of our system of representation. The mistake is to suppose that the application of language to the world consists of attaching labels that are, so to speak, self-identifying. In my view, the world divides the way we divide it, and our main way of dividing things up is in language. Our concept of reality is a matter of our linguistic categories.

A Make sure that you have seen what is meant by the triangle example. Can you think of any other such examples?

B In a modern art gallery, visitors were walking past a pile of bricks, thinking it was work in progress. When the pile was labelled, and the visitors realised that it was a piece of art, they stopped and looked at it. Were they experiencing it in a different way because of the label? Is this an example of what Searle is getting at?

C We tend to value clothes from a famous designer more than those which are not, even if the cost is the same. Is this another case of labelling or is this all about social recognition and status?

D Searle's last statement has echoes of the Sapir-Whorf hypothesis in it. Is Searle making a case for linguistic determinism? How does he suggest that language and thought are related?

E Do you think fewer people would fall in love or hate each other if they didn't have words for it? Would they perhaps experience love and hatred in a different way? Or is this simply taking the whole notion too far?

This is not the end of the story – language seems to be linked to experience in still more profound ways than this. We are all aware of the feeling that we are not understood; that nobody sees the world quite like us, and that we are in some abstract sense, alone. We have seen in this and earlier chapters that there may be good reasons for this. Despite what seems to be a very uniform world, we have no way of being certain if, for example, our perception of colour indicates anything meaningful about the world outside our minds. When we extend this argument to other sensations, it gets progressively more worrying. Modern science tells a similar story – our minds have contact with the world only through very specific and narrow channels of information – our senses. Our individual human awarenesses are located in worlds of experience that are completely isolated from one another. It's a scary thought.

It has been suggested that we can build bridges between the individual islands of our own experience through language. To some small extent, this must be true – using agreed symbols we stimulate the senses of another person, and we hope that they perceive our symbols. But we are not really interested in the transfer of symbols – what we want to do is transfer something of our world of *experience* to other people, and to receive some *experience* back. It is only because of our profound limitations that we have to do it via limited symbols. We long for a way to escape our isolation, a way to transfer content, directly and without distorting intermediaries, which we would soon do away with if we could.

As far as we know, all living creatures share our predicament. Like us, animals resort to symbols – they use coloured feathers, complex dances, mating songs, chemical markers and so on. We are fortunate in that our system of abstract symbols is highly evolved and able to represent far more complex experiences. With literature, and particularly with poetry, we can do remarkable things. But as far as we know, we are the only species which is miserable enough to recognise that for all its sophistication, we can never transfer experience.

> **A** Explain what is meant by 'experience' in the context of this passage.
> **B** Why should we want to transfer experience?
> **C** Why might we never be able to transfer experience?
> **D** Do you think we can, in fact, ever transmit experience, despite the pessimism above?

Where do we go from here?

Our quest for certainty is proving to be a long one, and the further we go, the more problems we seem to raise. This chapter has brought to light another raft of philosophical and scientific issues of enormous complexity. What do we do? We can't keep going like this!

Perhaps we should take a different approach, and instead of getting more and more theoretical, look to an area which has an immediate effect on our daily lives. We have been seeking knowledge, but have we ever considered if it is the right thing to do? Would we know what we should do with the knowledge that we find? Some of the recent developments in the history of humankind have not been encouraging. In other words, perhaps we should take a moment to reflect on ethical issues.

Further reading

A most profound and wide-ranging introduction to a range of language issue is Stephen Pinker's *The Language Instinct* (William Morrow and Co., 1994). For an entertaining guide to deceptive language, try William Lutz's *Double Speak* (Harper and Row, 1989). The problem of meaning is well covered in many philosophy texts – I can recommend as a very brief introduction chapter 5 of Thomas Nagel's *What Does It All Mean?* (Oxford University Press, 1987). Two more general overviews are provided in chapter 7 of Reuben Abel's *Man is The Measure* (The Free Press, 1976) and John Hosper's *Introduction to Philosophical Analysis* (Prentice Hall, 1953). A fascinating, less philosophical and more comprehensive guide is found in David Crystal's *Cambridge Encyclopedia of Language* (Cambridge University Press, 1992). Geoffrey Pullman's *The Great Eskimo Vocabulary Hoax and other Irreverent Essays on the Study of Language* (University of Chicago Press, 1991) remains an entertaining and informative peek at some areas and characters in linguistics.

As an introduction to the subtle and controversial aspects of language, it is hard to beat Noam Chomsky's *Language and Thought* (Moyer Bell, 1993) or the early chapters of *Powers and Prospects* (Pluto Press, 1996).

More about meaning

We can look into the way that meaning is constructed not only from individual words, but also from whole sentences. The problem is that we seem to get a lot more 'meaning' out of a sentence than appears to be in it, at least on a simple reading. That is, we always seem to go far beyond the available evidence to infer many things about the meaning of a sentence.

An extract from *Powers and Prospects* by Noam Chomsky.

...the gap between what the speaker/hearer knows and the evidence available becomes a chasm ... Take simple sentences, say, the following:

1 John is eating an apple.
2 John is eating.

In 2, the grammatical object of 'eat' is missing, and we understand the sentence on the analogy of 1, to mean (more or less) that John is eating something-or-other. The mind fills the gap, postulating an unspecified object of the verb.

Actually that is not quite true. Consider the following:

3 John is eating his shoe. He must have lost his mind.

But the sentence 2 does not include the case of eating one's shoe. If I say that John is eating, I mean that he is eating in a normal way; having dinner perhaps, but not eating his shoe. What the mind fills in is not an unspecified grammatical object, but something normal; that's part of the meaning of the construction (though what counts as normal is not).

Let's suppose that this is roughly correct, and turn to a slightly more complex case. Consider:

4 John is too stubborn to talk to Bill.

What this means is that John is too stubborn for him (John) to talk to Bill – he is so stubborn he refuses to talk to Bill. Suppose we drop 'Bill' from 4 to yield 5:

5 John is too stubborn to talk to.

Following the principle illustrated by 1 and 2, we expect 5 to be understood on the analogy of 5, with the mind filling the gap with some (normal) object of 'talk to'. The sentence 5, then, should mean that John is too stubborn for him (John) to talk to someone or other. But it doesn't mean that at all. Rather it means that John is too stubborn for anyone (maybe us) to talk to him (John).

For some reason, the semantic relations invert when the object of 'talk to' in 4 is deleted, unlike 1, where they remain unchanged. The same holds for more complex cases, as in 6:

6 John is too stubborn to expect the teacher to talk to.

The meaning is that John is too stubborn for anyone (maybe us) to expect the teacher to talk to him (John). In this case, parsing difficulties may make the facts harder to detect, though the sentence is still a very simple one, well below average sentence length in normal discourse.

We know all of these things, though without awareness. The reasons lie beyond possible consciousness. None of this could have been learned. The facts are known to people who have had no relevant experience with such [grammatical] constructions. Parents and peers who impart knowledge of language (to the limited extent that they do) have no awareness of such facts ... Just as dictionaries do not begin to provide the meanings of words, so the most elaborate multi-volume traditional grammars do not recognise, let alone begin to explain, even elementary phenomena of the kind just illustrated. It is only in very recent years ... that such properties have come to light. Correspondingly, it has become clear how little is known of the elementary phenomena of language. That's not a surprising discovery. As long as people were satisfied that an apple falls to the ground because that is its natural place, even the basic properties of motion remained hidden. A willingness to be puzzled by the simplest phenomena is the very beginning of science. The attempt to formulate questions about simple phenomena has led to remarkable discoveries about elementary aspects of nature, previously unsuspected.

Parlez-vous my language?

Advances in dentistry may brighten our smiles, computer technology may lighten our load and engineering may help get us around, but it is through language and literature that we come alive

writes Robert Dessaix in *The Age* (16 October 1999).

In the 1830s in England many factory owners argued against the building of railways on the grounds that making travel available to the masses would do nothing for increasing production, at least in their factories. Reform-minded industrialists thought travel might be of some practical benefit, making their workers healthier, happier and more productive. The high-minded spoke vaguely of train travel broadening the understanding of others, promoting tolerance and peace. They all had a point – they just had different notions of what sort of society was worth living in.

Debate about the teaching of foreign languages and literatures at our universities today follows much the same lines: the factory-owning class can't see much profit in it; the liberals hope it might provide a multicultural experience and open up trade opportunities at the same time; the high-minded say little and ponder retirement. Since the factory owners and their purse-proud surrogates in government and the universities rule the roost, the few lines allowed to operate have to justify their existence nowadays by catering to hordes of Sunday excursionists, and making their stations double as shopping arcades.

To what extent is learning a foreign language or literature the key? In today's Australia this basic question is left without a cogent, socially acceptable answer. In a society that has become a cross between a giant business conglomerate and a feudal principality (I speak as a Victorian, of course), those of us who would argue for a place in the sun for language teaching need, I think, to bite the bullet and assert other values entirely.

To argue for the value of learning Spanish, say, in terms of social or commercial usefulness is a lost cause. What does reading Lorca or writing an essay on Bunuel do for the corporate balance sheets? Why should taxpayers pay for this sort of refinement of the sensibilities? Even to argue in these profit-and-loss terms is to be complicit with the philistines now running the academic show, not to mention the country. Besides, they are right – learning a foreign language in Australia in 1999 is a useless exercise. It's all loss and no profit.

Many students and some staff won't be aware of how different things looked a few decades ago. At my state school, for instance, in the 1950s, when those who were not alive at the time keep insisting Australia was a 'monoculture' (and indeed cappuccinos and tom yum soup were hard to come by), we all studied Latin and French, some of us took German and Ancient Greek, and I was allowed to study Russian. At the Australian National University (ANU) in the years that followed, the range of languages on offer at different times was staggering: from regional Indonesian languages to Dutch and Polish, from Italian to Hindi. As Australia has become wealthier and more multicultural, the range has shrunk dramatically and in the next few months will shrink even further.

In those days of fuller employment, motivation was different, too. When I first took up Russian as a boy, walking into a newsagency in suburban Sydney buying myself a dictionary, I was not seeking knowledge to increase my career opportunities – there were none. When I enrolled in Russian at ANU, I was not seeking knowledge in order to serve some powerful institution in later life or to get in on the technological revolution (although in those post-Sputnik days Russia's scientific prospects were looking bright). I did it – although I wouldn't have used these words then and to use them in these anti-humanist times is almost embarrassing – to magnify my experience of being human. And, at a more mundane level, to decipher the script on the Russian stamps in my collection.

What has changed? In economic terms the employment situation has changed for the worse, of course, making my kind of motivation seem a self-indulgent luxury. In the cultural sphere, however, the changes have been even more profound. Where once 'education' had several meanings, it increasingly now means just 'pedagogy', the inculcation of knowledge to economic ends. Disagreement about the meaning of 'education' is hardly new – the Greeks were at each others' throats about precisely these questions two-and-a-half millennia ago: one school argued for the legitimacy of learning for learning's sake,

for education as the disinterested search for truths (not just facts), for what made the world work and humans human; the other school (the pedagogical) favoured learning for material achievement and advancement, for self-enrichment and power.

Both schools had a point.

The problem for language and literature teachers in our universities today is that they are expected to straddle both concepts of education at a time when the pedagogical arguments for language learning carry little weight. No one is arguing against the need to inculcate knowledge at the tertiary level: we want it drilled into our dentists, pilots and bridge-builders until they drop. The humanities, however, are there for a different purpose and there is a sort of barbarism – or perhaps it's philistinism, which is barbarism gone middle-class – about the notion that their value is of the same nature as that of dentistry or molecular biology. The life of the mind the humanities nourish may be impossible without engineers and good dentists, but the life that engineers and dentists make possible is scarcely worth living without a richly informed mental dimension to it.

Not only the culture of education has changed. Two other developments have worked against language and literature departments in our universities. First, Australians

now live in a distant khanate of the great American English-speaking empire. In the Roman empire you would have had to be highly eccentric to bother learning anything except Latin and Greek. Why learn Pictish or Aramaic when you could travel from the Scottish border to the Euphrates with perfect ease speaking just the two imperial languages? The odd spy or civil servant may have felt pressed to acquire a local dialect or two, but quite frankly, as a Roman vice-chancellor would no doubt have pointed out, there was no great call for Lydian from the Roman business community. And in the early 14th century, an Arabic-speaking scholar or trader could move with similar ease within the Dar al-Islam, the House of Islam, speaking Arabic with anyone he needed to make contact with from Spain to Southern China, from the Volga River to Zanzibar. A spot of Turkish or Persian might have helped here and there, but was hardly a requirement.

Today as Australians we live firmly within the Dar al-English, and any vice-chancellor or dean worth his or her salt should point this out. But when I first started travelling in the 1960s, it wasn't quite like that. I carefully learnt a bit of Finnish, quite a lot of Polish, and even a spot of Bahasa Indonesian to get around. I learnt some Spanish to go to Spain and Italian to go to ☞

Italy. I wouldn't bother now. The language of globalisation is English. Every day a billion people use it in one form or another. It's the world's lingua franca. To argue that you need Italian or French to conduct business in Italy or France is wishful thinking – hundreds of thousands of foreigners have lived there for decades without speaking a syllable.

Multiculturalism of the official Australian variety hasn't helped the language teachers' cause, either. Our brand of multiculturalism is not, after all, about individual Australians ceasing to be monocultural or bicultural – indeed, some of Australia's immigrant communities fervently wish to remain monocultural – but about immigration policy, about making migrants feel their heritage counts for something, about making them feel more at home.

But multiculturalism of the kind we all piously doff our caps to has made language learning even less necessary than it was just after the war. In the first place, who needs a cadre of Italian-speaking non-Italians when hundreds of thousands of Australians of Italian background already do it so well? With our kind of immigration policy, an educated bilingual speaker of any of 150 languages can be found almost instantly to perform any task. And in the second place, given our patterns of immigration, in Australia you are obliged to

speak English in a way in which you simply aren't in parts of Los Angeles, New York or even Canada. Even SBS [an Australian channel providing foreign-language programmes for Australia's ethnic communities] is basically an English-speaking television station – it has to be. If Turks want to watch a Greek movie – as I hope many do – then they will have to be able to read English subtitles.

I am not arguing here that 'things have got worse'. I am not evoking any Golden Age of Education or Britishness. There was no Golden Age, not even in Athens. My point is simply that things have changed, certain ideas about education are in eclipse, and under these conditions those of us who believe that universities should offer more foreign languages and literatures, not fewer, need to rethink our tactics. Defending ourselves in terms of social or economic usefulness will get us nowhere, unless perhaps we are in the field of two or three Asian languages.

If we do capitulate to the pressure to justify our existence in utilitarian terms, in no time at all we will find ourselves setting up stalls selling *Italian for Tourists, Italian for Businessmen* and quickie survey courses in Italian literature (in English, naturally). The microbiologists don't put up with this sort of huckstering, so why should we? To argue

the case for foreign languages from a different set of values we are going to have to use terminology some of us have been trained to think of as humanist, universalist and outdated. (It's not outdated, of course, it just isn't fashionable in certain circles, including the very circles that are currently being decimated.)

We're going to have to talk in terms of multiplying perceptions of the world, of refining our awareness of being alive, of seeing in colour instead of black and white, of opening doors to other selves we never knew existed – of multiculturalism, if you like, of a much richer, more real kind than the present model. Each new language learnt opens up a parallel universe. It's embarrassing, but these things have to be said.

It was Wittgenstein who proposed that 'the limits of my language are the limits of my world'. You don't have to be Wittgenstein to grasp that if you only have one word (let's say *depressed*) to describe your mental state, and can't wonder whether you are actually more dejected or suffering from ennui rather than depressed, or melancholy, triste, despondent, disconsolate or just plain glum, then your experience is drained of colour and possibilities. You're blocked from reinventing yourself. Does this kind of nuanced linguistic awareness have a cash value? None, I would suggest, that can be calculated by Treasury or Accounts. But it makes being here an adventure.

In our particular culture, too, a facility with language is still widely seen as a feminine skill. Whether its the Bush Tucker man painstakingly dropping his 'g's – he occasionally slips up, but not too often – or politicians resorting to stunted English for a working-class audience, or our sportsmen carefully speaking like half-wits in television interviews, the message is clear: a real man doesn't speak too well. Speaking well is an embroidering activity, supplementary to the real business of life, and is therefore women's business. (Showbiz personalities – jester figures in general – have a special dispensation, of course. They can even be black or homosexual and get away with it.)

One of the things learning foreign languages can do, as can serious literary studies, is to expand the sense of what it means to be masculine, something women have been waiting for since Adam. In a recent report there was an inspiring item about an experiment at James Cook Boys Technology High School in Sydney. The boys are discovering that they can dance, sing, and play musical instruments and enjoy it – and still be boys. They are less inclined to truancy and aggression in the playground, and, judging by the interviews, don't feel so limited to stereotypical behaviour.

If we feel cudgelled into arguing for some kind of social usefulness for language learning, getting rid of the barbed wire around dominant ideas of masculinity could be one area to explore. There must surely be more to being a man in Australia than is currently being publicly touted.

To what is studying a foreign literature the key? Barry Jones famously suggested to John Howard that, in his case, reading *War and Peace* could open the door to being a better Prime Minister, but we don't know the reasons he gave. In my case, reading Russian and French literature was the key to multiple ways of understanding the world. It's obvious: once you've read Tolstoy and Turgenev, for example, you will simply love differently. And talk differently, reason differently, tell different kinds of jokes, travel through life differently. You'll become hungry for things you never knew existed. How many dollars is that worth?

More importantly, perhaps, you'll find spaces opening up inside you in which to become serious about the things you love. And those spaces will be gradually furnished by what you read in utterly unexpected, vivifying ways.

Without these furnished spaces it's hard to see how imagination can take root. And without imagination all the cleverness in the world will leave our lives empty. To study a foreign literature, or cinematic or artistic tradition, is to take part in a vast conversation across generations and borders. And conversing is what the humanities are all about, surely. Not conversing in order to arrive at a set of facts, or to install a fashionable ideology in the minds of the young, but conversing for its own sake, about the most important things in the world – as we understand it, of course. That – not technological sophistication – is civilisation. To do it with a healthy set of teeth in our mouths, or using computer technology is a very fine thing, but our professional business is the conversation. It's a brilliant way of being alive.

High-minded arguments such as these will be sneered at by the book-keepers – by all those who think the life of the mind is a kind of effete luxury, or an entertaining adjunct to the real business of life. Those of us who think it is as much the real business of life as building casinos, maintaining an army, growing wheat and repairing the roads must start saying so – loudly. In these times old-fashioned values are suddenly radical again.

This is an edited version of an address given at a School of Languages Postgraduate Conference at Melbourne University.

Ethics is a code of values which guide our choices and actions and determine the purpose and course of our lives.
Ayn Rand

MORALITY, WHEN FORMAL, DEVOURS.
Albert Camus

A man without ethics is a wild beast loosed upon this world.
Manley Hall

That which is beautiful is moral. That is all, nothing more.
Gustave Flaubert

Morality is the best of all devices for leading mankind by the nose.
Friedrich Nietzsche

Pity is not natural to man. Children are always cruel. Savages are always cruel. Pity is acquired and improved only by the cultivation of reason.
Samuel Johnson

Because the human race is as much part of the Universe as atoms and galaxies, moral laws are as independent of you and me, and of whatever cultures helped shape our character and ethical convictions, as the laws of truth and beauty.
Martin Gardner

The first step in the evolution of ethics is a sense of solidarity with other human beings.
Albert Schweitzer

THE FOUNDATION OF MORALITY IS TO HAVE DONE, ONCE AND FOR ALL, WITH LYING.
Thomas Henry Huxley

Morality is suspecting other people of not being legally married.
George Bernard Shaw

A moral being is one who is capable of comparing his past and future actions or motives, and of approving or disapproving of them.
Charles Darwin

What is morality in any given time or place? It is what the majority then and there happen to like – and immorality is what they dislike.
Alfred North Whitehead

Introduction: what are ethics?

If you are particularly good at, say, history, then you are likely to be able to analyse sources intelligently, reconcile conflicting evidence, and convincingly analyse cause and effect with regard to the events of the past. If, in addition to your talent, you enjoy studying the subject then you may go on to study it at higher and higher levels, perhaps eventually becoming a professional historian. The same is true of many areas of knowledge.

The study of ethics, on the other hand, concerned as it is with questions such as 'How should we act?' and 'What is right and what is wrong?', seems very different. We do not study it as a subject in its own right, we probably couldn't say if anyone was 'good' at it, and it does not offer a career! Despite this, we all have a sense of 'correct' behaviour, though it may differ from person to person, and we all say things like 'He shouldn't have done that' or 'She did the right thing.' So what do we mean by 'ethics'?

For those who believe in God, the problem may seem to have an obvious answer – to act ethically is to act in accordance with God's wishes. But many believers feel that God's wishes are far from clear, and that the holy books do not give adequate guidance in many cases (for example, does loving my neighbour mean defending him by going to war against others?). So there is a need for a way of deciding what God's will actually is in a practical sense.

Atheists, of course, need to look elsewhere completely. Some might say that ethics is a set of socially and biologically imposed rules with the function of minimising conflict in society. If this is true then we might try to find the most effective rules possible (we certainly don't seem to have them yet). Perhaps the most radical view is that of ethics as nothing but a totally arbitrary system of rules and conventions imposed on a gullible community by those in political power. According to this way of thinking, we are all responding to social conditioning. If this is the case, the need to step back and examine our principles is even more pressing!

A Consider the following statements:

- You should hold your fork in your left hand.
- You should not waste your time.
- You should not lie.
- You should not use illegal drugs.
- You should take the first left to get to the theatre.
- You should control the money supply so as to bring down inflation.
- You should not jump a red traffic light, even if it is safe to do so.
- You should speak respectfully to teachers and parents.
- You should not drive a car recklessly.
- You should not use drugs.
- You should not engage in sexual relationships outside marriage.
- You should not steal.
- Your teachers and parents should speak respectfully to you.

B Which of the above are moral statements?
C Which of the above are pure conventions?
D Which of them should be made into legal requirements?
E What do we mean by a moral law?

We all have an intuitive feel for moral laws or standards (as opposed to legal or physical laws) and, surprisingly, there is often a good deal of agreement on these standards. Appeals to moral laws are commonplace. For example, we have all heard people arguing – they may insult each other and become abusive, but more often than not they make statements such as:

- Leave him alone – he isn't hurting anyone.
- There is a queue here – you can't just push in.
- Give me some of your chocolate – I gave you some of my juice.
- Hey, I was sitting there – that's my place.
- But you said you would help me!

These comments are interesting because they all assume something – they all appeal to some (unstated) standard of behaviour. In these cases there seems to be some notion of 'fairness' that is assumed by both sides of the argument. What is even more interesting is that the other person very rarely says, 'I don't care about the standards to which you appeal.' Instead they try to make some special excuse ('I have to push in because I have a really important meeting to go to' or 'Yes, but you had lots of juice but I only have a little chocolate') to justify their behaviour.

In other words, it seems that even people who are arguing are not arguing about the standards to which they should conform – they are arguing about how to apply those standards to a particular situation. They seem to agree on some sort of moral code; we all seem to have a sense of what this code is. The writer C. S. Lewis said that there must be, *'some sense of agreement as to what right and wrong are; just as there would be no sense in saying that a footballer had committed a foul unless there was some agreement about the rules of football'*.

At some points in the past, this rule about right and wrong would have been called a law of nature because it seems that nobody needs to be taught it – it is in everybody naturally. In his book *The Abolition of Man*, Lewis argues that despite differences, many moral standards are shared. He asks us to imagine what a completely different morality might mean, and whether or not such a thing would be possible. Can we find a society where people are proud of cheating on their friends or where it is considered good to steal from the poor? It is hard to imagine. Differences occur when different societies consider whom they should treat well, but they always agree that pure selfishness is a bad thing. Men have differed as to whether you should have one wife or four, but they have always agreed that you must not simply have any woman you liked.

Lewis claims that this simple observation means that moral laws exist in the same way as physical laws. He notes that whenever you find somebody who says that there is no such thing as a moral law, only arbitrary social conventions, you will find that they go back on this claim whenever it suits them. If these people, he says, break a promise to you then that is one thing, but if you break your promise to them then you'll find them complaining that it isn't fair. This means that they are appealing to certain standards of fairness which they expect everyone to agree on – otherwise what is the difference between a fair and an unfair agreement?

It is by arguments such as these that some have claimed that there are laws of human nature; that we all know them, and that morality is absolute, unchanging and constant.

> **A** Suppose a teenager is arguing with his parents about staying out late in the evening. Is it more likely that the argument is about:
>
> - what is a reasonable time to return
> - whether or not the parent has any right to insist on a reasonable return time?
>
> **B** Suppose that you come across someone about to take your watch from your desk. Is it more likely that the person will say:
>
> - that they just wanted to borrow the watch
> - that they dispute your right to own the watch.
>
> **C** How do these two examples relate to the idea of 'moral rules'?
> **D** Think about the last time you had a disagreement about right and wrong with somebody. Were you arguing about how to apply moral rules or the rules themselves?
> **E** Do you think that Lewis is right when he claims that these rules are universal and unchanging?

Whatever you think of the position that Lewis takes, his starting point is accurate. It is extremely rare to hear someone claim that they dispute your moral code – it is far more common to disagree about how to apply the moral code. These ideas should begin to sound familiar as they bring to mind some of the distinctions we looked at when we considered rationalism (Chapter 5). They also indicate that a closer look at the role of reason in ethics is in order.

The role of reason in ethics

Suppose your country is at war. Each individual needs to decide if they will fight, and possibly kill, for their country. Needless to say, there are strong disagreements about the ethics of the war, and arguments between pacifists and non-pacifists are common. For our purposes, we are interested in the types of disagreement between the two sides, and we find that there are at least two apparently separate reasons for disagreement; these are based in fact and in principle.

It may be that both sides have the aim of minimising the amount of overall suffering, but disagree as to how to achieve this goal. The non-pacifist may argue that the war will actually prevent more suffering than it causes; the pacifist may say that the war will increase the overall amount of suffering. The disagreement is about 'facts' and is open to settlement by evidence (although the evidence may be very difficult to obtain and interpret). On the other hand, it may be that the pacifist is uninterested in the overall suffering – he believes in the overriding sanctity of life and thinks that killing is wrong under any circumstances, even when it reduces suffering. If we ask him why he believes this he says, 'For the same reason as the non-pacifist wants to minimise suffering – I just think it is right.' This disagreement is of a different type; it is one based in principle, and it is hard to imagine that evidence will solve the dispute.

This distinction is very important, because arguments of principle and arguments about evidence are solved in different ways.

A If the disagreement is factual in nature, what facts, if they could be proven, would be likely to swing the argument in favour of:

- the pacifist
- the non-pacifist?

B If the argument were between a pro-abortionist and an anti-abortionist, both with the stated aim of reducing overall suffering, what facts, if proven, would be likely to swing the argument one way or the other?

C In either the pacifist/non-pacifist or the pro-/anti-abortion case, if the disagreement was one of principle, what evidence might help resolve the conflict?

Some people have taken these difficulties to be insoluble – this would mean that ethics, like art, comes down to a matter of personal choice. The prospects for finding the 'correct' form of morality would be bleak, and trying to persuade someone that one course of action is 'morally better' than another would be like trying to persuade them that oranges taste better than apples.

But surely we can try to make some progress with these problems? In cases where we need evidence, the problems are those of the social sciences. (Are unwanted babies less likely to be happy? Are the mothers of unwanted babies made unhappy by their children when they do not have abortions?) To be sure, these are very very difficult questions, but perhaps not insoluble. In the case of disputes of principle, we might ask for minimal standards of logical consistency. For example, what do we make of the pacifist in the previous case who is pro-euthanasia? Presumably, unless he is willing to change his mind on this issue, we can dismiss his argument for the sanctity of life as an inadequate defence of his principles. Similarly, if someone condemns homosexual acts on the grounds that 'they are not natural', then we can see that the consistent application of this principle would make flying or driving (or indeed chastity or contraception) immoral. On these grounds, we would not accept this principle as a reasonable one and we would seek an alternative justification for the belief.

In other words, when we think we have a justification for a course of action, we should look to see if:

1 there is any evidence we can collect to decide the case;
2 if any general principles suggested would lead us to moral conclusions which are either:

■ morally repellent (for example, some pro-abortion arguments can be applied to infants)
■ inconsistent with our other beliefs (for example, the homosexuality argument above).

If this is so, then we need to either modify our principle or accept what we initially thought was an unpalatable conclusion.

A In each of these cases, decide if the argument can be supported/refuted by empirical enquiry (finding and looking at evidence).

1 Counsellors should keep confidentiality – otherwise nobody will go to them for help.
2 Counsellors should keep confidentiality – it's a matter of respecting people's privacy.
3 We should tax the wealthy more than the poor – they are better able to afford it.
4 We should tax the wealthy more than the poor – it's the best way of generating substantial government revenue.
5 Euthanasia should not be allowed, or families will be pressurising elderly and inconvenient relatives to opt for it when they would rather not.
6 Euthanasia should not be allowed; the taking of life is wrong, even if it is your own.
7 Euthanasia should be allowed – we have the right to do what we want with our own bodies.
8 Euthanasia should be allowed – it is better to die than to live in misery.

9 Genetic engineering is immoral – we aren't meant to tamper with the basic machinery of life.
10 Genetic engineering is immoral – we would save far more lives by spending the billions currently spent on research on saving starving children in Africa.
11 Genetic engineering is moral – God put us here to understand and marvel at his creation.
12 Genetic engineering is moral – we can increase the quality of billions of lives in the future.

B Take the arguments that are based in principle rather than evidence. In pairs, one person should defend the principle while the other should attempt to show that it leads to unacceptable consequences, and that it should therefore be abandoned.

C It was suggested above that we can 'test' a moral principle by seeing if it leads to moral conclusions that are morally repellent. Explain why it could be argued that this is a circular argument, and decide for yourself if it is therefore possible to 'test' a moral principle or not.

So we can use reason to attempt to 'refute' an ethical argument. Let us look at this in more detail. Suppose we feel that abortion on demand (when there is no medical risk to the mother) is wrong, and that we wish to collect relevant evidence and test our principles to see if our belief is reasonable. One way of justifying our belief would be to suggest that (1) abortion is wrong because (2) abortion is murder and (3) murder is wrong. Of course, now I need to demonstrate the truth of (2) and (3), so I suggest that (2) is true because (4) the baby is alive and (5) murder occurs when a life is taken unnecessarily; (3) is true because (6) destruction of valuable things is wrong and (7) life is valuable. We might then also try to justify (4), (5), (6) and (7).

The argument can be shown diagrammatically, with the horizontal lines indicating that the statements are used in conjunction, and the arrowed lines indicating supporting reasons.

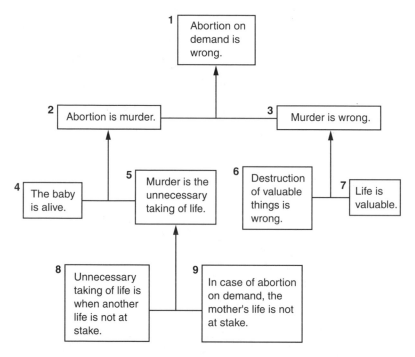

We could keep going; we could attempt to justify (4), (8), (9), (6) and (7) by going 'down' another layer and then another, and then another. But this would never end, and we have to stop somewhere. That somewhere is when we have reached the point where we believe the reasons no longer need justification – when they are 'self-evident'. You will recall that these statements are then the premises of our argument – they are the foundation on which the whole thing rests. In this case we have:

4 The baby is alive.
8 It is unnecessary to take life when another life is not at stake.
9 In cases of abortion on demand, the mother's life is not at stake.
6 Destruction of valuable things is wrong.
7 Life is valuable.

So are these 'obvious'? Can we take them as a reasonable platform on which to build our argument? Well, that depends on your point of view. Some may find them reasonable; others may find reason to disagree. Underlying (4) and (7) is the notion of life as a uniform quantity, but it could be argued that there is more to it than that – that an adult is 'more alive' than a baby, or that the life of an adult is more valuable than the life of a baby. This would need development to become a viable theory, but it does not seem to be out of the question – when a mother will die if her pregnancy continues, most (but not all) people deem it correct to abort the baby. (7) seems to equate animal life to that of humans – it might therefore need modification (but why are we more valuable than other animals?). Even if so modified, is there a reason we think life is valuable? Is it something to do with consciousness, or the ability to suffer, or the ability to reason? If so, perhaps we can take this premise a step further. (6) is highly contentious – what if the destruction of the valuable thing saved the destruction of other more valuable things?

It may be that the anti-abortionist will examine the axioms and be content, or make minor modifications, or it may be that the argument will be seen to be flawed for empirical or theoretical reasons. If this is the case, then it may be possible to construct another argument to support (1) in a reasonable manner, or it may not. If the latter, then it would be unreasonable to hold the original belief, and further thought would be required.

A Analyse the flowchart in the abortion case above.

- Is the argument reasonable?
- Do you agree with the premises? Explain your reasons.

B Construct a flowchart to suggest that abortion is not wrong.

C In the argument above, we have started from some/all of statements (2)–(9), and hence deduced the conclusion. Is this realistic? Is this actually how people derive ethical conclusions? Might it be more accurate to say that we have an emotional leaning toward/against abortion and we try to justify our (emotionally-held?) beliefs by starting from (1) and actually arguing downwards? If this is the case, is this an adequate way to argue?

D Construct flowchart arguments to suggest that the following are morally wrong and then construct arguments to suggest they are morally acceptable:

- murder
- suicide
- animal experimentation
- torture
- corporal punishment
- war
- promiscuity
- capital punishment
- racism

Defend your argument against someone who disagrees with you.

E In the arguments you have constructed, do you find any premises occurring again and again? What does this suggest to you?

It should be fairly clear that our choice of premises will largely determine what sort of things we think are right and wrong. Alternatively, we might say that we choose our premises carefully, so as to justify exactly the things we already think are right and wrong and thus to provide some coherency to our belief system. (There is a curious analogy here with mathematics which, as we have seen, often starts by noticing certain 'facts' (theorems) and then works out how to justify those theorems by judicious choice of premises/axioms – see Chapter 4. As maths is widely perceived to have little to do with morality, this is perhaps surprising.) In both cases, the foundations of our ethical arguments are our premises. It follows that the choice of premises is a crucial part of any ethical theory.

Choice of premises: ethical egoism and altruism

If it be right to me, it is right.

Max Stirner

We have made a vital distinction between principle and evidence. Now we might usefully look at the evidence to see what principles are most common in directly ethical actions. Consider your own personal experiences. What principles seem to guide the way people behave?

It is immediately striking that people act in their own self-interest and they do things in pursuit of their own personal goals. In (what at least seem to be) non-moral matters, this is absolutely clear – people earn money for their own benefit and spend it on food they enjoy, clothes they like to wear and on entertainment for themselves. In matters that certainly should be moral this seems to be the case, too. We say we should tell the truth (that others should tell the truth to us), but we are probably quick to excuse ourselves a 'white lie' when the need arises because we feel it is in our own interests to lie when we want to. We would probably say that we have a moral duty to save lives if we can – yet in practice we spend money on frivolous things or leave it in the bank rather than donate it to famine relief.

We might develop these observations into a theory that suggests that it is our own long-term happiness that is important, so we should behave in a way which turns out best for us in the long run. This is the theory of **ethical egoism** (notice that 'egotist' is an insult but 'egoist' is a theory of motivation). Some argue that this as a deeply immoral position, and one that can be used to justify terrible behaviour, but this is not necessarily the case. The philosopher Plato pointed out that ethical egoism does not suggest that stealing, cheating and dishonesty are moral behaviours, because these things wouldn't make you happier in the long term. By behaving selfishly, you will suffer fear of being caught, possibly punishment, and even in the unlikely event you achieve your goals in this way, you will enjoy the achievement far less than someone who made it there the hard way. Selfish actions will rebound on you, and in the long term you would have been better off by avoiding selfish behaviour.

> **A** According to ethical egoism, it is long-term happiness that is important. Do you agree with this idea?
> **B** Is ethical egoism a practical theory in terms of daily behaviour, that is, does it actually provide a guide for behaviour?
> **C** Is it possible for someone to act against their own interests?
> **D** Consider the rich person who gives large sums of money to charity, but says that she does so because it gives her business a good image, and so is in her long-term interests. Is this moral behaviour?

We can contrast the ideas of ethical egoism with those of **altruism**, which is based on the notion that we ought to sacrifice our interests to those of others. Ethical egoism suggests that altruistic actions simply do not happen, but this seems to fly in the face of our everyday experience. The fact of the matter is that many people do sacrifice their own interests to help others. Don't we regard altruism, not egoism, as the highest good? Consider the case of the soldier, safe in his trench, who spots a wounded colleague in distant enemy territory. The situation is such that any rescue attempt is very dangerous, and almost certain to fail, but he goes to help in spite of the risk. He succeeds and rescues the soldier, but suffers terrible, lasting wounds in the process. Is this not an altruistic act if ever there was one?

To answer this, let us consider the possible reasons that the brave soldier might give when asked why he went to rescue his colleague:

1 It was my duty.
2 It would have been awful to let him die.
3 He's my friend.
4 He once did the same for me.
5 I would have felt guilty if I hadn't.
6 I wouldn't want anyone thinking I was too scared to do it.
7 I thought it would be a good way to make my name.
8 I wanted to be in the running for a bravery medal.
9 I thought, on balance, that the potential gain outweighed the risk.
10 I wanted to achieve a benefit for myself.

Which of these would you regard as the most moral reason for acting? The ethical egoist would suggest that it doesn't matter; 1 to 9 are merely versions of 10. In 2, for example, the 'hero' is acting out of a desire to avoid the perceived 'awful' consequences of not acting; in 4 he is acting out of a desire to clear a debt. Similarly, we can suggest that all reasons ultimately boil down to 10.

Let's go one stage further and consider the most extreme case, where someone knowingly sacrifices their life for those of others. Let's return to our altruistic soldier. He is sitting around the fire with his fellow soldiers when a grenade lands in their midst. Without hesitation, the hero throws himself on the grenade, saving the lives of the others at the cost of his own. Surely this is altruism? Not according to the ethical egoist who argues that the soldier had nothing to lose – he was going to die anyway, and in this way he ensured that he would be remembered as a hero. So his sacrifice was in his interests. Alternatively, maybe the soldier was so desperately unhappy that the opportunity to limit his future suffering was a wonderful opportunity! Ethical egoism can explain it. However, now we are in a position to see why this theory is fatally flawed – it accounts for absolutely anything. This may appear to be a strength, but it is not. If our soldier had pushed his neighbour on the grenade, or run away, or done anything at all, we could say that he was acting in what he though were his own interests. The theory does not exclude anything, and it therefore cannot be said to explain anything.

The root of the problem is that if we see altruism as an excellent thing, then we can be egoistic by being altruistic. We can sacrifice our own interests if we perceive it to be in our own interests, and this covers any conceivable course of action. In other words, it can provide no guide to action – and so seems of little use as a moral theory.

A Consider the example of the soldier. Is there any action which could possibly prove that ethical egoism is incorrect? Pick any other situation – can ethical egoism tell you the correct course of action?

B Think back to what you know about science and the concept of falsifiability. How does this apply here?

If we reject the extreme of ethical egoism, where does that leave us with regard to altruism? Although we would certainly want to take others' welfare into account, it does not seem reasonable to live totally for others. So we need to find a way of balancing our needs with those of others.

Choice of premises: utilitarianism

Obligation, I think, can be compatible with self-interest provided it leads to the greatest good for the greatest number of people.

John Stuart Mill

Even though the extremes of egoism and altruism need to be moderated, they are both based on the principle of benefit, whether for self or for others. The concept of benefit is to be broadly interpreted, and should take into account as many factors as possible; in this context we often refer to benefit as **utility**. So both altruists and egoists attempt to maximise someone's utility, and perhaps the obvious compromise is to try to maximise overall benefit, for oneself and for others. This is, in a nutshell, the theory of **utilitarianism**. It seems like a common-sense approach, and is perhaps only a small step from the commonly held notion that we should be free to do what we want, as long as we do not harm anyone else. The problem with this, and one which utilitarianism seeks to address, is how we weigh up harm to others and benefit to ourselves.

Underlying utilitarianism is a very appealing notion of fairness (some have even said that it is a democratic theory of ethics). Utilitarianism states that we are all equally valuable – that all utility is equal; mine counts for no more than yours and it is sheer prejudice to take one's own point of view as the standard of judgement. It suggests that we should transcend our egocentric predicament and consider the welfare of everyone else as if it were our own (this idea is at the root of Christianity's 'Do unto others as you would have them do unto you'). Happiness is still the ultimate goal (so if you objected to this earlier, you may well still be unhappy with utilitarianism), but it is to be sought socially, not individually.

So how do we go about this? Faced with a number of choices, we calculate the net utility of each one, and choose the option with the biggest gain. It is simple in theory. Imagine we can measure happiness on a simple scale, with units of utils, so that +1 util is a small pleasure, but −50 utils is extremely unpleasant. Suppose, for example, that I am thinking of spending my money either on going to the cinema or giving it to a homeless person. If I go to the cinema I get a score of +5; by giving the money to the homeless person I get some satisfaction, say +3, and the homeless person also gets a score of +4.

- The egoist would go to the cinema; +5 being better than +3; the +4 is irrelevant.
- The altruist would give the money; +4 being the only important feature.
- The utilitarian would give the money; the +3 and +4 together outweigh the +5.

A In the example above, the utilitarian acts in the same way as the altruist. How would the util scores have to change so that the utilitarian would side with the egoist?

B Suppose this example was a real choice. How would you go about determining the number of utils to assign to each action?

C If I gave you $50, how many utils would this be worth to you? Compare your answers with a partner. If your partner gave a different score to you and I want to give away $50, then who should I give it to? Does this make sense?

D The notion that everybody's utility is equally valid sounds like an excellent principle, but is it really the case?

As soon as we begin to ask questions like these we see that the foundation of utilitarianism is not as straightforward as it seems. To make it work I need to be able to give a score to actions, and to place them in some sort of rank scale. But is this always possible? Even if I can do this, combining and comparing scores introduces a whole host of very difficult problems. If I give my trip to the cinema a score of ten (it was a really good film!) and the hungry beggar gives a meal a score of ten, then are they really of the same value? If the beggar finds out my score and changes his to twenty, then do we accept that as valid?

There may be valid ways of eliciting what decision-theorists call a **value function** – a meaningful ordering of alternatives – but there may not. If there is not, then we may have to retreat from a detailed calculus of utility to a broader, more general approach.

A Which is the better distribution between five people: 20, 20, 20, 20, 20 or 1, 1, 3, 5, 90? What would the perfect utilitarian say? Might there be reasons to disagree with the pure utilitarian analysis? If so, what are they?

B Consider the famous fictitious 'case of Sam'. Sam is an average, normal human being. He has a few friends, but no-one close, and he is unmarried. He has no living relatives. One day when he is in hospital for a regular medical check-up, it happens there are several medical emergencies occurring, and five people are going to die unless two kidneys, a liver, a heart and eight pints of blood can be found immediately. The people are all much-loved, with large families. What is the obvious utilitarian solution? Is it morally just? Explain your answer.

C Now imagine that one of the emergencies is likely to find a cure for cancer; another is central to the peace process in a war-ravaged part of the world; another is an actor whose work touches the lives of millions. Is it possible to find circumstances whereby Sam's life should, according to utilitarian principles, be forfeit?

D Make up an example of your own where it seems that utilitarianism leads to a terrible and unjust action. See how extreme an action you can justify via strict utilitarian principles.

Most people feel that such examples show that utilitarianism, as we have so far defined it, is flawed, running as it does against all our feelings of natural justice. This is a powerful objection, and unless one is prepared to allow Sam to be sacrificed, simple utilitarianism needs modification. One attempt to rescue the theory from these absurdities has been to require moral agents to look at the wider consequences of killing Sam and to **univeralise** – that is, to consider what would happen if everyone did such actions. Perhaps doing such a thing would lead to a community where everybody lived in fear and terror. Under these circumstances, utility would not be maximised, and so killing Sam would not be the right thing to do.

A Look at the example you just made up in which utilitarianism seems to go against what we feel is natural justice. Can you reconcile your example to the theory by universalising in this way?

B How wide a view should we take? Should we consider our immediate friends, the nearby community, the state or the world, and how far into the future should we look? What are the obvious problems here?

C If we begin to take an extremely wide view, what implications does that have for our lifestyle compared with, say, those who have little to eat? What would the utilitarian suggest is the right thing for us to do? Is this a problem with utilitarianism or our lifestyles?

D Is utiliarianism compatible with principles of natural justice?

It may well have struck some of you who have been reading this that utilitarianism rather misses the whole point of ethics. We have been arguing in terms of the outcome of the actions – and so whether or not we kill Sam depends on the effect killing him has. But not killing Sam purely because it doesn't do any good overall hardly seems like a moral position! Arguably it means that we are resisting murder not because we value Sam, or place a value on his life, but only because we can't find a way of making it worthwhile to kill him. For many, this is a fundamental and irresolvable flaw with the whole theory.

The root of this problem is at the heart of utilitarianism. In saying that no act is good or bad in itself, that it all depends on the outcome of the action, is to deny the importance of intention. Consider these two cases:

- I am about to get on a train when I am mugged, and my wallet is stolen. Instead of getting on the train I go to the police, who manage to catch the mugger, and I am about to press charges when I am told that the train crashed and I would have been injured or killed. That is, the mugger actually did me a favour by mugging me. Does this make the mugging a morally correct action?
- I see a sick man lying in the street in a deserted part of town. His condition is disgusting and repellent, but I feel it is my duty to help, and I take him to hospital. On the way we are in a car accident and he is killed. Is my action therefore immoral?

> **A** What would the strict utilitarian say about the two cases above? What do you think?
>
> **B** Can we modify utilitarianism to cope with the problem?

So what do we make of utilitarianism as a theory? One strength is that it recognises the need to view the world from the point of view of others. Another strength is that by basing itself on outcomes it attempts to offer clear guidelines for action. However, there are practical and logical difficulties in implementing anything like a strict utilitarian approach, and it is certainly worth considering other possible approaches which address some of the weaknesses.

Choice of premises: moral duty

In law, a man is guilty when he violates the rights of another.
In ethics he is guilty if he only thinks of doing so.

Immanuel Kant

Based as it is on happiness, utilitarianism is founded on the importance of our desires. For some, this is not a likely path to moral behaviour, as our desires are often impulsive, selfish and unreasonable. Many of the problems in the world are a result of people paying too much attention to their desires and not enough to other factors.

A strong contender for inclusion in any moral theory is the concept of **intention**. Simple utilitarianism makes no mention of it, but we instinctively take a rather dim moral view of someone who tries to do great evil but fails, even though there are no bad consequences. It seems that outcome alone is insufficient grounds for judging an action; the intention of the participants is key. (Interestingly, this is reflected in many legal systems where a *mens rea* ('guilty mind') is required in addition to an *actus reus* ('guilty action') for a crime to have been committed. The presence of the *mens rea* distinguishes between, for example, murder and manslaughter.)

The idea of intention seems rooted in common sense. Suppose, for example, that I offer to lend a friend my car. If I do so in the hope of reward, then you would not say that I was acting morally. A harder case to judge is the one where I lend the car because I like my friend. Is this a moral action? It certainly seems friendly and 'nice', but then so is smiling at your neighbour, and that is hardly a moral action! It has been argued, most famously by the philosopher Kant, that lending the car to a friend in this way is not a moral action. If I wanted to do it, if it was my desire to do so, then I was acting purely in my own interests, and (ethical egoists aside) few of us would want to say that such an action is moral. Kant goes so far to say that any action based in mere feelings cannot be a moral action.

This straightforward notion leads us to the idea of **moral duty** as a legitimate motive for action. There are times when we know what we should do and, irrespective of our feelings one way or another, the ethical action is clear. Suppose, for example, that my elderly parents need me to give them a large part of my salary each month so that they can afford to live reasonably comfortably. If I am paid enough so that I am not going to go hungry (and perhaps even then), then surely I have a moral duty to provide for them? I may not find it a very appealing prospect, and I may be reluctant to give up holidays or other things I value, but my duty is clear. Of course, I may actually be very enthusiastic about repaying my debt to my parents, but that is irrelevant. The point is whether or not I follow my sense of duty.

A Think of some situations where you would argue that intention is more important than outcome, or vice versa. Must intention play an important part in ethical theory?

B What do you think about Kant's rejection of desire as a basis of morality? Justify your answer carefully, giving examples where relevant.

C Kant claims that helping our friend because we like him is not a moral action. Do you agree?

D What would Kant say about the person who, seeing a sick person, was overcome with pity and went over to help them?

The idea of **moral duty** may sound very noble, but it needs to be scrutinised carefully. I am reminded of phrases such as 'Do your duty' which, in the mouths of the unscrupulous, really means 'Do as I tell you without question.' The concept of duty is a useless one unless it clarifies the way we should act. So what are our moral duties? Where do these impulses come from? Are they universal and unchanging, as C. S. Lewis argued earlier? Or do they change from culture to culture, and from time to time?

The danger here is that we answer these questions with reference to other schools of ethical thought. This is dangerous because we may end up following these schools of thought rather than trying to develop fully the duty theory. For example, if we say that our duty is to cause the greatest good for the greatest number then we are really just being utilitarian, and so we have gained nothing from the idea of moral duties. In order to clarify the idea, we need to avoid all other schools of ethical thought (which seems like a tall order!).

One philosopher who did manage to answer the question about what our duties are was Kant. In order to judge an act, he asks us to consider what principle governs the act, and then to imagine what would happen if everybody obeyed the principle. So far so good, but then Kant says that we judge if the action is good not by seeing if good effects are produced overall (this would be the same as utilitarianism) but by seeing if a **consistent world** is produced. To make it clear, consider the friend who asks if he can borrow my car. If I lend the car then the principle might be 'it is good to help friends when they ask,' and it is perfectly easy to imagine everyone in the world obeying this (notice I am not appealing to 'good' outcomes at all). So Kant would not forbid the lending of the car on moral grounds. On the other hand, suppose I have the urge to kill or lie or steal. If I generalise the principle 'you should kill/steal' then in the case of killing, after a brief period there will be no one left to carry it out; in the case of lying it is impossible to even state the law morally (since you should lie all the time). Thus it is unreasonable to generalise the principles governing your actions, and thus the actions are immoral. Kant called this notion the categorical imperative, and he stated it thus: *'Act only according to that maxim by which you can at the same time will that it should become a universal law.'*

A Think of a few cases where the concept of moral duty makes the moral course of action clear.
B Are there situations where the concept of moral duty is of no help?
C Try to apply Kant's reasoning to abortion, euthanasia, war, promiscuity, suicide and racism. Does his method come up with answers with which you feel comfortable?
D Explain Kant's thoughts on duty. What do you think about the insistence on a consistent world? What role does this give reason in ethics? Do you agree?

Does this help us make moral decisions?

You are free to choose, that is, invent.

Jean-Paul Sartre

We could go on to look at other ethical theories, or these theories in greater depth, and reams of profound books have done just that. But at this stage in our quest for truth and reliable knowledge, if other systems of knowledge are anything to go by, we might also have the sneaking suspicion that any system will present severe difficulties, and that a totally compelling theory may be extremely difficult to find. To be fair, some people find that one theory or another is powerful enough for them, but this is not an area where thinkers tend to converge, and there are some problems facing all the traditional ethical systems.

The influential French philosopher Jean-Paul Sartre pointed out one very real problem when he asked how we make a difficult decision in real life. He considered the case of a young man who, during the German occupation of France, wanted to leave England and join the Free French Forces to fight in the Resistance. However, he also did not want to leave his mother alone. How was he to make his choice? Sartre points out that Christian ethics are of no help. With a maxim such as 'Love thy neighbour,' whom was he to regard as his neighbour – his mother or the French Resistance? Utilitarians cannot decide – for how can the young man weigh up the specific and tangible benefit to his mother if he stays against the vague and abstract benefit to France if he goes? Kant's categorical imperative is also no guide – both universalised principles ('Everyone should leave to fight in the Resistance' and 'Everyone should look after their parents') seem consistent and plausible.

When Sartre said, *'No general ethics can show you what is to be done; there are no omens in the world,'* he meant that when we have a moral conflict, no moral theory will provide a reliable guide to behaviour.

A Is Sartre right? Is it impossible to find a moral theory which will tell us what is the right thing to do in all circumstances?

B Is it possible to resolve the case of the young man in Sartre's example?

C If Sartre is correct, where does this leave us in a search for moral guidance?

This critique of ethical systems focuses on the uniqueness of each human individual (as opposed to most theoretical systems which focus on abstract universal human qualities such as justice, utility, etc.). It stresses the primacy of freedom over reason because reason will not get us the answers we want or need – unless we are dishonest with ourselves (when Sartre would say we are 'acting in bad faith') we are forced to acknowledge that brute fact. This way of thinking has been termed **existentialism**, and provides a radically different approach to living and being in the world. Existentialism stresses the fact that we have to make choices, but that we have no clear, rational guidelines on which to make them; we are forced to turn away from reason as the final arbiter. It is important to note that rejecting a rational approach does not give us licence to do as we please. Sartre is very clear that with our freedom comes an over-riding responsibility to act morally, and many have felt that existentialism addresses humans needs in a personal and immediate way which no other system does.

A How do you resolve ethical conflicts? Are there any 'rules'? If so, why do you accept those rules and not others?

B Do you think any of the ethical theories we have examined in this chapter have all the answers?

C If we cannot rely on the traditional systems of ethics, what can we rely on?

D If we are free to choose our actions, what responsibility does this lay on us?

E Some may see freedom as liberating; others as extremely scary.
Sartre himself says that we find that we are free, but that we have no
choice about it – he writes that *'the truth is like finding you are free
but free in a prison'* and about the *'anxiety'* of freedom. What do you
think he meant when he said that we are *'condemned to be free'*?

It would be unfair to end our look at ethics without acknowledging
that there have been devastating critiques of the whole concept,
most notably in the form developed by the eighteenth-century
philosopher David Hume. His attack focuses on the role of
reasoning in ethics (and so might not be applicable to
existentialism, which leans on reason less heavily than the
traditional methods). Hume's penetrating point is a very simple
one: we cannot justify our choice of premises. Premises by
definition are simply stated (or they wouldn't be premises). For
example, suppose we want to explain why murder is wrong. We
can point to, for example, the utilitarian principle but Hume will
ask us why we accept that principle. We can say that we obey the
utilitarian principle because it leads to the greatest net pleasure,
but then Hume will ask why that is a good thing. And what can
we say? Is pleasure a good thing? Why is that? It seems
reasonable to me that my pleasure is good, but that is hardly a
guarantee of anything. Was Hitler's pleasure good? The Kantians
do not escape either – when they say that their theory is rational,
Hume asks why we should value rationality. And why do we?
Ultimately, to someone who keeps asking 'why?' in a moral
context (or probably any other), Hume says that we have to
acknowledge that we don't know. This seems to undermine any
attempt to ground ethics in objectivity.

Where does this leave us? Adrift in the Universe without a
moral compass? Some have felt so, and perhaps those thinkers
would describe their prevailing attitude as absurdism, whereby
there is no moral basis for passing judgement. So perhaps we
should just sit back and enjoy the show. But on the other hand,
maybe we are asking too much of any moral theory. Perhaps
Sartre was right when he said that a theory never makes moral
judgements, only humans do – to get hung up on theories is to
misunderstand the role they play in our lives. Theories are there
as guidebooks, not rule books; they can tell us the direction but
we must choose the path. Rather than seek to construct an
axiomatic system we should be looking for a way to construct
meaning for ourselves. So long as we do not expect too much of
philosophy, we will not be disappointed.

A What on earth does this last paragraph mean?
B What should we look for in a moral system? What role should
reason play?
C On the basis of this chapter, and all the theories and difficulties we
have seen, how should we live?

Where do we go from here?

The issues we have considered have been largely to do with individuals' moral choices. But we are more than individuals – we are part of a society, we live in groups and we have a government. Any ethical theory which claims to tell us how to live must surely take note of these facts, and address them directly. This means that any true ethical theory must have some impact on political theories, and what's more, political theories must be practical ones – a stiff test for any philosopher. So let us then turn to politics.

Further reading

It is well worth checking out some introductions to philosophy and then going on to look at some applied issues. Recommended introductions are chapter 7 of Thomas Nagel's *What Does It All Mean?* (Oxford University Press, 1987), chapter 8 of John Hosper's *Introduction to Philosophical Analysis* (Prentice Hall, 1953) and chapters 7 and 8 of Donald Palmer's *Does the Centre Hold?* (Mayfield, 1991). For a more detailed look at morality, I recommend Gilbert Harman's *The Nature of Morality* (Oxford University Press, 1977), and Jean-Paul Sartre's *Existentialism and Human Emotions* (Philosophical Library, 1957).

Three excellent studies are Jonathan Glover's *Causing Death and Saving Lives* (Pelican, 1977), and John Harris' *The Value of Life* (Routledge and Kegan Paul, 1985) and *Violence and Responsibility* (Routledge and Kegan Paul, 1988).

■ *Resource file*

RESOURCE FILE RESOURCE FILE RESOURCE FILE RESOURCE FILE RESOURCE FILE RESOURCE FILE RESOURCE FILE RESOURCE FILE RESOURCE FILE RESOURCE FILE RESOURCE FILE

Euthanasia: should it be legalised?

An extract from the *Pros and Cons Debates Handbook* by Michael Jacobson.

PRO: i) We put animals 'out of their misery' rather than let them suffer intolerable pain, yet we refuse the same merciful release to our fellow man. In spite of all that modern medicine and surgery can do to prevent disease, or abate it, many human beings still end their days by a slow and often agonising illness. Provided that strict legal precautions were observed (particularly regarding the crucial question of consent), a doctor should have the right to give an overdose of morphine to a patient who would otherwise die a lingering and painful death.

CON: i) A doctor cannot draw up a list of diseases which are invariably fatal. A steadily increasing proportion of cancer sufferers, until recently doomed, can now be cured. People with heart disease may live long and useful lives. It is impossible to make hard and fast rules when medical science is in a state of continual change and progress. The doctor's duty is to maintain life as long as possible by every means in his power.

PRO: ii) Although it may not be possible to draw up a list of diseases that are always incurable, a point comes in each individual case where a doctor knows whether a patient is beyond hope or not. The patient himself should be the best judge of whether life has become, for him/her, intolerable. If he/she wishes for release from suffering, it should not be denied. In Britain, suicide ceased to be a crime in 1961. Logically, euthanasia is merely a further step along this merciful path. The number of people recorded as committing suicide in Britain varies very little – averaging around 4200 a year. It may be doubted whether the number of patients seeking euthanasia would be anything like as much as even this relatively low total.

CON: ii) This argument is tantamount to a plea for the legalisation of suicide. If physical suffering is a valid excuse for cutting life short, then why not other forms of suffering? Unless a patient were aware of his condition, and deliberately asked for euthanasia, it would be an act of intolerable cruelty to let him/her know that such a measure was being considered. A request of euthanasia might easily be due to temporary depression; a person in great pain is not always responsible for his/her utterances. It is familiar ground that a high proportion of suicides are people who are 'calling for help' and do not really (in their subconscious minds) intend to kill themselves, but who go too far. Among those requesting euthanasia, the risk of irreversible error would be even greater.

PRO: iii) If the patient is unaware of the hopelessness of his/her condition, the decision should be taken out of his/her hands. The family doctor would know best, but to avoid any risk or error of judgement on his part, there should be consultations with a specially qualified medical assessor. If the doctors were in agreement that euthanasia was desirable, the final decision might then rest with the patient's relatives.

CON: iii) Doctors do not always correctly estimate a patient's recuperative powers and should not be saddled with the responsibility of making what is, in effect, a decision to murder. It could also be an impossibly heavy burden for relatives to have to be the final arbiters in cutting short the life of one linked to them by blood and affection. On the other hand, a legalised euthanasia would be a ready-made weapon for unscrupulous relatives, which no amount of legal precaution could adequately guard against.

PRO: iv) If we are to call it murder to take a patient's life with his/her consent, then we must call it theft to take his/her property with his/her consent, which is absurd. As for pain, no doubt it has its uses, if only as a danger signal. But not many of us would go on enduring a pain we could avoid. And none but a fanatic would advocate the cessation of human effort to alleviate or abolish pain.

CON: iv) Many religions teach that it is wrong to take a human life. Moreover, it is possible that pain itself has a significant place in the scheme of evolution and serves some mysterious moral purpose. A civilisation based on a high conception of the value of human life cannot countenance the deliberate taking of life where no crime has been committed by the sufferer. A large number of people supported the abolition of capital punishment in Britain, even for murder cases, and there was a far better case for it than for euthanasia.

PRO: v) In practice, 'mercy killings' by relatives have usually been treated with understanding and a measure of leniency in the courts. Even in the past, few of the culprits were sentenced to death, and the sentence was almost never carried out. Many unfortunate people are born who have no hope of ever leading a normal life or of being anything but a tragic liability to their families. Such people should not be forced to enter on a travesty of life, much less continue it.

CON: v) The danger of such cheapening of the respect for human life was seen under the Nazis, who had millions of people put to death for imaginary 'racial defects'. It is better that a few should suffer unwanted life than that the door should be opened, even to the slightest extent, to such ruthless practices.

The death penalty: should it be brought back?

An extract from the *Pros and Cons Debates Handbook* by Michael Jacobsen.

This article was published in 1987 in the UK where there is no death penalty.

PRO: i) Experience since its abolition has proved that the death penalty is a stern, though regrettable, necessity. Without it our lives and property have become less secure and crimes of violence have increased. In the present unsettled state of the world, its return is becoming more, not less, necessary. The police say that now criminals do not have to fear hanging, the numbers who carry guns when committing robberies or other crimes have risen enormously.

CON: i) The death penalty is an anachronism in the modern penal code. It is a relic of an age when all punishments were savage and vindictive and will be regarded by our successors with the same horror with which we now regard the hanging of little children for theft. Up to the early part of the nineteenth century, the death penalty could be, and was, inflicted for more than 200 different offences. Hanging is now recognised to be a revolting and cruel punishment. Its abolition was a major step towards our claim to be more civilised.

PRO: ii) The death penalty should be used to rid society of its enemies, instead of keeping them for the remainder of their lives as a perpetual charge on the public purse. Some of the countries which have virtually ceased to carry out the death penalty, e.g. France, have since found it necessary to draw back from its complete legal abolition.

CON: ii) The death penalty is not an effective deterrent. In fact the statistics of crime in all countries prove that violent punishment does not tend to bring about a decrease in violent crime. In spite of the death penalty, the average numbers of murders in Britain each year remained almost stationary for half a century – and the annual total (London had 204 murders in 1984 and 187 in 1985) has continued to be virtually static as well since the death penalty was abolished.

PRO: iii) The reformation and re-education of some types of criminal may be possible, and it is recognised that a high proportion of those convicted of 'unlawful killing' are 'one-off cases', not normally involved in serious crime; but a hardened murderer is beyond hope of reform. Are we to allow such people, ready to kill without compunction not once but several times, to live and return to society as a source of danger to their fellows on expiry of their sentences (even a life sentence may, in practice, sometimes amount to little more than 10–12 years)?

CON: iii) Out of about thirty countries that have abolished the death penalty, not one has reported any increase in murders, and several have reported decreases. A penal code based on the idea of education and reformation is much more likely to reduce the amount of crime. In the USA, neither the recent few years without executions nor the resumed implementation of the death penalty in several states has had any appreciable effect, one way or the other, on the already horrific murder rate (New York alone had 1392 murders in 1985). It is the tide of violent crimes that has continued to increase, not the number of murders, as such.

PRO: iv) If there is the slightest doubt in the minds of the jury, a verdict of guilty is not returned. Despite public concern over the possibility of mistakes, only one wrongful conviction and execution (that of Timothy Evans) is known out of the many thousands of murder cases in Britain since the last world war.

CON: iv) The death sentence is irrevocable. A mistake cannot be put right. Even a single mistake, among no matter how many thousands of cases, is one too many for a civilised society to chance.

PRO: v) Discrimination between degrees of homicide and the possibility of a verdict of manslaughter gives juries plenty of opportunities for clemency. It might be argued that a majority of murderers are insane – temporarily anyway – and that there is a case for revising the present somewhat restricted legal definition of insanity. But the prospect of facing the supreme penalty, not just a long jail sentence, is the only way to deal with the clearly threatening rise in those who commit murder in the course of other crimes. A life sentence is in some ways even more cruel than a death sentence, and there have been some convicted murderers who would actually have preferred the latter.

CON: v) Murderers did sometimes escape all legal punishment because the jury refused to convict, but this has become less likely now there is no death penalty. In many cases, death sentences were passed as an empty and cruel formality, when there was no intention of carrying them out. Very few murders are premeditated. Many are committed by people who are found to be insane – and no threatened penalty is likely to deter a lunatic – while in the great majority of those cases in which the murderer is held to be sane, the crime is committed under the temporary stress of violent passion or anger. That such people had to be condemned for premeditated murder, under the previous law, was a travesty of justice.

PRO: vi) That many people habitually signed petitions seeking clemency for convicted murderers was often merely the result of mass suggestion or hysteria – due, maybe, to newspaper 'hype'. It proved nothing.

CON: vi) That thousands were always eager to sign petitions for reprieve, even in cases where murder was definitely proved, shows how deep is the feeling that infliction of the death sentence is against the conscience of civilised man.

Abortion: should it be legal?

An extract from the *Pros and Cons Debates Handbook* by Michael Jacobsen.

PRO: i)   Legalised abortion is necessary to avoid the incidence of 'back-street' operations by ignorant or ill-equipped persons and the consequent hazards for women who have sought their help: infection, injury or even death. No responsible woman deciding to seek an abortion would ever make such a decision lightly. But one point on which she can reassure herself is that a child has no legal existence before birth and, in any case, is not even recognisable as a human being until relatively late in a pregnancy.

CON: i)   Life begins at conception, when the egg is fertilised by the sperm, and there can be no justification for ending that life. As the Roman Catholic Archbishop of Westminster wrote to Members of Parliament in 1985: 'The needs of some cannot be allowed to eclipse the rights of others.' Many women undergo abortions only through fear of disapproval, or perhaps even threats, from their family and friends or from the child's father. The operation is accepted reluctantly at a time when a woman's mind and body, even during the most normal pregnancy, both undergo significant additional stress.

PRO: ii)   Abortions are particularly necessary for the relief of pregnancies resulting from rape or incest or in girls below the legal age of consent. Figures for England and Wales in 1983 show that the number of live births to girls aged under 16 that year totalled 1249 and the number of induced abortions for the same age group was 4077. Over the preceding decade the annual total of such abortions had risen by 40% and the actual number of births had fallen by 250 – a conclusive indication, surely, of the extent of the misery which must have existed before legal abortions were available.

CON ii):   Violent end to an innocent life, one which is biologically half the own-child of the mother, is no answer to pregnancy caused by rape, incest or under-age sexual relations. Abortion is merely the easy way out. Statistically, moreover, it has been established that pregnancy follows rape relatively seldom.

PRO: iii)   Abortion should never be looked at simply as a form of birth control, as many critics claim it to be. The Abortion Act 1967 specifies that the termination of a pregnancy is permitted in order to safeguard the physical or psychological health of the woman involved. That many women thus spared can later go on to exercise normal procreation, without having suffered any lasting mental or physical harm from prior abortion, is shown by one statistic published in the mid-1980s, some 18 years after abortion was legalised in this country; by that time, it was calculated, about one woman in five bearing her first-born child, in Britain, had experienced a previous termination.

CON: iii)   The great majority of abortions in the UK are carried out on psychological grounds. Psychology, however, it still a science far less exact even than medicine; few doctors are trained in psychology, which points to a serious flaw in the legislation – because such training is not specifically required, by law, in those able to authorise an abortion. Little or no regard is paid to the woman's psyche after she has had an abortion. While there can be no grounds for suggesting that the lack of effective research into post-abortion, psychology might at least be partly due to doctors' fears of jeopardising their future career prospects, the fact remains that the comparative absence of studies on the subject is quite remarkable.

PRO: iv)   Selective abortion can minimise the number of handicapped people in the community who will never be able to enjoy the full quality of life.

CON: iv)   Abortion cannot be used to weed out 'imperfect' human beings, not only for the obvious moral reasons but also simply because of the other side of the equation: how do you define the perfect and who would be qualified to do so?

A   Pick one side of the three controversial cases examined in the Resource file. Look carefully at the arguments.

- Decide which are arguments of principle and which are arguments of fact.
- Construct diagrams similar to the one on page 236 to represent these arguments.
- Are the arguments supported by the ideas of ethical egoism, altruism, utilitarianism or moral duty?
- Do you accept the arguments? On what grounds do you accept or deny them?

12

Princes and governments are by far the most dangerous elements of a society.
Niccolo Macchiavelli

Democracy encourages the majority to decide things about which the majority is ignorant.
John Simon

The marvel of all history is the patience with which men and women submit to burdens unnecessarily laid upon them by their governments.
William E. Borah

DEMOCRACY IS A FORM OF GOVERNMENT THAT SUBSTITUTES ELECTION BY THE INCOMPETENT MANY FOR APPOINTMENT BY THE CORRUPT FEW.
George Bernard Shaw

It has been said that democracy is the worst form of government except all those others that have been tried from time to time.
Winston Churchill

Senator George H. Moses once complained to me that a man being considered for a Republican senatorial nomination was an 'out and out son-of-a-bitch'. Coolidge agreed saying 'That may be. But there are a lot of those in the country and I think that they are entitled to some representation in the senate.'
Calvin Coolidge

APPLAUSE, MIXED WITH BOOS AND HISSES, IS ALL THAT THE AVERAGE VOTER IS ABLE TO CONTRIBUTE TO PUBLIC LIFE.
Elmer Davis

Democracy does not guarantee equality of conditions – it only guarantees equality of opportunity.
Irving Kristol

We debated this bill for nine days. I think the world was created in seven.
Robert Byrd

It is the absolute right of the state to supervise the formation of public opinion.
Paul Joseph Goebbels

To rule is easy, to govern, difficult.
Johann Wolfgang von Goethe

Government is not reason. Government is not eloquence. It is force. And, like fire, it is a dangerous servant and a fearful master.
George Washington

Aims

- understand what is meant by political thought and action; and the nature of the concepts involved
- recognise alternative views of human nature and the implication for our view of government
- be able to discuss the legitimate role of government in social affairs
- understand the philosophies behind the communist, minimal state and liberal democratic approaches
- understand the strengths and weaknesses of the democratic system
- understand the meaning of the term 'human rights' and be able to suggest what those human rights should be.

Introduction

- Amnesty International calls for an end to human rights abuses in a particular country.
- The government increases income tax to fund an expansion in education.
- The United Nations condemns armed aggression by one country against another.
- Teachers go on strike for more pay.
- The unemployed stage a demonstration in the capital to protest against their plight.

In each of these cases, we have a **political** action. That is, we have organised groups trying to achieve their goals in the context of a broader society. This is what politics is about – the processes by which different groups pursue their interests, and the means by which societies regulate conflict between the groups (this is often called **government**). The whole means by which society is run is often called a **political system**, but in our daily lives we often focus on our immediate concerns and take for granted the political system in which we live. When we come into contact with government, it may be in negative ways – certainly it is difficult to pick up a newspaper in some countries without reading about some terrible case of political corruption. Sometimes even well-regarded politicians turn out to have been engaged in corrupt practices and, as a result, politicians tend to be held in extremely low regard. But politics is a vital part of our society, and anyone who has ever experienced the breakdown of government or the absence of political authority will know that it is a very frightening, and sometimes very dangerous, state of affairs. If we live in security and comfort, we may be blind to the fact that political systems are, in a very practical sense, vitally important to the values and quality of civilised life. If the system is stable and remotely efficient, there is the opportunity for peace and prosperity (even if it is unrealised), but where political processes fail to resolve differences between groups, armed conflict and war can follow.

Politics is a branch of sociology, and as such has two aspects – the descriptive and the normative. The descriptive involves collecting facts, making models and predictions etc. as in all human sciences. The normative is all about deciding how society should work. This is all about how to apply moral principles to groups' decision-making; often it is about the extent to which we have the right or duty to force some groups to do things against their will. Before we get into these issues, let's state the 'big questions' of political philosophy. See what you make of them both now and after you have finished reading this chapter.

A Can humans live peaceably without authority?
B What, if any, is the distinction between legitimate and illegitimate authority?
C What is the best form of government? Is it democracy?
D What is the best form of society?
E What should governments do/not do?
F What do we mean by terms such as 'social justice', 'equality', 'freedom' and 'human rights'?

A word of warning: we need to retain our awareness of the distinction between normative and descriptive statements, and avoid political dogma. In politics more than most other areas, we find people making illogical arguments based on poor reasoning and a desire to convince and persuade at all costs rather than on an honest and reflective search for truth. Terms such as 'socialist', 'conservative' and 'liberal' have been so over-used that they almost have no meaning, they are more anthems or rallying cries than statements of belief. Conservatives say that they want to retain the best of the past and socialists state that they want a fair society, or is it the other way around? The point is that it doesn't matter – everyone wants to retain the best of the past and everyone wants to have a fair society. The real debate starts when we acknowledge that there is a problem deciding what 'best' and 'fair' mean, and how to go about achieving these ideals.

As a concrete example of the danger of confusing rhetoric, labels and stereotypes with reality, consider the ideas of Karl Marx. Living in a Western liberal democracy, as I have done for most of my life, I find it easy to denounce Marxism on the basis of what has happened under communist parties in the mid-twentieth century, but a neutral reading of Marx suggests that some (but by no means all) of his ideas still have relevance. His ideas have been hijacked for political ends by both extremes of the political spectrum, and Marx himself remarked that by the end of his life, his ideas were being used in such contexts that he himself was not a Marxist!

Let us re-state an important value – in any search for truth we should examine ideas for their value and not be put off by the label. Even concepts with extremely negative connotations may have something to tell us if we approach them with open but critical minds. If we dismiss ideas out of hand, we can never learn from them – we can always dismiss them once we have seen precisely why they do not work.

Why do we need government anyway?

Why do we need government anyway?

Man is born free; and everywhere he is in chains.

Jean Jacques Rousseau

Rousseau's quote may be a slight exaggeration, but it contains at least a grain of truth. In our societies, rules govern almost every aspect of our behaviour. They tell us how we should behave, where we can and cannot go, how fast we must go to where we are allowed to go, and in what circumstances we are allowed to say certain things and not others. In some cases, we may even be told what we are allowed to wear. Furthermore, all these rules are enforced by threat of eventual loss of some freedom, property and maybe even life. Just breaking a simple rule, such as that which forbid nudity in public, can quickly lead to fines, loss of liberty and possibly loss of employment. So why do we put up with it?

Well, people do not always put up with it. Historically, and in some parts of the world today, people resist the imposition of rules they do not like, or do not feel are just, and try to overthrow a government and replace it with one that is 'better'. But how do they know which form is 'better' than another? Do we really need government at all?

When we attempt to answer this question, we quickly find that we have to make assumptions about human nature. What would we be like without government? One view is that that when left to our own devices, in our **state of nature**, we quickly descend to the level of animals – where might is right and there is continual fear of sudden and violent death. In his novel *Lord of the Flies*, William Golding suggests that unrestrained humans are fierce and savage. Thomas Hobbes wrote that under these circumstances our lives would be *'solitary, poor, nasty, brutish and short'*. This then gives a clear reason for government – to save us from ourselves. Governments remove our 'right' to do what we want, and we should be thankful for it! Hobbes suggests:

that a man be willing, when others are so too . . . to lay down this right to all things; and be contented with so much liberty against other men, as he would allow other men against himself.

This forms the basis of the **Hobbesian social contract**, which states that we give up certain things to the state in return for specified benefits. If you accept the basic premise, the logic is clear; my natural tendency is towards violence, and I will be violent towards you if I think that will benefit me. Unfortunately, the same reasoning leads me to recognise that you may well be violent towards me. In any unregulated society, therefore, unless you are confident that you are the strongest, you will live in fear, and therefore misery. Even if a group of people renounce violence to each other, there will always be the lingering suspicion that anyone who thinks they can get away with it will try something unpleasant. The only solution, says Hobbes, is to have an organisation strong enough to make sure that it is never in anyone's interests to use violence. This organisation is the government (the *Leviathan* of his famous work), which, according to this idea, legitimately wields absolute power.

A What do you think about the state of nature as Hobbes envisaged it? Is he correct?

B Does his view of the state follow automatically from his view of human nature?

C When would Hobbes suggest that a revolution to overthrow the government should take place?

D What do you think Hobbes thinks a government would do? Would it be likely to act in humane and noble ways?

Many thinkers have disagreed with Hobbes' fairly bleak view of human nature. Fifty years on, the philosopher John Locke suggested a radically different state of nature, based on Christian theology. For Locke, humans are created by God, and given basic human rights and basic moral obligations. The rights are to life, health, liberty and possessions; and the obligations are not to harm others with regard to life, health, liberty and possessions. Under these conditions, the role of government is far less than in the Hobbesian scenario. The government exists to stop offenders spoiling the idyllic state of nature, by punishment, and its legitimacy is granted by the will of the people. This is the **Lockean social contract** – the people submit to the government in return for the protection of their innate unalienable human rights.

A What do you think about the state of nature as Locke envisaged it? Is he correct?

B Does his view of the state follow automatically from his view of human nature?

C When would Locke suggest that a revolution to overthrow the government should take place?

D Locke suggests that the first possession, and one which is central to the other three rights, is one's own body and, by extension, this property right can be extended to that which we create with our bodies' labour. How does this translate into government policy?

It is interesting to note that when writing the American Declaration of Independence, the American Founding Fathers were strongly influenced by Locke:

We hold these truths to be self-evident, that all men are created equal; that they are endowed by their creator with certain unalienable rights; that among these are life, liberty, and the pursuit of happiness. That to secure these rights, governments are instituted among men, deriving their just powers from the consent of the governed; that whenever any form of government becomes destructive of these ends, it is the right of the people to alter or abolish it, and to institute a new government, laying its foundations on such principles . . . as to them shall seem most likely to effect their safety and happiness.

The USA has developed and adapted Lockean principles over the last few hundred years, and there has been much progress based on ideals of equality, human rights and government as a tool to serve the people. However, there are clear problems of distributive wealth, and Locke's convenient notion of property (who but a rich man would stress the unalienable 'right' to keep all you can get your hands on?) has led to a situation where wealth may not (quite) buy government, but certainly helps a good deal.

> **A** Some have argued that Hobbes and Locke are both right – they are describing different circumstances. One imagines a scarcity of natural resources, one an abundance. Which is which?
>
> **B** If this is true, what implication does this have for our society? For which classes of people (if any) is Hobbesian/Lockean theory correct, and what does this mean for law enforcement and social policy?

Some thinkers have argued that the authority of any state is illegitimate; that government is basically wrong, and that we should be able to negotiate our existence as individuals, and with the groups we choose to join. While this view seems to run against human nature (political power struggles seem to be built in to us just as they are built in to so many other animals) that is not to say we should dismiss its challenge. The view is that of **anarchy** and it does not mean, in this context, total chaos and disorder.

> **A** Do we need government at all? How did humans cope several thousand years ago?
>
> **B** What do you think an anarchist would say to the idea that we need government?
>
> **C** What would the hypothetical anarchist state look like? Would there be any social organisation at all?

How much should governments do?

We made no progress at all . . . and we didn't intend to. That's the function of a national committee.

Ronald Reagan

We are born in societies where the notion of government is taken for granted, and debate centres around the question of government action (this was not always so for as recently as the 1920s many governments took no responsibility for economic growth). In political life, as far as policies go, the questions are often on the extraordinarily difficult level of 'Will it work?' but for now we shall look at the more abstract level of 'Should the government be involved in this area at all?' The big question here is to do with social justice, and may be stated as follows: what is the legitimate role of the state in ensuring a fair distribution of resources among its citizens? The answers have been as varied as any in philosophical thought, and we shall consider only a few of the systems that have been suggested.

We shall start with the enormously influential ideas of Karl Marx. Although many of his revolutionary conclusions have been proven wrong by the passage of time, they still make for interesting debate. Marx's ideas are based on two thoughts:

- that individuals have little ability to develop material resources – it is only communities and societies that do so and, as a result, the wealth that is created belongs to the community or society
- that, historically, a small number of individuals in each society have managed to divert power and resources from the benefit of the community to their own benefit, and that the same individuals have then been in a position to set up systems of privilege and social institutions which protect that privilege ('army', 'police', even 'schools' and 'media').

From these ideas, Marx argues that the majority of people, the so-called **proletariat**, are working, generating wealth, but much of that wealth is siphoned off to the benefit of a so-called ruling class, and that this is a radically unfair way to run society. As an assessment of social problems, Marx's insights are still useful today.

A Is Marx accurate in his assessment of the society of your country?

B Who are the ruling class in your country? What are their lives like? Who are the poorest of the working class in your society? What are their lives like? Is this a fair system?

C Marx argues that the ruling class treats workers as profit-generating commodities, and that this leads to their neglect as human beings. Is this true in your society? Does it have to be true?

D If we take a global economy as the current society, which class do you fall into? What about the children in sweatshops around the world who are making running shoes they will never wear, basketballs they will never play with, and carpets they will never be able to buy? Which class are they in? Are there more of 'you' or more of 'them'?

You might think that Marx has a pessimistic, Hobbesian approach to human nature, that we are all just out for whatever we can get, but in fact this is not the case. Marx regarded the ruling class as somehow unnatural, and had a much more optimistic, Lockean perspective, arguing that humans are naturally imaginative, talented and aesthetic creatures who need to express themselves creatively in their work. However, he saw the capitalist system as fundamentally opposed to this. Under capitalism, workers do not work to satisfy their natural creative urges; they work for others to earn money. This is the distinction between intrinsically rewarding work (that which you would do for its own sake) and extrinsically rewarding work (that which you do because you have to earn a living). Marx denounced the latter as degrading and **alienating** – it divorces the worker from his true nature:

Consequently, he does not fulfil himself in his work, but denies himself, has a feeling of misery rather than well-being, does not develop freely his physical and mental energies but is physically exhausted and mentally debased . . . External labour, labour in which man alienates himself, is a labour of self-sacrifice, of mortification.

There seems to be some truth in this. What proportion of people enjoy their work and feel that they are doing something meaningful? Some, to be sure, but many probably do not. If we look at some of the things that people spend their working lives doing, we can see why Marx may have a point.

A There was a psychologist who was disturbed by children playing loudly in the road just outside his house. He wanted to get rid of them, but he knew them and suspected that asking them or even getting angry with them would just make the problem worse. So one day he went outside and told them how much he liked their noise, and that he would pay them $5 a day if they would keep it up. They were delighted, and for a week they continued to make noise; each day they took his $5. Then he told them that he was short of cash, and gave them $1; the next day he said that he really couldn't afford it, but that he had 50 cents for them. After that he gave them nothing. The children were very unhappy about this and went elsewhere.

How does this relate to intrinsic and extrinsic rewards, and what does it tell us about human nature and motivation? How does this fit into the Marxist approach?

B In a manufacturing society, many people work in factories. What does Marx think about that?

C Does the notion of an information society undermine the Marxist analysis?

D Are people really alienated from themselves in your society? Which jobs result in most/least alienation?

E What would Marx say about the corporations whose goods/ products are designed to wear out?

So far Marx has pointed out a lot of problems. That's easy, but what about solutions? At this stage his ideas seem far less compelling, certainly from a historical point of view. He suggests that revolution against injustice is justifiable (he actually thought it was inevitable), and that the new ideal society will have three important aspects.

- Production of resources will be geared to meet real human needs (food, shelter, clothing, medical care, education) rather than false needs, which benefit only a powerful ruling class (luxury cars, vast houses, excessive food, etc.).
- The means of production will be democratically and socially controlled rather than in the hands of a privileged few.
- No one will be forced to work in areas that inhibit the creative urges. The division of labour, whereby we have to specialise in one trade, will be over. We will be free to do one trade today and another tomorrow.

These ideas involve a large state presence in most areas of society. The state should decide which and how much of each commodity to make, who should make it, how it should be distributed and so on. This requires high taxation to fund, and is extremely unlikely to be efficient, but Marx would argue that the benefits to society outweigh the costs.

A Consider each of the aspects of Marx's ideal society in turn. Are they desirable? Are they practical? Are there any unacceptable consequences of the theory?

B What would life be like in this society under the best scenario and under the worst scenario?

C To what extent are any of these aspects present in the society in which you live?

D What are the problems with change by revolution? Is there always an alternative?

E What sorts of people (background, status, place in society) are likely to support Marxism? What sorts are likely to reject it?

F Does Marxism, as presented here, have any relevance today?

At the other end of the political spectrum to communism is the idea of the **minimal state**. The minimal state is one which does the absolute minimum to keep society together – it prevents violence, theft and so on, but it plays no role whatsoever in redistributing wealth and it has no legitimate right to undertake public works. There is something appealing about this idea, as any working person who has seen their taxes wasted on bureaucracy or government scandal will know, and some states are moving towards using private companies to do what has traditionally been government business. The idea is that, in Adam Smith's famous phrase, the 'invisible hand' of the market will create massive efficiency savings, boost the economy and make everyone better off in the long run. In Britain, refuse collection and prison services are two examples where recent governments have tried to bring in private enterprise to reduce state involvement. If expenditure can be cut, then tax cuts may follow, and perhaps this is what the people want.

The idea of minimal government has been also defended on grounds of social justice. The idea is, along Lockean principles, that we have the unalienable right to property; that our earned money is our property, and that avoidable taxation is therefore theft. The philosopher Robert Nozick has even argued that, when a citizen is working to give money to the state involuntarily, the citizen is in effect part owned by the state. On these grounds, Nozick puts imposed taxation on a par with slavery! In his exploration of the minimal state he acknowledges that, as a natural consequence, some people will become extremely rich and powerful and others will live in extreme poverty, but he argues that this unfortunate outcome is more just than mass state slavery.

A Are governments inherently less efficient than private enterprise? Why?

B Is redistribution of wealth from the rich to the poor a violation of human rights, in principle? Whose rights are violated?

C Does Nozick's notion of state slavery make any sense?

D What would life be like in a 'minimal state' under the best scenario and under the worst scenario?

E What sorts of people (background, status, place in society) are likely to support the minimal state? What sorts are likely to reject it? Does it help to talk about 'sorts' of people like this?

F Does the notion of the minimal state have any relevance today?

Many people feel that the redistribution of wealth is not only a right, but a duty of the state. We have seen the worst-case scenario in Ireland in the 1840s when the state refused to regulate market prices during a famine. Prices rose rapidly, a small number of food distributors got very rich indeed, and a million people starved to death. As Martin Gardner said, '*The hand of Smith proved to be a clenched fist with brass knuckles.*' Similar scenarios can be found around the world today. Perhaps there is a case for government intervention, and while the state should not tax the rich excessively, maybe it should redistribute wealth to some reasonable degree (of course, the terms 'excessive' and 'reasonable' are open to interpretation). (Even if it is moral to do so, some economists argue that high taxes lead to lower government revenue as rich people avoid taxes (for example, by moving overseas). Thus the moral question may be rendered irrelevant by the empirical fact.)

Many believe that the role of the state should go still further. In the mid-nineteenth century, labour laws were introduced in the USA to prevent children under twelve years of age working more than ten hours a day. The thinking behind this controversial move was that child labour was immoral and that the state should ensure that children are educated rather then exploited, even if this requires tax money to do. The laws were vigorously opposed by parents, factory owners, and even the church, who argued that that the state had no right to tell parents what to do with their children.

Today, most of us would support these labour laws, and argue that the state has a duty to legislate on such matters. This brings us to what is the most commonly held conception of a just and legitimate state – the **liberal state**. The liberal state is one with a large amount of free enterprise, which is largely in the control of private corporations and individuals, but where the state takes an active role in ensuring that the structural requirements for a prosperous and just society are in place. The German Social Democratic Party, when making the split with Marxism in 1959, put it succinctly: '*As much competition as possible, as much planning as necessary.*' Most have taken that to mean that there is a need for a state education system to ensure equal opportunities for future generations, a state police system to ensure laws are obeyed, state-financed welfare provision for those who cannot support themselves, and careful state monitoring in socially important financial matters such as unemployment, money supply, inflation, etc.

This arrangement is a judicious blend of free enterprise and state participation and every modern democracy, whether it calls itself socialist or capitalist, contains a mix of free markets and government-owned or regulated companies. Though some politicians campaign on a pro-capitalism or pro-socialism agenda, in reality there is usually a mixture of these extremes. In the USA, which claims to be a free market, there are government controls on food, medical drugs, discrimination, advertising, banking, working hours, working conditions, wage policies and education. There are also subsidies for scientific research, education, health care, the arts, and the line between state and the military, space agencies and energy authorities is so faint that it can hardly be seen. The reality is that in a complex and highly sophisticated technological world economy, governments and corporations both have a vital role to play, and anyone who says otherwise is probably engaging in political posturing.

Many people think that the liberal state is a hybrid – it attempts to combine the best of left- and right-wing philosophies in order to seek the ideal compromise between competition and co-operation.

As a philosophy, liberalism takes an optimistic view about the overall nature of humankind: it supports science and 'progress'; it values private property and use of natural resources; it supports the democratic rule of law; it is tolerant of diversity and peaceful reform. To those who live comfortably in these societies (and the fact that I have written and you are reading this book makes it very likely that we are two such people), this seems to be a very reasonable account of the principles by which a state should be run. Others who benefit less from these arrangements might feel differently.

The trouble is, of course, that the devil is in the details. *Precisely how much* should the government get involved? This is a difficult question, and perhaps one not answerable by philosophy.

A Why does the liberal state seem attractive? What are its best features?
B What would life be like in the liberal state society under the best scenario and under the worst scenario?
C What sorts of people (background, status, place in society) are likely to support the liberal state? What sorts are likely to reject it?
D What would be the dangers of the liberal state according to a supporter of the minimal state and a Marxist?
E In what respects does the state you live in resemble the ideal liberal state? Is it moving towards or away from that ideal?
F Consider education. How much should the government get involved? Should it leave education totally to the market or ensure there is schooling for all (see the UN Declaration of Human Rights)? Should it decide national curricula (many states do this)? Should it decide what goes on in individual lessons (this happens in France)? Should it set teachers' wages or exam grade boundaries?

Democracy

In America, anybody can be President. That's one of the risks you take.

Adlai Stevenson

The much celebrated practice of democracy is said to have originated with the Greeks. The city state of Athens instituted rule by the people (which is the meaning of the word **democracy**), as opposed to rule by the few (**oligarchy**) or by a king or queen (**monarchy**). But the Athenian system was not democracy as we might imagine it. For one thing, the word 'people' was narrowly defined – neither women nor slaves were allowed to get involved, and since two-thirds of the people were slaves, and half the remainder women, this meant that only one-sixth of the population were eligible to vote (perhaps it was an oligarchy after all)! It was also a **direct** democracy where anyone eligible could speak for themselves, whereas today all democracies are **representative** democracies, and citizens' participation is limited to electing a representative to speak on their behalf (or voting in an occasional referendum). Of course, direct democracy would be completely impossible today, but it had its problems even in Athens. One such problem was political apathy. It was not uncommon for there to be too few people in a political forum to make a decision, so slaves were sent to round up some more. Two slaves would take a rope, soak it in paint and, with the rope slung between them, walk down the street, one on each side. Getting paint on your toga was considered a disgrace, and so people would be herded towards the political assembly like animals!

This story still has relevance today. It reminds us that no political system is perfect and that we should neither accept the democratic principles without some examination, nor let the merits of today's democracies blind us to their theoretical and practical weaknesses.

The most obvious quality we prize in a democracy is theoretical fairness. Rather than being born into positions of power and leadership, leaders in a democracy must convince their fellow citizens that they should be entrusted with power. In theory, this gives everyone equal access to political power, and frequent elections provide a natural way of dealing with incompetents or those who abuse their power.

A Look at the leaders of various states around the world. Are some sectors of the population under-represented in parliaments and senates? Why is this? How fair is democracy?

B Can anyone succeed as a politician? Should anyone be able to succeed?

C Is democracy an effective way of avoiding incompetent and/or corrupt politicians?

The Greeks openly debated the merits of their system. The philosopher Plato argued that only a few citizens should ever get involved in political decision-making, for *'the multitude can never be philosophical'*. He believed that the task of running of a state was too difficult and skilled to leave to the masses, and that they should, instead, be ruled by an elite of wise men, whom he called **'philosopher-kings'**. This elite would govern for the sake of the people, but not be bound to them. The problem here, as Aristotle pointed out, is that philosopher-kings are hard to come by, and once in power have no reason not to become tyrants. Plato's problem is very much alive today. How competent/responsible are the masses in voting for their representatives? In a world where the issues facing governments are extremely complex and difficult, and where it is hardly unknown for politicians to break electoral promises, can citizens make an informed and accurate assessment of parties and candidates?

A related issue is the general level of education in a state. Martin Gardner notes that on 18 July 1967, *The New York Times* reported that a small town in Ecuador called Picoaza elected a foot powder as mayor. Yes, a foot powder! The story was that a company making deodorants had run an advertising campaign for their product (Pulvapies) with a slogan, 'Vote for any candidate, but if you want well-being and hygiene, vote for Pulvapies', and just before polling day had distributed leaflets saying 'For mayor, honourable Pulvapies'. Apparently, the powder had a comfortable majority.

This amusing story only serves to draw attention to wider issues. Look at recent leaders around the world. Are they really the most able? Or are they simply the wealthiest, the ones with most family connections, the most charismatic, the ones with the warmest smiles and the catchiest sound bites, who have won media support to help their case? Has your country ever elected a Pulvapies?

A H. L. Mencken said that democracy 'provides the only really amusing form of government'. Does he have a point? Is it laughable to expect the average person, busy with their own affairs, to find out enough to make an informed choice?

B If you live in a democracy, presumably you will be voting soon, if you have not already done so. What do you know about the major issues facing your country and the different options facing the government? Do you know anything about the proposed policies of the candidates, and how realistic they are, or how likely they are to be able/willing to implement them?

C In what ways does the system of representative democracy resemble Plato's solution of philosopher-kings? Does representative democracy have the drawback that Aristotle suggested?

D In Australia adults have a legal obligation to vote. Why do you think this obligation was introduced? Is it a good thing?

A further interesting issue in relation to democracies is the attention given to minorities. In a speech to the party faithful in the UK in the mid-1980s, Margaret Thatcher said that she acknowledged that 15 per cent of the country was unemployed and wanted an increase in benefits, but that 85 per cent of the population was working and wanted a tax cut. The links with morality are clear; Thatcher was appealing to some vaguely stated and questionable utilitarian principle (does a tax cut for 85 per cent of people lead to a greater increase in happiness than a welfare benefit for 15 per cent?) and she saw no over-riding moral duty towards the less well-off minority. Of course, a very real danger of democracy is if the people want and vote for something terrible. Hitler was an enormously popular leader, but does this legitimise what he did? Most people would say that it did not, and we would do well here to remember that while the principle of democracy is founded on certain moral principles of equality, sometimes other principles may over-ride them. The mandate of the people is not a *carte blanche*.

The problem is compounded by the truth of Dan Bennet's remark that *'an elected official is one who gets 51 per cent of the vote cast by 40 per cent of the 60 per cent of voters who are registered.'* It may well be that the government is elected because it has more votes than any other party, but still has the support of well under 50 per cent of the population! The mandate of the people may not be a real mandate at all.

> **A** How much attention should Mrs Thatcher have given to the 15 per cent in the example above? Suppose that by helping them she would have alienated the 85 per cent and lost the next election. Should this factor play a part in her decision-making?
> **B** To what extent is duty to the majority subject to fairness to the minority?
> **C** Suppose a democratic government facing election soon has two choices. The first is to keep taxes low to keep the electorate happy for a few years, but risk serious long-term problems (ten years in the future). The second is to impose unpopular taxes for five years, which will ensure long-term prosperity. What is the danger here? Do you think this ever happens in real life? Is there a solution to this problem?
> **D** Look again at Dan Bennet's remark above. What percentage of the population voted for the official who is elected? How legitimate was this official? Is this an argument for compulsory voting?

Finally, in light of all these issues, how would you feel if your school were to become a democracy? Each student, all teachers and all support staff would have one vote, and all major decisions would be taken on the basis of a vote. Would this result in a better school? What if the democracy extended to the classroom, and students voted on working practices, homework, exams and which teachers they wanted? What effects would this have on the students and the staff?

Could democracy be applied to the running of a hospital (patients vote on their treatment), a business (workers vote on the directors), or the organisation of a family (children vote on what the family does)?

> **A** What, if anything, do these analogies tell us about the problems of democracy in a state?
> **B** Where are the analogies strong and where are they weak?

Most people, if asked to defend democracy, would mention the notions of fairness, equality and maybe human rights. You would probably agree that these are laudable qualities and sufficient justification for democratic systems. In other words, you are basing your justification on ethical grounds. This is all well and good, but ethics are highly contentious, and we have seen that some difficult dilemmas can arise when ethical considerations come into play. It is therefore interesting, and perhaps rather reassuring to the supporters of democracy, to see that there is a different line of support for the democratic ideal based on a completely different approach.

The ideas which follow were initially proposed by Karl Popper, who also put forward some very influential theories on the nature of science. To understand his argument, you must first consider a society almost as a living human; it has goals of some sort (which may not be entirely consistent), constraints, and many different and possibly conflicting needs. In short, it has problems to solve. What then is the best way for a government to organise the society? Popper suggests that we can leave ethical considerations to one side and simply organise a government which is most capable of achieving its ends; the nature of those ends should be a separate issue.

So the question is, what is the best way of creating an organisation which can achieve its ends? Popper's argument consists of a number of stages.

- Recognise that the problems facing a society are extraordinarily complex and continually changing. Government is about trying to solve these problems.
- Because these problems are so hard, the solutions may be unexpected, hence a wide range of solutions should be considered when attempting to solve a problem.
- Hence we need a system whereby a vigorous exchange of diverse ideas is possible, indeed encouraged, and where incompatible and conflicting aims can be freely expressed. Everyone must be free to criticise proposed solutions, most importantly those of the government.
- Because these problems are so difficult, it is very unlikely that they will be adequately solved; even if they are, circumstances may change and what was once a solution may cease to be one.
- Most solutions will therefore be inadequate; this is inevitable and should be conceded immediately. Thus we need a system whereby errors are picked up as a matter of course – that is, the institutions of government must be built that way.
- Policies are normally suggested and implemented by those committed to them; large-scale policy changes will therefore involve changes of people, too. Hence, a government must be removable and replaceable at reasonable intervals.
- For this to be true, there needs to be a possible alternative government – ideally several of them, all with different approaches to problem solving.

Popper argues that the ideal government must therefore engender an 'open society', and that this is quite close to democracy. That this approach is not based on concepts such as 'equality' but leads to the same conclusion has been seen by some as a resounding vindication of the democratic ideal.

A Is Popper's argument valid? Is it sound?
B Is this really a model based on reason rather than ethics, or are there some normative judgements hidden in the argument?
C Popper is better known for the concept of 'falsification' in the philosophy of science, but he always saw himself as advocating a unified philosophical approach. What are the links between his scientific and political approaches?
D Do the ethical considerations behind democracy provide a weaker or stronger justification than the reasoned approach above?

Human rights

A What are your human rights? Should you have the right to:

- life
- food and water
- employment
- shelter
- meaningful work
- equality
- think what you want
- a holiday every few years
- own a car
- have children

- education
- liberty
- freedom from torture
- freedom from discrimination
- own property
- live where you want
- education to degree level
- own a television
- adequate medical care
- decide your child's education

B What other rights do you have?

C Are these rights unambiguous? Are they universal? Are they absolute?

Given that we seem to have so many rights, a statement like MacIntyre's at the start of this section is a little surprising. It might even sound rather threatening – certainly we do not want our rights to be treated as if they were completely imaginary! However, we can take his statement as a friendly reminder that human rights are not present in the world in the same way as mountains and lakes; they are not there waiting for us to find them. Rather they are political devices of our own making and, as such, reflect our deeper moral beliefs about the value of life and so on. When we say 'I have a right to be heard,' we cannot point to the right; what we are doing is using the words to appeal to a commonly-held belief system about the relative importance of certain things. Of course, in reality there may be a great deal of disagreement over rights. Robert Nozick, for example, thinks that the right to property and freedom over-rides other moral claims, but many people strongly disagree, and this highlights the constructed nature of rights. What should we pick as our fundamental rights? This is too big a question to attempt to answer fully here, but let us instead consider two examples of rights and see how they fit into the wider social picture.

It is sometimes considered self-evident that 'equality between all citizens' is a fundamental human right. Thomas Jefferson, in the American Declaration of Independence, wrote that it is *'self-evident, that all men are created equal'* and similar statements can be found in the United Nations Declaration of Human Rights. Certainly such a right denies racism, sexism and homophobia. But obviously humans are not equal in every way – you are stronger or smarter than some people, and some people are stronger or smarter than you. So what does political equality mean in a practical sense? How should society act on this human right?

Those who believe in the redistribution of wealth and lean to the left of the political spectrum argue for equal distribution of money (unsurprisingly, it tends to be poorer people who argue for this, and richer against). Certainly, if we look at the wealth

distribution around the world, where in 1999 Bill Gates alone
was wealthier than Zimbabwe, Ghana, Iceland, Panama, Costa
Rica, Kenya, El Salvador and the Dominican Republic combined,
it may seem that there is a case for this.

> **A** Should we interpret the right to 'equality' as the right to an equal
> share of all resources? Should governments therefore distribute
> wealth evenly?
>
> **B** Are there other ways of interpreting the right to 'equality'? Are they
> 'better' interpretations?
>
> **C** How can we know if one interpretation is 'better' than another?
> What does this tell us about the concept of 'rights'?

Aristotle's objection to sharing wealth evenly remains powerful.
He points out that our natural sense of justice is aggrieved *'when
either equals are awarded unequal shares or unequals equal shares'.*
What we often seek is not so much equality of reward, but
rewards commensurate with what we feel we deserve. If a
teacher gives all his students the same grade then he is probably
being unfair to at least one of them. Discrimination is not in itself
unjust; it is unjust only when it is done according to unjust
criteria. But what are just criteria?

Many feel that equality of opportunity is the answer to this. If
everyone has the same chance to succeed, then those at the top
deserve to be there. For those who have struggled hard to
succeed this seems fair; for those who struggled hard but failed, it
is less obviously so. Equality of opportunity only makes sense
when all the competitors start off with equal opportunities, but
genetics and family upbringing ensure that this is never so. In
short, equality is intuitively appealing, but elusive and difficult to
define, let alone implement socially.

> **A** Is the previous paragraph correct? Is equality of opportunity
> realisable? Or could it be one of those cases where the words are
> just a slogan rather than having any real meaning?

Now consider another basic human right – that to freedom of
action and thought and to determine your own destiny. We
should remember that this is a recent and quite limited
innovation. In the past, and in many parts of the world today,
governments limit freedom strictly and intervene in daily life to
direct the activity of citizens (in ancient Sparta this included
compulsory physical exercise).

The libertarian John Stuart Mill argued that such intervention
constituted a gross violation of liberty. Even if every single person
bar one believed exercise to be good for the body, then that one
person could never justifiably be forced to change his ideas. He
wrote *'all silencing is an assumption of infallibility'*, and that this is a
dangerous and unacceptable assumption, because *'there is no such
thing as absolute certainty'.*

This is an interesting argument as it seems to imply that if we
had certainty we might be justified in forcing people to do as we
thought, or rather knew to be best. Of course, we have seen that

certainty has proven to be a rather difficult thing to find (of this we can, ironically, be certain) and most directive, illiberal governments have been absolutely disastrous for their citizens and those of neighbouring states. Many tyrannies express the chilling desire to 'make people free' – and to kill them if they resist such efforts at enlightenment. This is, perhaps, one of the ultimate justifications for liberal democracy as an expression of freedom and liberty – despite its problems it is preferable to the alternatives. It is simply the least bad.

Having said that, it does seem that perhaps states should have the right to persuade, or even force, people to do things which are in their own interests, if only they could see it. The philosopher Isaiah Berlin wrote:

It is possible, and at times justifiable, to coerce men in the name of some goal (let us say, justice or public health) which they would, if they were more enlightened, themselves pursue, but do not, because they are blind or ignorant or corrupt.

He argues, however, that the danger is clear. It becomes easy:

to conceive of myself as coercing others for their own sake . . . I am then claiming what they truly need better than they know it themselves . . . Once I take this view, I am in a position to ignore the actual wishes of men or societies, to bully, oppress, torture them in the name of their 'real' selves.

Perhaps then the state should give up its right to tell people what to do in their own interests because there are far more dangers in starting down that road than there are in letting people do as they like.

A When we say that human rights exist, what do we mean? Obviously they don't exist in the same way as, say, the Sun. But do they exist in the same way as, say, the law of gravity? If these rights exist then what sort of 'truth' do they represent?

B Are human rights inalienable, or is it possible to forfeit such rights under certain circumstances? If so, how?

C Read the 'Just rewards' article on page 272, and discuss the best way of rewarding citizens in a just society.

D How should states ensure that the principle of equality is followed? What should be forbidden, and what should be encouraged (or made compulsory)?

E Is affirmative action a way to ensure equal access to jobs for all members of society?

F What happens when my freedom to protest in front of parliament infringes your freedom to drive past? What happens when my freedom to smoke infringes your freedom to breathe unpolluted air?

The questions in F above show that freedoms do not exist in isolation. The questions both relate to the general paradox of freedom, or paradox of tolerance. How much do we tolerate someone whose views are intolerant? Do we allow freedom of speech where that freedom means that people preach hatred, racism and violence? Should those who deny the terrible fate of the Jews in the Second World War be allowed to speak?

Different people have held different views. Noam Chomsky argues that you are either 100 per cent for free speech or 100 per cent against it – you cannot decide if speech should be free on the basis of what the person is saying. He points out that Stalin allowed free speech when he agreed with what was being said! Supporting free speech does not mean supporting the speaker, and like Berlin, Chomsky sees far more danger in preventing highly objectionable beliefs from being aired. On the other hand, it is illegal to shout 'Fire!' in a crowded building (when there is no fire that is) for obvious reasons, and thinking along these lines we might argue that inciting racial hatred and inflaming social tension is equivalent to doing just that.

A What should we do when rights conflict?
B How much should we tolerate other views?
C Does freedom over-ride all other liberties? If not, when does the state have the right to curtail freedom?
D Voltaire said, *'I disapprove of what you say, but I will defend to the death your right to say it.'* How does this relate to free speech? Do you agree?

Designing the perfect society

How can anyone govern a nation that has 246 different kinds of cheese?

Charles de Gaulle

In 1974, the English philosopher John Rawls suggested a novel approach to help us determine the ideal society. He asks us to imagine that a group of people is about to arrive at a hitherto uninhabited island and that they are to form a society and set up a government. We can decide for them all the details of their society – the form of government, the laws, the economic structure, and so on. What kind of society and government should this be? How do we decide what is fair?

Rawls suggests that we can decide the fairest system by imagining that we are going to have to live in the new society, but that we have no idea as to the role we will be given – we may be the President, but we may also be homeless (if there are such people in our system). Nor do we know our intelligence, race, gender, social status, age or indeed anything about ourselves. He refers to this as the 'veil of ignorance' behind which we have to decide about the society. The aim is clear – Rawls wants us to see what we would want for ourselves and to set it in place for everyone. So will we want slavery? No, because we might turn out to be a slave. Will we want protection for labourers? Yes, because we may turn out to be labourers.

A Do you think this is a good way of determining fairness?
B Rawls suggests that the veil of ignorance idea ends up advocating a liberal democracy. Do you agree?
C Design your perfect society from behind a veil of ignorance. Describe what features, if any, you would implement which are radically different from those in countries in which you have lived.

Where do we go from here?

I will be amazed if while reading and discussing the last two chapters, someone has not mentioned religion or God. These are concepts which form the basis of very powerful paradigms, which are at the root of many of our beliefs, and which we have so far neglected. Perhaps the next chapter should have been the first one, as beliefs in this area traditionally shape those in all others.

Further reading

A tremendous personal view, largely concerned with practical matters in the USA in the last century, is given in chapters 7 to 9 of Martin Gardner's *The Whys of a Philosophical Scrivener* (Oxford University Press, 1983). A brief overview can be found in chapter 9 of Donald Palmer's *Does the Centre Hold?* (Mayfield, 1991) or in Alan Brown's *Modern Political Philosophy* (Penguin, 1986). An extraordinarily powerful attack on Marxism can be found in Karl Popper's *The Open Society and its Enemies* (Princeton University Press, 1971); an easier introduction to the great man can be found in Bryan Magee's *Popper* (Fontana Modern Masters, 1973). The minimalist state is defended in Robert Nozick's influential *Anarchy, State and Utopia* (Basic Books, 1974) and the interesting, but at times dense, John Rawls' *A Theory of Justice* (Harvard University Press, 1971) discusses the veil of ignorance.

More technical but still fairly readable is T. Ball and R. Dagger's *Political Ideologies and the Democratic Ideal* (Longman, 1998), and M. Forsyth, M. Keens-Soper and J. Hoffman's (eds) *The Political Classics – Hamilton to Mill* (Oxford University Press, 1993) contains the classic thoughts of Hobbes, Locke, Hume and Mille all in one handy volume.

Just rewards

An article by Michael Albert from www.zmag.org

In a desirable economy, what income does each actor get to enjoy? What is the basis for remuneration?

Rewarding property?

This is called profit and in this case individuals own the means of production and pocket profit based on the output of those means of production. This leads to someone like Bill Gates having more wealth than the entire GNP of Norway, or, if you prefer, 475 billionaires together having more wealth than half the world's population. Being born rich due to inherited property doesn't reward a person for something worthy that he or she has done nor even provide incentive to do something he or she otherwise might not have done. There is thus no moral or economic rationale for it other than aggrandising the few.

Rewarding power?

Folks reading this probably don't think people should be rewarded based on their ability to extort a greater share of society's product due to their power. A thuggish economic actor using racism or sexism or a monopoly on some asset shouldn't be able to translate that power into income. Sure, in an economy where extortion is a norm we wouldn't want to say that unions shouldn't be allowed to demand and use their power to win higher wages against the power of owners and others. But in a good economy where everyone is subject to new norms and not battling for advantage, surely we agree that we wouldn't want owners or unions or any other actors to be gaining income based on relative power. Rewarding power is no more moral, ethical or economically efficient than rewarding ownership.

Rewarding output?

Controversy arises over how to reward output. That is, do we reward someone on the basis of what they produce? A perfectly sensible and humane person reading this essay might think, roughly, each economic actor ought to get back a share of output equal in value to what they themselves produce for the economy. This has even been the slogan of very radical movements. And it seems fair: if you don't put much into society's economic product, you shouldn't take much out. If you put a lot in, you should take a lot out. Otherwise, someone else gets value you put in, or you get value someone else put in, instead of each getting back only the amount of our own contribution.

But, suppose Sally and Sam are picking oranges. Sally has a good set of tools. Sam has a crummy old set. They go into the fields for eight hours. They work equally hard. They endure the same conditions. Sally's pile when the day is done is twice as big as Sam's. Should Sally get twice Sam's income? If she does, we have rewarded her luck in having better tools. Is that moral or efficient?

Suppose Sally is very large and strong and Sam is much smaller and weaker. They have the same tools. They again go into the fields for eight hours. They again work equally hard. They again endure the same conditions. Sally's pile is again twice Sam's. Should Sally get twice Sam's income? If she does, we have rewarded her luck in the genetic lottery: her size and strength. Is that moral or efficient?

Now suppose we compare two people doing mathematics investigations, or creating works of art, or doing surgery, or doing anything else socially desirable.

They work equally hard under the same conditions. One has more of some relevant natural talent and the other has less of it. Should the former be rewarded commensurately more than the latter? Clearly, there is no moral reason to do so. Why reward someone for genetic luck on top of the benefits the luck already bestowed them? More controversially and interestingly, there is also no incentive to do it. A potential recipient of bounty for innate talent cannot change her natural talent in response to the promise of higher pay. The natural endowment is what it is, and being paid for it won't cause us to change our genes to increase it. There is no positive incentive effect.

But how about education, or learned skills? Shouldn't improving our productivity be morally rewarded, and also an incentive to promote it? That seems reasonable but not in proportion to the output the education permits, rather in proportion to the effort and sacrifice it required. We should reward for the act undertaken, such as *enduring* schooling. We should provide a proper incentive for undertaking that act. But that is very different from looking at lifetime output and saying we will reward in accordance with that.

Rewarding only effort and sacrifice!

Suppose we reward effort and sacrifice, not property, power, or output. What happens? Well, if jobs were like now, those doing the most onerous or dangerous or otherwise debilitating work would be highest paid per hour of normal effort. Those with the most comfortable conditions and circumstances would be lowest paid per hour of normal effort.

But shouldn't a surgeon get paid for all those years of schooling, as compared to a nurse or a janitor, say, who has less schooling?

Sure. Whatever the level of effort and sacrifice the years of schooling entailed, the surgeon should be paid for that while schooling herself. Later, the surgeon should be paid in accordance with the effort and sacrifice expended at work, just like the janitor in the hospital should. In this event, each person should be rewarded according to the same norm paid according to effort and sacrifice expended at a worthwhile job that contributes to society.

But then no one will be a surgeon is the reply. Folks will prefer being a janitor.

Why? Imagine you are just out of college. You now have to choose – will it be medical school for six years followed by being a doctor for forty, or would you prefer being a janitor in the local hospital for the full forty-six years? More exactly, how much do you have to be paid to go to medical school instead of being a janitor for the first six years, in light of the quality of life you will have then and later? Or, vice versa, how much would you have to be paid to opt to be a janitor for the first six years rather than to go to medical school? And then, how much would you need to be paid to do either of the jobs as compared to the other for the remaining forty years?

To ask these questions is to answer them and to reveal that the motivational effects of payment according to effort and sacrifice are exactly right if we are discussing a world in which people are free to choose their jobs without encumbrances from history or limiting institutions. Of course, not everyone will seek these specific jobs, but the thought experiment is easy to translate to all other realms.

In short, other things being equal and all options open, you need and deserve more pay to provide you the incentive to do that which requires greater effort and sacrifice – way more to be a janitor than a student. But you don't need nor do you deserve more pay to do something that is more fulfilling, more empowering, or yields more output, assuming it doesn't require greater effort and sacrifice – you need less to be a doctor than a janitor.

Just reward is that those who put out more effort and sacrifice at a needed set of tasks for society get more income. Those who put out less for society, get less income. That's the goal we propose for a participatory economy: just rewards or payment according to effort and sacrifice.

My religion consists of a humble admiration of the illimitable superior spirit who reveals himself in the slight details we are able to perceive with our frail and feeble minds.
Albert Einstein

There is no greater fool than he who says 'there is no God', unless it be one who says he does not know whether there is one or not.
Bismark

THERE IS ONLY ONE RELIGION, THOUGH THERE ARE A HUNDRED VERSIONS OF IT.
George Bernard Shaw

I do not seek to understand that I may believe, but I believe in order to understand.
Anselm of Canterbury

There is no God. This negation must be understood solely to affect a creative deity. The hypothesis of a pervading spirit co-eternal with the Universe remains unshaken.
Shelley

The further the spiritual evolution of mankind advances, the more certain it seems to me that the path to genuine religiosity does not lie through the fear of life, and the fear of death, and blind faith, but through striving after rational knowledge.
Albert Einstein

I AM AN AGNOSTIC; I DO NOT PRETEND TO KNOW WHAT MANY IGNORANT MEN ARE SURE OF.
Clarence Darrow

To you I'm an atheist; to God, I'm the Loyal Opposition.
Woody Allen

A year spent in artificial intelligence is enough to make one believe in God.
Alan J. Perlis

My atheism, like that of Spinoza, is true piety towards the Universe and denies only gods fashioned by men in their own image, to be servants of their human interests.
George Santayana

I believe it because it is absurd.
Tertullian

Christian fundamentalism: the doctrine that there is an absolutely powerful, infinitely knowledgeable, Universe-spanning entity that is deeply and personally concerned about my sex life.
Andrew Lias

By the end of this chapter you should:

- **appreciate the different approaches that are possible to religious questions**
- **understand some of the arguments for and against the existence of God, and have some insight into the debate which is generated by competing claims**
- **understand the role of faith and belief in the context of religious knowledge**
- **be able to justify a personal position on the question of the existence of God.**

Introduction

In any search for truth, the issue of religion will arise at some point. You may have already seen that religious values, or lack of them, permeate our thinking about many issues, and most people naturally feel a deep personal interest in the whole question of God. There may be people who are indifferent to the possibility of God's existence; if so I have never come across them. And it would be strange to be indifferent to an area of knowledge which claims to explain the nature of right and wrong, the purpose of life and what happens to us after death. What more important and exciting questions can there be?

Although religious questions are asked universally (every single culture throughout history has, as far as we know, had the concept of one or more deities), there have been no universally accepted answers. Opinions vary from atheism (the belief that there is no God), to theism (the belief that there is one God), to polytheism (the belief in several gods), to pantheism (the belief that the Universe is God), and agnosticism (the lack of belief one way or another), and within each 'ism' there are numerous, sometimes strongly conflicting, beliefs. A full investigation is more than we can offer here – instead we focus on the most commonly-held belief; namely, that there is one omnipotent, benevolent, and personal God who takes an active interest in humanity, and ask the central questions: Is there a God? How can we know?

Before we even start to answer the questions, we find that we are already in controversy. The philosopher A. J. Ayer dismissed the whole concept as meaningless, since *'no sentence which purports to describe the nature of a god can possess any literal significance'*. (Ayer was a **logical positivist**, which meant that he would only accept as meaningful statements which could be verified by empirical evidence. The logical positivists' approach is now regarded by most as extreme and fairly barren.) Similarly, in the eighteenth century, David Hume suggested that rational inquiry can play no part in religious matter. Of the whole concept of divinity, he wrote, *'Commit it then to the flames, for it can contain nothing but sophistry and illusion.'*

It will come as no surprise that many believers have accused this sort of philosopher of monstrous conceit and have suggested that it is philosophy, or in extreme cases, philosophers, who should be cast into the fire! St Augustine's view was that humans must rely on God, not reason, to guide them to the truth, and in response to the 'stupefying arrogance' of philosophers who believed they could work out the great questions without an appeal to God, wrote *'What sort of an awareness of truth is there in this material flesh?'*

Those are the extreme views. These days most people would agree that there is a middle ground between philosophy and religion; certainly it would be foolish to dismiss the possibility out of hand. Arguing that both faith and reason are divine gifts, the great Christian philosopher St Thomas Aquinas rejected the idea of an inherent conflict between them. He saw them as complementary, even harmonious tools with which to study God. The Prophet Muhammad expressed a similar sentiment when he said *'God has not created anything better than reason, or anything more perfect or more beautiful than reason.'* This whole course is based on the principle that we need to maintain an open mind and to try to apply honest reasoning where we can. Let us therefore see how far reasoning will take us, and if it proves to be an insufficient tool then let us recognise that and examine the alternatives.

A What are your religious beliefs (if any)? Do you know why you believe what you do? Is it a set of beliefs (or lack of beliefs) you have come to yourself, or one that you have absorbed from your culture unquestioningly?

B Do you believe that reasoning should play a part in determining religious beliefs?

C Look at the different meanings of 'exist' in the following sentences:

- Trees exist.
- Protons exist.
- Dragons exist.
- Ghosts exist.
- Pain exists.
- Dinosaurs exist.
- Energy exists.
- Love exists.

Which statement is most like 'God exists'?

D Would any of the following demonstrate the existence of a God?

- If believers lived on average 25 years longer than atheists.
- If prayers of believers were answered.
- If children started to quote the Holy Book as soon as they learned to talk.
- If believers were more successful in life than atheists.
- If believers could perform miracles.
- If believers after death were seen to fly up into the sky and disappear.

Can you think of any empirical test that would prove that God existed?

Many brilliant thinkers have argued passionately that God exists; many have argued that He does not. Some of the arguments have been debated for the best part of 800 years, and still inspire new defences and counter-attacks from both sides. We will review some of the more popular arguments and then stand back and take stock of what, if anything, we can conclude.

Arguments for the existence of God

The fool hath said in his heart 'There is no God.'

Book of Psalms 14.1

Imagine you are walking in a sandy desert, miles from civilisation, through what you believe is completely uninhabited land. There have been no signs of human life for days; just sand in all directions, and the odd camel. Suddenly, in the distance, something small and shiny on the ground catches the light; you walk over to it and you find a camera. You were sure that there were no humans in the area, so you have two options. Either you were wrong, and the camera was put there by humans, or it somehow sprang into being by some mysterious, purely natural forces. Which choice is the more reasonable?

In this case, we clearly require human intervention (neglecting the camel possibility) because the camera could not have come into being in an accidental way. The lens exactly fits the camera body, the shutter opens for exactly the right length of time to create a detailed image on the film, the film is itself a very clever way of recording visual images, and there is a viewfinder lens for humans to look through to see the image they are recording. In short, the camera shows unmistakable signs of design, and what is more, design for human use. For many people, exactly the same argument applies to the world. It is clearly designed, so there must be a designer, and God is that designer. In fact, the argument arguably applies with far more force. You think a camera is complex? Look at the eye! Look at the brain! A single human brain is the most complex physical structure known to man, far, far more complex than the most sophisticated supercomputer. If a camera is designed, surely a brain must be designed?

For many people, the argument from design, or teleological argument (from Greek *telos* meaning 'goal' or 'end'), means that a compelling argument in favour of God's existence is all around them. It is in the intricacy, beauty, and design of the natural world.

The most famous counter-argument against this proof comes from Charles Darwin, and in essence it is very simple (note though, that it is an argument against the teleological argument, not an argument against the existence of God). Darwin makes a distinction between the concepts of **order** and **design**, suggesting that not everything which shows order must have been designed. As an example, consider walking along a river. You notice that as you walk further, the rocks in the river seem to be getting bigger; that the river is well-ordered in this respect. But no designer is needed to explain this ordering, and the whole process is completely and convincingly explained by geographical theories of fluvial transportation and deposition – sorting rocks of different sizes is simply the result of natural physical processes. Similarly, Darwin argues that we can explain the order in nature through purely physical processes; that a designer is unnecessary. This means that we can account for the world without God, and that the apparent design of the world is no evidence for a creator.

Of course, the order in the natural world is far greater than that in a single river and Darwin's basic idea needs a lot of detailed work before it becomes convincing, but most, though not all, scientists working in biological fields believe that the evidence for it is convincing.

One variety of the argument from design that is at least partly immune to Darwin's criticisms goes by the name of the **anthropic argument**. This argument notes from a scientific point of view that very slight changes in any one of several aspects of the Universe would have made it impossible for us to exist, or even have evolved. If the Earth were a little closer or further away from the Sun; if the atmosphere were a little thinner; if the Sun were hotter or cooler; if the structure of water were a little different; if the electron/proton or neutron/proton mass ratios were different; if the ratios between the four fundamental forces were different; if there were different numbers of spatial dimensions and so on, we would not exist. All these and dozens of other conditions must be fulfilled for us to be able to survive or evolve. What is the probability of that happening? Extremely low runs the argument, and this provides evidence that we are not here by pure chance. Astronomer Fred Hoyle said that it looks as if *'someone has been monkeying with the laws of physics'*. Others argue that the logic is incorrect; given that we are here, it is absolutely certain that these things are the way they are. If they were not, we would not be here, and it is a trick of conditional probability that it appears unlikely.

A The following argument has been made against Darwin's idea of evolution: The human body is vastly more complex than a jumbo jet. But we say that 'natural events' led to humans. Well, could natural events lead to even a jumbo jet? Could a natural event like a whirlwind sweep through a scrap yard and somehow assemble all the parts for a jumbo, ready for take-off? If not, then natural events can neither account for jumbo jets nor humans.
Evaluate the validity of this analogy.

B Augustine of Hippo, the fifth-century bishop and philosopher, anticipated Darwin by well over a thousand years, suggesting that God created the Universe with built-in organising principles through which all forms of life and non-life developed. So is evolution consistent with belief in God? What would scientists today make of Augustine's claim?

C What do you think of the anthropic argument? Is it persuasive?

D Let us grant the argument from design its full force, and accept that the Universe was indeed designed. What can we conclude from this fact? Are we inevitably led to the existence of an omnipotent, benevolent God, or could God be of a completely different nature?

A second argument often put forward in favour of God's existence has been called the argument from first cause, or the **cosmological argument**. Like the argument from design, it is based in everyday experience. When we ask 'Why did this happen?' we always feel there is a cause, even if we cannot find it. And when we have found the cause, we can, like the proverbial curious child, ask why that happened, and so on. For example, in attempting to answer the question, 'What causes the stars to twinkle?', we can imagine a (very truncated) sequence which starts 'stars twinkle because the light comes through the atmosphere; coming through the atmosphere causes twinkling because of the process of refraction; refraction is caused by...' and which eventually ends '...because that is the way the Universe is made'. In any explanation we either keep on going, or we stop somewhere, and this argument suggests that the somewhere is God. Most famously stated by Thomas Aquinas, this argument can be expressed in the following logical form:

1 Every event is caused by some event prior to it.
2 Either the series of causes is infinite, or it stops with a first cause which is itself uncaused.
3 An infinite series of causes is impossible.
4 Therefore a first cause, which is uncaused and which is God, must exist.

This common-sense approach has also been subject to stinging criticism from David Hume, who we have by now seen several times before, and who disputed 1, 3 and 4. Hume thought that 3 is simply false, and another example of limited human understanding, and the need to impose human order on the Universe. If we can conceive of an infinite future, why not an infinite past? It is not logically or empirically clear why 2 should be true, so we should not accept it. He also argues that even if 1, 2 and 3 are true, why does this lead to God? Couldn't the Universe have created itself, uncaused? A related difficulty lies in the contradictory nature of the argument. Premise 1 seems to rule out the possibility of anything uncaused at all, which would rule out God immediately.

Recent attempts have been made to defend Aquinas against these charges, and it is fair to say that despite Hume's penetrating comments, debate is still alive and well in some philosophical quarters.

A Current scientific theory suggests that the Universe began in a 'big bang' several billion years ago. It also suggests that some events on the quantum-mechanical scale are genuinely uncaused. Are either of these facts evidence for or against the argument from first cause?

B What do you think of part 2 of Aquinas' argument? Is it possible to imagine an infinite past? Is this harder to conceive of than an infinite future? If so, why?

C Some have argued that trying to find the first cause is like trying to find the smallest positive number – a meaningless task. Given any number (state of the Universe), you can always find a smaller number (earlier cause) but you can never find the smallest number (first cause) because there is no such thing. This is obvious when you think of a number line – no matter how close you get to zero, you can always 'zoom in' and get closer.
Is this a helpful analogy? Is it possible to imagine that every single event has a cause, but that there is no first event?

D Let us grant the first cause argument its full force, and concede that the Universe was indeed caused by God. What can we conclude from this fact? Are we inevitably led to the existence of an omnipotent, benevolent God, or are there other first causes equally consistent with design?

The final argument we shall consider, and one that has had great popular appeal over the centuries, is the **argument from miracles**. According to this argument, miraculous happenings throughout history, such as Jesus rising from the dead, milk flowing from a stone statue of Ganesh, or sudden remissions of deadly diseases, are evidence of divine intervention because only God could cause such things to happen. Like the other two arguments, there is something very appealing about this line of thinking – some events seem so incredibly unlikely, implausible, or even impossible for humans, that some sort of divine agency must be responsible.

However, like the other two arguments, there are problems. Firstly, let us consider exactly what we mean by a miracle. Presumably it must be something which cannot be explained by an natural or scientific laws, so in this context we do not mean such miracles as the 'miracle of birth', wonderful and awe-inspiring as this may be, as it requires no divine intervention. Most physical and biological processes are reasonably well understood and there is every indication that those which are not will be explained by careful and painstaking scientific investigation. No, a miracle must be something which is beyond scientific explanation. Suppose, for example, I find that my cup of water has turned into wine. What can I make of this? Is it a miracle? It certainly seems to be unaccounted for by the known laws of nature, but that may well be because we don't know the correct laws of nature. In past times, thunder and lightning were explained with reference to gods – they were thought to be miraculous. Now we believe otherwise. In the late nineteenth century, it was found that photographic plates kept in total darkness became exposed. At the time this was inexplicable, but in fact this 'miraculous' incident opened up the whole field of radioactivity to scientific study. To invoke God as the explanation for events which are not explained by science is possible (the God-of-the-gaps approach), but this inference is vulnerable to advances in knowledge.

It could be said that some events seem not only miraculous, but take place in such contexts that natural laws must be inadequate to explain them. For example, the Bible recounts that the sound of Joshua's trumpet caused the walls of Jericho to fall, and the Sun to stop still in the sky for several hours. By any account, this would have to be a miracle; how could the laws of science link a trumpet call with the motion of the Sun? If the story is true, even the most fervent atheist would have to admit that this is a good case for divine intervention. But is it true? We were not at Jericho at the crucial time. How can we know?

In *On Miracles*, David Hume, writes that when we listen to stories of such miracles, we should weigh up two possibilities. Firstly, that the account is genuine and the event is indeed miraculous; secondly, that those making the report are deluded, credulous, or dishonest and that the event is not miraculous. This approach may seem rather brutal, but it would be foolish and simply incorrect to suggest that lying, exaggeration and gullibility are even rare, let alone miraculous:

No testimony is sufficient to establish a miracle unless the testimony be of such a kind that its falsehood would be more miraculous than the fact which it endeavours to establish.

So which is the more likely? There are no prizes for guessing where Hume stands on the matter, but what do you think? Hume argues that some deception is far more likely than a miracle, but it could be said that he is open to the charge of circularity. We do not know the likelihood of a miracle happening – if we did, then their occurrence would not be in dispute (a zero probability means miracles never happen; any other probability confirms the possibility of their occurrence). So how do we evaluate the probability? This question clearly illustrates the paradigmatic nature of religion – if we are atheists then the probability is zero, but if we are theists then the probability may, depending on our particular beliefs, be reasonably high. Under some circumstances then, by Hume's own account we may feel that the miracle is the better explanation, especially if the source is very trustworthy.

Perhaps all we can say is that the argument from miracles is hardly likely to win converts from atheism, and conversely, the problem of miracles is hardly a problem for any theist! Despite these issues, it is probably fair to say that if certain miracles were to be reliably witnessed at first hand, even the most zealous atheists would need to re-examine their beliefs, but that these miracles have not (yet?) happened. If someone appeared to us, telling us that he was God, with the ability to repeatedly perform under scrutiny such 'impossible' things as changing water into wine, reading minds, and predicting the future publicly, precisely, and unambiguously, then many would say that the claim was a strong one. The existence of God could still be avoided in several ways, but these ways would also be problematic.

A Sometimes scientists are accused of arrogance because they believe that science has all the answers. How does this relate to the notion of miracles as being beyond the realm of science?

B Even if we grant the difficult-to-satisfy criterion that an event must be inexplicable by science, where does that get us? Does an event that is 'inexplicable by science' necessitate divine intervention?

C The science fiction writer Arthur C. Clarke wrote that *'any sufficiently advanced technology is indistinguishable from magic'.* Do you agree? What implication does this have for the argument from miracles?

D In Hume's critique, we are required to assess the probability of a miracle. How do we do that? What are the problems with Hume's argument?

This is by no means a complete catalogue of the rational arguments which attempt to support the existence of God, nor an exhaustive report of the subtlety, complexity or richness to which they can be taken. They do, however, give a flavour of the genre and should inspire further research for the interested. We now turn to the arguments offered in the other direction.

Arguments against the existence of God

*Your Highness, I have
no need of this
hypothesis.*

Pierre Simon de
Laplace
(to Napoleon on
why his works on
celestial mechanics
make no mention
of God)

The most extreme defence of atheism has been to claim that it
needs no defence. The thrust of this argument is that the
existence of God is like the existence of Father Christmas – the
notion is so far-fetched and lacking in rational or empirical basis
that our base position should be that of atheism, and that the
burden of proof is on the theist. This sort of statement, which is
arguably circular and certainly more aggressive than persuasive in
nature, goes to demonstrate that the whole role of argument
within the religious context is sometimes so clouded in emotion
on both sides of the divide that rational discussion is difficult. This
sort of argument is made when the speaker is less interested in
the truth than in scoring rhetorical points, and since it is the
former which interests us here, we shall go ahead and examine
theism for strengths and weaknesses.

The first argument against the existence of God is based around
a set of questions which are collectively known as the **paradoxes
of omnipotence**. Proponents argue that these paradoxes
demonstrate that the very concept of an omnipotent God is
inconsistent and hence impossible. The argument is quite radical
as it claims to demonstrate not only that there is no God, but that
there could not be a God, just as there could not be a square
circle or a married bachelor. The questions are those such as:

1 Can God make a stone so heavy he cannot lift it?
2 Can God make himself omnipotent and not omnipotent at the
   same time?
3 Can God create another omnipotent being?
4 Can God cease to be omnipotent?

You can immediately see the problems – 2 seems downright
absurd, and no matter how you answer the others there seems to
be some limit placed on God's power. For example, in 1 if God
can't make such a stone then there is something He cannot do
(make the stone) and so He is not omnipotent; if He can make a
stone that He cannot lift then there is something He cannot do
(lift the stone) and so He is not omnipotent. Either way we have
a dilemma.

Responses to these have been to either engage them directly or
to acknowledge their force but to deny their relevance. We will
turn to the latter tactic in the next section; for now let us see
what we can do to resolve the paradoxes. Many have said that
these objections have something of a word game nature to them
and suggest that none of these questions generate paradox when
looked at correctly. In the stone case, for example, to say that
'God cannot create a stone which is too heavy to move' is a direct
and harmless consequence of 'God can create and move stones of
any weight at all.' In case 4 a common response is to say that God
cannot cease to be omnipotent any more than He can cease to
exist, but that this inability is not a contradiction of His
omnipotence but an expression of it.

A separate but related issue to do with the nature of God is His omniscience – that is, His knowledge of all things at all times. The argument goes as follows: if God is omniscient then He knows what you are about to do; if He knows what you are about to do then you must do it (otherwise God would be in error); if you must do it then you have no freedom (since you couldn't do anything else). But we know that we have freedom, and hence God cannot be omniscient. There are several possible responses to this, although the response that we do not, in fact, have free will at all seems closed to most believers (see Chapter 6). An interesting line is taken by some who have placed God in time (as opposed to the more common conception of God as timeless) and said that His omniscience only extends to what can be known, which does not include the future. Thus, God's omniscience does not include knowledge of my future choice. Critics of this approach ask how this God makes prophecies, and ask what it means for God to have been 'younger' in the past. The arguments seem endless; certainly they have been going on for several hundred years.

A Why does the third paradox of omnipotence (above) provide an argument against the existence of God? Is there any way that two omnipotent beings can exist at the same time?

B Some philosophers have suggested that omnipotence should be defined as the ability to do all logically possible things rather than just all things. (Descartes famously disagreed and thought that God could do the logically impossible.) Why do we place such an important role on logic? What does it mean to say that God must obey the laws of logic?

C Other thinkers have argued that God's omnipotence and freedom are incompatible. Do you agree?

D Take the argument that suggests that omniscience is incompatible with free will. Identify the premises, formulate them in propositional form and test them for validity. If the logic is valid then the argument is sound, unless you can fault one or more of the premises. Which of them are open to doubt?

E Is there any way that theists could jettison free will and still believe in a benevolent God?

It is, I think, fair to say that these problems fail to strike a chord with many, even those who acknowledge the force of the arguments. They do not seem to resonate with human experience. Maybe the atheist needs a more personal, immediate and less abstract argument if he is to persuade any waverers.

The atheist points to the problem of evil as just such an argument; the idea being that an omnipotent, perfectly good God cannot exist simultaneously with evil. Since evil does exist, an omnipotent, perfectly good God cannot. Notice that this argument does not rule out God in general, but just a specific type of God. If God is good, how can evil have come about? Even if we can answer that, if God is good, why doesn't He stop it? Over the centuries, the questions have been asked from far more than an intellectual point of view. Anyone with any knowledge of the world sees and feels the vast amount of suffering and pain that there is. John Stuart Mill obviously felt it keenly when he wrote, in *Nature*:

Nature impales men, breaks them as if on the wheel, casts them to be devoured by wild beasts, burns them to death, crushes them with stones like the first Christian martyr, starves them with hunger, freezes them with cold, poisons them by the quick or slow venom of her exhalations, and has hundreds of other hideous deaths in reserve ... all this Nature does with the most supercilious disregard both of mercy and of justice, emptying her shafts upon the best and noblest indifferently with the meanest and worst; upon those who are engaged in the highest and worthiest enterprises.

Unfortunately, increasing knowledge about the world has not given us any reason to doubt the description painted here; if anything it reinforces it. We find wasps whose stings paralyse but do not kill their prey; this in order to provide fresh food for the eggs which are laid in the body of the victim when they hatch. The still-living insect is eaten from the inside outwards. We find cats whose 'play' with mice we would call torture if they were human. All over the animal kingdom we find predators whose only way to survive is to rip other animals limb from limb. When we turn to human life, we may be lucky enough to find ourselves in a position of comfort, but looking around the world, this seems to be the exception to the rule. And it has been far worse in the past. If the world has been designed, then it is difficult to see how the design could have come from a good God. William James points out that *'to the grub under the bark, the exquisite fitness of the woodpecker's organism to extract him would certainly argue a diabolical designer'.*

A possible defence recognises that evil exists, but suggests that it is all worthwhile because good comes of it (interestingly this makes God a utilitarian). The analogy can be made with a doctor who must inflict pain to ensure recovery. It may hurt in the short-term, but in the long term it will be in our interests to undergo the treatment. Similarly, God's ultimately good plans for us can only be realised through a certain amount of suffering. There are several problems with this. Firstly, we might question whether or not good arises from evil. Does the wasp eating its way out of a victim bring more good to the world than pain? Can we somehow justify the brutality and agony of the Holocaust, or more recent atrocities in Cambodia, Indonesia, the Balkans, Africa, East Timor and Central America? To say that these are all for the good seems a little far-fetched. Leibnitz famously suggested that we live in *'the best of all possible worlds'* but the argument is remembered more for its implausibility than anything else.

Even if we grant that good does come of evil, we still find the existence of evil to be a real problem for theists. To take the doctor analogy further, we recognise that the doctor may be forced to inflict pain, and we do not blame the doctor because we recognise her limited ability to stop it. But what do we make of the doctor who, when it is within her power to heal the patient painlessly, decides to inflict agony and torture? *That* is the true situation with an omnipotent God, who *can* make us achieve His goals without pain, but seems not to have done. It is very hard to see how this explanation makes evil compatible with a just, loving and omnipotent God.

In short, the idea that evil is necessary for good, or somehow begets good, is difficult to sustain. If we are to resolve the problem of evil, we will need to look elsewhere. Perhaps the most widely held and most plausible defence offered by believers is that which suggests that evil is caused not by God but by human freedom. Taking omnipotence to mean 'ability to do all that can be done' or 'ability to do all that is logically possible', this argument suggests that in giving us free will God had no choice but to give us freedom to commit evil. Freedom and inability to commit evil are logically inconsistent – if you have one you can't have the other. Being a little bit free is like being a little bit pregnant – it's impossible. Either we are totally free, and free to commit evil acts, or we are not free at all. God wanted to give us free will, and to do that He had to give us the capacity for evil. He is responsible for that, but we are responsible for the evil itself, not Him.

Of course, this argument is not free from controversy. A simple way out is to deny that we have free will at all. This renders the discussion irrelevant, but few people would want to go that far. Let us take free will at face value. Is the problem then resolved? Can we forget about the problem of evil?

We should at this stage distinguish between **natural** evils and **moral** evils; the former are those which occur naturally without human intervention (earthquakes, floods, plagues); the latter are those inflicted by people on other people. Now the freedom defence clearly does not apply to natural evil, but let this pass for now. If we can deal with even moral evil then it will be a huge step forward, and if it is humans who are responsible for pain and suffering then is God not excused? Have we not solved the problem?

Maybe not. Atheists may point to, for example, the terrible acts of free tyrants and the price paid by sometimes millions of innocent victims, and still maintain that this is incompatible with a good and just God, and that even if we get our 'just rewards' in the afterlife, this is not really justice. If I have suffered terrible torture, or seen my children die horribly, then a happy afterlife does not 'make up' for this; justice cannot be doled out like ice-cream. Nor does the suggestion of an eternal punishment for my torturer or the murderer of my children provide me with comfort; the deeds have been done. The only thing that God could do would be to prevent these terrible things from happening in the first place. And, says the atheist, the fact remains that He does not.

At this stage, we may have reached a stalemate. The believer says that the price is worth paying; the atheist says that it is not. The two sides differ in their assessment on the relative values of freedom and suffering, and they may have to agree to differ.

A Consider the argument against God's existence based on the problem of evil. Identify the premises, formulate them in propositional form and test them for validity (as we did when looking at rationalism). If the logic is valid then it is sound, unless at least one of the premises is wrong. Which of the premises are open to doubt?

B St Augustine said that there is no such thing as evil, merely the lack of good. Thus there is no problem of evil. Let us make an analogy. Imagine a blind man wondering why he has been born blind. If we tell him that he is not really blind, he merely lacks vision, are we solving the problem? What do you think of this solution? Or is this a poor analogy? If so, why?

C Could the problem of evil be resolved by blaming it on 'the devil' or some such creature?

D Is the commentary on page 284 too harsh when explaining the problem of evil by arguing that it is for the greater good? Can the argument be made to work? If so, how?

E No one suggests that God created humans free to do anything at all. For example, we cannot fly unaided, or stand in the middle of a furnace unharmed. Might there be a way for God to construct a universe with morally free people who physically could not commit such atrocities as we do? And if so, since God created this world when He could have created that one, does this undermine the free will defence?

F It is suggested that God is responsible for giving us the capacity for evil, but that we are responsible for the evil acts themselves. Let us make two analogies that involve giving guns to adults and children:

- I gave the man the gun; I was responsible for giving him the capacity to shoot someone, but he is responsible for the act itself.
- I gave the eight-year-old child the gun; I was responsible for giving him the capacity to shoot someone, but he is responsible for the act itself.

Is there a difference between these two cases? Which analogy is closer to God giving us free will? Is either analogy helpful? Can you think of a better one?

G Where do you stand on the problem of evil?

Once again, we have given an account of only a few of the arguments, and explored these only superficially. It is fair to say that the problem of evil, at least, is a major difficulty for believers who feel the force of the argument as keenly as any atheist. The Christian writer C. S. Lewis wrote on the problem of evil when his wife Joy was dying of cancer. He asked 'Are the tortures that happen necessary?' and answered:

If they are unnecessary, then there is no God or a bad one. If there is a good God then these tortures are necessary. For no even moderately good Being could possibly inflict or permit them if they weren't.

Christians admit the problem, but do not give up hope: *'We are perplexed, but not in despair'* (2 Corinthians 4:8).

Should we believe in God?

> *The leap of faith, in its inner nature, remains opaque. I understand it as little as I understand the essence of a photon.*
>
> Martin Gardner

In his autobiography, Bertrand Russell tells us that as a young man he believed in God until he was eighteen, when he decided that the argument from first cause was invalid, and became an atheist. Then he tells us about an incident in his fourth year at Cambridge when he converted back to believing:

I had gone out to buy a tin of tobacco and was going back with it along Trinity Lane when suddenly I threw it up in the air and exclaimed 'Great God in Boots! – the ontological argument is sound!'

Later he came to the conclusion that his insight had been mistaken, and reverted to atheism.

Despite our commitment to reasoning and rational inquiry that we reaffirmed at the start of this chapter, most of us find Russell's approach rather strange. Though we may admire his open mind and willingness to admit his errors, most people simply do not respond to the rational arguments for and against the existence of God in this way. We may find them interesting, and may even get into heated arguments about them, but for many these arguments do not really touch us or the core of our beliefs. William James expressed it well:

The arguments for God's existence have stood for hundreds of years with the waves of unbelieving criticism breaking against them, never totally discrediting them in the ears of the faithful, but on the whole slowly and surely washing out the mortar from between their joints. If you have a God already whom you believe in, these arguments confirm you. If you are atheistic, they fail to set you right.

A similar statement can be made with regard to all the arguments against the existence of God. So we are in a position where atheists are satisfied that their arguments have falsified theism; theists say much the same thing in reverse and neither side gives much ground. One is reminded of competing scientific theories where the evidence is inconclusive, but the difference here is that in the case of religion no more evidence seems to be available, at least in this life. If you already believe then the arguments are persuasive, but reason isn't going to make any converts on either side. As a result, it may be more accurate to say that the arguments are expressions of our beliefs rather than reasons for them.

So where does this leave us? If you already lean one way or another, you may be satisfied that you have the truth. For anyone who is unconvinced, the most obvious stance might be to subscribe to agnosticism whereby we do not believe but nor do we disbelieve. Some thinkers see this position as the only reasonable option; others have scorned it as indecisive. The Danish philosopher Søren Kierkegaard, noting that the Latin for agnostic is *ignoramus*, said that he was not surprised that there were so many ignoramuses, but amazed that they would suggest that their stance had any value! Martin Gardner suggests that agnosticism is pretty much the same as atheism, asking *'Is there any significant difference between not believing in God and believing there is no God, or not believing in an afterlife and believing there is no afterlife?'*

For those who remain undecided, perhaps their approach should be to acknowledge reluctantly that reason cannot provide the answers. Maybe they need to put reason aside, look for other means, and find out what Martin Luther meant when he wrote:

Whoever wants to be a Christian should tear the eyes out of his Reason . . . Reason must be deluded, blinded and destroyed.

In one sense, this is hardly surprising – even in the 'most reliable' fields of knowledge we have seen that reason does not get us all the way to certainty. The sciences have the unsolved problem of induction; even mathematics has Gödel's theorem; other disciplines have their own troubles. Why then should we expect more from religion? What sort of God could be proven to exist anyway? On the other hand, to hear a scientist or mathematician saying that they have put reason to one side and tried other means would be tantamount to saying that they stopped practising science or mathematics, so we should be careful not to push the analogy too far.

So, if the seeker needs to look to something other than reason, what is there? What else can he use? Perhaps reading this you will breathe a sigh of relief (or despair, depending on your persuasion) to see faith mentioned at last (as the foundation for so many people's religious beliefs, it may be surprising that it has taken us so long to get here, but perhaps the arrival is all the more satisfying for the long journey). The seeker looks to faith. As has been said in a different context, reason serves as a ladder to be thrown away once it has been used and found wanting; and given that the ladder was not long enough to cover the gap between the seeker and where he wanted to go, what choice did he have? Paradoxically, perhaps abandoning reason, at least momentarily, is the most rational thing to do.

So we have two choices: either we stay where we are, safe and secure but possibly with that nagging feeling that we have missed something, or we attempt to cover the gap with a leap of faith, and hope that there is something on the other side to meet us. Those who say they cannot make the leap using reason point to Psalm 14.1, which says *'The fool hath said in his heart, "there is no God".'* Miguel de Unamuno explained his experience of God this way:

God goes out to meet him who seeks Him with love and by love, and hides Himself from him who searches for Him with the cold and loveless reason.

For atheists this is simply absurd. They argue that emotion plays no part; that desperately wanting something has no impact whatsoever on its existence, and that whenever faith has stood against reason, reason has prevailed. From this point of view, the whole concept of the leap of faith makes little sense – the seeker has acknowledged that the evidence does not warrant belief, but then goes on to believe anyway! Atheists see this as blind dogmatism – the determination to believe no matter what the evidence says – and do not accept the leap as in any way valid.

Many believers, on the other hand, argue that the dogmatism comes with the insistence to cling to reason. They do not argue about evidence one way or another, and they feel that the whole application of reason is simply inappropriate. For them, their faith is as natural as their sense of wonder when they look at the stars, and they argue that once the leap of faith has been made, things make sense again; they say that believing does not mean irrationality! They suggest that it is as if you want to cross a river. If all you have is a ladder which won't reach across, you have to get wet to reach the other side. Once you are on the other side, you can dry off again. St Augustine put it like this:

Faith is to believe what we do not see, and the reward of this faith is to see what we believe.

A powerful proponent of the need for faith is Kierkegaard, who argues that philosophy should begin not with doubt, but with wonder. The scepticism that arises from doubt cannot be resolved by reason, but only by a resolution of the will. We can decide to have faith.

Perhaps this is the resolution of whether or not we should believe. After looking at all the options, and studying them well, it is still simply our choice.

A Explain the differences between having religious feelings, religious beliefs, religious faith and religious knowledge.

B The atheist might say that faith is simply believing when there is no reason to, and that therefore faith in God is no different to faith in Santa Claus. What arguments might be made against this?

C The believer says that in many cases you can only see what is there once you know it is there; that *'seeing is believing'* should be *'believing is seeing'* (we have seen this idea over and over in this course). The leap of faith, he argues, is therefore hardly controversial. Is he right?

D How do you feel about faith? If you believe, to what extent is your belief based on faith and to what extent on reason?

E Does God exist? Justify your position.

Billions of people have believed and do believe in God and it is interesting to see why they do so. Despite what we have said here, only a minority who go through the rational arguments, find them inconclusive and then make the decision to take the leap of faith. For most the process is entirely different and some have likened coming to God to the process of falling in love – exciting, scary and involving trust and faith. They say that 'you just know' when you are in love; that their reasons are based in emotion and intuition and it is the same with God. The leap of faith is not a leap that is consciously made; rather it is something that is felt, perhaps even lived. Perhaps it has nothing to do with knowledge.

Where do we go from here?

In recognising faith, and seeing that for some, reasoning and looking at evidence is sometimes not enough, we may have hit on a theme that has been hinted at in previous chapters. We have seen, in several guises, that the dreams of both rationalists and empiricists to rely totally on reason or perception to arrive at truth have not been realised in practice. In the religious context, faith and the feeling that 'there must be a God' come to the fore – so perhaps the role of feelings and emotions is one that we have so far overlooked. As humans we live in a world of feelings and may base much of our lives around them. Certainly, they are worthy of closer examination.

Further reading

Check out the philosophy or religion section in any bookshop and you will be spoiled for choice; here are a few personal favourites. An excellent brief overview can be found in chapter 5 of Donald Palmer's *Does the Centre Hold?* (Mayfield, 1991). A very personal account of the defence of faith against the problem of evil and doubt is in chapters 10 to 16 of Martin Gardner's *The Whys of a Philosophical Scrivener* (Oxford University Press, 1983).

Arguments for and against the existence of God are covered very readably in Todd C. Moody's *Does God Exist?: A Dialogue* (Hackett Pub Co., 1996). The challenge posed by science is well covered by Cambridge scientist and theologian John C. Polkinghorne in *Belief in God in an Age of Science* (Yale University Press, 1999).

The parable of the gardener

Based on an idea by Anthony Flew

A brother and sister return to their family home after a long absence. Nobody has lived there for years, but they go back for a holiday every now and then. In the garden they find, to their surprise, that among the weeds a few of the old plants are surprisingly vigorous. In fact, as they look at the other deserted gardens around them, theirs seems very different indeed. It seems almost planned and tended.

The brother says 'A gardener must have been coming and looking after these plants' but when they ask their neighbours they find that none of them has ever seen anyone working in the garden. The brother says that the gardener must have worked while people slept, but the sister replies 'Why would he do that? Someone would have heard him and, besides, anybody who cared about the plants would have kept down these weeds.' The brother looks around, sees how beautiful it is and says 'But it's so lovely here! There is purpose and design in this garden. If we look carefully enough I am sure we will find evidence that the garden has been tended lovingly.'

And so they examine the garden ever so carefully. It is a very big garden, and as they look they find that, while some of it is ever so beautiful, there are parts which seem untended, perhaps even ruined on purpose. The brother takes both parts as evidence of the gardener, but the sister remains unconvinced. 'I am sure that this is just natural' she says. 'We do not need a gardener to explain this.'

The brother and sister sit up at night and watch the garden carefully, but no gardener is seen. 'Perhaps he is an invisible gardener' says the brother. So they set up an electrified barbed-wire fence. But no shrieks ever suggest that some intruder has received a shock. No movements of the wire ever betray an invisible climber.

The brother is still convinced. 'There is a gardener,' he maintains, 'a gardener who is invisible, intangible, insensitive to electric shocks, a gardener who makes no sound, a gardener who comes secretly to look after the garden which he loves. Otherwise how do you explain why this garden is so different to the others?'

The sister replies 'I can't explain why it is so different, but just how does what you call an invisible, intangible, eternally elusive gardener differ from an imaginary gardener or even from no gardener at all?'

Consequently, after all this, when the brother says 'I still believe a gardener comes' and the sister says 'I don't believe there is a gardener' their different words now reflect no difference as to what they have found in the garden and no difference as to what they would find in the garden if they looked further.

Is there really much difference between the belief of the brother and the sister?

TO UNDERSTAND VIA THE HEART
IS NOT TO UNDERSTAND.
Michel Eyquem de Montaigne

Reason's last step
is recognising that
an infinity of things
surpass it.
Blaise Pascal

The mind leads, the
emotions follow.
Ayn Rand

Feelings are not supposed to be logical.
Dangerous is the man who has
rationalised his emotions.
David Borenstein

People who are
sensible about love
are not capable of it.
Douglas Yates

**Anger is never
without a reason,
but seldom a good
one.**
Benjamin Franklin

I hate to lose more
than I like to win.
Jimmy Connors

THE HEART HAS ITS REASONS
WHEREOF REASON KNOWS
NOTHING.
Blaise Pascal

**Love is the only
way to grasp
another human
being in the
innermost core of
his personality.**
Victor Frankl

No one is truly
literate who cannot
read his own heart.
Eric Hoffer

People think love is an
emotion. Love is good sense.
Ken Kesey

Depend on it Sir,
when a man knows
he is to be hanged
in a fortnight, it
concentrates his
mind wonderfully.
Samuel Johnson

*If you can once engage people's pride, love, pity,
ambition (or whatever is their prevailing passion)
on your side, you need not fear what their reason
can do against you.*
Lord Chesterfield

By the end of this chapter you should:

- be able to offer various ways of defining and characterising emotions and feelings
- be able to discuss the relationships between emotions and physical signs of emotions
- be able to comment on both traditional and modern views of the interplay between emotion and reason
- understand what we mean by the feeling of intuition
- understand the role of qualia in our emotional experiences
- understand why our emotions are not 'raw' but products of our engagement with the world.

Introduction

If we have been on a journey looking for certain knowledge, then perhaps it is rather strange that it has taken us so long to get here. As we saw in the last chapter, there are certainly times when we rely on our feelings and on reflection. This may not be such a bad idea – after all, our emotional knowledge has many advantages over other forms of knowledge. We do not need language to express it; we do not need to apply reasoning to it; we do not need to use our senses to perceive it. Looking back over the course perhaps this should have been the place to start rather than end. After all, what is going on inside us is perhaps a more obvious place to look for certainty than anywhere else! Why then has it taken us so long to realise that?

There has been a philosophical tradition of separating feelings and emotions from other aspects of human life, especially reasoning, and this has usually downplayed the role of emotions. In Plato's metaphor, wisdom and passion are two horses pulling the chariot in different directions; they oppose each other and only one can prevail. The common view has been that we must overcome our emotions and listen to 'the voice of reason'. Anyone operating under today's technological paradigm may view the emotions as a troublesome remnant from humanity's savage past – they are for small children and stupid adults. Problems are solved by the application of reason, by the appliance of science and by appeal to the 'higher' faculties. Phrases such as 'If only he would stop being so angry and listen to reason' or 'Will you just calm down and stop being so emotional?' are common enough, and they tell us about how we view our feelings and reason.

This negative approach has rubbed off on those areas that deal with this aspect of our 'inner life', especially when they malfunction. In many cultures, emotional unbalance is a source of shame in a way that a broken leg is not (it has been said, for example, that neurotics build castles in the sky, psychotics live in them and psychiatrists collect the rent – but few would mock 'regular' doctors in the same way). We often do not examine our emotions with the care that they deserve – we merely experience them passively. As a result, we sometimes tend to have stereotypical and perhaps even naïve views of what emotions are, and what role they play in acquiring knowledge.

A To what extent are emotion and reason separate things?
B Do you agree that we tend to treat the two as separate things and that emotion is often looked at with suspicion, if not dismissed outright?
C Emotion has appeared in some guise in all of the previous chapters. Look back through them and make a summary of how. In light of this, what role have we already seen for the emotions?

Having noted the relatively low status of feelings as vehicles of knowledge (rightly or wrongly), we should remember that we have been looking at human knowledge, and our search for certainty is very much a human search. In our everyday lives we use our feelings as guides all the time, and they are worthy of study. A view of human nature that ignores our feelings is short-sighted – although the title *homo sapiens* (literally, *thinking man*) encourages us to do just that. Emotions should form an important part of our search for knowledge, but this is not to say that they should be immune to rational criticism. We will be vigilant for problems of knowledge, but we will not dismiss the emotions. Instead, we shall try to find a place for these complex and difficult things.

To start, let us consider the various feelings that humans have.

Classifying the emotions and feelings

The seven emotions: pleasure, anger, sorrow, joy, love, hate, desire.

T'oegye (Korean philosopher 1501–1570)

The six emotions: fondness, dislike, delight, anger, sadness, joy.

Hsün Tzu (Chinese philosopher, third century BC)

The two lists of emotions above immediately alert us to the familiar problem of language. A dictionary definition says that feelings and emotions are particular types of mental states, but this is hardly helpful. If we are to discuss feelings and emotions in a meaningful way, we need to decide how we are going to name and classify the experiences we have, and how we are going to communicate clearly. To start with, what is the difference between a feeling and an emotion? Rather than refer to a dictionary, let's look at how we actually use the words.

A Here is a list of things you can feel. Add some others.

joy	relief	hungry	certainty
love	wonder	happy	tired
sadness	wonderful	helpless	irritated
anxious	grief	hopeful	dizzy
afraid	energetic	merciful	longing
lust	dread	lucky	relaxed
envy	empathy	content	embarrassed
rapture	disgust	pity	surprised
angst	apathy	vulnerable	amused
gratitude	sympathy	guilty	horrified
jealous	sweaty	hatred	excited
confident	cold	sleepy	annoyed
compassion	stupid	anger	proud
awe	ashamed	bored	nervous

B How many different types of love can you think of? What does this tell you about the list?

C Psychologist Mihaly Csikszentmihalyi has pinpointed an interesting sensation/emotion, which not everyone has experienced. He calls the effortless physical or intellectual state associated with an exceptionally high level of expertise at a particular task as 'being in flow':

You yourself are in an ecstatic state to such a point that you feel as though you almost don't exist. I've experienced this time and again . . . I have nothing to do with what is happening. I just sit there watching in a state of awe and wonderment. And it just flows out by itself.

He says that this feeling is common among many, including athletes, composers, surgeons and engineers. Diane Roffe-Steinrotter, an Olympic gold-medallist skier, said that during her performance she 'felt like a waterfall'. Have you ever had such an experience?

D If you said 'I feel. . .' and finished the sentence with a word from the list above, it would make sense. Does that mean that every item in the list is a feeling?

E It is clear that the feelings above are of several different types. Identify a few types of feeling that are distinct from each other.

F Distinguish carefully between emotions, feeling and moods.

A very interesting mood is the existential 'angst', which has been described as 'the mood in which we rediscover our freedom and autonomy'. To get at this complex feeling, let me describe the experience I have when I am driving on a motorway – the sudden and rather sickening realisation that I could quite easily swerve into the oncoming traffic, almost certainly causing a serious, if not fatal, accident. Nothing is actually stopping me other than myself (irrespective of ethics, laws, expectations, etc.). I could do it. A similar feeling happens while waiting for a train – I could throw myself under the wheels. You can probably come up with similar situations, but the conditions do not have to be extreme. You could start dancing on the table now, ignoring your teacher's requests to stop; he or she could join you. Or anyone could rip up their books and throw them in the air. In everyday life we may sometimes think that we have no options, but the reality is that we always have many, many choices. The awareness that these choices are real is what we can call angst. Some describe angst as liberating, others as oppressive.

There are many ways of classifying emotions, but we can quickly identify a few likely categories. The list makes clear that we use the words 'feeling' and 'emotion' in different ways, because the feelings of being hungry, sweaty, dizzy, sleepy and cold are not what we would call emotions in themselves (although we may certainly have an emotional reaction towards, say, hunger). These physical feelings can be separated from the others, which seem more mental in nature, and we will not consider them any further (note, however, that the categorisation is not without its own problems – where would you put the feelings of being relaxed or lust?).

The rest of the items on the list seem likely candidates for emotions, though we might wonder about putting certainty in the same category as anger. Imagine the state of feeling either condition – they seem rather different. Perhaps the same could be said of fear and awe.

Here are two suggestions that have been made for further classifying the emotions. We can distinguish between:

- the instinctive emotions, such as anger or love
- the social emotions, such as guilt or shame.

We can also distinguish between:

- the inward-looking emotions, such as fear, where we are 'drawn into ourselves'
- the outward-looking emotions, such as wonder, where we are drawn 'out of ourselves'.

The classifications are interesting because they emphasise two very different aspects of emotion (remember there are always problems of classification – it is never neutral). The first one stresses the origins of the emotions, and perhaps leads us to ask which emotions are 'under our control'. The second takes a less scientific and more humanistic approach, asking about the nature of our experience in relation to the world.

A Plot the emotions in the list above (and any others that you care to name) on the axes.

B Is it easy to classify the emotions on either axis? If not, what, if anything, does this tell you about the classifications?

C Where does 'certainty' go?

D Are there any 'better' classifications of emotions?

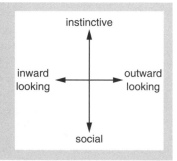

Before we leave the idea of classification, having done our best to achieve some sort of clarity in our thinking, let's remember that our descriptions are not the real thing; that any classification is an aid to insight, not a description of reality, and that however useful a map is, it is not the territory. As G. K. Chesterton says:

Man knows that there are in the soul tints more bewildering, more numberless, and more nameless than the colours of an autumn forest ... Yet he seriously believes that these things can, every one of them, in all their tones and semitones, in all their blends and unions, be accurately represented by an arbitrary system of grunts and squeals. He believes that an ordinary civilised stockbroker can produce, out of his own inside, noises which denote all the mysteries of memory and all the agonies of desire.

What is an emotion?

It is no longer my moral duty as a human being to achieve an integrated and unitary set of explanations for my thoughts and feelings.

Bronwyn Davies

Now that we have considered feelings and emotions, and bearing in mind the warning of the last paragraph, we need to tackle head-on this very difficult question. If we are going to appeal to emotions as a way of knowing, and if we are going to hold that they are a vital part of human nature, then we ought to try to understand precisely what it is that we are talking about. It is clear that an emotion is some sort of experience, but what kind precisely? We have suggested earlier that 'blue', or colour in general, is an experience, but this seems to be a completely different type of experience.

The scientist Edward O. Wilson has defined an emotion as *'the modification of neural activity that animates and focuses mental activity'* which may not be incorrect, but which seems to miss the vital human element – the experiential part of an emotion. To define an emotion in this way is like describing music as a collection of air vibrations – helpful for scientific experiment but not for philosophical inquiry.

If we are, in this section at least, to focus on the human side of emotion then we should notice immediately that emotions are bound up with our bodies – they have a very visceral component. When we are angry or frightened, for example, our heart thumps; blood is re-routed from the gut and skin (which is why we feel 'butterflies') to the muscles; our breathing speeds up; and adrenaline releases fuel from the liver. Now the conventional wisdom is that physiological manifestations are expressions and results of inward emotion – after all, the two go together. So surely the emotions cause the changes in the body?

However, an alternative has been suggested. Try to imagine as vividly as you can some extreme emotion, which has a very strong bodily effect (say anger, nervousness or fear – recall an experience you have had). Now try to subtract these bodily feelings. What are you left with? William James, who first suggested this experiment in 1884, suggests that all that is left is 'a cold and neutral state of intellectual perception' – that is, a thought with no emotions at all. On the basis of this, he argues that our emotions do not cause our bodily responses but are in fact caused *by* them. So according to this, something happens and the external event produces bodily responses (elevated heart rate, etc.). The perception of these events in their totality then constitutes the experience of emotion. What this means is that emotions are purely and simply our experience of a bodily reaction to an event.

> **A** Is the thought experiment correct? Try it yourself and see if you agree with James.
> **B** This theory (which psychologists call the James–Lange theory, as C. G. Lange argued a very similar case) seems to reduce emotions to experiences of our bodily reactions to our surroundings. What is your emotional reaction to this theory?
> **C** If James is correct, then each distinct emotion is associated with a distinct set of bodily responses. Think about your emotional experiences to determine if this is the case.
> **D** Does the theory cover all emotions, or are some not correlated with physiological effects?

There seems to be an element of truth to James' idea – presumably the thrill of, for example, a rollercoaster is to do with the effect on our bodies, and it is well known to runners that the release of endorphins during exercise can cause a natural high. So physical effects can cause emotions. However, subsequent experiments have shown that it is more complex than simply cause and effect; that there is more to emotion than response to bodily effects. For example, when injected with adrenaline, most subjects in a psychological experiment said that they felt elevated heart rates, butterflies, that they were clammy, and so on – but not emotional as such. Some said they felt 'as if' they were angry, but they were clear that they were not. Some careful thinking indicates that our whole awareness and knowledge of a situation must be involved. For example, if we are on a rollercoaster then we may experience exhilaration; if we are in a serious car accident from which we walk away unscathed but which duplicates the physical experience of the rollercoaster, then our emotional experience is likely to be very different. We cannot separate the emotions from the intellect and knowledge in a simple way. So we should delay an answer to the question of what an emotion is until we have looked into this in a little more detail.

Emotion, reason and knowledge

> *The practically real world for each of us, the effective world of the individual, is the compound world, the physical facts and emotional values in indistinguishable combination. Withdraw or pervert either factor of this complex result, and the kind of experience we call pathological ensues.*

Stephen Pinker

There is one uncontroversial sense in which knowledge and feeling are separate things – my desire to be famous is not the same as the knowledge that I am famous; my grief at my friend's death is not the same as my knowledge that my friend is dead. This much is clear. There is, however, a long tradition of working up such distinctions into complete dualistic accounts of human nature. This has led to the commonly-held notion that emotions are hot, urgent and irrational impulses that come from the body, and reason is the cool, reflective analysis that comes from education and civilisation. In this way of thinking, our emotions are 'forces' or 'substances' of some sort. If we examine the way we speak about the emotions, we find that the metaphorical way we conceptualise them reflects this. Consider the following:

- She could barely contain her joy.
- Don't bottle your rage up – go on, let off some steam!
- There isn't an ounce of goodness in her.
- She has a really nasty side to her.
- Her mother's death hit her very hard.
- Compassion welled up inside her.

If we liken ourselves to boats, then under this model the emotions are the tides. They push us around, whether we like it or not, and we have no control over them. Moreover, they are not dependent on cognition, reason or perception. We can use our reason to try to keep the emotions in check, though we need to be careful not to go too far because the emotions are the source of wisdom, innocence, authenticity and creativity, and to repress them is dangerous. The 'dark forces' can overwhelm us at times, and we are helpless before them.

This 'tidal view' paradigm dominates the way western societies view emotions, as witnessed by so many films, songs and self-help books. There is an element of truth in this paradigm – there are times when someone is literally out of control through grief, rage, hatred or guilt – but is anyone ever out of control from hope, compassion or gratitude?

A Why is it that the notion of a reasonable man 'giving way' or 'losing control' to his emotions is a very popular theme in films and books, whereas the reverse seems rather dull and uninteresting? What does this say about our popular culture?

B Have you ever been out of control due to strong emotions? How did it feel?

C Which emotions can 'take over'? Do they have a common characteristic?

So far we have considered the very strong impulses – rage, grief, fear – all of which can be overwhelming. But we might also say that we are helpless before our emotions in a different, perhaps more subtle way. Imagine that you are in a situation where you feel awe (it doesn't matter if it is the view of some mountains; the stars at night; a mathematical insight; anything will do). Is it your decision to feel awe? Did you choose to feel it? Can you control your emotions?

The same argument applies to any emotion. When it happens, did you choose it? Imagine times you have felt disgust, happiness or hope. Were you in control? Most people say that they were not. This is sometimes taken as evidence for the view that we are helpless before our emotions, and that they are irrational.

However, if we take a slightly broader conception of the role of reasoning in emotions then we can see that this is not necessarily the right interpretation of the evidence. Let's look more closely at rage and relaxation. Answer the following questions:

When might we go into a frenzy of rage?

- When our family is threatened.
- When someone tells us a joke we find funny.
- When we see a terrible injustice.
- When we have won a valuable prize.
- When our lives are threatened.
- When we see a good friend unexpectedly.

When do we feel relaxed?

- When we are on holiday.
- Just before bungee-jumping for the first time.
- At the end of the day before sleep.
- In a traffic jam on the way to the airport.
- After exercising.
- During an argument.

The answers to these questions tell us something important – that we only go into a frenzy, that we only feel relaxed, when it is 'reasonable' to do so. We do not go into a frenzy of rage when we hear a funny joke; we do not feel relaxed during an argument. Instead we feel 'appropriate' emotions relevant to the situation at hand. In other words, there has to be a reasoned judgement before we 'know' what emotion to feel. Reason must operate on something – as we have seen it does not operate in a vacuum, but requires premises and logic – so we need the input of the senses so that the reasoning can take place. In retrospect, this is perhaps rather obvious – we cannot feel emotion about something if we don't know anything about it. So the emotions are not separate from our more familiar ways of knowing. In fact, they cannot be or we would be as likely to feel joy over a terrible tragedy as we would grief.

A Consider the emotion of 'jealousy'. If I am to be jealous, what judgements must I make?

B Choose another emotion and identify what must be rationally understood before the emotion can be felt.

C Here is a quote from Bertrand Russell that some people find moving:

I must, before I die, find some means of saying the essential thing which is in me, which I have not yet said, a thing which is neither love nor hate nor pity nor scorn but the very breath of life, shining and coming from afar, which will link into human life the immensity, the frightening, the wondrous and implacable forces of the non-human.

Small children would not find this moving, nor would many adults. Much of this comes down to individual temperament, but suppose we found a thousand people who said that they did find it moving. Would these people have anything in common, such as education or intellectual ability? What rational processing must go on before such a statement can be moving?

D Are there any emotions that require no rational processing?

This idea is reflected in some criminal codes, where there is the concept of 'reasonable provocation'. Under some circumstances, a 'reasonable man' may 'reasonably' become 'uncontrollably angry and violent'. Adultery of a spouse (but not a fiancée), for example, or a blow to the face (but not a boxing of the ears) are often considered reason enough.

So it might appear, at the moment, that emotion comes after empirical data has been processed rationally. In this sense, we might think that emotion is derivative from these two primary ways of knowing. This is not so surprising – in our long search for certainty we have not yet managed to find direct, unmediated 'facts' so maybe we were asking a bit much from emotional knowledge.

But this cannot be the whole story. There is a world of difference between my knowledge that, for example, 'there are nine planets in the solar system' and, my knowledge that 'my friend is dead'. Even though both pieces of knowledge convey information, and both require certain rational interpretation for me to understand them, my relationship to the pieces of knowledge is quite different. Even ignoring the question of how our bodies respond to emotionally charged information, my friend means something to me in a way that the solar system does not. In a human sense, information about my friend *signifies*. This may be the key to getting a handle on the slippery nature of emotions. I can know anything about anything, but I can only feel about things/people that have some personal impact on myself. (A possible exception is the emotion of wonder – do the stars or mountains have any personal impact on me other than the emotion they evoke?)

To make this clearer, let us perform a little thought experiment. Imagine a person with no emotions. For this person, the world exists as it is, with no shades of approval or desire. For him, everything is of equal value; he has no liking for any thing or any person, and no dislike either. The world is neutral to him, and no activity or project has anything to commend itself over inaction. This may sound boring to you, but it is not for him, any more than it is interesting. Now we ask, what is this person's engagement in the world?

The answer must be none. This person can have no engagement in the world for such an engagement would necessarily indicate that some part of the world was more important to him than another, but we know that this cannot be the case. In fact, he would have no interest in any human relationship, in any work or in any play. He would have no desire to live or die. It seems then, arguably, that far from some Spock-like character, this emotionless being is an impossibility. It is hard to see if we would even want to call such a person alive. Even if he were alive, would he be a person? With no emotions there can be no goals, and no being-in-the-world, as some philosophers have called it.

> **A** What would it be like to be this emotionless being?
> **B** Could a race of sentient but emotionless aliens exist?
> **C** Do all animals therefore have emotions? Does this question present the above account with difficulties? If so, state the difficulties precisely, and try to offer a solution.

It seems then, that the key is to focus on our relationship with the world, and what our emotions do to represent that. To our imaginary, emotionless man, the world is not differentiated; metaphorically it is all a neutral grey. But our world is 'lit up' according to our purposes and priorities, and emotions are the lights.

> **A** This view suggests that emotions play a central role in our cognition and in our interactions in the world; that they represent important features. If we focus on this idea of 'representation', then we are reminded of empirical knowledge and the way that our senses provide us with a map of the world. Compare the emotions to some qualities which we have seen may appear to be in the world but are, in fact, in our minds. Are there analogies to be made between the emotions and concepts such as 'colour', 'pain', 'brightness' and so on?
> **B** The philosophers Sartre and Heidegger have said that moods *'disclose features of the world to us'*. What features might they mean by this? Could they mean something other than the 'obvious' physical features? How does this relate to what we have said here?
> **C** Explain in your own words, and with your own examples, this view of emotions. Do you agree with it?

This view may answer the charge that the emotions are leftovers from our pre-sapient days. Rather than mere distractions, they are vital characteristics of any human being engaged in a physical world which is indifferent to human needs. Though enigmatic, the poetic and coherent logic of emotional experience is therefore a central aspect of human life.

Intuition

The seeds of wisdom that are to bear fruit in the intellect are sown less by critical studies . . . than by insights . . . and flashes of intuition.

Carl von Clausewitz

You may have noticed that in focusing on emotion we have passed by an important class of feeling – 'intuition'. It does not seem to be an emotion, but all of us know the experience of a hunch, a feeling that we can't explain, and it seems to be very different from the feeling of anger or cold. We start with a few examples.

Case 1: Tony is a relationship counsellor. He is currently seeing Andy and Barbara who are having terrible problems. They both attend their session every week without fail, say all the right things and appear to be making progress, but Tony feels there is something wrong with Andy's approach. He doesn't know why, but he has a hunch that Andy doesn't really want to save the relationship. Tony engineers a situation to get Andy on his own for a minute and he asks him directly. Andy admits he is having an affair and is thinking of leaving Barbara.

Case 2: Igor is a physicist, and has spent the last few months working with a team on the design of a complex and costly experiment. His role was minor, and he is confident that he completed his work correctly, but he has had doubts that the overall design is sound. He and his colleagues have discussed the matter, but Igor cannot pinpoint the problem, and the experiment goes ahead. Everything seems to work, but as the results come in it is clear that they are not adequate, and that some fundamental part of the design was, after all, flawed.

Case 3: Jaya is a young woman with a ten-month-old daughter, Nidhi. She spends each day looking after her, in a routine of feeding, playing, sleeping and so on. Recently, she has begun to worry about Nidhi's health, even though she seems perfectly happy and healthy. The family can see nothing wrong and thinks that Jaya is worrying about nothing. But she is sure, so she takes Nidhi to the doctor for tests. Although the doctor can find nothing wrong from an initial examination, further tests reveal a mild infection of the sinuses.

Case 4: Henri Poincaré was a mathematician working around 1900. He wrote in his diary:

For fifteen days I strove to prove that there could not be any functions like those that I have since called Fuchsian functions. I was then very ignorant; everyday I seated myself at a worktable, stayed an hour or two, tried a great many combinations and reached no results. One evening, contrary to my custom, I drank black coffee and could not sleep. Ideas rose in crowds; I felt them collide until pairs interlocked, so to speak, making a stable combination. By the next morning I had established the existence of a class of Fuchsian functions, those which come from the hypergeometric series; I only had to write out the results, which took but a few hours.

> **A** Recall a time when you had a powerful intuition that turned out to be right. How do you explain it?
> **B** Does your intuition ever mislead you?

We have all had feelings like these – feelings which can't really be justified at the time, but which are strong and, as it turns out, correct. We will distinguish this particular feeling from others by calling it an **intuitive feeling**, or simply, **intuition**, and we ask what is the nature of this feeling and how does it generate knowledge in such an apparently magical way?

Of course, we immediately run into a problem here, which is that the very nature of intuition means that it is partially beyond explanation – if we could explain it, it would not be intuition any more! If Jaya had noticed that Nidhi's nose was blocked, or had Poincaré solved his problem in the usual way, then these would be familiar examples of the use of evidence and reason. By their very nature, specific incidents of intuition are inexplicable. This leads some to claim that intuition is some sort of sixth sense, mystical or magical in nature. But we need to be a little careful in coming to rash conclusions prematurely. Even if we cannot completely explain specific incidents, we may be able to make some general progress towards understanding the phenomenon.

Consider what has actually happened – a conclusion has been reached without a conscious, logically defensible process. In other words, you seem to know something without knowing how you know it. Put like this, it does not seem so strange, but notice that this is quite radically opposed to the model of reasoning that we have seen in earlier chapters, where we carefully set up 'pyramids' of logical reasoning in order to justify a conclusion.

Consider the following questions:

- How do you know how to catch a ball?
- How do you know that nothing in this sentence breaks the rules of grammar?
- How do you know that you are happy today?
- How do you know how to write your name?
- How do you know how to indicate to someone that you find them attractive?
- How do you know that $1 + 1 = 2$?
- How do you know how to keep your heart beating?
- How do you know that pleasure is better than pain?
- How do you know that you love your favourite type of music?
- How does an animal know anything at all?

In each of these cases, we might be hardpressed to explain our answer in a conscious, logically defensible way. But to ask for justification in these cases seems rather to miss the point of the activity. Do we really need to find a deliberate, logically valid way of justifying our answers to these questions? Is such a justification even possible? Perhaps intuition is, by its nature, opaque and we should be content to leave it there.

However, remembering that we have tentatively defined knowledge as justified, true belief, and having spent a good deal of time looking at the nature of reasoning and justification, we should be suspicious of 'knowledge' that we know without knowing how we know it. If we don't know how we know, then we can't justify our knowledge. But not requiring justification for knowledge opens the door to all sorts of trouble (as the justification is often the way we determine whether or not we will accept the knowledge as likely to be true). If we do not ask for justification, then we are driven to the unpalatable conclusion that we must let intuition be the final arbiter of questions such as:

- Is the Earth flat?
- Are women superior to men?
- Are blacks superior to whites?

The history of thought shows that trusting intuition can be a very dangerous thing as well as a marvellous one.

A Can you say when we should rely on intuition and when we should not? Are there clear cases when it is appropriate to use intuition and others when it is not? Or do we need intuition to answer this question?

B If we refer to knowledge as justified, true belief then we might say that intuition seems to fall down on the justified part. Or does it?

C You are not able to state the rules of grammar (they are not known in totality), but you obey them nearly all the time when you speak. Does this mean that your grammatical knowledge is based on intuition? If so, does the fact that we learned our language skills mean that we also learned our intuition?

D If intuition is not rational, it may be irrational or non-rational. Alternatively, it may be rational after all. Which of the three options do you go for? What is the difference between the first two anyway?

If we are to rely on intuition in at least some cases, then the obvious question to ask is whether or not it is likely to give us reliable knowledge. Our examples have all suggested that it does, but that may say more about our examples than about our intuition. We have seen that all the other ways of knowing have some fundamental problems, or at least limitations. This means we should suspect that intuition is unlikely to be a totally certain path to truth.

Answer the following problems about everyday situations. Do not analyse the problems but go with your gut reaction:

A You are jogging along and you drop a tennis ball. Does the ball land:

    1 directly below the point where you dropped it
    2 behind the point where you dropped it
    3 ahead of the point where you dropped it.

B If you drop a solid metal ball the size of your fist from a tall building, it takes eight seconds to hit the ground. How long will a solid metal ball twice as big take?

    1 4 seconds
    2 16 seconds
    3 8 seconds.

C You go to a party where there are 40 people. How likely is it that any two of them will share the same birthday?

    1 Very likely – about a 90 per cent chance.
    2 Quite likely – about a 50 per cent chance.
    3 Very unlikely – about a 10 per cent chance.

D Consider the plan view shown here. It shows, from above, a ball attached to a string being swung around a central point A. When the ball is at B, the string is cut. In what direction does the ball go?

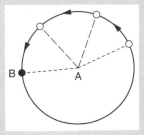

E Suppose you have a toy boat with a metal weight on it floating in a tank of water. You mark the water level on the side of the tank. Then you take the weight off the boat and drop it in the water. Where is the water level now?

1 Above the original water level.
2 Below the original water level.
3 At the same level as the original water level.

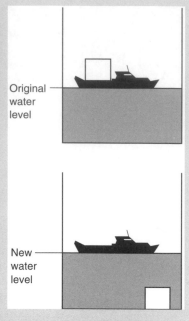

Original water level

New water level

F Although you feel fine and perfectly well, you go for a routine check-up with your doctor. After examining you, she tells you that it seems that you have a very rare disease – only one in 10,000 people suffer from it. To be sure, she administers a test. The test is not perfect – but if you have the disease, the test is 90 per cent likely to spot it, and if you do not have the disease, the test is one per cent likely to tell you that you do.

When the test comes back it is positive. How likely are you to have the disease?

1 Very likely (90 per cent or more)
2 Reasonably likely (50 per cent)
3 Very unlikely (1 per cent).

Now, if you have had formal training in these areas, go back and answer the problems by analysis rather than by intuition.

Although these six questions can be answered by mathematical or physical analysis, they are well within our everyday experience, and so we should find we have an intuitive idea about the answers. Surprisingly, what we find is that most people get most of the questions wrong. Problem E above was presented to three exceptional physicists – Robert Oppenheimer (leader of the Manhattan project to develop the atomic bomb), Felix Bloch (Nobel Prize laureate) and George Gamow (a renowned quantum theorist), and they all got it wrong when doing it by intuition.

A What does this tell us about intuition?
B These examples were based in a certain type of problem. Why do you think intuition seems a poor guide here when these types of problems are so familiar?
C Are there other areas where intuition would be a better guide? How do you know? (Remember that we have a tendency to remember the times that things worked rather than when they did not; if our intuition was correct once but failed nine times then we may tell the story of the success, whereas in reality it has a 90 per cent failure rate.)

While intuition clearly has elements that are valuable and mysterious, and despite what we have said above, it seems a little far-fetched to claim that intuition is independent of reason. To go back to our earlier examples, Tony's intuition was a very reasonable one in the sense that it was clearly based on his experience as a counsellor and the situation at hand. He didn't suddenly get the intuition that the important factor was the alignment of the stars or the colour of his shirts. And we would be astonished to find that Igor had an intuition about Jaya's child, or that Jaya had a flash of inspiration which helped Poincaré solve his problem. We have intuition in areas with which we are familiar. This suggests that intuition and reason may not be so far apart after all.

A Have you ever had an intuition in an area about which you know very little?

B Intuition often seems to operate with regard to people – you just have a feeling that someone is not honest, or upset, or whatever. But we can have intuitions about people we have only just met, so does this disprove what has just been said?

Recall for a moment an example from Chapter 8 on empiricism.

Imagine you are in a noisy room with lots of people talking – including you. You can't hear the other conversations, but suddenly you hear your name mentioned across the room. This seems very strange . . . you couldn't hear the conversation, but you heard your name.

In this case, the best explanation seems to be that there are all sorts of unconscious things going on in your mind – processing, interpretation, filtering and so on – and that you become aware of things which are deemed to be 'important', but not of anything else (it is puzzling to ask 'deemed by whom?'). Perhaps intuition works in the same way – it is the result of a complex train of analysis of which we are only ever dimly aware (at best). In the first example above, perhaps Tony noticed, almost subconsciously, that Andy appeared nervous when certain things were mentioned, and perhaps he had seen similar cases in the past where the man was having an affair. His subconscious mind then pieced together the evidence and hence the hunch.

In this case, intuition only seems like a problem because we can't explain it. The real problem is not the intuition, but that we do not have access to certain parts of our thinking processes. If we regard our brains as information-processing devices, then perhaps intuition is nothing more nor less than unconscious empiricism and rationalism.

Emotional quotients and multiple intelligences

Anyone can become angry – that is easy. But to be angry with the right person, to the right degree, at the right time, for the right purpose, and in the right way – that is not easy.

Aristotle

Traditionally, the intelligence quotient (IQ) has been seen as a good measure of 'intellectual ability' – whatever that means (IQ is not without its inherent problems, as we have seen). In schools it tended to be those students who did well in IQ tests who did well in examinations, and who, it was presumed, went on to be successful in later life (however that is defined). Of course, there were many exceptions to the rule but, by and large, it was thought that this was the case. However, experiments at Bell Labs in the USA threw up some interesting results. The researchers found that the most productive engineers were not those with the highest IQ. In a highly technical setting, one would assume that intelligence would be a key factor so this was a very surprising result. Following this discovery, there has been a great deal of interest in broadening the concept of intelligence.

The term **emotional quotient** (EQ) was coined in 1990, and is now a commonly used term used to describe the degree of control a person has over his or her emotions. EQ is often contrasted with IQ, and is usually thought to be independent – that is, an IQ score is no indicator of EQ score.

High-EQ people are supposed to enjoy high levels of self-awareness, and to use their self-knowledge to manage their lives skilfully. Most theorists believe that developing EQ is much like going to the gym – the more you practise the skills the easier it becomes. They tend to identify five areas of emotional knowledge:

- knowing your emotions
- managing your emotions
- motivating yourself
- recognising emotion in others
- handling relationships.

The focus of the EQ concept is very much one of success and self-improvement. As such, it is a little beyond our scope. Nevertheless, we can ask some interesting preliminary questions.

A In Chapter 6 on social sciences we saw that the concept of IQ is a problematic one. This does not mean that we deny differences in ability, but that there are problems with the idea. Do such problems affect the EQ concept?

B We use the same word, 'emotion', in this section as the section on emotion, reason and knowledge on page 298, where we were more interested in 'engagement with the world'. Are we using the word to describe the same thing in each case, or is the concept different in each case?

Psychologist Howard Gardner has written extensively on the multi-faceted nature of intelligence, arguing that ability in several areas fulfils the requirements to be called a distinct intelligence. His theory of **multiple intelligences** (MI) has been refined over the years and is the basis of development plans in many US schools. Gardner lists several basic intelligences:

- musical
- bodily-kinesthetic
- logical-mathematical
- linguistic
- spatial
- spiritual
- interpersonal
- intrapersonal.

As far as the emotions go, we can see that these come under the categories of intrapersonal and interpersonal intelligences. Intrapersonal intelligence is the capacity to understand yourself and subsequently to act adaptively. Those who have high ability in this area will have:

- an honest, accurate, and comprehensive picture of themselves
- an awareness of their inner moods, motivations and desires
- self-discipline tendencies
- healthy self-esteem.

Interpersonal intelligence is the capacity to quickly grasp and evaluate the moods, intentions, motivations and feelings of other people. Those who have high ability in this area will have:

- sensitivity to facial expressions, gestures and voice qualities
- ability to discriminate among many personal cues
- expertise in responding effectively so as to achieve their goals.

> **A** To what extent do you think that the intelligences mentioned above are separate and distinct qualities?
>
> **B** Are the MI and EQ theories compatible?
>
> **C** EQ and MI are both models for understanding certain aspects of our cognitive processes. As such they represent the phenomena they are trying to study. Are they good representations? Do they leave anything out or include too much? What are the inevitable problems of representation?

If there is a good deal of truth to these theories – and certainly they seem to resonate with many people– they may lead us to look at the whole concept of 'knowledge' in a broader way. Perhaps we should not be focusing on what may now seem the narrow idea of 'justified, true belief', and we should place the ability to handle our emotions and interpersonal relationships in the category of 'knowledge'. This would mean that we would have to expand our definition, but arguably this is now well overdue.

A Few would suggest that we should have university degrees in knowing about our emotions, so should we expand our definition of knowledge in this way? If so, what would 'knowledge' mean?

B Is the whole MI/EQ idea making a simple point – that knowing how to do something is different to knowing that something is the case?

C Does it matter if we classify emotions as knowledge?

D MI and EQ are very much focused around 'happiness' and 'success' rather than knowledge. Bearing this in mind, what, if any, are the implications of these theories for our knowledge and our ways of knowing?

Emotion, experience and culture

Modern man is estranged from being, from his own being, from the being of other creatures in the world. He has lost something – what, he does not know; he only knows that he is sick unto death with the loss of it.

Walker Percy

Despite what we have seen in the previous two sections, we have missed out an important part of the study of emotions. Without denying anything that has been said, there is more to feeling than a relationship with the world, or a 'reasonable' response to the world. It *feels like* something to be angry, or disgusted, or in love – and, of course, we are all intimately acquainted with our own 'inner lives'.

Perhaps we could put it rather crudely:

$$Emotion = \frac{recognition\ of}{an\ event} + \frac{recognition\ of\ my}{relation\ to\ that\ event} + something\ else$$

The 'something else' of the equation is the thing that dominates our sense of the emotion – it's what the emotion *feels like*. Imagine the feeling of embarrassment. It is quite distinctive, it has a certain 'taste' and cannot be mistaken (and is separate from the sensation of shame, which often accompanies it). These feelings cannot be reduced to anything else – they are 'simple' in this respect, and we call them **qualia** (the singular is quale). They are notoriously difficult to describe to someone who has never felt the emotion (in this they are like the more 'physical' qualia such as the sensation of 'blue' or the smell of freshly-ground coffee). Given that they are so basic to our emotions (and other sensations), there is not much that we can say about them in themselves – they just 'are' and they are the building blocks from which we construct our inner world.

However, even if we cannot say much about the nature of qualia themselves (how qualia can come about from a physical substrate is probably the outstanding problem in the philosophy of mind), it is interesting to examine their role in an emotion. Imagine the last time you had a blazing argument with someone (if you ever have!), preferably when you were shouting and really furious. Try to recall the qualia – most people use words such as 'boiling' or 'trembling'. Now, could you be said to be really angry without that feeling or is it an essential part? It seems that the sensation is a crucial part of the emotion, but philosopher George Pitcher has asked us to imagine two situations:

- Helen arrives home to find Ingrid setting fire to her house. If Helen rushes violently at Ingrid, then must she be having the 'boiling' sensation of anger that we mentioned in the last paragraph?
- James is being interviewed for a job and is anxious to make a good impression. One of the interviewers, Katy, makes an insulting comment, and after that an observer might notice an icy tone creep into James's voice when he addresses Katy. Is James angry?

Now different people interpret the thought experiment differently, but many agree with Pitcher that Helen and James are both angry, though neither is having qualia of the sort we described above. Helen will likely admit she is angry, though James may not. But then that means that both are angry without the quale of anger, which seems like a contradiction.

A Is it possible to be angry without realising it? Can you think of a similar example from your own experience? What about other emotions?

B Might we get around the problem by suggesting that there are (at least) two distinct types of anger – the 'hot' type and the 'icy' type, and that the quale associated with each one is different? Or would James still not have the right quale?

C Does this mean that emotions are not experiences?

D We offered a simple model above:

$$Emotion = \frac{recognition\ of}{an\ event} + \frac{recognition\ of\ my}{relation\ to\ that\ event} + qualia$$

Do we need to adjust the model in light of what we have said? If so, how?

E Are your emotional qualia the same as my emotional qualia? While we can never be sure about this one, what seems the most reasonable answer? (What does 'same' mean here?)

F Are your emotional qualia the same as those experienced by somebody from a different culture who speaks a different language?

The cultural aspect suggested in Part F of the questions above is a fascinating one. Anthropologists have studied cultures where grief is expressed in entirely different ways – the Inuit-Ifaluk tribe 'cry-big' at a death and a bereaved mother may pound her chest with her fists, while a Balinese equivalent may be far more restrained and even outwardly cheerful. What are we to make of this? Do people from different cultures really experience their emotions differently?

Those who have met and known people from a genuinely different culture seem to agree that emotional lives are broadly the same around the world, although the external displays, behaviours and rituals may vary significantly. The Ifaluk, for example, believe it is healthy to express grief energetically, whereas the Balinese believe that sad feelings are dangerous to the health and so they try to distract themselves. While the emotions may not be as different as they appear, that is not to say that they are precisely the same.

Evidence for this claim can be found in many places. Martha Nussbaum notes that, *'Finns cultivate and prize the emotions connected to solitary contemplation of forests; and the sense of wonder and smallness that arise.'* Few of those born in Calcutta have experienced these forests, and so we can say with some confidence that the emotional lives of these two groups will differ, at least in this respect. We can also point to an ancient Greek words for love, *erôs*, which has a connotation of longing to own and control and which carries no implication of being loved back, and ask if this reflects an experience of love that is nuanced from ours? (It is also interesting to note that there are two other words in ancient Greek – *agape*, the selfless love for all people and *philia*, a mutually reciprocated love, which may or may not be platonic in nature.) There is a certain kind of highly self-conscious romantic love (which seems, in films, to involve lots of holding the back of one's hand to one's forehead, and fainting), which may require a relatively luxurious and pampered lifestyle. Based as it is in the idealisation of the perfect and pure chaste female, might we not conclude that this romantic love involves emotional experiences which are simply not available to many of us today?

And, of course, today's experiences of love are hardly the same the world over. If one is raised in a culture where sexual relations are considered dirty and embarrassing, then one's experience of love and sex will be different to someone brought up where these things are considered natural and wonderful.

> **A** Consider your own emotional life. Do you think that the way you experience love, disgust, disappointment or any other emotion has been shaped by your culture?
>
> **B** Can you imagine having a different emotional life?
>
> **C** There is a popular stereotype that women are 'more emotional' than men (in extremes, some men say that women are 'irrational'; women counter that men are 'emotional cripples'). In light of what has been said above, and in your experience, to what extent, if any, is the stereotype true?

Perhaps all this suggests that emotions are not as 'raw' and 'immediate' as we had imagined, but that they are filtered and moulded by our paradigms as surely as are all our thoughts. This may be a disappointment but it is hardly a surprise – did we really expect emotions to be pure and 'true' in some abstract sense? If our emotions are about our being-in-the-world, and the relations we have to the world as we find it, then they must be linked intimately to our needs, perspectives and individual histories. If they were not, how could they be as important to us as we know they are?

In saying this, we should remember to neither demote nor elevate the emotions to some separate and special type of experience. They are entwined so closely with reason, perception, culture and language that we should not think of all these as separate categories, but as the stuff of human life. We give the last word to Stephen Toulmin:

Is the primary task ... to find formal solutions to abstract problems, and impose those solutions on the raw material of the world, as we experience it? Or is [it] to get acquainted with the world of experience in all its concrete detail, stating our problems and resolving them later in the light of that experience?

Where do we go from here?

In our search for certainty and truth we seem to have asked many, many questions, and to have found very few certain answers. We are getting to the stage where we are going to have to make some choices about what we think are the best answers, but this is a task that we must do as individuals.

Further reading

The argument about classifying emotions is explored in Paul Griffith's *What Emotions Really Are* (University of Chicago Press, 1998); the existential viewpoint is found in Jean-Paul Sartre's *Sketch of a Theory of Emotions* (Methuen, 1962). Robin Hogarth's *Educating Intuition* (University of Chicago Press, 2001) is a beautifully written and wide-ranging overview of current thinking on the topic of intuition. For a concrete context, you could try *Reading People* by Jo-Ellan Dinitrius and Mark Mazzarella (Vermillion Press, 1999). Martha Nussbaum uses her own life, poetry, literature and music to bring to life her difficult but exceptional *Upheavals of Thought* (Cambridge University Press, 2001).

My favourites for mixing science and sensitivity are chapter 6 of Stephen Pinker's *How the Mind Works* (Penguin, 1997) and Thomas Lewis et al., *A General Theory of Love* (Vintage, 2001). Howard Gardner's *Frames of Mind: The Theory of Multiple Intelligences* (Basic Books, 1983) is a best-seller and can be found in the self-help section of most bookshops.

Emotions

Paul Harkin

Since at least the time of Homer, the emotions have had pretty bad press. The *Iliad* opens with an account of 'the rage of Achilles', whose anger and wounded pride have such devastating consequences. Slightly later, the Greek tragedians offered their audiences characters such as Medea, a woman apparently so much in the grip of her spiteful jealousy, that she is prepared to sacrifice her own children to ensure her revenge.

Plato also took a fairly dim view of the emotions, regarding them as agents of tyranny which enslave the true and rational part of our nature. And it is to Plato that we originally owe the idea that reason and emotion are distinct and opposed faculties or aspects of the human psyche. The Stoics who followed him claimed not merely that the passions are disruptive and uncontrollable forces, but that they involve false attributions of value to things (and people) in the world. Such attributions, in the form of love of family and friends, for instance, make us vulnerable, since we care what happens to them. When, thanks to the Stoics' own brand of therapy, we rid ourselves of these false conceptions, we can remain clear-eyed and unperturbed – 'Stoical', as we would say – in the face of our fate, and theirs.

Later, Hume, Kant and then Freud, each in his own way confirmed the gulf between reason and passion, and the events of our own century testify to the terrible potential of hatred in its different forms. We are, as a result, well primed to share the dim view of the emotions which has been our cultural inheritance. It is the view of Bertrand Russell, in his History of Western Philosophy:

'...most of the strongest passions are destructive-hate and resentment and jealousy, remorse and despair, outraged pride and the fury of the unjustly oppressed...'.

While it is, of course, undeniable that emotions can be unruly and that they can and have had dreadful consequences, the good news is that many philosophers and psychologists have for some time been urging us not to infer from these facts any sweeping negative conclusions about the emotions. Better news still is that – contrary to appearances – we do not in fact hold such negative views ourselves. Our own thinking about the emotions is more ambiguous, perhaps even contradictory. We sometimes speak as if we endorse Plato's view, but in other respects our sympathies are quite different.

Literature offers some pertinent examples. In *The Adventures of Huckleberry Finn*, Huck's moral education – or at least the moral precepts he has been brought up to believe – tell him to turn in the runaway slave Jim. His emotions, however, will not allow him to follow the dictates of principle, and betray his new friend. Readers of the episode, as Twain intended, are on the side of Huck's emotions. Huck himself remains unsure.

We should not take this, however, as confirmation of a conflict between brute emotion on the one hand and reasoned precept on the other. The assumption that these are distinct and opposed forces is mistaken from the start. More generally, we do not think emotions are merely sources of potential danger; danger which can only be averted when harnessed to the constraining influence of reason. If we did, why would we think it a defect – as we surely do – to lack or be incapable of certain emotions? Camus' anti-hero Mersault, for example, (in *L'Étranger*) is notable, above all, for his emotional alienation, his inability to feel. Contrary to the Stoics, who wanted us to get rid of our emotions, we, in many respects, are anxious to feel more of them.

Underlying the wholly negative view of the emotions we can discern three basic claims:

First, emotion and reason are distinct and opposed parts of the psyche. What is emotional is irrational, and conversely, what is rational is not emotional. This is the account offered by Plato (in the Republic) in the form of his 'tri-partite' conception of the soul.

Secondly, it follows from this that there is no question of emotions being appropriate or inappropriate. We can contrast this with the case of beliefs, where we assume that questions of appropriateness do apply (for instance; are beliefs in an immanent Apocalypse appropriate to the available facts?)

Thirdly, if the previous two points are right, they imply a picture of the sort of thing an emotion is. divorced from thought and reason, it must be something of the character of a sensation or feeling – akin to the appetites, perhaps, and the feeling of hunger.

So here we have an account of what an emotion is (a sort of sensation) and of the value it has (i.e. not much, given what it is). In case anyone should think these views are of strictly historical interest, I offer the following (not unrepresentative) quotations from the editor of Living Marxism, writing recently on the subject of the media's handling of the death of Princess Diana:

'An atmosphere which puts feelings first is hardly conducive to any cool assessment of what has actually happened, never mind a critical discussion of the hows and whys behind the events. [...] Public debate was debased by an editorial elevation of feelings over facts and the insistence that the heart should rule the head'.

Here we find the same suspicion of the emotions, the same carving-up of the psyche into warring factions that we find in Plato. Lying behind Hume's view that emotion has mistakenly been allowed free rein in this particular instance – with disastrous results – is the more general suggestion that that could not but have been the outcome. It is reason that brings understanding, not emotion. The example of Huckleberry Finn should, however, already give us grounds for discontent with this easy formula.

One of the commendable developments in more recent philosophical writings on the emotions is that there has recently been a consensus that each of these three claims is false. To see why, we need to begin with the issue of what an emotion is. The temptation to think of emotion as a feeling and hence akin to a sensation, is a strong one. After all, emotions differ from thoughts, above all in how they feel. When you're angry, you feel a particular sort of way. It might seem natural, therefore, to conclude that emotions are feelings. However, for some years now, philosophers have argued against this line of thought. There are at least three considerations which can be offered against it.

In the first place, what are the feelings that are involved? Take anger, there are feelings corresponding to various physiological changes: increased heartbeat, blood rushing to the larger muscles, the release of adrenaline, and so on. In addition, there is much that is unfelt: neuron firings and complex patterns of electrochemical and neurotransmitter activity. The difficulty is that if we consider the felt changes, it is clear that none of them is distinctive or definitive of anger. Many of them are shared with fear and other emotions.

In addition, experimental evidence also seems to support the suspicion that we could not easily identify our emotional states if this were the only basis for such judgements.

The second point is this: if feelings were the basis of our identification of our emotional states, our judgements would be inferences; we would infer the identity of the state we were in from the feelings. But while there may be some instances where this is the case, it is not the typical route to such knowledge; we seem to know 'from the inside' and not by inference. Confronted with a large lion, for example, I do not need to observe the sensation of adrenaline release, note my quickened pulse, feel the shaking in my legs and conclude from these that I am afraid. I know that without reference to these things. There must, therefore, be more to emotions than feelings.

The third point is that when we actually look at what is distinctive about different emotions, it seems clear that what distinguishes them is the thoughts that they comprise. Take fear: to fear something is to believe that it is threatening or dangerous. Or pride: to be proud is to think something is of value or deserving praise and to believe it is related to you in an appropriate way. Having these beliefs is what makes your emotion fear or pride. This is not to say that an emotion just is a set of beliefs (though the Stoics did think something like that). Most philosophers and psychologists would now say that thoughts and beliefs identify and in part constitute emotions, but that other factors such as feelings, dispositions, pain and pleasure and so on, are also necessary. This view of the emotions – cognitivism, as it is known – therefore claims that beliefs are necessary but not sufficient for emotions. Having the beliefs alone isn't enough.

But even this much is a significant advance on Plato, Hume and the rest. For if my emotion (fear, say) is based on the belief that the object of my fear is dangerous and threatening, then, since that belief can be rational or irrational (appropriate or inappropriate to the facts) so the emotion itself can also be appropriate or inappropriate. If we accept this, all three of the claims above must be false. Since emotions are based on beliefs, they are not merely sensations, they can be appropriate, and furthermore it is a mistake to characterise the 'rational' and the 'emotional' as mutually exclusive, to think of them as distinct capacities, because they are in fact, intertwined.

Many psychologists and neurologists concur. Antonio Damasio, for instance, argues that neurological research reveals that patients whose emotional capacities are impaired as a result of brain lesions are also impaired across a range of cognitive capacities, such as the ability to prioritise, to deliberate, evaluate and make decisions. At the level of the brain too, it seems, emotion and reason are inseparable.

Although this new consensus on 'cognitive' theories of the emotions is welcome, there remains much disagreement and many unanswered questions. Some philosophers have wondered how the emotions of animals and young children fit the theory, since we hesitate in attributing beliefs to them. Others have recently rejected the cognitivist approach altogether and attempted to put feelings back at the centre of emotions.

And then there is the issue of emotional education. Psychologists and writers such as Daniel Goleman (in his best-seller, *Emotional Intelligence*) are interested in how the emotions are educated. This is an issue that also preoccupied Aristotle, one of the few early philosophers to have endorsed the cognitive view. But if, as cognitivists claim, beliefs are not sufficient for emotion, what else has to be changed in order to educate someone's emotions? It is one thing to get someone to believe that spiders aren't dangerous, but another to get them not to be frightened by spiders. Some therapies, however, achieve high levels of success in treating such recalcitrant emotions. But does such change amount to education? Education involves a transformation of understanding. Cognitivism seems, however, to concede that this will not be enough. How, then, can there be real education of the emotions? This issue is of abiding general importance as well as being relevant to all putative 'philosophical therapies', from Stoicism to the present day.

15

> CONVICTIONS ARE MORE DANGEROUS FOES OF TRUTHS THAN LIES.
> *Nietzsche*

> To know one's ignorance is the best part of knowledge.
> *Lao-Tse*

> Believe those who are seeking the truth. Doubt those who find it.
> *André Gide*

> I must, before I die, find some means of saying the essential thing which is in me, which I have not yet said, a thing which is neither love nor hate nor pity nor scorn but the very breath of life, shining and coming from afar, which will link into human life the immensity, the frightening, the wondrous and implacable forces of the non-human.
> *Bertrand Russell*

> But the fact that some geniuses were laughed at does not imply that all who are laughed at are geniuses. They laughed at Columbus, they laughed at Fulton, they laughed at the Wright Brothers. But they also laughed at Bozo the Clown.
> *Carl Sagan*

> When the student is ready, the teacher will appear.
> *Ancient Buddhist proverb*

> Examinations are formidable even to the best prepared, for the greatest fool may ask more than the wisest man can answer.
> *Charles Caleb Colton*

> MOST PEOPLE ARE OTHER PEOPLE. THEIR THOUGHTS ARE SOMEONE ELSE'S OPINIONS, THEIR LIVES A MIMICRY, THEIR PASSIONS A QUOTATION.
> *Oscar Wilde*

> We shall not cease from exploration
> And the end of our exploring
> Will be to arrive where we first started
> And know the place for the first time.
> *T. S. Eliot*

> If a man will begin with certainties, he shall end in doubts; but if he will be content to begin with doubts, he shall end in certainties.
> *Francis Bacon*

Introduction

As I write, I am sitting at my computer having just finished the main body of this book, and I am wondering how to conclude it. Of course, I have had lots of thoughts about this already, and several pages of preliminary notes are here beside me. They cover a fairly wide range of ideas, but they seem to focus mainly on the concept of truth. It appeared to me while writing the other chapters that this would be a good way to bring the threads together and tie up all the loose ends. But now that I come to it, it seems to me that to write such a conclusion would be to go against the whole spirit in which I have tried to conduct this inquiry into knowledge. Such a conclusion might suggest logical closure when there are wide horizons of imagination and wonder to explore. It might create the illusion of authority where there should be measured independence and originality of thought. If this is to be more than an abstract game to you, then the conclusion must be as much yours to make as mine.

A tidy conclusion is inappropriate for other reasons, too. This is not an introduction to a specific field of philosophy, nor simply a collection of ideas that I think are interesting (although there has been some overlap with these categories). Its purpose has not been to give you lots of answers. Instead I hope to have introduced you to some questions that have been considered important over the centuries, to have mentioned a few of the answers that have been suggested, and to have indicated how we might recognise a good answer. One reason that the questions are considered important is that they don't go away. They come up again and again in different circumstances, and at odd times. Once you know they are there, you can't get away from them – in everyday discussion, while reading novels, when watching the television or reading a newspaper – they are everywhere and they are one of the things that makes life interesting.

Another reason that the questions are important is that the answers make a difference to how we experience our lives. On the grand level, if you have grasped the problems of free will, or perception, then the world will be a more subtle, slippery thing for you. Your awareness of paradigms will impact all your relationships, and your stance on political, religious and ethical matters will determine the values by which you live your life. On the practical level, if you are sensitive to the value-laden nature of language, then you will be less likely to be a credulous and gullible consumer. If you know how to reason, then you will be less vulnerable to fraud. If you are aware of paradigms, then you will be more creative. So I think what we have attempted to do is important for us as individual human beings. These ideas should stay with us, inform our thinking and be guides to action.

What good then is a conclusion when this is really a beginning?

Before finishing, however, it is perhaps worth glancing back over our shoulder to see how far we have come in our search for reliable knowledge. Has the search been successful? Well, maybe we have moved forward here and there, but in terms of finding solid, fixed certainties, we may be forced to admit that we have accomplished precious little, if anything. If we are honest then we might admit that we have even gone backwards in some places; that where we once had certainty, conviction and confidence we now have scepticism, reservation, and perhaps even confusion. To some, this is a sign that we should never have started on our quest. *'Why have we just confused ourselves?'* ask the sceptics as they point to the inconclusive debates, unsettled questions and unsettling ideas.

Of course, as the writer of this book I am hardly likely to subscribe to this way of thinking! Someone once described education as the 'progressive discovery of our own ignorance'. If this is correct, then we have been well educated by our quest and we can call it a resounding success. We have been on a philosophical journey where the sceptics would have had us stay at home. If on our journey to date we have raised more doubts than we have dispelled, so be it. Real, honest doubts are worth more than the illusions we once took for truths. Voltaire was correct when he said, *'Doubt is not a pleasant condition, but certainty is absurd.'*

If this book has served its purpose, then you will continue the search for your own answers and your own questions. The journey is an exciting one, and as far as we know we humans are the only ones in the Universe that can make it. We should not waste the opportunity.

The problem of individuality

'Among humans,' said Pablo Picasso, *'there are far more fakes than originals.'* Our age is an age of conformity. Today, no-one who does not conform can feel comfortable. Whenever individual thought arises, it is a struggle to make it heard. From early childhood, we are bombarded with facts, opinions and the thoughts of others until we find it very difficult to think at all, except in the terms that others have thought before us. Most of us entirely abandon the search for originality. Our capacity for individual thinking has been smothered in a unending flood of clichés, and so conformity has become the order of the day.

It is natural to ask why we all accept this situation. Why is individual thinking so feared? Why is it so avoided? The answer is simple: to be an individual requires courage and strength. Conformity, by contrast, requires nothing but a nodding and easy assent to whatever everybody else thinks. The individual thinker is alone, with only himself to rely on. The individual must have the courage to say: 'Here I am. I am different to the rest, and I am not afraid of being different. And I will remain different until the day I die.' It requires strength to maintain that position.

The position of the conformist could not be more different. He feels safe because he has made sure that he is with the majority. He cannot be singled out because there is nothing for which to single him out. And he need not bother with leaving his mark on the world, with creating anything new, because in one sense he will not die. He will live on in the millions of people who are just like him. He is immortal.

It is perhaps natural that we always seek the easiest solution to a problem. But it is not a good thing that we do so, because the easiest solution is to do what most people are doing. The individual thinker is prepared to go beyond the easy and obvious solution. He is prepared to question. As a result he is often shunned and sometimes loathed by those who know him. Why? Because he is a danger. He is a threat. By showing that he relies on his own judgements and values, and not those of others, he demonstrates a great power. As well as the burden, his is the freedom of individuality. The conformist, trapped in the ideas of others, hates nothing more than someone with the freedom he does not have.

Today, as throughout history, the individual thinker's life will not be an easy one. It may even be a dangerous one. It is unlikely that he will be nailed to a cross, but make no mistake, the means of suppression are there, though they are rather more subtle. And so it is as true as it ever was that individual thinkers are likely to lead the lives of outcasts. And it is as true as it ever was that we desperately need those with the courage and strength to live independently. In our age of information and conformity, the vast majority of people live passively, dominated by things outside of themselves and alienated from their human potential. We need individual thinkers.

Things are not improving. What little individuality is left is being diluted more and more. Perhaps one day there will be none, and something precious and vital will have been lost. I hope you can see what I mean when I ask: are you real, or just another fake?

Further reading

The irony of suggesting further reading in the light of the previous section does not escape me, but I cannot resist suggesting a few personal favourites. Bryan Magee's wonderful *Confessions of a Philosopher* (Phoenix Books, 1997) takes an autobiographical thread through many issues and gives an excellent overview of philosophical inquiry. *Mortal Questions* by Thomas Nagel (Cambridge University Press, 1999) takes a more analytical approach to issues as diverse as death, the absurd, moral luck, sexual perversion and massacres in war. Much of William James' writings in the early twentieth century remain fascinating – a useful collection can be found in *Pragmatism and Other Writings* (Penguin, 2000); to my mind it is the *other writings* (which cover ideas such as the stream of consciousness, worthy lives, empirical experience and the moral life) which are most interesting.

We have considered qualities such as reason, justice and truth and seen that these relate to human experience in certain ways. A totally different way of approaching the thinking life is to take the human experience as central, and to see what emerges. This is, very roughly, what the existentialists have done, and a fine introduction is William Barrett's *Irrational Man* (Anchor Books, 1962); a more detailed, but also more difficult, text is Davis Cooper's *Existentialism* (Blackwell, 1990).

Acknowledgements

■ Photo credits

Thanks are due to the following for permission to reproduce copyright photographs:

Cover Andrez Dudinski/Science Photo Library; **pp.48–49** *all* Courtesy Ronald Feldman Fine Arts, New York.

■ Text credits

Text extracts reproduced by kind permission of:

pp.12–13 *Zen and the Art of Motor Cycle Maintenance* by Robert M. Pirsig published by Bodley Head. Copyright © 1974 by Robert M. Pirsig. The Random House Group Limited and HarperCollins Publishers Inc; **pp.15–16, 17** *Six Easy Pieces* by Richard Feynman. Copyright © 1997 by the California Institute of Technology. Perseus Books Publishers, a member of Perseus Books, LLC; **pp.28–9** *On Science and Uncertainty* by Lewis Thomas, 1990, www.Discover.com; **p.36** *The Sovereignty of Good* by Iris Murdoch, Routledge, 1991; **p.40** 'High and Low Thinking About High and Low Art' by Ted Cohen, *Journal of Aesthetics and Art Criticism*, 51:2 (Spring 1993), Blackwell Publishers; **pp.42, 42–3** *Love's Knowledge: Essays on Philosophy and Literature* by Martha Nussbaum. Copyright 1990, 1992 by Martha C. Nussbaum. Oxford University Press, Inc; **p.43** 'The Artworld' by Arthur Danto, from *The Journal of Philosophy* LXI 19, October 15, 1964, Columbia University; **p.43** 'Carnage and Glory; Legends and Lies' by Michael Norman, *The New York Times*, July 7, 1996; **p.44** 'Must Art Tell the Truth?' by Douglas Morgan, from *Journal of Aesthetics and Art Criticism*, vol. 26, 1967, Blackwell; **pp.48–50** 'What the Whole World Likes Best', Christina Lamb/Times Newspapers Limited, London, December 29, 1996; **pp.50–51** *How Proust Can Change Your Life* by Alain de Botton, copyright © 1997, by Alain de Botton. Pantheon Books, a division of Random House, Inc; **pp.55, 60–61** *A Mathematician's Apology* by G. H. Hardy, 1940, Cambridge University Press; **pp.66–7** 'It Ain't What you Prove, it's the Way that you Prove it' by Chris Binge; **p.71** *Miss Smilla's Feeling for Snow* by Peter Høeg. First published in 1992 by Munksgaad/Rosinante, Copenhagen. First published in Great Britain in 1993 by Harvill. Copyright © Peter Høeg and Munksgaard/Rosinante, Copenhagen, 1992. English translations copyright © Farrar, Straus & Giroux Inc. and The Harvill Press, 1993. The Harvill Press; **p.103** *The Language Instinct* by Stephen Pinker, copyright © 1994 by Steven Pinker, William Morrow, HarperCollins Publishers Inc; **p.111** *Behaviourism* by James Watson. Copyright © 1924, 1925, by The People's Institute Publishing Company. Copyright © 1930 by W. W. Norton & Company, renewed 1952, 1953 © 1958 by John B. Watson. W.W. Norton & Co. Inc; **p.113** *The Mismeasure of Man* by Stephen Jay Gould. Copyright © 1981 by Stephen Jay Gould. W. W. Norton & Co. Inc; **pp.119–21** 'Testing: A Case Study in the Social Sciences' from *Descartes Dream* by Philip Davis and Reuben Hersh, 1986. Pearson Education Limited; **pp.122–23** 'Is Economics a Science?' by Arthur Williamson and Seamus Horgon, *Chemistry New Zealand*, February 1992, no.46; **p.131** *Kafka and His Precursors* by Jorge Louis Borge, Penguin Books, 1964. Laurence Pollinger; **pp.132, 138–39** *Practising History* by Barbara Tuchman, copyright © 1981 by Barbara W. Tuchman. Alfred A. Knopf, a division of Random House, Inc; **pp.141–43** 'Is History a Science?' from *The Nature of History* by Arthur Marwick, 1970. Palgrave and Lyceum Books Inc; **pp.144–45** *Memoirs found in a Bathtub* by Stanislaw Lem. Copyright © 1973 by the Seabury Press. The Continuum International Publishing Company Inc; **p.148** 'The Non-Substantial World of Modern Physics' from *New Pathways in Science* by Arthur Eddington, Cambridge University Press, 1935; **pp.150–51** *The Man Who Tasted Shapes* by Richard Cytowic, copyright © 1993 by Richard E. Cytowic, Abacus, 1993. Little, Brown and Company, and Mews Books Ltd; **p.154** *The Universe and Dr Einstein* by Lincoln Barnett, copyright © 1948 by Harper & Brothers. Copyright © 1948 by Lincoln Barnett. Revised editions copyright © 1950, 1957 by Lincoln Barnett. HarperCollins Publishers Inc; **pp.163–64** 'Bats: Sight and Sound' from *The Blind Watchmaker* by Richard Dawkins, © Richard Dawkings 1968. Pearson Education Limited; **pp.165–67** 'How do we know anything?' from *What Does it All Mean? A Very Short Introduction to Philosophy* by Thomas Nagel, copyright 1987 by Thomas Nagel. Oxford University Press Inc; **p.170** *Life on the Mississippi* by Mark Twain. Reissue edition Bantam Classic and Loveswept, 1997. Random House Inc; **p.181** *A Brief History of Time* by Stephen Hawking, copyright March 1998 by Bantam Doubleday Dell. Transworld Publishers (a division of the Random House Group Ltd.) and Writers House LLC (as agent for Stephen Hawking); **pp.182–84** 'The Harmony of the Spheres' by Paul Davis from *Time*, 1996 with the permission of the author, the Australian centre for Astrobiology at Macquarie University, Sydney; **pp.187–90** 'Japanese Politeness, the Interplay of Language, Culture , and Thought', by Eileen Dombrowski; **p.192** *Human Universals* by Donald Brown, McGraw-Hill College Division, 1991. The McGraw-Hill Companies; **pp.193–95** *Body Ritual Among the Nacirema* by Horace Miner, Irvington Publishers, 1993; **pp.196–97** 'The Loss of the Creature' from *The Message in the Bottle* by Walker Percy. Copyright © 1958 by Walker Percy. Farrar, Straus and Giroux, LLC; **p.203** *Mokusatsu* by Heathcote Williams; **p.204** *Good Bones and Simple Murders* by Margaret Atwood, Nan A. Talese. Copyright of O. W. Toad Ltd 1992; Murder in the Dark © Margaret Atwood 1983. Time Warner Books UK; **p.207** *1984* by George Orwell; **pp.207–8** *Language* by Edmund Sapir, Harcourt Brace and World, New York, 1921; **p.209** *The Deeper Meaning of Liff* by Douglas Adams, Macmillan, London, UK, 1992; **p.217** *Powers and Prospects* by Noam Chomsky, Pluto Press, 1996; **p.218** *Tractatus Logico-Philosophicus* by Ludwig Wittgenstein and D. F. Pears (ed.), Routledge & Kegan Paul, 1995; **pp.219, 219–20** *Philosophical Investigations* by Ludwig Wittgenstein (trans. Anscombe). Pearson Education Inc., N.J.; **pp.221–22** *Men of Ideas* by Bryan Magee (copyright © Bryan Magee 1978). PFD on behalf of Professor Bryan Magee; **p.225** *Powers and Prospects* by Noam Chomsky, Pluto Press, 1996; **pp.226–29** 'Parlez-vous my Language?' by Robert Dessaix, from *The Age*, 16 October 1999; **pp.249–51** *Pros and Cons, Debates Handbook*, by Michael Jacobson, Routledge & Kegan Paul, 1987; **pp.272–73** 'Just Rewards' by Michael Albert, www.zmag.org; **p.287** *The Varieties of Religious Experience* by William James, Random House, 1999; **p.291** *The Parable of the Gardener* by Anthony Flew; **pp.314–15** *Emotions* by Paul Harkin, The Philosophers' Magazine.

Every effort has been made to trace all copyright holders, but if any have been inadvertently overlooked the publishers will be pleased to make the necessary arrangements at the first opportunity.

Index

Abel, Reuben 127, 135

abortion 234, 236, 251

absurdism 247

Adams, Douglas 209

Adams, John 32

Adler, Stella 32

Agathon 124

agnosticism 275, 287

Akiyosho Kitaoka 158

Albert, Michael 272–3

Alchin, Nick 46–7

alienation 258

Allen, Woody 274

altruism 239–40

ambiguity 212

American Declaration of
    Independence 256, 267

anarchy 257

anger 308

angst 295–6

Anselm, Saint 274

Aquinas, Saint Thomas 276, 279

Aristotle 263, 268, 308, 315

arts 30–51

    Alchin: Is 'beauty' just
      'biology'? 46–7

    artistic truth 40–4

    de Botton: *How Proust Can
      Change Your Life* 50–1

    definition of 32–7

    evaluation of 37–40

    importance of 31–2

    Lamb: What the whole world
      likes best 48–50

    mimesis 34–5, 43

    morality in 35–7

assumptions 80–3, 171–3

atheism 180, 275, 282, 283,
    285, 287, 288–9

Atwood, Margaret 204

Auden, W. H. 2

Augustine of Hippo, Saint 276,
    278, 286, 289

Austen, Jane 124

axioms 56, 57, 62–4, 93

Ayer, A. J. 40, 275

Bacon, Francis 316

Barnett, Lincoln 153–4

Baylock, J. 72

Beecher, Henry Ward 30

belief 6–7, 287–9

Bennet, Dan 264

Bergson, Henri 146

Berkeley, Bishop George 155–6

Berlin, Isaiah 139, 269

Binge, Chris 66–70

Bismarck, Otto von 274

Bissell, Claude T. 94

Bohm, David 14, 25

Bohr, Niels 39

Bonaparte, Napoleon 124

Boorstin, Daniel J. 2

Borah, William E. 252

Borenstein, David 292

Borges, Jorge Luis 131

Brilliant, Ashleigh 168

Brown, Donald 192

Browning, Robert 131

Byrd, Robert 252

Camus, Albert 109, 116, 230

capital punishment 250

Carlyle, Thomas 132

Carr, E. H. 126, 128, 129, 142

Casimir, Hendrik 25

causation 104–6, 133–5, 140

Chase, Alexander 94

Chesterfield, Lord 292

Chesterton, G. K. 2, 72, 214,
    297

Chomsky, Noam 104, 111,
    113, 216, 217, 225, 270

Churchill, Winston 127, 134,
    252

Clarke, Arthur C. 14, 281

class conflict 130

Clausewitz, Carl von 302

Cleopatra's Nose 134

Cobban, Alfred 143

cognitivism 315

Cohen, J. M. 30

Cohen, Ted 39–40

Cole, K. T. 146

Collingwood, R. G. 124, 132

Colton, Charles Caleb 316

compatibilism 109

computers, and human
    intelligence 64

Confucius 2

Connors, Jimmy 292

Coolidge, Calvin 252

Copernicus, Nicolaus 178

cosmic calendar analogy 4–5

Croft, Tony 206

Cronkite, Walter 168

Csikszentmihalyi, Mihaly 295

culture

    emotions and 310–13

    paradigms and 184–90

Cytowic, Richard 150–1

Damasio, Antonio 315

Danto, Arthur 43

Darrow, Charles 274

Darwin, Charles 110, 180, 230,
    277

Darwin, Erasmus 22

Davies, Bronwyn 297

Davies, Paul 182–4
da Vinci, Leonardo 2
Davis, Elmer 252
Davis, Philip and Reuben Hersch 119–21
Davy, Humphrey 198
Dawkins, Richard 163–4
death penalty 250
de Bono, Edward 90
de Botton, Alain 50–1
deductive logic 73–4, 77–81
de Gaulle, Charles 270
de Laplace, Pierre Simon 108, 282
de La Rochefoucauld, François 2
democracy 261, 262–6
Democritus 2
Dennett, Daniel 109, 110
Descartes, René 58, 148, 154–5, 283
Dessaix, Robert 42, 226–9
determinism 107–13, 133, 135, 205, 208–11
Dewey, John 38, 131
Dillard, Anne 154
Dirac, Paul 22, 62–3
distribution of wealth 261, 267–8
Dombrowski, Eileen 187–90
Drummond, William 72
duty 243–5

economics 122–3
Eddington, Arthur 148
egocentric predicament 167
Einstein, Albert 14, 22, 72, 150, 168, 274
    on mathematics 52, 62–3
    on relativity 24–5, 180
    on truth 18, 234
Eliot, T. S. 316
Elton, G. R. 125
emotions and feelings 34, 292–315

angst 295–6
classification of 294–7
definition of 297–8
emotional quotient (EQ) 308
and experience and culture 310–13
Harkin: Emotions 314–15
intuition 302–7
multiple intelligences (MI) 309
qualia 310–12
and reason and knowledge 298–302
empiricism 146–67
    Dawkins: The Blind Watchmaker 163–4
    Nagel: What Does It All Mean? 165–7
    optical illusions 157–62
    rationalism 154–5
    senses, interpretation of 150–4
    senses, limitations of 149–50
    senses, reliability of 147–8
    sensory data, philosophical explanation of 154–7
    solipsism 165–7
    tabula rasa 100, 155
environmental determinism 110–13
ethical egoism 238, 239–40
ethics 230–51
    abortion 234, 236, 251
    altruism 239–40
    capital punishment 250
    decision-making 245–7
    definition 231–3
    ethical egoism 238, 239–40
    euthanasia 235, 249
    intention 243–4
    Jacobson: Pros and Cons Debates Handbook 249–51
    moral duty 243–5
    pacifism 234

reason, role of 234–8
    utilitarianism 240–3, 244
euthanasia 235, 249
Evans-Pritchard, E. E. 143
evil, problem of 283–6
evolution 180, 183
excluded middle, law of 93
existentialism 246
experience
    emotions and 310–12
    language and 221–3
experimentation
    natural sciences 16, 19, 21–2
    social sciences 97–100

facts 8, 96–7, 126–31, 150–4
faith 288–9
fallacies 87–9, 105
feelings see emotions
Feynman, Richard 14, 15–16, 17, 22
Fiedler, Edgar R. 94
Fitzgerald, F. Scott 168
Flaubert, Gustave 230
Flew, Anthony 291
Frankl, Victor 292
Franklin, Benjamin 292
freedom 8, 268–70
free will 107–10, 285
Freud, Sigmund 180
Frisch, O. R. 16
Frost, Robert 40
Fuller, R. Buckminster 14, 168

Galbraith, John Kenneth 94
Galileo Galilei 14, 72
Gallagher, Winnifred 97
Gangstead, Steven 46–7
Gardner, Howard 309
Gardner, Martin 230, 261, 263, 287
Gates, Bill 268

Gauguin, Paul 30
genetic determination 110–13
geometry 68–9
German Social Democratic Party 261
Gide, André 316
God, existence of
    arguments against 277, 282–6
    arguments for 277–81
Gödel, Kurt 63–4
Goebbels, Paul Joseph 252
Goethe, Johann Wolfgang von 52, 146, 252
Golding, William 255
Gould, Stephen Jay 113
Goya, Francisco de 72

Hailsham, Lord (Quintin Hogg) 72
Haldeman, H. R. 198
Hall, Manley 230
Hardy, G. H. 55, 60–1
Harkin, Paul 314–15
Hawking, Stephen 181
Hawthorne effect 98–9
Heidegger, Martin 302
Heisenberg, Werner 180
Hersch, Reuben, Philip Davis and 119–21
Hightower, Cullen 146
Hilbert, David 63
historical determinism 135
historiography 125
history 124–45
    causation 133–5, 140
    definition of 125–6
    facts, basic 126–8
    facts, interpretation of 129–30
    facts, selection of 128–31, 135–6
    Lem: Memoirs found in a Bathtub 144–5

Marwick: The Nature of History 141–3
    personalities, in 132–3
    quantification 138–9
    Tuchman: Practicing History 138–9
Hitchcock, Alfred 30
Hitler, Adolf 264
Hobbes, Thomas 255
Høeg, Peter 71
Hoffer, Eric 292
Hogan, Seamus 122–3
Holmes, Oliver Wendell 168
homosexuality 235
Housman, Alfred 126
Hoyle, Fred 141, 278
Hsün Tzu 294
human intelligence, and computers 64
human rights 256, 267–70
Hume, David 37–8, 156, 247
    on religion 275, 279, 280–1
Huxley, Aldous 124
Huxley, Thomas Henry 23, 230

idealism 156
identity, law of 93
imagination 17
inductive logic 74–5
    problem of induction 75–7
intelligence quotient (IQ) 120–1, 308
intention 243–4
intuition 302–7
intuitionism 93
Ionescu, Eugène vii
Irving, David 136

Jacobson, Michael 249–51
James, William 284, 287, 297–8
James–Lange theory 297–8
Jefferson, Thomas 267

Jensen, Robert 52
Johnson, Samuel 230, 292
Jung, Carl 31
justice, social 257–9

Kafka, Franz 42, 131
Kant, Immanuel 156–7, 243, 244, 245, 246
Kesey, Ken 292
Keynes, J. M. 94
Khrushchev, Nikita 124
Kierkegaard, Søren 287, 289
King, Martin Luther 2
knowledge 2–13
    cosmic calendar analogy 4–5
    definition of 6–8
    emotions and 298–302
    Pirsig: Zen and the Art of Motorcycle Maintenance 12–13
    reasons 9–10
    and truth 3–4
    types of 8–9
Knowles, Professor 143
Knox, Ronald 156
Koestler, Arthur 14, 52
Komar, Vitaly, and Alexander Melamid 48–50
Kristol, Irving 252
Kuhn, Thomas 21

Lamb, Christina 48–50
Lange, C. G. 298
language 29, 153, 198–229
    Atwood: There was Once 204
    Chomsky: Powers and Prospects 225
    and culture 187–90, 205
    Dessaix: Parlez-vous my language? 226–9
    Gulf War journalism 202
    and human experience 221–3

importance of 199–200

linguistic determinism 205, 208–11

and meaning 214–21, 225

miscommunication 211–13

sentence structure 212–13

and thought 205–11

translation 210, 215

and values 200–5

Williams: *Mokusatsu* 203

Lao Tzu 94, 316

Larson, Bill 96

lateral thinking 89–90

Lem, Stanislaw 144–5

Lewis, C. S. 232–3, 244, 286

Lias, Andrew 274

Lincoln, Abraham 220

linguistic determinism 205, 208–11

Locke, John 155, 256

logic

deductive 73–4, 77–81

inductive 74–5

scepticism about 92–3

logical fallacy 89, 105

logical positivism 211, 275

Long, Lazarus 100

Luther, Martin 288

Macchiavelli, Niccolo 252

Mach, Ernst 127

MacIntyre, Alasdair 267

Magee, Brian 221, 222, 318

Marwick, Arthur 141–3

Marx, Karl 254, 257–9

Marxism 130, 260, 261

Maslow, Abraham H. 31

mathematics 52–71

axioms 56, 57, 62–4

Binge: It ain't what you prove... 66–70

creativity of 59–61

definition of 54–6, 63

geometry 68–9

Høeg: *Miss Smilla's Feeling for Snow* 71

importance of 53–4

nature of 56–8

prime numbers 59–60

theorems 56, 57, 63–4

truth of 58, 62, 63–4

Matisse, Henri 35

McIlwain, C. H. 124

meaning 84–6, 214–21, 225

Melamid, Alexander, and Vitaly Komar 48–50

Mencken, H. L. 264

Mill, John Stuart 240, 268, 284

Miller, D. C. 22

mimesis 43

mimetic theory of art 34–5

Miner, Horace 193–5

Mises, Ludwig von 2

Monod, Jacques 184

Montaigne, Michel Eyquem de 292

moral duty 243–5

Morgan, Douglas 44

Mozart, Wolfgang Amadeus 107

Muhammad 276

multiculturalism 228

multiple intelligences (MI) 309

Mumford, Lewis 30

Murdoch, Iris 36

Nagel, Thomas 165–7

natural sciences 14–29

falsification 18–19, 21

game analogy 15–16

as human endeavour 16, 20–2

reductionism 23–4

scientific method 16–20

Thomas: On science and uncertainty 28–9

truth and 24–6

universality 23–4

nature/nurture debate 110–13

Newton, Isaac 25

Nietzsche, Friedrich 30, 230, 316

non-contradiction, law of 93

Norman, Michael 43

Nozick, Robert 110, 260, 267

Nussbaum, Martha 36, 42–3, 312

opinions 8, 37–40

optical illusions 157–62

Orwell, George 198, 207

pacifism 234

pantheism 275

paradigms 21, 116, 168–97, 298

assumptions 171–3

Brown: *Humans Universals* 192

choice of 174–5

culture 184–90

definition of 169

evaluation of 175–6

grand paradigms 177–84

Japanese language 187–90

Miner: *Body Ritual Among the Nacirema* 193–5

paradigm shift 178

Percy: *Ways of Reading: An Anthology for Writers* 196–7

riverboat pilot paradigms 169–71

thinking, effect on 171–4

Pascal, Blaise 292

Patton, General George S., Jr. 168

Peattie, Donald Culcross 30

Percy, Walker 196–7, 310

Perlis, Alan J 274

Peter, Laurence J. 94

philosopher-kings 263

Picasso, Pablo 35, 40, 318

Pinker, Stephen 103, 112–13, 210, 298

Pirsig, Robert M. 12–13

Pitcher, George 311

Planck, Max 20

Plato 52, 54, 153, 238, 263, 293, 314

Poincaré, Henri 14, 94, 303

Polanyi, Michael 22, 198

politics 252–73

   Albert: Just Rewards 272–3

   democracy 261, 262–6

   descriptive 254

   distribution of wealth 261, 267–8

   government, need for 255–7

   government, role of 257–62

   human rights 256, 267–70

   liberal state 261–2

   minimal state 260–1

   normative 254

   social contract 255–6

   social justice 257–9

   state of nature 255

polytheism 275

Popper, Karl 265–6

prime numbers 59–60

proletariat 258

Psalms, Book of 277

Pugh, Emmerson 116

Pullman, Geoffrey 210–11

qualia 310–12

quantification 138–9

Quayle, Dan 198, 220

Rand, Ayn 230, 292

rationalism 58, 72–93, 154

   application in real world 81–3

   arguments 77–8, 81–6

   assumptions 80–3

   deductive logic 73–4, 77–81

   definitions 84–6

empiricism and 154–5

   fallacies 87–9

   inductive logic 74–7

   lateral thinking 89–90

   logic, scepticism about 92–3

   meaning 84–6

   problem of induction 75–7

Rawls, John 270

Reagan, Ronald 257

reason 16, 234–8, 292, 298–302

reductionism 23–4, 100–4

Reichenbach, Hans 198

Reid, Kate 30

relativity, general 24–5

religion 274–91

   agnosticism 275, 287

   anthropic argument 278

   argument from miracles 280–1

   arguments against the existence of God 282–6

   arguments for existence of God 277–81

   atheism 275, 282, 283, 285, 287, 288–9

   belief, need for 287–9

   cosmological (first cause) argument 278–9

   faith 288–9

   Flew: parable of the gardener 291

   paradoxes of omnipotence 282

   problem of evil 283–6

   teleological (design) argument 277

Robbins, Tom 124

Roffe-Steinrotter, Diane 295

Rousseau, Jean-Jacques 255

Ruskin, John 30

Russell, Bertrand 52, 59, 76, 183–4, 287, 300, 314

Rutherford, Ernest 14

Safire, William 2

Sagan, Carl 20, 168, 316

Samuelson, Paul A. 94

Santayana, George 136, 274

Sapir–Whorf hypothesis 205

Sartre, Jean-Paul 245–7, 302

Schlesinger, Arthur M. Jr. 2

Schopenhauer, Arthur 149

Schweitzer, Albert 230

scientific method

   natural sciences 16–20

   social sciences 113–18

Searle, John 221–2

Shakespeare, William 40–2, 198

Shaw, George Bernard 72, 230, 252, 274

Shelley, Percy Bysshe 274

Simon, H. A. 58

Simon, John 252

Simonson, Lee 133

Singh, Devendra 46, 47

slavery 260

Smith, Adam 260

social contract 255–6

social determinism 133

social justice 257–9

social sciences 94–123

   causation in 104–6

   Davis and Hersch: *Descartes' Dream* 119–21

   definition of 95

   determinism 107–13

   environmental determinism 110–13

   experimentation 97–100

   free will 107–10

   genetic determinism 110–13

   Hawthorne effect 98–9

   Hogan: *A reply from an economist* 122–3

   nature/nurture debate 110–13

normative statements (value) 96–7

positive statements (fact) 96–7

reductionism 100–4

scientific method, applicability of 113–16

scientific method, limitations of 116–18

statistical data 100–4

Stroop technique 99–100

Williamson: *An account from a chemist's point of view* 122

Socrates 171

solipsism 165–7

Sontag, Susan 94

Sowell, Thomas 94

Spencer, Herbert 198

Spinoza, Benedict de 109

Stevenson, Adlai 262

Stirner, Max 238

Stoics 314

Strathern, Paul 37

Stroop technique 99–100

Sullivan, John W. N. 52

syllogism 171

Szent-Gyorgy, Albert von 168

tabula rasa 100, 155

Taylor, A. J. P. 129, 132, 135

Tertullian 274

Thatcher, Margaret 264

theism 275

thinking
language and 205–11
lateral 89–90
paradigms and 171–4

Thomas, Lewis 28–9

Thompson, Charles 168

Thoreau, Henry David 146, 198

Thornhill, Randy 46–7

T'oegye 294

Tolstoy, Leo 30, 132, 134–5

Tomlinson, John 42

Toulmin, Stephen 313

translation 210, 215

Trotter, Wilfred 14

Truesdell, C. 52

truth
artistic 40–4
mathematics and 58, 62, 63–4
natural sciences and 24–6
premises and 80–1
slipperiness of 3–4
validity and 79

Tuchman, Barbara 138–9

Turnbull, Herbert Westren 52

Twain, Mark 168, 170

Unamuno, Miguel de 288

Uncertainty Principle 180

United Nations Declaration of Human Rights 267

utilitarianism 240–3, 244

validity 6, 79

value judgements 21, 96, 97

veil of ignorance 270

verificationism 167

Vico, Giovanni 52

Voltaire (François-Marie Arouet) 270, 318

von Leibnitz, Gottfried Wilhelm 284

Washington, George 252

Watson, James 111

Watts, Alan 94

wealth, distribution of 261, 267–8

Welles, Orson 30

Welty, Eudora 117

Weyl, Hermann 52

Whitehead, Alfred North 230

Whorf, Benjamin 205, 207–8, 209, 210

Wilde, Oscar 36, 39, 72, 316

Williams, Heathcote 203

Williamson, Arthur 122

Wilson, Edward O. 297

Wittgenstein, Ludwig 109, 198, 211, 218–20

Xenophanes 24

Yates, Douglas 292